The Light of Egypt

or

The Science of the Soul and the Stars

VOLUME I

BY

THOMAS H. BURGOYNE

Zanoni, 𝄞

"Write the things which thou hast seen, and the things which are, and the things which shall be hereafter; THE MYSTERY OF THE SEVEN STARS, which thou sawest in my right hand."

Revelations, Chap. I, 19 and 20.

The Green Dolphin Bookshop
7915 S.E. Stark Street
Portland, Oregon 97215

REPRINT EDITION 1969

The first edition of THE LIGHT OF EGYPT was copyrighted in 1889 by the Religio-Philosophical Publishing House of San Francisco, California.

The following editions were published by Henry Wagner M.D. the Astro Philosophical Publishing Company of Denver, Colorado, some sixty years ago. The 1963 edition is a reprint of the fifth edition together with additional material taken from original manuscripts by the same writer, Thomas H. Burgoyne. The 1965 edition and 1969 edition are reprints of the 1963 edition published by H. O. Wagner, P.O. Box 20333 Montclair Station, Denver, Colorado, 80220.

H. O. Wagner.

Kessinger Publishing's Rare Reprints
Thousands of Scarce and Hard-to-Find Books!

-
-
-
-
-
-
-
-
-
-
-
-
-
-
-
-
-
-
-

We kindly invite you to view our extensive catalog list at:
http://www.kessinger.net

Dedication

To the Budding Spirituality of the Occident and
The Rising Genius of the Western Race,
This work is respectfully dedicated.

Very Truly
T. H. Burgoyne.

The symbol upon the cover of this book THE LIGHT OF EGYPT is complex in meaning. It is the symbol of Spiritual Initiation, and means, literally, "I have pierced the illusions of matter, and I am conscious that I am Divine." The seven stars represent the seven Principles of Nature. The serpent represents the objective phenomena of life, and the arrow piercing the serpent represents the human soul which is conscious of its origin, power and destiny.

The name Zanoni means: — Zan, a star; oni, a child of or son of; thus Zanoni, son of a star.

The double zee ($\mathcal{Z}$) means completion.

PREFACE

For nearly twenty years prior to the year 1881 the author was deeply engaged investigating the hidden realms of occult force. The results of these mystical labors were considered of great value and real worth by a few friends who were also seeking light. Finally, he was induced to place the general results of these researches into a series of lessons for private occult study. The whole, when completed, presenting the dual aspects of occult lore as seen and realized in the soul and the stars, corresponding to the microcosm and the macrocosm of ancient Egypt and Chaldea, and thus giving a brief epitome of Hermetic philosophy as taught by the Hermetic Brotherhood of Luxor, Egypt.

The chief reason urging to this step was the strenuous efforts being systematically put forth to poison the budding spirituality of the western mind, and to fasten upon its mediumistic mentality, the subtle, delusive dogmas of Karma and Re-incarnation, as taught by the sacerdotalisms of the decaying Orient.

From the foregoing statement it will be seen that this work is issued with a definite purpose, namely, to explain the true spiritual connection between God and man, the soul and the stars, and to reveal the real truths of both Karma and Re-incarnation as they actually exist in Nature stripped of all priestly interpretation. The definite statements made in regard to these subjects are absolute facts in so far as embodied man can understand them through the symbolism of human language, and the author defies contradiction by any living authority who possesses the spiritual right to say, "I know."

During these twenty years of personal intercourse with the exalted minds of those who constitute the brethren of light, the fact was revealed that long ages ago the Orient had lost the use of the true spiritual compass of the soul, as well as the real secrets of its own theosophy. As a race, they have been, and still are, traveling the descending arc of their racial cycle, whereas the western race have been slowly working their way upward through matter upon the ascending arc. In December 1880 they reached the equator of their mental and spiritual development. Also at this time the sun left the sign Pisces and entered the sign Aquarius thus ushering in the Atomic Age and a new dispensation of spiritual thought to meet the needs of the budding Sixth Race of the Fourth Round of humanity. Today, the world is experiencing an awakening of the intellectual, religious and spiritual senses and is also experiencing the second coming of the Christ as prophesied in Scripture. Therefore, the author feels this is the proper time to present the occult knowledge put forth in this book, during this period of change, the great mental crisis of the western race.

Having explained the actual causes which impelled the writer to undertake this responsibility, it is also necessary to state most emphatically that he does not wish to convey the impression to the reader's mind that the Orient is destitute of spiritual truth. On the contrary, every genuine student of occult lore is justly proud of the snow white locks of old Hindustan, and thoroughly appreciates the wondrous stores of mystical knowledge concealed within the astral vortices of the Hindu branch of the Aryan race. In India, probably more than in any other country, are the latent forces and mysteries of Nature the subject of thought and study. But alas! it is not a progressive study. The descending arc of their spiritual force keeps them bound to the dogmas, traditions and externalisms of the decaying past, whose real secrets they cannot now penetrate. The ever living truths concealed beneath the symbols in the astral light are hidden from their view by the setting sun of their spiritual cycle. Therefore, the writer only desires to impress upon the reader's candid mind, the fact that his earnest effort is to expose that particular section of Buddhistic Theosophy (esoteric so called) that would fasten the cramping shackles of theological dogma upon the rising genius of the western race. It is the delusive Oriental systems against which his efforts are directed, and not the race nor the mediumistic individuals who uphold and support them; for "omnia vincit veritas" is the life motto of the author.

These lessons, on the occult forces of Nature, are from the original manuscripts written some eighty years ago by Thomas H. Burgoyne for use of members of the Exterior Circle of the Hermetic Brotherhood of Luxor, with the approval of M. Theon, the Grand Master and his brother adepts. To these lessons, have been added additional material from other manuscripts and private letters by the same author.

Today, the incoming forces of Nature are rapidly finding new expression in all branches of scientific thought, long before there are any textbooks to show the way. Old thoughts, time and space are being annihilated quickly and new truths are taking root. We are entering an age of unprecedented intellectual and scientific advancement, many undreamed of changes are taking place in all walks of life.

In response to the demand for scientific occult thought to meet the needs of the new dispensation, the knowledge in this book is now being presented for public use, with the full consent and approval of the Hermetic Adepts and the Guardians of "The Wisdom of the Ages," the Hermetic Brotherhood of Luxor, Egypt. It is their prayer that the thought expressed herein will greatly aid mankind in learning the real eternal truths of life and thus hasten the day when all nations will join in one universal brotherhood under the fatherhood of the One Eternal God.

After the first edition published in 1889 THE LIGHT OF EGYPT went through five editions and was published by Henry Wagner M.D. under the name of The Astro-Philosophical Publishing Company, Denver, Colorado. It has been out of print for about sixty years. It is hoped this new edition will receive as hearty a welcome as the early editions.

Please note Mr. Burgoyne's style of expression. This book is not intended as a literary master-piece, a product of the mind, but is an earnest attempt to clearly and truthfully express spiritual thought and ideas in our human language. To change his style is to change the intended thought. He was an Initiate of Esoteric Masonry and a natural born mystic who was able to understand and verify the truth he teaches in all of his writings; "Omnia Vincit Veritas" was the life motto of Thomas H. Burgoyne (Zanoni).

CONTENTS

The Science of the Soul and the Stars in Two Parts

PART I

The Science of the Soul in Three Sections

The Science of the Soul—Section I

The Genesis of Life

The Science of the Soul—Section II

The Transition of Life

The Science of the Soul—Section III

The Realities of Life

PART II

The Science of the Stars

PART II

The Science of the Stars

CONCLUSION

PART I

THE SCIENCE OF THE SOUL

INTRODUCTION

At the very first step the student takes into the hidden pathway of Nature's mysteries, he is met face to face with this startling fact, that all his preconceptions, all his education, all his accumulation of materialistic wisdom are unable to account for the most simple phenomena that transpire in the action and inter-action of the life forces of the planet on which he lives. As a chemist, he may pursue the atoms of force until they become lost within the realms of the imponderable, "the great unknown," or, as it has been facetiously christened amid the groans of scientific travail, "the aching void." But he can get no farther. As a physicist, he may decompose light and sound into their component parts, and, with scientific accuracy, dissect them before your very eyes as a surgeon would his anatomical subject. But no sooner is this point reached, than the shy molecules and timid vibrations become alarmed as it were at man's daring presumption, and fly into the realm of the infinite unknown. There, in "the aching void" to sport in delight, safe from man's intrusion. This realm of the unknown imponderables is the universal ether, an infinite ocean of something, which science created in her frantic endeavors to account for the material phenomena of light and heat, and for a time she was infinitely pleased with her own peculiar offspring. But it has become a restless phantom, a grim, unlovely spectre, which haunts the laboratories of her parent, night and day, until at last science has become frightened at her own child, and tries now in vain to slay the ghost of her own creation. She dares not enter the "aching void" she has called into existence, and there pursue and recapture the truant atoms and timid vibrations of this sublunary sphere.

Therefore, at the very outset of his pilgrimage through these vast and as yet "scientifically unknown" regions, the student had better unload, so to say, all the heavy and useless baggage of educated opinion and scientific dogmas that he may have on board. If he does not, he will find himself top heavy, and will either capsize or run off the track and be buried amid the debris of conflicting opinions. The only equipment that will be found useful, and will repay the cost of transportation, is an unbiased mind, logical reasoning, genuine common sense, and a calm, reflective brain. Anything else for the voyage upon which we are now about to embark, is simply so much useless, costly lumber. Hence, so far as modern science and theology are concerned, the less the student has, the better it is for him, unless he can use his scientific acquirements merely as aids in climbing the spiritual steps of Occultism. If he can do this, then he will find science a most valuable auxiliary aid. But this achievement is an exceedingly rare gift, and one that is seldom found. It is also a most delusive snare, because nine out of every ten seriously cheat themselves into the belief that they possess this ability, whereas in reality they are woefully deficient. Hence it is always a safe course to mistrust the absolute impartiality of our opinions and reasoning.

Before starting out on such a mighty and important undertaking, we must draw the reader's attention to the chief obstacle of the voyage, and the one which he will have the greatest difficulty in surmounting. This hidden rock upon which so many otherwise profound students of the Occult have become shipwrecked, is the non-realization of the duality of truth, viz., the truth of appearances, and the truth of realities. The former is relative only. But the latter is absolute.

We do not mean merely taking for granted that truth is dual, and so assenting to the statement; but we mean that the great majority of Occult students fail to realize this conception within themselves. Know that; every thing is real upon its plain of manifestation.

If we possess half of anything, we know by the laws of common sense and logical reasoning that there is another half somewhere. No subtle twist of metaphysical sophistry can cheat us into the belief that we possess the whole when we know and see that we have just exactly half and no more. Further, when we look at any known thing we know that to possess the attributes of a thing it must possess three dimensions, viz.; length, breadth and thickness. This being so, we also know that it has (broadly speaking) two sides, an outside and an inside. The outside is not the inside any more than the boiler is the steam which drives the engine. This logical process of reasoning is the only chart that has so far been prepared for the Occult explorer. It is vague and probably very unsatisfactory, so far as details are concerned, but when used in conjunction with his conscious intuition — the only true compass man has by which to guide himself in his winding, uneven path upon the shores of the Infinite — he never need fear being lost or failing in his endeavors to know the truth.

In order to carry out the same line of reasoning a little further, let us take a type of architecture, say the Gothic, and mentally examine some well known handsome specimen of this structural conception. The world's thought will say, "what a beautiful building; how imposing and grand; what a triumph of man's mechanical skill!" So it appears to the world, and upon the plain of appearances, so it really is.

Consequently, it is a truth for the time being. But when examined by the light of Occult science, we find this truth is relative only, that it is only true upon the external, transitory plane of material phenomena. We see that, in addition to being the result of man's trained mechanical ability, it is also the external form of his mental ideal. It is, in fact, the phenomenal outcome of his creative attributes. When we look at the solid building, from the earth's plane, we see only the outside of a thing having length, breadth and thickness. Now since we know that there must be an inside, we must enter the interior plane before we can see it, and therein we shall find that it exists within the subjective world of its architect. The solid stone edifice will, in time, crumble to decay, fall, and finally not one material atom will remain to indicate the place whereon it stood. Hence it is not permanently real, it is only a passing appearance assumed by matter under the moulding forces of man's mechanical ability. As soon as the forces which gave it form become polarized by the restless oceans of planetary magnetism, it will dissolve and finally vanish "like the baseless fabric of a dream." But though the external structure of stone and mortar is lost within the soil of the earth, the idea which created it is eternal, because it was a spiritual reality. Therefore, we see that the absolute truth (the eternal reality) appears to be the non-reality. upon the plane of matter, while the material structure appears to be the only thing which is real. It is these delusive appearances that have created the almost hopeless confusion regarding the exact meaning of the terms "Spirit" and "Matter." Science refers all she cannot grapple with to some of the undiscovered forces of "Matter," while theology refers all that she cannot explain to the unknowable workings of the "Spirit." Both are right, and both are wrong. And as we shall have to explore the territory belonging to both of these terms during the progress of our journey, we will in this place briefly add that spirit and matter, as we know them, are but the dual expression of the one Deific principle, due to differences of polarity. In other words, a unity under two modes of action. This duality can only be comprehended in its true relationship when viewed from both planes and realized by the science of correspondences, which science is but a material system of symbolism from which we can justly regulate our conceptions of all things.

Plato once said, "Ideas rule the world." So far Plato was right; for, before the divine idea was evolved from within the divine sensorium of the Infinite One, the universe was not. Hence the result of the divine idea was the evolution of a pure symbolic form.

Just as symbols are the product of ideas, so, in their turn, ideas are the symbols of thought, and thought itself is but the symbolic response of the Ego to the pulsating throb of the Deific will, the divine radiant soul of the Infinite One. Back of this we cannot penetrate, even in our most exalted conceptions. Hence all serious study and meditation as to the nature and existence of God is unprofitable and cannot bring the student any substantial return either in this world or the next, seeing that the Infinite can never be comprehended by the finite. Therefore, we must rest satisfied with the certain knowledge that we can by one grand chain of sequences trace the transmission of thoughts, ideas and symbolic forms to their source.

Thus the angelic world is but a prototype or symbolic expression of the divine sphere of the Infinite. The celestial world is a reflection of the angelic world. The spiritual world is a prototype and symbolic outcome of the celestial heavens. The astral world is the reflection of the spiritual sphere. And lastly, the material (our world) is but the concrete shadow of the astral kingdoms.

Hence the reader can perceive that we, in our present state, are a long way down in the scale of creative life. But if we are, we know by the laws of our being that we can and shall win our way back through this valley of the shadow, this plane of inverted images and delusive appearances, into the bright realms of our former state, those spheres of pure angelic life where alone exist the ever living reals of all the infinitude of apparent realities.

THE GENESIS OF LIFE

CHAPTER I

THE REALM OF SPIRIT

Involution

"Being, Uncreated, Eternal, Alone," says Dr. John Young, when speaking of "the Creator and the creation;" certainly no inspired writer ever penned a more sublime truth than is contained in the above words.

Pure spirit is diffusive, non atomic, uncreated, formless, self-existent being. Silent, motionless, unconscious, Divinity; possessing in its sublime purity the one sole Deific attribute expressible in human language as absolute and unconditioned potentiality.

Such is the realm of spirit, which, for the sake of linguistic convenience, has been termed by the Occultist "the realm of unmanifested being." With the first emanation of this inconceivable state we have now to deal. The Kabbalah, of the early Jewish rabbis, contains long and elaborate treatises upon the various emanations of the ten sephiroth, which for the most part are written in such an allegorical style as to be practically useless to most Western students, and even to Oriental minds are unsatisfactory, and in many respects misleading. The first emanation from this realm of spirit (formless being) claims the student's closest attention. It forms the Deific keynote of the divine anthem of creation. This first emanation, called by the Kabbalists the Crown, means, when stripped of its mystical veil, simple and naked activity or motion. Thus we see that the first action of Divinity (unconscious mind) is thought, and thought implies vibration or motion. At the moment the Deific mind vibrates with thought there springs forth, from the infinite womb of creation, the duad of all future greatness. This duad is the Kabbalistical twins, "Love and Wisdom," which, in turn mean the attributes, attraction and repulsion of force and motion. They are male and female, co-equal and co-eternal, and express themselves externally as activity and repose.

No matter how recondite or abstruse our speculations may be, when the orbit of our metaphysical meditation is complete we shall find ourselves face to face again with our original starting point, which is this infinite triad of Love, Wisdom and Crown, or, in other words, the one primal force containing unlimited potentialities within itself. Back of this we cannot go. With this divine trinity or Godhead, as students and investigators of Nature's occult mysteries, we must rest contented, consoling ourselves, whenever necessary, with the certain knowledge that the nearer we appear to approach the great white throne of the Infinite One, the further does that divine center recede from us. If this were not so, there could be no such thing as eternity for the atoms of differentiated life. Consequently, the immortality of the soul would be an empty dream, a mere figment, hatched by some infernal power within the overheated imagination of poor deluded man.

Before going further, the reader should commit to memory the following primary doctrines, taught by the Occult initiates of all true wisdom. They are doctrines to us in our present state, in so far that we cannot demonstrate them externally by any known form of experiment.

I. "The whole universe is filled with the Deific presence of God." That is to say, the universe is permeated with the pure, motionless, formless, spirit of Divinity.

II. "The universe is boundless and unlimited, a circle whose circumference is everywhere and whose centre is nowhere." The universe is dual and consists of the manifest and the non-manifest. Hence Deity is progressive in his infinite scheme of spiritual unfoldment.

III. "The divine one life principle emanates from the pure vortices, the central Spiritual Sun of the manifested universe. From this mighty inconceivable center of life emanate the spiritual rays of the Father, scintillating with divine activity, whereupon the vast, motionless void, the awful universe of God's silent, formless spirit, becomes alive with an infinite number of subordinate universes." Which means, the rays of Divinity are brought to a focus at various points in space. These points or foci form the spiritual centers of smaller universes. An example of this can be seen upon our material plane by observing that primary suns throw off a series of secondary suns. These secondary suns throw off planets, and the planets become the parents of moons. By the science of correspondence, "as it is above, so it is below." Remember these facts.

The divine purpose of creation is the differentiation of the unconscious formless One, and the grand outcome of this divine purpose is the ultimation of Deific Intelligencies; separate minds reflecting the divine idea of the universal mind, conscious, individualized mentalities possessing immortal souls capable of eternal progression, who, as differentiated life atoms of the Creator, the grand Arbiter of the whole, become themselves secondary creators and the arbitrators of the destinies of worlds.

The processes of creation are dual, and consist of Involution and Evolution. The one is inseparable from the other. Paradoxical as it may appear to the uninitiated, it is, nevertheless, a divine truth that the Evolution and ultimation of spiritual life is accomplished by a strict process of Involution; from the without to the within, from the infinitely great to the infinitely small.

To better understand this mystery we must have recourse to a series of symbols. Accordingly, we conceive the divine focus of the primal essence as the spiritual center of a universe. This Deific ray constitutes a triune Godhead, from which emanates the pure white light of the formless One, or in other words, this center constitutes a realm of sephiroth, a sun-sphere of living potentialities, divine beings infinitely beyond the highest archangelhood. As such we may conceive it floating as a speck in the infinite ocean of divine love, surrounded by the effulgent brightness of the nameless Crown. This divine sphere is passive in such a state. Nirvana reigns upon the blissful radiance of its motionless bosom. But the time now approaches when its mission in the scheme of creation must commence. The moment arrives, and as soon as the first creative pulsations of thought vibrate, the whole sphere of motionless, formless, white light flashes forth sparkling with living energy. And now, behold what a change has taken place. The soft, white light has ceased to be and in its place there is raying forth in every conceivable direction mighty oceans of force; each ocean differing in velocity, color and potentiality. The passive has become active, and the motionless has commenced to move, traversing the void of space upon the wings of light. Deity has become refracted; a portion of the infinite soul decomposed, and its original unlimited potentialities resolved into a series of active but limited attributes. This is related in the mystical language of the Kabbalah as the evolution of the seven active sephiroth from the first trinity, Love, Wisdom and Crown. It is

THE REALM OF SPIRIT

Symbolical Illustration
of the
Divine Harmony of Nature's Laws

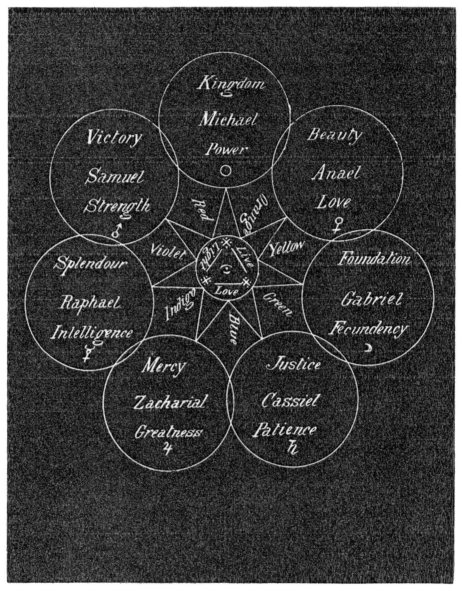

"In the beginning was the Word,
And the Word was with God,
And the Word was God."—St. John, Chap. I, vi.

these seven active sephiroth that constitute the seven principles of Nature. They form seven points or sub-centers around their parent center, the Spiritual Sun, and are the seven worlds of angelic life from whose divine matrix issue all the life atoms of their universe.

From the foregoing the reader will see, that when the dawn of any universe commences, the pure formless essence is indrawn from the realms of the unmanifested into their sun-sphere of creative life previous to being involved by the deific will of the angelic hierarchies, and by such contact it immediately undergoes a change. It is formless no longer but atomic, and endowed with an attribute or state it had not before, viz., polarity. This polarity at once evolves a sort of partnership, and equally divides the formless substance into two parts, each a necessary attendant upon the other in manifested existence. One is positive, the other, of course, negative. The positive ray is that which constitutes the living spiritual fire of all things, and its atoms are infinitely fine. The negative ray is ever tending toward a state of repose or inertia, and its atoms are coarse and loose as compared with those of the positive ray. It is the substance formed by the negative ray that constitutes every species of matter, so-called, from the inconceivably fine etherealized substance, which composes the forms of the divine archangels of the sun, down to the mineral veins of dense metal in the earth.

Therefore, when speaking broadly of spirit and matter, the terms are perfectly unmeaning in an occult sense, for that which we call spirit is not pure spirit, but only the positive or active attribute of that which we term matter. Hence matter is so far unreal, it is only an appearance produced by the negative ray, and this appearance is the result of polarity or mode of motion; the positive is straight and penetrating, the negative is round and enfolding.

With this brief but necessary digression we resume. From the seven angelic states before mentioned, spiritual involution commences. Each one of the seven spheres is a reflection of one of the seven refracted principles, which constitute the divine mind of the angelic creators. From this reflection spring forth angelic races, second only in mental power and potentiality to their parents. Then, in turn, are produced still lower celestial states, each state or sphere corresponding in nature, color and attribute to the sphere from which it was born or reflected. But though each state in the descending scale is similar by correspondence, it becomes less in size, more material; the spiritual potencies of its angelic races are weaker, that is, less active, because they are more and more involved within matter as they descend in the scale. Thus does involution proceed; involving state after state, and sphere after sphere, forming a series of circles whose line of motion or descent is not in the plane of its orbit; hence the form ultimates itself as a spiral until the lowest point is reached. Beyond this, motion is, impossible, and the infinitely great has become the infinitely small. This is the great polarizing point from which the material world is reflected. It is the lowest possible spiritual state of life, which formed the first ethereal race of human beings upon our planet, and thus ushered into existence the famous golden age of mythological celebrity.

EXPLANATION OF THE DIAGRAM

The central triad represents Love, Wisdom and Crown, The Trinity of God. The seven-pointed star, the seven rays issuing therefrom. The seven circles show the seven angelic worlds formed from the seven active principles. The names Cassiel, Michael, etc., are cabalistical names for the sephiroth (the secondaries or ruling intelligencies, who, after God, actuate the universe), while the words above and below show their attributes.

CHAPTER II

Evolution

The term evolution is from the Latin e and volvo, which means to roll from, or unroll, and the evolution of matter means precisely what the term implies, viz., unfolding, expanding, opening and evolving. The whole of which can be summed up in the word progression.

Matter, per se, is the polar opposite of manifested spirit. It is the reaction of spiritual action. It is energy in a state of rest. It is force and motion in an exact state of equilibrium; in short, matter simply means solidified spirit. When two imponderable equal forces from opposite directions meet each other, both powers become polarized, force is resolved into inertia, motion is transformed into rest; in other words, spirit becomes matter, its refinement or its density depending upon its degree of etherealization.

The progression and ultimation of the life forces latent within matter, must be accomplished by a process of unfoldment. The potentialities, in order to expand and put forth their infinite possibilities, must EVOLVE, and this is so, because they have become incarnated by the opposite forces of enfoldment. But having become involved in the degradation of the material, by the fall, and cast into "the bottomless pit" or crystallizing point in space, the only possible means of return to the original pure spiritual state is through the progressive cyclic pathways of material unfoldment.

The evolution of matter, like everything else within the realms of manifested existence, must have some point of commencement. If matter is, as previously stated, but the manifestation of spirit — the negative ray externalized and in a state of crystallized inertia — then matter must be the first offspring of spirit, and both combined must comprise the all of all things, yea, even Deity itself; for an infinite creator cannot get beyond his creation, nor exist apart from himself, because the great law of polar opposites is the direct emanation from his own divine nature. Consequently, HE must also be governed by the self same laws and principles which control his creative activities, and when traced to their source we have seen how beautifully simple such primal laws are, viz., "Wisdom and Love," and, convertibly, male and female, positive and negative, activity and repose. Briefly stated there is but one law, one principle, one agent and one word. This sacred law is SEX, a term wherein may be summed up the grand totalities of the Infinite Universe.

Sex is dual, and finds expression in the phallus and yohni of animated Nature. This same sexual law operating throughout Nature limits the sources from which our knowledge of Nature can be obtained; in other words, there are but two sources from which knowledge of any kind is received; one is subjective, the other objective; the former gives us knowledge of the spiritual or causal side of the cosmos, the latter gives the material side, which is the world of effects, on account of its being evolved out of the former, as the poet hath said;

> "The outward doth from the inward roll,
> And the inward dwells in the inmost soul."

The great first cause has evolved out of himself the esoteric, or subjective world; and out of the subjective, by a simple change of polarity, which at once brings forth a change of energy and substance, he has evolved the objective world. Therefore, the antecedents of the objective are to be found in the subjective world.

We have now completed the cyclic outline of our present research, and, as a result, we know that the point of commencement in material evolution which we have thus far been seeking, lies hidden within the realms of spirit, of which realm we have already spoken, in chapter one.

In order to clearly comprehend Nature's processes in the unfoldment of matter, a careful study of the seven creative principles is very necessary, not studied as so many intelligencies or states of conscious life, but as seven principles or forces, which, though unconscious and blind in their activities throughout their different spheres of operation, yet act strictly in harmony with each other as the refracted parts of a whole, fulfilling the creative design. These seven principles are not in themselves intelligent, but are simply powers directed by intelligence, just as the electric current is a power which, when governed by intelligence, becomes a medium for the expression of that intelligence and capable of transmitting its master's thoughts and desires, instantaneously, to any part of the globe that has been prepared to receive them. The intelligence which directs these powers by the laws of harmony are the seven angelic worlds mentioned in the previous chapter, and as they are a perfect epitome of the divine law, it necessarily follows that the objective world of matter must be a perfect epitome — a solidified expression of its progenitors, and must contain within itself the latent attributes of its spiritual source.

Powers, like individuals, are limited in their activities. For instance, before electricity can manifest itself as light or power it must have something to act upon, a point of contact or rapport, at the point or place of manifestation. As stated in the above illustration of the electric current, the place and object of such phenomena must have been prepared for the expression of such power. Hence the necessity (if we may use such a term) of the objective world being a perfect epitome of and containing the latent attributes of the higher and more interior worlds of cause.

If this were not so the perfect evolution of matter would be an impossibility, because no subjective power, state or principle can act or react upon an objective form unless a portion of itself lies within that form. We must carry this line of reasoning a little further.

Man, in his physical body, is a perfect epitome of the planet upon which he lives, while the celestial worlds find their perfect expression in his soul, and these worlds, in turn, are but the higher and more interior expression not only of man's physical organism, but of the earth on which he lives. We see, therefore, how beautifully harmonious Mother Nature is, even in her most secret parts. She has made every known "thing" dependent upon a something else, and all things, therefore, are mutually dependent upon each other. Evolution is dependent upon involution; the objective upon the subjective, and man is dependent upon the earth. All contain the same eternal seven principles; the subjective, in its imponderable essences; the objective, in its solids, fluids and gases; and man, as the spirito-natural medium and meeting point between the two great worlds, treasures up the seven mineral qualities in his body and their magnetic counterparts in the odylic sphere of his soul. In this recondite sense alone can we fully understand the occult axiom of the ancients; "Man is a microcosm — a universe within himself."

The seven principles of Nature correspond in their chemical affinities to the seven prismatic rays of the solar spectrum, and also present

a perfect correspondence to the seven progressive states of manifestation, which have been very appropriately termed the "The Life
Waves." It is these waves of cosmic life energies that carry out the
grand ascending scale of material evolution.

When a "wave" commences, it, at once, sets in motion, its evolutionary activities. These forces produce a series of responsive vibrations
within that realm of force which forms its material correspondence, and
thus acting and reacting upon each other like the ebb and flow of the
tides, these forces produce another scene in the sublime drama of external life. These waves, seven in number, succeed each other in the
following order;

    I. The Spiritual or realm of creation, symbol of The Word.
    II. The Astral or realm of design, symbolic of The Idea.
    III. The Gaseous or realm of force, symbolic of The Power.
    IV. The Mineral or realm of phenomena, symbol of The Justice.
    V. The Vegetable or realm of "life," symbolic of The Beauty.
    VI. The Animal or realm of consciousness, symbol of The Love.
    VII. The Human or realm of mind, symbolical of The Glory.

The student will form a clearer idea of these mighty principles, if
we travel over the same ground again in an explanatory manner;

I. The world of creation signifies the angelic world from which
the original impulse first emanated. This spiritual impulse travels
around the whole of the future orbit of the "system" about to be
evolved, and prepares the spaces for the reception and manifestation
of a less ethereal force.

II. The world of design is the subjective cause-world in the astral
light, containing all the germs, forms and ideals possible for that system to ultimate.

III. The world of cosmic force is the ever circulating oceans of
mundane, sub-mundane and super-mundane forces, with which
"science" is only just becoming acquainted in the forms of light, heat,
magnetism, universal ether, electricity, and chemical, atomic and solar
energy.

IV. The world of phenomena needs no explanation, it being the
world of matter.

V. The world of life is the fluidic, the first forms of all things, that
is, organic forms "wherein there is life" are vegetables, and they originate in water, the grand matrix.

VI. The world of consciousness. The first rudimentary expression of consciousness, generally termed instinct, manifests itself in the animal kingdom. It is intelligent mind expressing itself through the lower forms of etherealized matter.

VII. The world of mind contains the human principle, Man being the culminating point of material evolution. In this realm the mind begins once more to assert its supremacy over matter, here life conquers death; hence the very significant symbol of the Kabbalah, wherein this state is termed "The Glory." See chapters V and VI, La Clef.

The processes of ultimation by the means of involution and evolution are inversely related to each other; the former (involution) is the original action, while the latter (evolution) is only the reaction; a necessary consequence of the former.

Before attempting to explain those occult processes connected with the evolution of matter, which are silently at work within the unseen womb of Nature producing the endless series of causes, the activities of which externalize themselves in an infinite variety of forms, it is necessary to briefly review the ideas expressed in chapter I, "The Involution of Spirit," wherein we pointed out that, originally, our solar system was "without form and void," (Genesis I, 2) that is to say, it had no material objective shape; that previous to its external manifestation, it must have existed subjectively as an ideal form; and that this ideal form is but the symbolic expression of the ethereal forces projected during the evolution of thought. This is as far as we are permitted to go along the line of actual spiritual facts. But in carrying out the same chain of reasoning, we are led to the conclusion that if we could only penetrate, even for a single moment, the sacred adytum of Nature's greatest of all mysteries, we should find that even thought itself was only due to the throbbing pulsations of the soul, and that these pulsations, in their turn, were but the sympathetic response,— the expansion and contraction—of the spiritual respiration in harmonious obedience to the action and reaction of its divine Ego.

The primary ideas which we derive from Chapter I, are as follows; I. That the macrocosm is the objective image of the divine subjective idea, and the microcosm is a reflection of the macrocosm. II. That the former, as a whole, is essentially without form, not only because it consists of such an infinite variety of forms, but because of the endless succession of progressive manifestations of these forms; hence, being without essential form, it is unlimited. III. That the latter, though a perfect epitome of the former, is finite, and as such possesses a form as a symbol of its limitations.

NOTE: We do not claim any originality for the ideas put forth upon this subject, because they have been known to at least a thousand generations of the Hermetic Initiates, in fact the great Hermes Trismegistus says distinctly, that, "The Universe is from God, and man is from the Universe," which means, the macrocosm is a reflection of Deity, and man is an image of the macrocosm. It can have no other rendering.

Neither Pythagoras nor Socrates ever wrote upon the sacred science. They were essentially thinkers, in fact the vows of the former to the great hierophants of Egypt prevented him from externalizing truth as Plato did.

Though Plato was the pupil of Socrates, he gives forth the Pythagorean philosophy in its entirety, in the form of allegory. The only mystery about the matter is, where did Plato's teacher obtain his Pythagorean wisdom? The only reasonable solution to this query is, to suppose that he obtained it from his attendant daemon. Our conception of the teachings of Pythagoras and Socrates can only be obtained by a knowledge of the fact that both Plato and Pythagoras were initiated — hence Plato simply wrote that which these old sages only thought. "The primordial essence," says Plato, "is an emanation from the Demiurgic mind," which mind, "contains from eternity the idea of the natural world within itself." He further asserts that, "He (the Demiurgus) produces the divine idea out of himself by the power of his will."

Thus only re-expressing the self same Hermetic doctrine elaborated by old Hermes at the very dawn of Occult philosophy.

So far, we have simply followed out the ideas presented in chapter I. "The Involution of Spirit," upon the descending arc of their manifestation, in order to point out to the reader the realm wherein the final separation of the divine unity takes place, and assumes the dual forms of energy, termed "Spirit" and Matter." Having reached this point of differentiation, (the polarizing point, as we term it) we must now turn our attention to the altered mode of motion, the changed polarity, so to say, of these two forces and examine the processes of their action, which are silently at work in Nature's invisible laboratory, gradually externalizing themselves as solid forms cognizable by our physical senses. Then we must show how these forms are ultimated as crystals; primary, molecular crystals; which constitute the first physical foundation of material phenomena from which issue the infinite variety of concrete crystallized forms found here on earth.

NOTE: The polarizing point, as we term it, seems to be an impenetrable mystery to most Occult students. The chief difficulty is in grasping the essential idea that change of energy is simply due to the necessary re-action of all action. The true conception is difficult to express in words, so we will try to illustrate it. If a ball is thrown up into the air spinning round its axis, directly the force which projected it becomes exhausted it will become stationary for one single instant, and then, obeying a different force, re-action sets in and it falls to the ground revolving in exactly the opposite direction. The stationary instant is the "polarizing point."

In order that the laws of crystallization may be clearly apprehended, we must state at the commencement that crystallization means death. By death, we do not mean death in the ordinary acceptation of the term, but we mean the lowest possible minimum in the activities of force—the state we call inertia. This much being granted, we are assumed to be at the beginning of our subject, and also of physical creation.

The first act in creation, according to the Hebrew cosmogony, was the creation of light, Genesis I, 3., "and God said, let there be light, and there was light." As we have already seen, the boundless realm of universal ether containing unconditioned potentialities, requires but the faintest ripple or impluse of the divine mind to set it in vibration, and, instantly, there flashes forth LIGHT, heat, magnetism and molecular force; in short, our universe begins the grand march of cosmic evolution. The first logical effect of this vibration was light, a disruptive centrifugal force, and its correlatives radiating in straight lines, in all possible directions from a center, while from each line of force minor rays radiate at every possible angle to the axial ray. We have, thus, at the very outset of our conception, a complete and perfect network of rays, or lines of energy, moving at the rate of light, 185,000 miles per second through the formless, motionless, ethereal, medium of space.

It will help us in our conception, if we call to mind the fact that matter, to produce in us the sensations we refer to matter, must possess at least three dimensions, viz.; length, breadth and thickness, and each of these dimensions requires at least two equal forces for its expression; also, that all these six equal forces must be concentrated upon a single impenetrable atomic point, and, lastly, this impenetrable atomic point must also consist of two equal forces. Therefore, to produce a single grain of solid matter, a solitary minute crystal, it requires the complete polarization of eight rays of cosmic energy.

Our first duty, then, is to discover our impenetrable atom. When two equal forces coming from opposite directions meet each other, both become polarized, a state of inertia is produced, and an atom, a veritable material atom, is the physical result of this change of energy. From the infinite network of rays produced by the first vibrations of light, it is easy to conceive of the instantaneous evolution of an unlimited number of material atoms from the equally unlimited number of opposing rays of force. Now, we have our necessary atom, which, after all, is nothing but an unknowable something.

This polarized something, however, gives us the first dimension of material forms. It is a point in space, and if we now take two more equal forces at this polarizing point, we have another atom, which, although it gives us nothing in the form of a solid, yet will supply us with the second dimension, viz., a straight line or a point extended by

Fig. 1   Fig. 2

an additional point. Let us now take our impenetrable atomic point, consisting of a single atom, and suppose that four equal forces are concentrated upon it, one from the right and its opponent from the left, one from above and its opponent from below (see fig. 1), and the result is, we possess an ideal form, but still no solid; we have both length and breadth, but no thickness, hence it is only a higher form of the second dimension. But, instead of four, let us now suppose that we have six equal forces concentrated upon our impenetrable atomic point. In addition to those which come from above, below, right and left, we have two more which come from the rear and the front. (see fig. 2) Force 1 comes from the right, its opponent 2 from the left; 3 comes from above, its opponent 4 comes from below; 5 comes from the rear, its opponent 6 comes from the front. Now, what is the result? We have length, breadth and thickness; we have six equal sides; and our unknowable atomic something has become transformed into an ultimate molecule, whose crystallized substance is a cube. It has all of the elements of a solid form, though it can be measured only by the imagination, since microscopes are not yet powerful enough to reveal the first original forms of crystallization. Man's physical senses are too dull to perceive such things but it may be this atomic age will produce some electrical or atomical instrument sensitive enough to detect an original atom of matter. But such wonderful transformations as take place can be seen only by the eye of the spiritual soul whose piercing sight can penetrate the mysteries of Nature's Workshop, the astral light. It is from this source that the principles contained in the above illustrations were obtained.

We see, therefore, that logically it requires six equal forces, meeting at an atomic or impenetrable point, to produce solid dimensional matter. It may, of course, be many more than six, just so they approach in pairs from opposite directions. The only difference would be in the form of the crystal. By keeping in your minds that the atomic point can be made by forces from all possible directions, you will see that as the possible angles are infinite, so the possible crystals are infinite. all in strict conformity to the mathematical law, "each kind of crystal is the type of the substance it forms."

So far, we have spoken only of the three external dimensions recognized by science. There are seven dimensions, in all. In this chapter we shall speak only of the fourth, which was first introduced to the notice of science by Prof. Zollner, in his "Transcendental Physics." No matter how solid any external object may appear, it is not so, for every molecule of which it consists forms an extremely small atomic system of satellite atoms, revolving around their one primary atom, which forms the impenetrable point of every crystal. There is space between every one of them. It is these unoccupied spaces that form the fourth dimension of matter. Note; the above was written some seventy years ago, now that our atomic age is getting into the serious study of the hidden forces of Nature all sorts of undreamed of phenomena are being brought to light. Only time will show how far man may go in exploring the universe.

To de-materialize objective matter and resolve it into its original elements requires the application of an external force powerful enough to polarize the cohesive affinity of the atoms. If in the de-materializing process, electricity is the force used, the form is destroyed, as far as the external plane is concerned. This change releases atomic energy. But, if the force is magnetic, the object is only etherealized, and in this state matter can be made to pass through matter, and the instant, the magnetic dissolvent is withdrawn the object will reassume its original objective shape.

We need scarcely add, that, in this natural fact lies the secret of spiritual materializing phenomena of modern spiritualism, and it forms the true foundation of all magical manifestations of a physical nature. A strong physical medium, even though a helpless tool under the control of a very questionable class of invisibles, can produce phenomena equally as well as the living adept. The only difference is, that, the medium cannot control either the spirits or the phenomena, whereas the adept commands both at will and thus accomplishes his desire. Of all creatures, MAN alone, has the God given ability to consciously develop his spiritual senses (become an Adept, truly understand life) so as to be able to use them in observing the operations of the true laws of life and thus learn the causes of what we experience here on earth.

If rightly used, this occult knowledge could correct many human errors, raise the moral and spiritual standards of men and thus aid in the actual establishment of a sincere fraternal society of all men here on earth.

If it were possible to reduce magical science to a technical formula the following would be, within certain limits, scientifically correct; "As the density of the atoms is to the mass of the substance, so is the power of cohesion to the form of the article." Master that magical receipt and you will be able to work wonders.

From the principles elucidated in this chapter, the reader will perceive that if all the forces of the universe were balanced, the external result would be a complete stop in the progressive work of creation. The variety of substance would be endless; there would be an infinitude of crystals, and our earth would be nothing but a dead crystallized sphere. All forces, when balanced, make crystals, but no motion. Crystallization is the negation of motion. It is death. In our next chapter, our energies will be directed toward the polar opposite of the inert crystal, therein will be disclosed the origin of physical life.

CHAPTER III

THE ORIGIN OF PHYSICAL LIFE

"Mighty oaks from little acorns grow."

When we speak of the genesis of life, we must be understood to mean "the origin of physical life" and not the genesis of life within the divine super-celestial sphere of God's infinite creation.

Man, his constitution, from whence he came, and whither his cyclic journey will carry him, is all that embodied man can hope to understand during his sojourn upon the external planes of matter. The exalted adept craves no more, in fact he cannot obtain any absolute knowledge beyond this, because it is impossible for him to realize anything beyond himself. The perfect man, while incarnated within the astral vortices of humanity, cannot pentrate and know the details of truth belonging to the purely angelic state. Before he can do this he must be forever translated from the astral sphere of the planet which gave him birth, and, he himself, become the angel. The mightiest hierophant (Hermes Trismegistus) this world has ever produced has only been able to speculate as to details within these exalted states, and such speculations without corroborative testimony, are as valueless, when used as the foundation for a system of thought, as the speculations of any religious enthusiast. The only difference between the two consists in the different planes occupied by the respective speculators.

The involution of spirit, and the re-active evolution of matter, are based upon absolute laws, which man may realize for himself. That one form disappears only to give place to another more perfect, is a fact observed throughout Nature in all her departments, and those who possess the attributes of soul-sight in a sufficiently developed state, can perceive the hidden potentialities latent within the outward form. This being so, and we assert of our own spiritual experiences that it is true, then we know that previous to this evolution which we can distinguish taking place all around us, there must have been a process of involution, by which these latent potentialities became involved within external matter. From nothing, nothing can be produced; it is therefore only the blind, unreasoning atheist who can crédit such an illogical creed as the one which has been thus summarized,—

> "From nothing we came, and whatever our station,
> To nothing we owe an immense obligation.
> Whatever we do, or whatever we learn,
> In time we shall all into nothing return."

To the cold, heartless supporter of this soul annihilating system of nothingness, who flaunts his superficially learned authority under the plausible name of Agnostic, we reply with the fully realized consciousness of a deathless, progressive immortality,—

> From an infinite source midst realms of light,
> An offspring from God, my soul took its flight;
> To gain amidst matter, with its trials and pain,
> The knowledge to carry it homeward again.

The immutable laws of Nature may be traced backward into remote eras of sun formation, or carried forward beyond the purview of the present into the equally dim vistas of the eternal future, by those who can see and realize for themselves the planes of both cause and effect. To be able to do this we must attain unto the soul state of equilibrium where both realms unite, where there is neither cause nor effect, but where the two are one. It is from such a state that the teachings contained in this work were derived, and as such we desire them to be closely studied.

The genesis of life must be viewed from the seven planes of its manifestation, to be thoroughly understood. These planes, taken in the order of their cyclic evolution, are as follows; I. Celestial; II. Spiritual; III. Astral; IV. Mineral; V. Vegetable; VI. Animal; VII. Human. From the seventh or human state the life atoms again pass through the astral and spiritual to the celestial; the complete cycle of necessity being composed of ten great cycles, corresponding to the well known Kabbalistical "Sephiroth." At present, we shall only speak of I, IV, and V, these three constituting the foundations from which the others arise.

I. The Celestial State

Of this state it is impossible to give more than a general outline, containing, as it does, the mystery of those inconceivable laws, by the operation of which the Ego becomes a self acting entity. It must suffice to say, that it is this state of celestial life wherein is located the purely embryonic center in the divine arc of progressive being.

This is the point where the diffusive intelligence of the infinite spirit becomes differentiated and atomic; yes, we repeat the word; the divine Ego of the human soul is absolutely atomic. It is a self-existing absolute atom of Jehovah-God, (a Christ Child) which it is impossible to alter, transform, absorb or annihilate, from the supreme moment of its differentiation. It is as eternal and immortal as the infinite, of which it forms a part. But though atomic, it is only so as a purely spiritual conception, a point of radiant light, free from matter, and incapable of uniting itself with it except by means of reflection.

The process of differentiation now claims our attention. This process is consummated within the celestial matrix of angelic parents. By "angelic parents" we mean those divine entities who dwell within the various spheres of purified angelhood.

NOTE: We do not use the term angel in the sense implied by ordinary lexicographers, who interpret the word as "a spirit, servant or messenger," but we use it to mean the highest and most interior state of life which it is possible for mortal mind to grasp. It is infinitely above the so-called spiritual sphere.

The twin souls, male and female, or heavenly Osiris and Isis, (father and mother) form two halves, the masculine and feminine attributes of the divine Ego. They have their alternate cycles of activity and respose. During the cycle of their fruitful activity, the two natures respond with intense vibrations to the divine anthem of creation which creates an influx of the formless, motionless spirit into the celestial sensorium until the whole sphere becomes radiant with the scintillations of spiritual harmony. Obeying the creative impluse, these streams of spiritual force flow along the convergent poles from the various centers of the sphere, each force from the male being met and balanced by that of the female, the contact producing, by the exact equilibrium of the masculine and feminine natures, the living, external sparks of immortal life. In other words, these angelic vibrations transform the formless intelligence, which has been indrawn, into active eternal Egos. As man on earth is the natural outcome of the procreative powers of earthly parents, so the divine activities of the Ego are the spiritual results, in one sense, of the creative attributes of angelic progenitors in the celestial worlds. But we must not be misunderstood upon this point. The Ego is not created in the angelic state; it is only differentiated. The Ego never had an actual genesis; it is coeval with Deity. The celestial harmony or vibrations merely endowed it with spiritual activity, aroused it from its unconscious state, and propelled it forward with the motion of eternal life.

These newly differentiated atoms remain within the paternal soul sphere until the vibrations have ceased. They then become attracted by the reactive energy, and are withdrawn from their celestial matrix and carried by the spiritual currents to the embryonic state of the Seraphs. Their next descent is to the paradisiacal worlds of the Cherubs, where the bisexual Ego becomes the Adam and Eve of Scripture. In the process of time, these pure twin souls, unconsciously obeying the internal impluse of their evolutionary tempter, become attracted towards matter. Up to this point they are pure and innocent, knowing neither good nor evil. Therefore the divine Ego, which is incapable of descent into matter, projects the two souls outward as spiritual monads into the vortex of cosmic evolution, where they become separated and ultimately incarnated within the mineral round of a planet, which is the lowest point in the arc. In making this descent each monad passes through every state in the soul world, then through each of the four realms of the Astral Kingdom before it appears in the external mineral plane. In this state they constitute the hidden fire of matter, latent force, atomic energy.

IV. The Mineral State

Having arrived at the mineral state, we must now ascertain the origin of its motion—its life—since we know that within the mineral lies concealed the potencies of an immortal being.

In the chapter upon the evolution of matter and the laws of crystallization, we endeavored to show that forces, all balanced, produce crystals, and in their production motion comes to an end. Now, to help us in our search for physical life, let us again press into service our six equal forces, our cubic atom, and let us imagine that one of its forces is not equal to its opposite, i.e., the two are not balanced. Say one is less, and that it is the force coming from "before." It is evident that the point will move forward in a straight line, and that the weaker the force coming from the front, the greater will be the velocity of this movement, forward. Now, if this force coming from the front be a mite less than its opposite, its motion will be infinitely slow. Now, let us assume that two of the six forces are less than their opposites. Say the one from the "front" and the one from the "left". It is evident that we should have motion in a curve. But inasmuch as all the others are the same as when we assumed our point, it is plain that this motion in a curve will be in the same plane of surface, and will, in time, describe a circle. But let us assume also that another force is less than its opposite. Say the one coming from "above." What have we now? Our original point with three of its forces less than their opposites. The result will be motion, not motion in a straight line, but in a curve, but not a curve in the same plane of space, and hence it can never describe a circle, but will form a spiral. This spiral is life. That is to say, it is the motion of life. Just keep clear in your mind that if one-half of the primitive forces that make an impenetrable point are less than their opposites, and you have the essential idea of a life force.

Chemical force is death, that is, balanced, still and motionless. The spiral motion is the type of life. It is the motion of life. It is a spiritual screw, with all the mechanical advantages of a screw in penetrating the universe of matter. The spiral varies in magnitude from the infinitely great to the infinitesimally small. Conceive the lesser forces to be but an infinite fraction less than their opposites, then the spiral will be almost infinite in its sweep of curve, and will require almost an eternity to reach its culminating point. On the contrary, the greater the diversity in power the less will become the curve, until we have the infinitesimally small spiral that will culminate almost instantly. Thus between these two extremes we have every phenomenon of life, from that of the tiniest insect to the great cosmic life of an astral universe.

V. The Vegetable State

Since we have found that motion is the life of matter, we must now seek for a still higher form, the immediate product of matter. We therefore ask the student to mentally bridge the distance between the formation of a crystallized atom to the evolution of a planet with its gaseous envelope, called its atmosphere. This done, we will carefully notice the evolution of the first rudimentary forms of vegetable life from which primal forms all the infinite variety of the vegetable kingdom are evolved.

Having made the assertion that the spiral is the motion of life, it will be as well to see if the vegetable kingdom will substantiate our assertion. As some sort of external evidence, then, let us call to our aid the phyllotaxy of plants (as it is technically termed). On the stems of plants the leaves are so placed that a line wound around the stem, and touching the petiole of each leaf, would be a spiral. Where the leaves are in two rows, the space between two opposite leaves is just half a circle or circumference of the stem, and where there are three rows, it is one-third of the circumference, and so on to a regular successive series in different plants which express the ratios of 1-2, 2-5, 3-8, 5-13, 2-21, 13-34, 21-55. The external facts, demonstrated by botanical science, not only confirm our assertion, but also tend to show that vital force is subject to measurement in the plant.

In order to understand how the vegetable evolves from the mineral, not only must the spiral motion of life be held in view, but the various changes of atomic polarity must also be clearly apprehended. As, for instance, the atoms of oxygen and hydrogen by a certain combination produce water. In this union both become polarized, and form a substance which is the polar opposite of their original inflammable states. From this change of polarity we have clouds, oceans and rivers. When the vapor from these waters is drawn upward by the heat of the sun, an infinitely small fraction becomes decomposed into its gaseous state. Although decomposed, the atoms are actually the same as they were previously, after combining in the substance known as water. They have only received a different angle of motion. Whereas before they rotated in a circle, they now ascend and revolve in the form of a spiral. In this ascension from earth they attract or are attracted by the atoms of carbonic acid gas, and instantly a violent rotation among the various atoms is produced. They combine and lo - another transformation has taken place; a new thing has been produced, viz.; a molecule or germ of physical life. Under the control of a central atom of fire, the predominating forces being oxygen and carbon, this union produces another change of polarity, and they become re-attracted to the earth. Here, water or moisture receives them, and a species of vegetable slime is the physical result. When this vegetable product has served its purpose and decays, its liberated atoms arise in their spiral and, in turn, become attracted, or themselves attract, some one or more of the atoms of air with which they have a natural affinity. The same process of polarization is repeated, with some slight variation, and a still higher germ of life is evolved, viz.; the lowest form of the lichen. From the liberated atoms of the lichen spring forth still higher types of the same family until the climax is attained, when, by a higher and more ethereal attraction, the polarized germs bring forth the next higher form of vegetable life. Thus, as the ages roll on, from this original form develop species, classes, and families of vegetation, and from these evolve, through the medium of water, a still higher round in the gamut of being; insect, reptile, animal, and lastly, MAN. After ages of development, we have Man of today.

Space will not admit of our going into further details of this exceedingly interesting subject. Volumes might be filled in recounting the writer's personal experiences in this department of life, watching with intense interest the weird but beautiful transformations of Nature. Much that has been left unnoticed here, should be made the subject of the student's private meditation, and personal research.

CHAPTER IV

It has been well said by an eminent Occultist, "man is most ignorant of those things which are most manifest."

In some departments of Nature this is true, and probably in no other "manifested" department of his being is this truth more strikingly apparent than in that which relates to his sexual nature. He is aware that animal nature is divided into two great classes, male and female, but he knows almost nothing of the spiritual principles which underlie this physical expression of sex. He is fully aware that the union of the two organisms is necessary for the purpose of procreation, but he is fearfully ignorant of those interior processes which produce the actual germs of life. He is more or less acquainted with the fact that in the lower stratas of animated existence bi-sexual organisms are the general rule, and that, occasionally, this bi-sexual nature becomes manifested among men, as seen in the hermaphrodite, but he is quite at a loss to account for such "monstrous" productions. Hence it may be truly said that "man is most ignorant of those things which are most manifest." Therefore, in order to enable the general reader to clearly grasp the various connecting links in the mystical ramifications of sex, to see their perfect harmony, and to understand their relation to each other, we will first speak of the origin of sex; secondly, describe, as clearly as possible its nature and functions; thirdly, point out the relation of the sexes to each other; and, lastly, present a brief application of the whole as it relates to Man, the Universe, and the Immortality of the Soul.

I. The Origin of Sex

Deity is a unity that expresses or manifests itself as a duality. This is the eternal trinity of life.

The infinite ocean of formless spirit within its latent bosom contains all that is, was, or ever can be. Therefore it contains all the elements of sex in their primal state. When the first pulsations of that thought which evolved "the divine idea" became manifest, Nature arrayed herself under the two modes of motion, action and reaction.

The in-breathing and out-breathing of this divine thought, in the earliest dawn of creation, thus instituted the first spiritual attributes of sex. Each function of the Deific soul, which we designate as inspiration and expiration, or action and reaction of the universal life current, thus became differentiated for all eternity as the primary fundamental principle of Manifested Being. The Kabbalistical initiates, of the ages that are gone, formulated this same biune spirit as Love and Wisdom. Love, as the negative or feminine ray, is content and ever seeks to enfold. Wisdom, as the positive, masculine ray, is restless and always in pursuit. The feminine forces are ever striving to encircle the atom, and the masculine forces striving to propel it in a straight line. From this dual action of the spiritual potentialities, is born the "Spiral," the motion of life and symbol of eternal progression.

We cannot attempt any explanation of how the first Deific forms of sexual life become ultimated, nor of the why and wherefore of this celestial existence. It is enough for us that we are enabled by the laws of correspondence to trace the origin of sex to the shores of the great fountain of all existence, and to proclaim it to the world as the first principle of that great central Ego (God) from which all manifested egos derive their being. In order that we may comprehend somewhat of the mysteries of sex as we see them manifested in humanity, we must descend from these practically inconceivable heights of celestial glory and seek for the links of this continuous chain within the highest states of life approachable by the embodied human soul, viz., the angelic sphere of the soul world. Only in these states can we obtain any definite idea of the interior significance of sex, and its mighty importance as a factor in the immortality of the human soul. The first link of this celestial chain, as we have seen, lies concealed within the bosom of the Infinite One. What the succeeding ones may contain we cannot tell, but that they will bear a perfect correspondence to the angelic state we are certain, making due allowance for the difference of their respective states. Therefore, since we know the origin of sex, we will consider its correlatives which we have designated, as inspiration and expiration.

II. Sex, Its Nature and Functions

In the previous chapter we have described in a very brief manner the actual differentiation of the human Ego, as a deific atom of life.

We need not, therefore, repeat any of the description there given, but we will add that it must be a self evident fact that each Ego contains within itself all the primary elements of sex, in a latent condition. These attributes have not as yet been subjected to the requisite conditions for their evolution. In this state, then, there is neither love nor wisdom manifested within the Ego. It cannot know happiness when it is ignorant of sorrow. It cannot form any conception of rest before weariness has approached. There can be no real love for the Ego when it has never experienced the various contrary conditions by which love is distinguished. The wisdom of the Ego in this state is equally latent, since it possesses no means of arriving at a true knowledge of its various surroundings. In this state, we behold the spiritual atom in its primal condition wherein the power of God hath just created it. It is the first spiritual Adam. The various series of states through which this divine Ego must penetrate in order to evolve its soul sphere, are the necessary means by which the internal potentialities of sex must be awakened. When this transpires, the divine Ego becomes pregnant with the dual forms of its own organic life, and the twin souls are born, the male and female elements of its being, which are represented in Genesis as Adam and Eve, knowing neither good nor evil. A beautiful description this of the embryonic human souls. These twin souls are the absolute expression of the masculine and feminine rays of which every absolute atomic Ego is composed. The masculine ray contains a portion of the feminine elements or there could be no reaction of its forces. The feminine ray must likewise contain a portion of the masculine qualities for the same reason. These twin souls contain a portion of each other. They constitute the sun and moon, so to say, of the Ego's creation, and when once they become differentiated they are as eternal and immortal as the EGO which called them into existence. They can be neither absorbed nor annihilated by time nor eternity. They constitute the divine idea of their deific parent, and as such they become the divine expression of Love and Wisdom upon this earth.

NOTE: This statement requires some slight qualification. We mean that no foreign or outside influence can absorb or annihilate the sexual qualities of the soul. It is therefore true that the masculine and feminine attributes of the soul cannot be destroyed as a whole. But the masculine portion may attract its feminine portion or soul mate, and by the intense selfhood of its own dominant forces virtually destroy her manifested existence. This absorption however, is a very rare occurrence and only transpires in the case of those magical adepts of the astral plane who have attained their psychological powers by a complete polarization of all the truly human elements of their internal natures. Such magical adepts become the concentrated centers of spiritual selfishness, but teach the external masses that self is the very demon they have conquered. These occult processes have transformed them into sexless beings, who are neither human nor divine, and yet they profess to be the guardians of "the secret doctrine" of "the sacred science."

In this latter capacity they have formulated much erroneous philosophy, since they are self-magnetized and self-deluded by their own positive idea of Nature to such an extent that they cannot penetrate beyond their own astral spheres, nor receive any knowledge which elevates the soul to higher views and truer conceptions of God's infinite resources. It is from this magical school of thought that mankind have received the doctrines which teach that sex is only the appearance of matter, and not a spiritual reality; whereas, nothing in this mighty universe is so manifest and so eternal as the male and female expressions of the divine soul. These adepts profess to have blended the two; but they have simply polarized the feminine, and created a conscious selfhood of the other.

It is impossible for the absolute Ego (the twin soul) to descend into more outward conditions than the paradisiacal state. So in order to attain the full development of its internal attributes, its own soul, expressed as the male and female elements; each unit is projected outward upon the subjective arc of the great cycle, where, after passing through innumerable spheres and states of life, each finally reaches the polarizing point of creation, in the mineral, which is the turning point in its cycle of necessity. From this point its journey back again is traversed upon the objective arc until it reaches the climax of material forms.

We see, therefore, that the nature of sex is to give perfect expression to the two grand attributes of deific life; Love and Wisdom; that to attain this end the divine soul of the absolute Ego becomes differentiated as male and female, each conscious of itself, each a perfect expression of the positive and negative forces of its being. When once this differentiation is completed, then, they exist as the divine idea of the microcosm and constitute its universe, even as the myriad creations of space constitute the divine idea of the Deity. This being so, each portion of the dual soul maintains forever the perfect symbol of its internal qualities and always gives expression, in its outward form, to the symbol of its internal nature. Like produces like.

The function of the soul is to awaken and round out those qualities and attributes which are latent within; and as we have seen that there are two sets of soul qualities, one the necessary outcome of the other, we see the harmony and the philosophy of the twin forms of life

to express them. Both male and female, as we have endeavored
to show, possess the necessary positive qualities for the perfect subju-
gation of material forces. Hence it is, that, when the twin souls are
projected on their journey into matter, they travel upon divergent
lines, along the subjective arcs of the soul's evolution. These lines (if
it were possible to measure them) would form two sides of an equilat-
eral triangle with mineral as a base, while the apex would indicate the
absolute Ego or point of projection. The return journey between the
mineral and man forms a similar triangle, in reverse, which would indicate the objective arcs of the soul's evolution. When both arcs are
combined they represent the mystical seal of King Solomon, the
double trinity, or six pointed star. This completes two acts in the
grand drama of life. The closing tableau in the first act represents the
stationary forces of the crystallized mineral and the second act the
external conditions of human life.

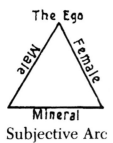
Subjective Arc

Objective Arc

Solomon's Seal

The third and last act in the human cycle briefly reviews the
whole of the previous two arcs and evolves another six pointed star
which represents the higher and lower planes of manifestation. (This
last act is the transit of the soul through the seven super mundane
spheres of disembodied existence from man to the angel.) But, in its
grand outlines it is also a spiritual trine whose closing tableau represents the reunion of the twin souls symbolized by St. John as the
celestial marriage of the lamb. Thus, we begin with the one divine
monad or Ego and in the course of its expression and of the gradual
evolution of its sexual attributes, we see it slowly transform into a
trinity. This trinity, in the sub-cycles of its evolution, forms three triangles, which constitute the symbol of its forces three times expressed
upon the three sub-cycles of its journey. These three sub-cycles are the
subjective arc or the cycle of unconsciousness, the objective arc or
cycle of intelligence, and the ethereal arc or cycle of soul conscious-

ness. The results so far of our present research show that the origin of sex begins with God; that the nature of sex is the manifestation of his biune spirit, and its functions are the spiral motion of its evolutionary forces that awaken and round out its latent possibilities.

It now becomes our duty to consider the third section of our subject, the relation of the sexes to each other.

III. The Relation of the Sexes to Each Other

Male and female exist in Nature as the representative expressions of wisdom and love. Their functions correspond exactly with their sex, and in actual life it may be truly said that woman is ever the center of the love element of humanity. Her thoughts and desires constitute the index of her mission on earth. In her, we behold the gentle, yielding, loving nature which softens and harmonizes man's positive spirit of aggression. In her delicate nature we see the lovely center of maternal care and affection. She is the weaker portion of the dual soul upon the physical plane, but her physical weakness constitutes the great center of her spiritual strength. As the weaker sex, we may think that her true place is that of subjection to man, but, on the contrary, her more delicate forces become her most potent weapon, and instead of being the subject she ascends the throne of the conqueror. Man becomes a pliable medium in her hands, and is led a willing captive by her subtle power and resources.

In man we behold the positive, aggressive Lord of Creation, that portion of the soul which becomes the restless explorer of Nature seeking for wisdom. Man's will is electric, penetrating and disruptive. The will of woman is magnetic, attractive and formative. Hence they express the polar opposites of Nature's forces.

The twin souls are related to each other primarily as brother and sister, and finally as man and wife. In this latter state their true meeting place is the plane of embodied humanity, but, during the present cycle, very few of these spiritual unions take place. But, whenever the two halves of the same divine Ego do meet, love is the natural consequence; not the physical sensations produced by the animal magnetisms of their sexual natures, but the deep, silent emotions of the soul; the responsive vibrations of their internal natures toward each other; the blissful silence of two souls in perfect rapport wherein neither careth to speak. This spiritual love is the outcome of their divine relationship, and should never be set aside nor crushed by any worldly considerations. But, on the contrary, wherever possible, these pure intuitions of the soul should be obeyed. They cannot deceive nor lead astray, because the soul never makes a mistake when claiming its own. Should circumstances in life or any other material consideration prevent their rightful union, the fact that they have actually met will constitute an invisible connection, a spiritual rapport, between them which no earthly power or device can break. Deep down within the secret chambers of the heart the image of the loved one will be treasured and its continual presence will poison and corrode everything which pertains toward an ephemeral affection for another. If a female should marry under these circumstances, and become the mother of children, it will frequently transpire that the actual germs of spiritual life will be transmitted by this absent one. The external husband only provides the purely physical conditions for the manifestation of the spiritual offspring of the true Lord. The rejected soul-mate, the spiritual bridegroom, is the real father, and very often the child born will resemble the image of its true parent.

By far the most important of the various relations of the sexes toward each other is that which pertains to their sexual intercourse. Untold misery, suffering and crime are born into the world through the sensual depravity of mankind on the one hand, and their benighted ignorance of human nature upon the other. We are sorry that such a delicate subject cannot be properly treated in the present work, so we will only add that man and wife should harmonize with each other, both in physical temperament and in magnetic polarity. No marriage union should be thought of where these essential points of comparison are wanting. Neither wealth, fame, nor worldly position, can compensate for the lack of natural harmony. Discordant unions are the harbingers of sorrow, crime and disease. Sexual union between inharmonious souls evolves the seeds of every species of wickedness and sexual disorder. It may not become apparent to the producer thereof, but it exists within the spaces of human life ready to spring into concrete form under the first favorable conditions.

Let those who deliberately misuse their sexual nature, to satisfy licentious wicked desires, stop in the deadly path. Such thoughts and actions lead to madness and actual death.

The purely Martial man will prove a continual curse to the cold-natured Saturnine woman, and vice versa. This may not be any fault of the man or woman, but it is the discordant polarities of their astral constitutions. The same will hold good between natures of the Earthy triplicity and those born under the Airy triplicity. A true knowledge of the science of the stars is necessary to determine conjugal harmony or discord. Now, the various sections of our subject are completed, and it only remains for us to apply the logical outcome of the principles of sex as they affect man, the universe and the immortality of the soul.

As we view the outward forms of man and woman we cannot fail to observe the perfect harmony between the external appearance and the internal cause. Their organisms are the concrete image of the principles concealed within. It would be the extreme height of absurdity for us to believe that a materialized form bears no correspondence to the forces which created it. The form cannot exist without an internal cause, and the internal cause is powerless to produce any external form apart from the reflected image of itself and its functions. Under these circumstances it must be self-evident that every male organism is the absolute outcome of masculine forces, and every female organism the product of feminine qualities. Therefore, a male soul cannot be born into the world under the cover of a female form. Neither can a female soul be ushered upon the planes of humanity imprisoned within the masculine body. These are Nature's simple facts, which ought to be apparent to every thinking mind. But it seems that such is not the case, for we are seriously informed by certain theosophical writers that during the various incarnations of the human soul within the human form, man may incarnate in the form of a woman, and vice versa. We can only say that such unutterable nonsense is almost beneath the notice of any sane mind, and those who make such ridiculous assertions are not only bound to the external plane of appearances, but are completely ignorant of the true light of Occult Science.

It often transpires that we find men who appear to possess true feminine natures, and women who seem to be masculine in temperament, but this is not really the case. It is only an appearance caused by the combined influence of pre-natal conditions, and stellar positions at birth. The Buddhistical conception of man and woman rounding out until sex becomes obliterated, is probably the most transcendental delusion that ever originated within the oriental brain; therefore, we will take no further notice of such mystical folly.

The human form, as male and female, is the material culmination of Nature's sexual expression. Upon this plane she can go no further, for beyond this limit we step within the spaces of the ether where Nature continues her wonderful expression of sex in strict harmony with the laws of correspondence to the planes below. While dealing with the forms assumed by man, we must briefly notice those vital secretions which form the physical conditions for re-production of his kind. The seminal fluids are the most ethereal of all physical secretions, and contain the very quintessence of human nature. The sexual organism exists as a factor in procreation, therefore, the organs have their proper functions and use or they would not be present. To suddenly and completely suppress their natural functions will do a great deal of physical and spiritual harm, because the reaction will create violent discord within the ethereal constitution. In fact, the complete suppression is almost as bad as excessive use or lustful indulgence. It is only one of the two extremes, nothing more. When the sexual organism is evolved above the physical plane of its manifestation, the seminal fluids are absorbed by the magnetic constitution and the etherealized atoms help to build up the spiritual body of man. But when this is not so these seminal germs, if not passed off amid the other secretions from the body, live and germinate a swarm of elemental lifeforms which rob the organism of a portion of its vitality.

To obey the laws of Nature is the only safe and sure road to evolve the spiritual senses of the soul, and one of these laws is the rightful union of the sexes. Celibacy in itself is not a natural state; it is purely artificial, because it ignores one of the principal elements of our being. Therefore, there is great spiritual danger in a celibate life, and nine tenths of the mystical manias and spiritual saturnalia of past history have originated among celibates. It is well to remember this at the present day, as there is some considerable danger of history repeating itself.

Celibacy, as a quick means of artificially stimulating and producing certain so-called spiritual powers and mediumistic states, is a successful method, so far as mere psychological results are concerned, but one that is fraught with terrible danger. It is a method that should be discouraged in all cases wherein the spiritual constitution of the organism is in a negative conditon. Under the most favorable circumstances it is a very questionable practice unless the spiritual nature is sufficiently active to absorb and use the etherealized atoms of the seminal fluid which has become dematerialized by the magnetic activities of Occult training.

Any species of "forcing" the attributes of the soul, renders their manifestations weak and unhealthy, hence liable to error and delusion. It is upon this basis that we account for the spiritual absurdities of many oriental mystics. Their severe asceticism renders them the unsuspecting prey of every imaginable species of Occult delusion. Celibacy, then, must only take place when the animal nature has been evolved so far upward toward the higher principles, that the sexual propensities are susceptible of extending their vibrations to a higher plane of action. In this case, celibacy becomes an absolute necessity of further Occult progress. Herein, we see once more the paradox of truth. Upon one plane it becomes a delusion and a snare, but upon a higher plane it contains all the elements of a glorious truth. Consequently no being, human or divine, can lay down any hard and fast line to guide the various processes of spiritual development. Each organism requires a system that is peculiar to itself, each soul a training specially adapted to the plane it occupies. From this it will be seen that nothing more than the general principles of Occult training can be given. From such outlines each must adapt such rules and exercises as are applicable to him as he learns from self study and practice. And only those who are themselves spiritually enlightened can see the true state of the soul and, physician-like, scientifically, prescribe for its various disorders.

When we regard the mystical ramifications of sex as represented in the universal creation of suns, stars, moons and planets, we see the same principles at work throughout every department of their being, even to their shape and the form of their orbit. The suns are masculine, and represent the cosmic male spirit. The planets are feminine, and consequently become the fruitful wombs of progressive life. The moons are neither the one nor the other; they are the conflicting offspring of disturbing forces within the sun and its planet. They are the lowest organic expression of planetary life, and as such represent the state of the hermaphrodite. So, both in man and in the universe, the potentialities of sex swing the mighty pendulum of thought and motion.

The grand object which the divine Ego seeks to realize in the evolution of the human soul, is the complete differentiation of its latent attributes. The soul must become the expression of both its qualities, and must express the true nature of the biune spirit; hence male and female evolution is the outcome. Each soul rounds out and completes, so to say, its own section of the Ego, and in doing this it becomes individualized as a complete expression of one ray of the divine idea, hence it has a perfect identity with its source. Both male and female complete the whole, and are related to each other as Osiris and Isis; brother and sister; their individuality, in the form of their spiritual identity, is forever preserved, and their united as well as their separate consciousness becomes an attribute of their glorious immortality. Without sex there cannot be eternal life, and to absorb or destroy these principles in the human organism brings about a divorce between man and his divinity, and thus robs conscious humanity of its deathless immortality.

IV. The Mystery of Isis

The human organism, in its more interior sense, is the mystical uterus of Isis, (that is, the human organism is the uterus of Nature), ever pregnant with the Holy Ghost, (the incarnated soul), which, when the period of gestation is completed, (the cycle of evolution), shall give birth to the Son of God, whose kingdom is not of this earth, but of Heaven (this means, the soul which has attained its immortality, is a Son of God, etc., whose future state of being is the boundless realm of Spirit.) I and the Father are one, meaning that the human Ego is but an atom of the Father, is not the same idea as the more interior state of Adeptship or being at one with God. This at-one-ment is the mystical Atonement of the Christ (Spirit) within the human soul, (you are at peace with your spiritual conscience.) These ideas if meditated upon, will reveal unto you the whole mystery of Christ and the immaculate conception. The idea of the human organism being the mystical womb of Nature, was the cause of the Ancient Priests of the sanctuary elaborating the magnificent funerals, the cremation of the Hindoo, the Greek and Roman rites, and embalming of the Egyptians. It was the most important ceremony of Ancient times, because the most mystically important and the most sublime rite that the soul can pass, from matter to spirit, or "back to the Father's home."

From the Phallic symbolism of ancient sex-worship, through the dual power of love and hatred, lust and brutality, the same law holds true. Sex is the great primal law of Nature, both visible and invisible, objective and subjective. The powers of love and hatred in man, are feminine and masculine. The man or woman who cannot love is an inhuman monster; there is nothing human about them, except the outward physical form of humanity, which is but the lamb's clothing that ill conceals the ravenous wolf within. It is only the truly human that can truly love, and in loving let their souls transcend all lower passions. Lust is not love. Lust is the animal or passional appetite, with nothing human about it, and woe be to those whose love cannot rise above the plane of lust.

The deliberate use of so-called "CHECKS" against conception, is a fearful crime, and should never, under any circumstances, be resorted to. The vital germ-seeds so wasted will not leave you, but, like famished vampires, they will germinate within the odyllic soul-sphere. Your cruel act has separated the Divine spark from them; only the animal portion remains, and they become the spiritual elementaries of your own creation, who, like parasites will suck your life away.

If you are not perfectly confident and certain that your sexual passions are pure and respond only to that one whose soul-affinity you possess, then at once and forever debar the passion completely, and lead a life of celibacy, for the soul cannot evolve healthy psychic powers where the tainted mildew of either lust or an impure life is allowed to remain. If psychic powers are developed in such a state, they are abnormal and impure, mere spiritual fungi of the soul, more tender than hothouse plants, because they are forced and reared under artificial conditions and, consequently, liable to wither and die upon exposure to the first blighting currents of the Astral light, when disastrous results always follow.

Read, mark, learn and inwardly digest these great fundamental truths. There is no middle course for the Neophyte who aims at the practical realization of the occult powers of his soul. It is either heaven and the ultimate glories of eternal progression, or it is hell and ruination, with the terrible surroundings of the Black Magician and almost a certainty of final extinction in the elementary spheres of the soul-worlds.

True it is, that so-called spiritual gifts do not depend upon moral purity, but the utility of these attributes do; hence, avoid the curse of (irresponsible) mediumship. Trust to no controlling spirit guide. ALWAYS remain the complete master of your own organism at any cost. Once you submit to hypnosis or any control, it is difficult to free yourself, and the oftener you submit the weaker you become until you are no longer able to make any decision for yourself, you have been robbed of all will power. You have become a helpless tool and must do as you are told. The modern spiritualistic seances, or spirit circles, are often, very often, nothing but steaming hotbeds of vice and spiritual impurity. Not all are such; far from it, but only the sacred family circle at home with kindred souls, whose blameless lives and moral purity form an impassable barrier to either elemental or elementary, is spiritual intercourse safe. There, and there only, can Spiritualists obtain anything worth knowing or be free from danger.

We now approach a most sacred subject and one the most vital to both man and woman, because it deals with the fundamental principles of their being, and explains how, through the magical attraction of human passions, they may become the unconscious instrument of untold evil by launching upon an already over-suffering humanity, cruel monsters in human form.

There are many spiritualistic teachers who assert that nothing exists in Nature but the human, but God forbid that we should accept as human that which is yet animal. The occultists cannot afford time to moralize upon the mysterious laws of Nature. He knows that such laws exist, and that alone concerns him. The teachers conception of that which constitutes good and evil, morality and immorality, is not the standard the occultist can accept for one moment.

In the first place it must be understood that the offspring of the average of human beings, under average conditions, will be quite human, and more or less intellectual according to the accidental conditions that surround their prenatal state. But parents of small spirituality and under the dominant influence of the animal passions, are to be considered as below the average of mankind. It is chiefly of this class we shall speak.

In the second place, it must be known that there are vast realms and races of beings existing in, on and around our planet who are invisible to most people. These beings are neither elementary nor elemental spirits, but aireal beings, possessing a very powerful affinity to man. There are seven grades of them corresponding with the seven planetary states, and, consequently, corresponding with the seven great divisions of the human race. It is this class of beings that can and do become incarnated in the human organism. The class of persons who most frequently are the means of incarnating these beings are those of large animal propensity and small spirituality. The conditions are generally sexual intercourse when the male is in a state of intoxication or both may be so. When thus inflamed with drink, lust and other vile passions and thoughts, there is no possible chance for anything human. When conception takes place under these conditions, an inhuman soul is the result. It is from such unions as these that the inhuman Neros and Nana Sahibs of history originated. Remember, that social position or artificial education, cannot alter the natural result. People of this class are numerous, from the highest to the lowest, and "dope" addicts are under the same laws and penalty.

The second class of individuals who may be the means of such incarnations are nervous, sensitive people, who are actually obsessed by elementaries during sexual union, because, by such obsessions, the elementaries seem to realize and enjoy the excitement of their lustful passions. In all such cases inhuman incarnation is the result. Should conception take place under these conditions, the only remedy these people have is to abstain completely, or prevent, by the moral purity of their lives, the possibility of elementary obsession. And lastly, a woman may, during the period of gestation, magnetically attach an evil being to her otherwise human child, who will obsess it completely during life, and doubtless lead it to the scaffold or asylum. This magnetic attachment is caused by some sudden, extreme exercise of her passions.

Enough has now been said to enable the thoughtful student to see the great mystery of sex, completely. He now knows the use and abuse of sex; understands how to become the parent of good, noble, intellectual human souls for his family and how to avoid causing the production of monsters.

Continuing the same laws, we now leave the physical and enter the spiritual or magnetic states of being and find sex still remains the supreme law. That same principle which manifests itself as parental instinct and ferocious passion in the animal; and as affection and lust, jealousy and hatred in the human; blooms out into its own pure state in the Angelic or celestial condition, as Love and Wisdom, in this most interior state. Its attributes in all exterior states of angelic or spiritual existence are intuition and reason, the feminine and masculine qualities of each human soul.

Magnetism is of two kinds, viz.; animal and mineral, and each kind is dual, or male and female, positive and negative. It is the Astral fluid containing the properties of the body with which it is connected; hence, sex always predominates the very soul-force of Nature, because it is through the agency of this Astral fluid that all the various phenomena are produced, it is the actual cause of every effect in both the material and spiritual planes of existence. This force is the indispensable agent of every Adept, Magician or Mesmerizer, and the cause of all magnetic and occult phenomena. It pervades every atom of the vast universe and all of life including planets and stars are subject to this double law of sex, action and repose. Just as night rests humanity from the day's activity, does this force restore the equilibrium of the spiritual and cosmic planes of Nature.

The magnetic and Astral fluid is androgyne or bi-sexual, (exactly like the human soul) because equilibrium is but the resultant of two forces eternally re-acting upon each other, this is life. When these two forces expand and remain so long inactive as to equal each other and come to complete rest, the condition is death. The same soul-force, in the hands of the expert magician, has control over life and death, for, if the magician wills a thing and his will is sufficiently strong, that thing is done, this is the positive action. Mediumship is the reverse, the negative or passive, it is the feminine which receives.

Now we come to the last mystery of the Grade of Eros. It is the climax of the potential powers of sex, and embraces all the previous teachings in the recognition of the human organism, as the grand mystical uterus of Nature. It is the sacred Yoni of the glorious Isis, the Universal Mother. It is this mystery that explains the immaculate conception of the Christ child, or Divine human within us. It is the immortal soul begotten of the Father, enclosed or incarnated in the flesh, (the human organism.)

The Virgin Womb, which shall give birth to the immortal Son of God, when the period of gestation (human incarnation in or on this material plane) is completed. This period of gestation is, of course, the great cycle of necessity; for, "except ye be born again ye cannot enter the Kingdom of Heaven." Certainly not. The human soul, while incarnated in the physical organism, is within the womb of Nature and it is only when its full time has elapsed, and it has gained its immortality, that it is re-born into the realm of spirit. It has burst the bonds of flesh and blood; escaped from its mother's womb, the uterus of Nature, and is free again.

And now, dear reader, that we have finished our chapter on sex; can you spare the time to close the book and calmly, quietly and seriously contemplate on what sex really means?

Let your soul rise as high as possible, in pure, holy thoughts; thinking only of that mysterious something in life which is able to develop beautiful, fragrant flowers; delicious, luscious fruit and nourishing grain foods; all from tiny seeds placed in the ground.

How this is accomplished is far beyond our understanding. Yet, men and women are high above the products of the soil, the birds, the fish and the animal kingdom. We have freedom of thought and action, and should keep out of the mire. If we honestly desire the good, noble things of life, we can live as we think and thus help to make a glorious heaven here on earth; a real, sincere, friendly brotherhood of men and women; free of greedy, selfish and immoral strife and ill will toward each other. Why not try for it?

Truly, this is the eternal prayer of all upright men and women, to have peace and harmony here on earth.

THE SCIENCE OF THE SOUL—SECTION II
THE TRANSITION OF LIFE
CHAPTER I

INCARNATION AND RE-INCARNATION

Probably no truth has been more completely inverted by the ignorant and concealed by the learned than that of re-incarnation. In every age it has been thought necessary by the priesthood to over-awe the uneducated masses by some species of pious jugglery, and the popular theory of re-incarnation, as understood and taught at the present day, is a typical example of truth thus perverted.

By re-incarnation we mean, as now currently understood, the doctrine of the re-birth of the human soul in various human forms and personalities, in different ages, upon the same planet.

NOTE: The reader must bear in mind that the doctrine of human re-incarnation is not, strictly speaking, a doctrine of Occultism. It is a theological doctrine of oriental sacerdotalism, formulated by the priesthood either to conceal the real truth, or to account for what they themselves could not comprehend or explain. This same thought is expressed by Ranga Hilyod, a very ancient sage of India, in his book, Illuminated Brahminism, The True Theosophy.

In every bundle of theological chaff there is, undoubtedly, concealed a grain of genuine truth. This is particularly the case with this doctrine. Up to a given point its teachings are those of truth itself, but beyond this point the doctrine of re-birth into physical conditions becomes one of the greatest delusions with which the mystical student has to deal. To those who are purely upon the plain of appearances it possesses an almost irresistible attraction because it appears to account, in a most rational and philosophical manner, for the wide difference manifested in the mental, social and moral conditions of humanity. Upon the external plane it seems to settle the question of good and evil, and harmonizes all our inequalities with what seems divine justice. All these delusive appearances, however, are but empty shadows of the phenomenal world. They can only deceive those who are entirely upon the external plane and who have accepted such teachings without verifying the doctrines for themselves. There are two methods of verification; one, the actual experiences of the soul, the other, the response of the soul to the thoughts and ideas we derive from an author's work. Unfortunately, this latter kind of verification is subject to very serious drawbacks. A mediumistic nature may respond to error because of the more potent thought of the writer, or, if over-sensitive may be superficial enough to respond to an erroneous idea through pure sentiment. These means have been seized by the Inversive Brethren to enable them to fasten upon the sensitive minds, and mediumistic natures of the western race, these erroneous, delusive doctrines of karma and re-incarnation. The most finely spun ideals of "the higher life," of "Devachan," of "The Masters," and of "blissful Nirvana," have been and are being presented by a host of sentimental, spiritually sick, mystical writers to explain "the glorious mysteries" of Nature and "the secret doctrine" of all religious philosophies, of which they themselves, in real truth, know very little, apart from the mediumistic ideas which are projected toward them by the Inversive Magi. The whole craze is merely a metaphysical delusion cast over their mentalities by means of a magnetic glamor to deceive them and their readers.

The reader must not suppose that because a person studies the various branches of Occult science, tries to lead an ideal life, and, after acquiring a very large stock of booklore-occultism, begins to write and publish works upon mystical subjects, that the person is beyond the worldly plane. On the contrary, this class are the most external of all, because they become dominated by the thought forms of certain Occult leaders upon the physical plane, and their sensitive natures become absolutely blind to the real spiritual truth. We have seen numerous examples of this among the popular writers upon Modern Theosophy. The soul alone is capable of penetrating the realm of shadows, and seeing through the inverted images to learn the real truth.

It seems very strange that the external followers of "the path" which leads to physical re-incarnation, can be so blind as to imagine that this earth is the only place within God's infinite universe whereon divine justice can be satisfied, and due punishment meted out to the evil doer. The life beyond is far more real, far more earnest, and a much more conscious life than here on earth. Surely, then, the soul can work out its redemption there better than here. Surely, the soul ought to be granted the privilege of knowing for what wrong it is being made to suffer, but this is not the case according to the fallacies of esoteric Buddhism. But alas; the spiritually blind are blind indeed.

They that have eyes to see let them see. For modern Buddhistic Theosophy cannot perceive in the slightest degree, beyond the dull veil of external matter.

As a typical example of such material conceptions, we will quote from a publication professing to give the secret doctrines of all religions, The Mystery of the Ages, by Marie, Countess of Caithness. In a footnote upon the subject of Karma, page 143, the writer says; "Karma is the law of consequences, by which every act receives its exact recompense in the next life when the soul is born again. But unless the same soul passes on through a succession of earth lives such a recompense is impossible, and neither could it expiate or make amends for the injuries it may have done to others unless again brought into contact with them."

So thoroughly materialistic are the ideas conveyed in the above extract that one would think that esoteric Buddhism was nothing but materialism run to seed. According to such erroneous theories we are to believe that recompense for evil doing is impossible except by physical re-birth. Such writers are so destitute of the higher spiritual perception that they cannot comprehend any process of repentance and purification except upon the material earth, while incased within a material organism. We can only say to the followers of such, that when authors set themselves upon such a pinnacle of knowledge as to declare what is not possible within the mighty spaces of spiritual existence, they ought to be in a position to verify their assertions. If they cannot do this, then they are simply boasting pretenders to a state of knowledge and spiritual development which they do not possess, and seeing that their teachings do not in any sense agree with the actual experiences of those who have penetrated the realm of spirit, and investigated the mysteries of life for themselves, we challenge their right to speak with such authority. How different from such ideas are the real truths of Nature. How different are spiritual realities from such oriental theories and dreamy speculations. The talented author of "Art Magic" and "Ghost Land", who for years had investigated the various unseen realms of life for himself, gives the world the brief results of his life-long research in the latter work. Speaking upon re-incarnation this author says; "To my dim apprehension, and in view of my long years of wandering through spirit spheres, where teaching spirits and blessed angels guided my soul's ardent explorations, this brief summary of our pre-existent states explains all that the re-incarnationists have labored so sedulously to theorize upon. The universal and reiterated assertions of myriads of spirits in every stage of a progressive beyond, convinced me there was NO return to mortal birth, NO retrogression in the scale of cosmic being, as a return to material incarnations undoubtedly would be, and all the demands of progress, justice, and advancement, are supplied by the opportunities offered the soul in the sphere of spiritual existence."

NOTE: At the time these books were written (1875-76) modern theosophists knew nothing of the Buddhistical theories they have since adopted. Our author refers to the re-incarnation theory of the Spiritualists of France. Not until the Theosophical Society removed its headquarters to India did it go crazy after India's subtle delusions.

The same author concludes the chapter of his experiences in the following eloquent words; "I have stood on the threshold of glorious lands, where my eyes could perceive the radiance of celestial spheres, the memory of whose brightness will warn and beckon me upwards forever."

The personal experiences thus narrated correspond exactly in their results with those of the present writer, and also with many other true spiritually initiated Occultists with whom we are associated. Can the carefully tabulated results of all our united labors count for nought? Is it possible that the unanimous but legitimate conclusions of scores of spiritual investigators, each and all of whom were specially qualified for research by reason of their own soul development, are false and delusive? Must the result of our own personal research and actual experiences of the soul within the realm of spirit be cast away as unreliable, simply, because they conflict with an old fossilized theory of some priestly metaphysicians? Not so, dear reader; not so. "Prove all things," saith the apostle, "hold fast that which is good;" and such is our humble intention, and our advice to all students searching for truth.

We repeat what we have so often said to those who have studied under our care, that re-incarnation, as taught by modern writers, is nothing but a theory of the physical intellect. In other words, it is the metaphysical outcome of intellectual force destitute of spiritual intuition or truth. It is an attempt of external mind to harmonize good and evil and nothing more. It contains nothing approaching to the pure intuitions of the spirit in its composition. It was formulated to deceive, by cunning priestly minds, in the first instance, and afterwards accepted as a divine truth by those who possess nothing but their intellects to guide them in their gropings for truth. Knowing as we do the Why and Wherefore of its present diffusion of error, we challenge all esoteric Buddhists to produce one single individual, a responsible medium who has penetrated the realms of spirit for himself, who can truthfully say that the theory agrees with the actual results of his own personal investigations. From the beginning to the end, this re-incarnation and Karma doctrine of Buddhism is a purely external theory which tries to explain the apparent contradictions of physical Nature; hence it is destitute of spiritual proof, or of the possibility of spiritual proof, and it is palmed off upon the mental currents of western thought as emanating from supposed holy (?) mahatmas. But we deny in toto that such a theory is taught or ever has been taught, as a true theory, by any real adept. The magical hierophants of the Inversive Magi, are beings we consider not worthy of the name of Adept, because they are the legionaries of the Dark Satellite, and as such are only adepts so far as the mysteries of practical magic are concerned. They cannot penetrate beyond the astral zones of the cosmic and magnetic elementals, hence they know absolutely nothing of the higher states of the soul world, or of the mysteries of angelic life. They deny their very existence, and substitute a delusive Devachan, and dreamy Nirvana of nothingness in their place.

Before going any further we would impress upon our student the fact that there is not a single doctrine within the whole range of Occult science that is not susceptible in its interpretation to the well known Latin proverb, "cum grano salis." Further, that every truth is a paradox when viewed from different planes; this latter fact is especially true regarding re-incarnation.

We now commence at the point where we left off in our previous chapter, in the descent of life into external conditions. From this point we see it enter and successively pass through the mineral, vegetable and animal life waves of the planet. In obedience to the higher and more interior laws of its own especial round, the divine attributes are ever seeking to unfold their involved potentialities. No sooner is one form dispensed with, or its capabilities exhausted, than a new and still higher form is brought into requisition, each in its turn becoming more complex in its structure and diversified in its functions. Thus, we see the atom of life commencing in the mineral of the external world, working upward and outward. The grand spiral of its evolutionary life is carried forward slowly, imperceptibly, but always progressively, through the higher states. There is no form too simple, no organism too complex, for the inconceivably marvellous adaptability of the human soul in its divine struggles of progressive life.

Throughout the entire cycle of necessity, the character of its genius, the degree of its spiritual emanation, and the state of life to which it originally belonged, are preserved with mathematical exactitude. These states correspond, in a general sense, to the four ancient elements, Fire, Earth, Air, and Water. Yet, as a matter of purification alone, each atom must pass through and be a part of all these states upon its upward journey. Not only so, but before the human monad can possibly attain the climax of its material evolution, which is the grand terminus of its earthly incarnations, it must also have passed through certain phases of its existence upon each planet to which its microcosmic nature in the embodied man shall bear a mathematical correspondence. Thus, between the mineral and man there is a perfect scale of life; no one form being parallel with another in the grand chain of cosmic being. Even the insects count, in the links, as progressive states. In the whole of this chain are seven worlds through which the soul monad migrates, and from whatever point or planet it commences its toilsome cosmic journey, the seventh planet is the end of its material orbit, and the sphere wherein it attains the human form divine. Here it becomes conscious of life, able to learn and understand. In no case does the soul monad commence as a mineral and attain unto the animal or human plane upon the same planet. It rests or becomes latent on each alternate planet. For instance, the mineral atoms upon this earth will undergo a purely impersonal cycle upon Venus, which is their next sphere, and then become incarnated within the vegetable plane upon the next planet, and so on; while the mineral atoms of the planet Mars, when they reach the Earth will be purely impersonal beings and will not incarnate here as objective forms but will pass their cycle in the astral spaces, then enter into material conditions again upon Venus. Thus, the soul monad has four objective states, and three subjective states. The objective states are as; 1-3-5-7,

viz.; the mineral, vegetable, animal and man. The subjective states are
as; 2-4-6, negative states of its embryonic being. The awakening to
conscious life with ability to think and understand is carried out by
the soul after it attains the objective human form or seventh (7) state.
The next state is beyond matter. "Once and only once," saith the law.
After the human state, Nature shuts the door behind her. Eternal progression is the anthem of all creative life.

NOTE: We have omitted to note the exceptions to the general laws of re-incarnation
which have been set forth. There are three classes of exceptions in which re-birth
within the human organism may be the usual course.

Class I. Cases of abortion, or of still-born children. These, not having attained consciousness of external human life, may, and in fact generally do, become re-incarnated.

Class II. Cases of natural born idiots. Though it is very rare that even
idiots are so lost to all external consciousness as to make re-birth necessary to them.

Class III. Cases of special "Messianic" incarnation by exalted souls, for the
special purpose of enlightening the race. The laws which govern this mystery
are unknown to all except the highest adepts. Such an incarnation transpires about
every 600 years, and never twice in succession to the same race. In all cases of
Messiahship these glorious souls are conscious of their mission from the moment
of birth, though doubtless they wisely keep such precious knowledge to themselves as a protection against the tender mercies of the dominant priesthood of
their generation. This class may be called cases of conscious re-incarnation. The
same spirit is never so incarnated more than once. Hence the stories of Buddha's
numerous incarnations are pure fiction.

When we apply these laws to external life we can gauge the soul's
past history with an accuracy which is truly marvelous. Thus, for
instance, the truly Martial individual belongs to that state of life known
in Occult phraseology as Fiery, and consequently those peculiar and
especial attributes were "rounded out" upon the planet known as Mars.
That is to say, the fiery characteristics of an atom belonging to that
state of life corresponding to the Fiery triplicity, were evolved through
various organic forms during its cycle of incarnation upon the planet
of Mars. On the other hand, a Saturnine individual, during its sojourn
upon the Martial planet was but little attracted to the Maritial forms
of existence. In fact, the soul monad, at that particular stage of its
journey, passed through a kind of impersonal coma instead of an active
evolutionary life. This was because there was but little affinity between
itself and the planet. Consequently, the planet had not sufficient attractive power to project the impersonal soul into the more outward
forms of organic being. The same may be said of each planetary char-

acteristic. Their latent or active expression in the embodied individual reveals to the initiated mind the whole of the soul's past history during the various stages of its impersonal planetary life. A careful study of this fact will do much to explain the deeper mysteries of Astrology. The planets at a person's birth do not make him what he is; they only harmonize with his conditions.

During the process of the soul's involution, the monad is not actually incarnated in any form whatever. The soul descends into earthly conditions down the subjective arc of the spiral, and re-ascends upon the objective arc. Rebirth commences, as before stated, when the objective mineral state is reached. The process of the monad's descent through the various realms, is accomplished by a gradual polarization of its Deific powers, caused by its contact with the gradually externalizing conditions of the downward arc of the cycle. At each step the soul becomes more and more involved within the material. "The sphere of re-incarnation," embracing the birth in an external form, its transient life there, then death, and then, the same soul's re-birth in a higher and more perfect form of life, is really comprised between the Mineral plane and Man. Between these two planes, the soul must pass through countless forms and phases. It is an absolute truth that, as an impersonal being, "man lives upon many earths before he reaches this one. Myriads of worlds swarm in space where the soul in rudimental states performs its pilgrimages until its cyclic progress enables it to reach the magnificently organized planet, whose glorious function it is to confer upon the soul, self-consciousness." At this point alone does the soul become man. In every other step, of its wild, cosmic journey, it is but an embryonic being, a fleeting, temporary shape of matter, an impersonal creature in which a part, but only a part, of the imprisoned soul shines forth; a rudimental form with rudimental functions, ever living, dying, then sustaining a brief spiritual existence only to be re-born again, and thus, to sustain the successive round of births and deaths. New organs and new functions are acquired with each birth, to be utilized by the gradually expanding soul as a means of further development. We see it in the fire of the flint and as atomic energy, and as we watch the revolving sparks of the mineral soul, we can see it burst forth to the sun light in the garb of the lowly lichen. It guards the snow white purity of the lotus, and animates the aromatic glory of the rose. It is the butterfly springing from the chrysalid shell, and the nightingale singing in the grove. "From stage to stage it evolves; new births and new deaths; anon to die, but sure to live again; ever striving and revolving upon the whirling, toilsome, dreadful, rugged path until it awakes for the last time upon earth; awakes once more a material shape, a thing of dust, a creature of flesh and blood, but now a man." The grand, self conscious state of humanity, is attained, and the climax of earthly incarnation is reached. Never again, will the soul enter the material matrix or suffer the pains of material re-incarnation. Henceforth its re-births will be in the realm of spirit.

Those who hold the strangely illogical doctrine of a multiplicity of human births, have certainly never evolved the lucid state of soul consciousness within themselves. Had they done so, the theory of re-incarnation as held by a vast number of talented men and women, well versed in worldly wisdom, would not have received the slightest recognition at the present day. We would strongly impress the fact, that, an external education is comparatively worthless as a means of obtaining a true knowledge of Nature. Remember, that though the acorn becomes the oak, and the cocoanut the palm; the oak, though giving birth to myriad others, never again becomes an acorn, nor the palm the juicy nut. So it is with man. When once the soul becomes incarnated in the human organism, and thus attains the consciousness of external life, man becomes a self responsible being, accountable for all his actions. This accountability constitutes his earth karma, (which is explained in chapter III) and the reward or punishment, as the case may be, is consciously and divinely administered in the state which each individual soul has prepared for itself. The soul is not ignorantly ushered again into the world, completely unconscious of its past load of karma. Such a means of redemption, instead of being divine, would be void of justice. It would be diabolical. When human laws punish the criminal, he is conscious of the misdeed for which he is suffering. If this were not so the punishment would be horribly unjust. For this reason we do not punish irresponsible children, nor insane people. It is thoroughly useless, however, to deal any further with such a transcendent delusion. We will, therefore, only say that all the so-called re-awakenings of latent memories, by which certain people profess to remember certain past lives can be explained, and in fact are only really explained, by the simple laws of affinity and form.

This subject will be dealt with in the chapter upon Mediumship, Chapter IV.

Each race of human beings is immortal in itself; so likewise is each round. The first round never becomes the second, but those belonging to the first round become the parents or originators of the second. Each round constitutes a great planetary family which contains within itself, races, subraces and minor groups of human souls. Each state formed by the laws of its karma, and the laws of its form, and the laws of its affinity; a trinity of laws. At the expiration of one round, the polar day of evolution is brought to a close and the life wave leaves the shores of the planet. The second round of humanity; offspring of the first, does not commence until the human life wave, having gone around the whole planetary chain again reaches the planet, a period of 15,552,000 years as stated in La Clef Hermetique, Chapter V.

The embryonic, impersonal soul becomes the man, just as the acorn becomes the oak; and as the oak gives birth to many acorns or embryonic oaks, so does man, in his turn, become the means of giving birth to many souls. There is a complete correspondence between the two.

From what has been said the student will perceive that each round of humanity becomes more numerous. As the population increases the expanding material knowledge of each succeeding generation makes it possible for our earth to sustain a greater number upon a given surface.

CHAPTER II

THE HERMETIC CONSTITUTION OF MAN

The reader, by this time, should be somewhat familiar with the origin, nature and activities of the divine Ego which gives birth to the spirit monad of man. All things originate as the objective outcome of the divine and subjective idea. The human Ego is the offspring of that celestial harmony, a differentiated atom of diffusive formless spirit. It was brought into being through the angelic activities of parental souls who are representative of Love and Wisdom, intelligence and truth, within the sun sphere of creative life. We have endeavored to make these points as clear as possible, because of their primary importance in realizing, that, the point in the arc, which is claimed by the Buddhist cult and their followers as the origin of the soul's formation, is not so, but is, in fact, only the great turning point, the bottom rung of Jacob's esoteric ladder, upon which the soul makes its ascent and descent.

The Theosophists of the human re-incarnation school, while admitting the absolute divinity of the Ego, fail to account for the genesis of the soul which the Ego evolves, otherwise, than in matter. So far as we have been able to learn, not one of them has any conception as to how, when or where, the differentiation of the Ego takes place. Although, they hold, that, there is a spiritual evolution preceding all material evolution, they consider that the first spiritual manifestation of the soul is an arcane mystery, known only by the highest adepts. These adepts of the Buddhist Cultus, however, totally ignore the state of angelhood, they deny its existence, because they, in their concentrated sphere of absolute selfhood, can form no conception of such a state. The charge of spiritual selfishness has often been made, even by theosophists, against the teachings of their mahatmas, and there is good foundation for the charge when their teachings are critically examined. Such a state is as much above and beyond the grasp of their minds as the doctrine of Nirvana is beyond the grasp of the African bushman. They are particularly fond of applying to outsiders that proverb which intimates that there are more laws in heaven and earth than are dreamed of in man's philosophy, but they fail to apply this truism to their own august selves.

In our chapter upon re-incarnation, we briefly pointed out the actual sphere of re-birth within objective forms, and in doing so, many important features were omitted which appear to belong to that subject, but which in reality belong to the present one.

Re-birth within progressive forms is not for the sole purpose of evolving and energizing the latent powers of the human soul, as so many ignorantly imagine. If this were true, and man alone was the sole object of development, it would constitute the basis of absolute selfishness. We can safely assert that such human exclusiveness is only an appearance as there is nothing approaching to selfishness in the creative design. When we penetrate below this plane of appearances, we find countless realms of beings, equally as immortal as man, going through their cyclic rounds, obeying the same universal law as ourselves. These realms constitute stepping stones for external humanity in its journey towards the infinite. The organisms of humanity, in their turn, form the evolutionary spheres or material means by which these same realms pass through their cycles of progressive life. If we make use of certain planes for our soul's advancement, it only follows as a matter of reactionary law (justice) that we should render an equivalent service in return, hence, the importance of a true knowledge of our hidden or Hermetic constitution.

Man, as we behold him by means of our physical senses, appears to us a wonderful specimen of mechanical skill and architectural beauty. Each organic part is so exquisitely formed, and in such perfect unison one with another, and each with the whole. There is little wonder that the human organism has been taken as the finite type of the unknown infinite. If this be true upon the external plane, it is infinitely more so upon the internal plane. Here, bone, flesh, blood, and hair, the externals of the outward body, are seen to be nothing but the crystallizations of ethereal force, held together by mental being. Not held together as a matter of necessity, for the sake of its own especial evolution, but simply as the natural outcome, the physical reaction of its ethereal activities. In order to present a clear and definite picture of what man really is, we will formulate his Hermetic constitution, as follows;

A. A physical form fourfold in its composition, consisting in a general sense, of bones, blood, flesh, and hair. This form, as a whole, is composed of an infinite number of separate organic cells, each cell constituting a minute system of its own, which in its turn has been formed by the crystallization of imponderable forces around a living spirit entity.

B. An electro-vital body, seemingly composed of pale phosphorescent light, enclosing a glittering skeleton framework of electric fire. This is the purely electro-magnetic form, inseparable from the physical body during life, because this latter depends for its continued existence upon the active presence of the physical form. The pale phosphorescent light presents a very perfect outline portrait of the physical body, while the fiery skeleton shows the interior electro-nervous system of the organism. The branches of the nerve system, spreading out in every direction from the great trunk lines of the brain and spinal column, present to the trained spiritual sight the appearance of an infinitude of fine pencil rays of light darting in straight lines with inconceivable rapidity toward every point of the compass.

C. An astral form, so called because it is composed of the magnetic light evolved by the planet. This astral light differs in quality and degree upon every orb in the universe. It is generated from the universal ether of space, and it may be said to be the ether under a change of form and capacity. It is the soul of the material planet, consequently, the cause world of that planet's external phenomena. To give a better and truer idea of this almost unknown astral light we will illustrate. We say that water is the universal material fluid. This is a truth, but some water is salty, some brackish, some bitter, others sulphuric, sweet or fresh. This is exactly the case with the astral fluid. It differs upon every star. It is this difference that constitutes the strikingly different qualities of planetary influence. With this slight digression we resume. This astral form presents a perfect image of the external personality, even to style and condition of the clothing worn at the time. This form is easily separable from the physical organism, and constitutes the true or real personality. By personality we do not mean the individuality or identity of the person, but we mean the persona, or appearance assumed by the soul during its sojourn within the material vortices, or planes of cosmic force. This form is under the direct control of the mental being animating it, and, under suitable conditions, can be made to assume (temporarily) any ideal image or form within the grasp of the dominating mind. When the astral double is absent from the physical body, the latter, if awake, performs whatever it may be engaged in doing, in a purely automatic or mechanical manner. At the same time it is susceptible to any pain or injury which may befall the absent double. The astral is also specially susceptible to magical operations. Probably nine tenths of all black magical injury are operated by means of or upon this ethereal form.

D. The animal soul is that section of the animating entity incarnated within the microcosm, which constitutes the lower arc of its universe. This animal soul is formless as regards its separate expression, and can be traced only in the lower lines and shadings of the human countenance. It is the seat of the selfish, brutal desires, which are, in themselves, lower than the human sphere but are evolving upward through it from the animal. Their activities are strictly confined to the astral and material planes.

E. The spiritual body, per se, is a finely etherealized organism which in the majority of the present generation is either latent or embryonic. This body constitutes the human form divine in the higher sphere of the soul world where man becomes the angel. It is the white robe and golden crown given the elect in the Apocalypse of St. John. In other words, it is the soul's expression of the heavenly raiment of the purified man.

F. The divine soul is that section of the entity incarnated within the microcosm which constitutes the higher arc of its universe. This soul, like the lower one, is formless as to its separate expression, and can be traced only in the higher lines of the human countenance. It is the seat of the good, unselfish, noble aspirations, and of all those actions which spring forth spontaneously to aid the weak, the suffering and afflicted, unassociated with any interested motives of self.

G. The pure spirit entity itself, called the divine Ego. This is the divine atom of life, the vital spark, the central controlling spiritual sun of the microcosm. It is never incarnated within the form until the seventh state or perfect manhood is attained.

The above are the exact divisions of the human constitution, as viewed from without and within. Upon the surface this division will not appear to differ very materially from the septenary formula of the Buddhist cult. But, in reality, there is all the difference which exists between Cause and Effect. The chief point of difference will be found in the fifth principle as they term it, and which is called also the human soul, manas or mind. Mind, though correct in some respects, is, to say the least, a very vague and unsatisfactory term to express intellectual capacity or the power of thinking and reasoning, and reducing the objects of thought to a science. For this reason; mind exists as a motive force all the way from the mineral to man, and, surely Buddhists will not say that rocks contain (mind) their fifth principle. It is upon this point in particular where, in the opinion of the student of Hermetic philosophy, that Esoteric Buddhists make a very serious mistake. It is the evolution of this "principle," we are told, that gives us the power of understanding; without this, we should be upon the plane of the animal and act from mere instinct. When this principle is active, man becomes noble, humane and capable of understanding, or, in other words, instead of being a creature of instinct only, he becomes a reasonable being. We question the whole of such teachings. For instance, a man may be the intellectual giant of his age, so far as mere mental capacity is concerned, and yet at the same time be the most selfish, unjust and immoral. History teems with such examples; while, at the same time, some of Nature's noblest souls have been those whose intellectual abilities have been very much below the average of the race. There are intellectual animals among mankind, human only in form; while on the other hand, there are many demented human beings whose souls are akin to the angels. "This fifth principle," we are told on page 175 of "The Mystery of the Ages," "is the highest principle of the animals." But, Hermetic initiates deny this in toto. They assert that this "principle" is no principle at all, but merely a form; that in real fact, there are only three principles in an active state, viz.; animal, human and deific. The remaining four are merely forms or reactions. It is the action and reaction of these principles which produce every class of mental phenomena in existence, be it vegetable sensitiveness, animal instinct, human reason or deific perception. They form the three primary colors of the soul's spectrum; while the remaining forms are simply complementary reactions.

The Hermetic constitution of man consists of three active principles, all emanations from the one universal principle, and four secondary reactions. This constitution will correspond to the trinity of the ancient Gnostics and the modern spiritualists, as consisting of body, soul and spirit, in the following manner; Body, (A and B); Soul,

(C and D); Spirit, (E, F and G). It also corresponds to the quaternary or fourfold constitution of the Kabbalists and the Greek speculators on Egyptian Theosophy, who taught that there is a body, an astral or magnetic body, the animal soul, and the divine soul. Body, (A and B); Astral body, (C); Animal soul, (D); Divine soul, (E, F and G). And so may we proceed with every system of which we have any knowledge. The only contradictions are the appearances upon the surface, chiefly due to an insufficient use, or to a misuse of terms. In reality, there is no difference in any system, when it is traced to its primal source. The same may be said of the Buddhist constitution, when understood in its true spirit. The radical differences are due to their gross misinterpretation of the one fundamental law; one truth. one principle, one agent (law) and one word.

We must now briefly sketch the Hermetic constitution, and present the four fold teaching of the Western initiates. Man consists of three duads and the Ego, a total of seven, which stand in the relation of Refraction and Reflection to each other. They are as follows;

First duad	Second duad	Third duad
A. Reflection, Physical body.	C. Astral body.	E. Spiritual form.
B. Refraction, Electro-magnetic form.	D. Animal soul.	F. Divine soul.
	G. The true Ego.	

The whole of these three duads are controlled and carried forward in their cyclic orbit by the Divine Ego, the absolute atomic spirit entity. Thus, the three duads and the Ego constitute the fourfold microcosm of the Hermetic schools. This is the most perfect system that can be formulated in words because the duads travel in pairs. At death we lose A and B. Then, during our purgatorial process through the sphere of purification in the soul states of the disembodied humanity C and D are gradually thrown off. Not separated, as one would quarter up an orange, but gradually thrown off, atom by atom, as they are ready to move forward upon their progressive journey. The unprepared atoms are liberated and sent forward upon their own special lines, and all gross matter eliminated. The animal principles are no portion of the purified soul and are dispersed as separate cells within the cause world, and ultimately nothing is left but the trinity, E, F and G, the Spiritual form, the Divine soul, and the true Ego; or rather the dual E and F, because the true Ego G does not become a part of the duad until it has ascended beyond these soul spheres. At this point, man is the positive or male spirit of the Ego; woman, the negative or feminine. The true angel requires the spiritual union of both principles.

Man, as he appears to the outward sight, is, as we have shown, very different from the being within. He contains a universe of life within his organism; countless myriads of spirit atoms are evolving through him and are as independent of him, in reality, as man is of the planet which gave him birth. The truly human being is the most interior or spiritual soul. The whole of the lower nature and the external organism are only the various realms of being which the human monad has conquered and subjected to its imperial rule during its cyclic journey. We should say, to be true, that the externals are the reflections of those elemental states moulded more or less rudely by the human soul after its own divine form. The millions of separate entities within the human sphere are no more the real man than the forty million inhabitants of France were Napoleon who ruled them with his imperial will.

A few words now regarding the WILL and the REASON, and we must close. WILL is universal, and it is as impossible to point out where it begins or where it ends as it is to separate the colors of the rainbow. The power of the WILL upon the external plane depends upon the strength of the electro-vital constitution B. While upon the spiritual plane WILL depends upon the activity of the spiritual constitution E. Within the astral plane the potent WILL must have both of these (B and E) well developed to be successful. If B alone is potent, only the elemental realms can be contacted. If only E is active, then the higher or spiritual world will be contacted, not the astral. Under these circumstances nothing but mediumship can be attained. The true form of training, then, is to evolve that which is the most latent, so as to bring about the equilibrium. In the great majority of cases, of course, it is the spiritual that requires evolving. Considering the WILL as a universal power, it naturally follows that the strength of our WILL must depend entirely upon the capacity we possess for absorbing and reprojecting this power. In fact, Man's WILL is only limited by his capacity to absorb the one Universal Will. This WILL is not, it itself, a principle; it is only an active result, viz.; transcendental matter in rapid motion. Everything utilizes some portion of this WILL in its own peculiar way.

The reason, manas, or mind, is simply mental capacity, and like the WILL, is not a principle but a result. Intellect is the offspring of innumerable and constantly changing causes or combinations of force never repeated under exactly the same conditions, consequently, no two people are exactly alike. The seat or mainspring of reason, intellect, understanding, and mind, is consciousness; and whether it will be good or evil, will depend upon the respective activities of the animal and divine souls. The higher the soul evolves, the more spiritual the understanding becomes, until perfect rapport with the divine spirit is attained. This is the true at-one-ment. Man made perfect.

From the foregoing the student must perceive that a man may be a perfect intellectual genius upon the physical plane, and at the same time be a veritable idiot in a spiritual sense. Very many intellectuals are standing before the world today and being accepted as the grand repositories of absolute knowledge because most of mankind are wholly engrossed in worldly affairs and are spiritually asleep.

CHAPTER III

KARMA

"If we are ever to know anything clearly,
we must be released from the body,
that the soul by itself may see things by
themselves as they really are." Socrates.

We need scarcely say that we fully agree with the above remarks
of Plato's teacher. While in the body we are completely fenced in by
delusive appearances, and had the Greek sage been alive today those
prominent individuals who so loudly and glibly speak and write upon
the subject of Karma would have been very greatly inconvenienced
by the Athenian's terrible logic.

"Karma is the law of consequences,—of merit and demerit", say the
Buddhists. "It is that force which moulds our physical destiny in this
world, and regulates our period of misery or happiness in the world
to come." We are also further informed that "Karma is the cold, inflexible justice which metes out to each individual the exact same
measure of good and evil at his next physical re-birth that he measured
to his fellow-men in this." Not only so, but this karma at death remains somewhere or other down upon the astral planes of the planet,
like an avenging demon, waiting anxiously for the period of Deva-
chanic happiness to come to an end, in order to re-project the poor
unfortunate soul once more into the magnetic vortices of material incarnation, where, with its load of bad karma hanging like a millstone
round its neck, it will in all human probability generate a still greater
load of this theological dogma, and consequently, at each re-birth it
will sink deeper, unless the spiritual Ego can bring it to some consciousness of its fearfully sinful state. How this may transpire is not
very satisfactorily explained. If the human soul only receives punishment for the sins and wrongs it inflicted upon others during a previous life, then, surely, the soul when it first became incarnated must
have started on its human journey without any karma to suffer for.
One is naturally led to ask, then, how it first began to commit sin? For
we are distinctly told that what we now suffer at the hands of others
is only a just repayment for our own past sins. If, then, we had no
past sins, we should be perfectly free from trouble. We are distinctly

taught that the first or pre-adamite men, i.e., those of the golden age, were perfect. How, then, did this abominable karma get a start in the world? This question it is our duty to fully explain in the present chapter.

We have given a general idea of the Karma of Theosophical Buddhism, and before revealing the origin of this Oriental delusion we will present the Hermetic doctrine of Karma.

I. Karma is not an active principle, but, on the contrary, it is crystallized force. It is the picture gallery or cosmic play of Nature.

II. Karma constitutes the scenery, essence and mental imagery of a person's past existence. It is a picture of their acts while on earth that become living realities to them in the soul world.

III. The karmic sphere of an individual's existence, exists as the astral life currents along which the soul has traveled and which become crystallized forms, expressive of the actions and the motives which prompted them. Therefore, our past karma constitutes the soul's past history in the astral light, and can be deciphered by the properly trained lucid, and even by some mediumistic clairvoyants.

IV. Karma is the offspring of everything; everything possesses pictorial records of its past evolutions; stones, plants, animals and men. It is by means of this karma that the Psychometric sensitive can read the unwritten past of small karmas. Without karma, the powers of Psychometry would be useless. On a grander scale exists the karma of moons, planets, suns and systems. Races of men, species of animals and classes of plants, also evolve special racial karmas which constitute their astral world.

V. The harmonies and discords of cosmic evolution generate their special karma just the same as thoughts and emotions produce corresponding reactions.

VI. Karma is absolutely confined to the realms of the astral light, and consequently, is always subjective. Therefore, Karma can exist only as long as the soul, which generates it, is attached to the same planet. When a soul leaves the planet its karma disintegrates. A soul cannot carry its karma around the universe with it, because this astral light differs in quality and degree upon each separate orb. See Chap. II.

VII. When a soul enters the spiritual states of the soul world (which Buddhists term Devachan), the power of its earthly karma can never re-attract it to earth; its influence over the soul is forever lost.

The lower can never control the higher, when once they exist apart. To assert that past fossilized karma can re-attract the soul from the realms of spiritual happiness and re-project it into the mire of earth is to exalt matter to the throne of Deity, and degrade pure spirit to the level of a passive brute substance.

From the above seven statements it will be seen that the Hermetic initiates assert that karma is not the primary law of consequences and destiny. It is not an active principle, always at work, re-adjusting Nature's ridiculous mistakes. Nature never yet made a mistake. On the contrary, karma is shown to be a result; the subjective outcome of innumerable laws and forces, and in this life it is utterly powerless to effect either good or evil, so far as our destiny is concerned upon the external plane. But, upon the interior plane, that is, upon or within the astral sphere of the disembodied soul world, this karma becomes the Book of Life from which all our actions in this world are judged. At death, we are surrounded by and compelled to exist within our own karma. We are forced by the laws of magnetic affinity to work out our own redemption, ever face to face with the grim idols of our earthly past. The foul, unlovely pictures of every unclean imagination will haunt us, and set our very souls aflame with the consciousness of every injustice and wrong we have committed. The only redeeming feature will be the good karma, the kind unselfish thoughts and noble aspirations we have evolved; all our true, unselfish love for our fellow-creatures will spring up like flowers at our feet, and help to aid and brighten our path upward and onward through the spheres of purification and purgatory. At last we shall enter the sphere of immortal life where those whom we have loved below may be waiting to greet us.

We have asserted that karma is utterly powerless to effect either good or evil in so far as the material destiny is concerned. While this is true within certain limits because karma is but the astral record of the past, yet this statement requires explanation. It is not the actions we commit, that can, in themselves, bring happiness or misery, benefit or misfortune to the person, but it is the effects which our actions have upon others that really produce immediate material results. The precise effect which any action will have depends entirely upon the peculiar mental states surrounding us at the time and our own intentions. For instance, in one age it may be considered a very meritorious action to roast a poor helpless medium under the name of a witch, but at another period such an action will be followed by an indignant spirit of public resentment, and a terrible penalty will be imposed by the law of the state to satisfy the public sense of justice. The praiseworthy actions of one age become the criminal acts of another. We see, therefore, that the result of any action upon the material plane depends upon the physical, moral, mental and spiritual development of the race. This is not the case, however, within the astral soul world, where absolute justice is the universal law. The mighty hero of a thousand fights, who dies surrounded by all the pomp and vanity of public worship, comes face to face with the fearful reality that he is, nevertheless, a blood stained murderer, and as such he must work out his own salvation amid trial and suffering. His purgatorial state will depend in a great measure upon his motives, and the consciousness of his earthly actions. If he was a true patriot, who fought against cruel oppression simply for the love and liberty of his country and people, his conscience will deal very lightly with him. But if love of fame and martial glory were his chief motives, and constituted the greater part of his karma, then so much the worse for him.

The reader will notice that in the Hermetic definitions of karma, the soul when working out its past iniquities is perfectly conscious of its task, and knows the true why and wherefore of its suffering. Not only so, but it has also the certain hope of final emancipation, not, however, until, as the parable says, "thou hast paid the uttermost farthing." Herein, then, is the truth and justice of Nature's laws revealed. But in the definition of Buddhism, this justice is absolutely wanting. In their outrageous scheme of esoteric philosophy, millions of souls upon the earth are perfectly ignorant of what they are suffering for. They are ushered into the world for the purpose of undergoing the fiery torments of their old fossilized karma, and are completely ignorant of the fact. How can the average mortal work off his bad karma when he does not know that he has any, nor what he is working and suffering for? If we cruelly abuse a dog when it is full grown for some offense committed when a puppy, it would be considered an outrageous piece of cruelty, because the dog would be perfectly ignorant of what the punishment was for. The same may be said of inflicting punishment upon the material man for some forgotten offense of his infancy. The reader should ever remember that no punishment is just, when the one punished is ignorant of the cause. Punishment under such circumstances not only ceases to be just, but becomes diabolical injustice. The common justice of humanity condemns such a proceeding. If this is true, how much more severe must be the condemnation of that justice which is divine?

At this stage of our subject, the student will doubtless ask, "if human suffering is not the result of previous karma, what is the real cause of so much misery in the world?" To this we reply, human suffering is the result of innumerable laws, which in their action and reaction produce discord at certain intervals in the scale of human development. For all practical purposes, they may be classed under two heads as primary and secondary. The primary cause is that of racial evolution. Each round and each race of the round of human beings, requires different external conditions in order to evolve its chief attributes; for each round and race become the special means by which a certain one of the soul's attributes is rounded out or developed. Let us illustrate. The first or primal race were those of the Golden Age. They were a purely ethereal race of beings, and cannot be strictly classified with what we know of humanity, nor can they be said to have been really incarnated in gross matter at all. For this reason, their penetrative power was very small; hence, though highly spiritual, they were correspondingly simple; they lived an ideal life amid semi-spiritual surroundings. The second race, that of the Silver Age, penetrated deeper into matter than their Golden Age forefathers, and their bodies, consequently became more dense and less sensitive. Toward the termination of this race, and the beginning of the third or Copper Age, the equator of our racial arc was reached in the descending scale. Here it was, that the first murmurings of a mental storm began to manifest themselves; emigrations and partings took place between what had previously been a united people, and consequently separate national interests began to evolve. When our earth reaches the equinoctial points of the year, storms and tempests abound. Upon a higher plane, it is the same with the progress of man around the cycle. With the Copper Age race a still further descent took place, and a still greater increase of self-interest was evolved; from the national was evolved that of the family. Kings ascended thrones and sacerdotal systems were formulated; the strong began to assert their greater force, and the weak gradually sank into subjection. A still further descent and we come to the fourth race, the bottom rung in the cyclic ladder, and fittingly known as the Iron Age. This was the turning point of the seven races wherein the soul attains its greatest penetrating power; spirit can descend no lower. Kings and their priestly counsellors became true despots, and the people were helpless and oppressed.

Next comes a higher evolution. The fifth race, beginning at the end of the fourth, reaches up to the equinoctial line of the mental arc in the ascending scale, and consequently another stormy period commences. All is strife and turmoil. It is the struggle of the oppressed against the oppressor. It is not the gentle mental storm of the Silver equinox, because a spiritual period of light had preceded that era, but it is the storm of war and bloodshed; of a fierce democracy battling for the divine rights of man against usurped authority. It is thus because the Iron Age of oppression has preceded it. We are at the present day passing through this fearful equinocial period. The fifth race is coming to a close, and already forerunners of the sixth race are among the people, aiding in the spread of glorious truth.

A spiritual, intellectual and scientific awakening is now taking place. All peoples of the world are seeking truth and justice. While the scientific world is producing miracles in their efforts to annihilate time and space, and solve the many hidden mysteries of life. See La Clef, Chapter VI. The sixth race of human beings now externalizing here on the earth will develop intuition as a sixth sense, perception through spiritual sensation, and learn to consciously use it in their daily lives. They will intuitively know a thing without any material evidence to support their knowledge, yet will find the truth upon application or verification of the information received.

The secondary causes of human suffering are man's ignorance, and the re-actions of his animal nature. That is to say, man makes the conditions that are necessary for his progress by alternately struggling with and yielding to his own animal desires. But for this nature and the experience the soul gains thereby, material incarnation might be dispensed with. The state of suffering depends upon the race, as before stated, but the effects of that suffering are in exact fulfillment of Mother Nature's requirements. Mighty causes produce mighty effects; results, let us say, and vice versa. This law is absolute. To every action there is an equal and opposite reaction. Every spiritual atom of life is the direct result of a cause. These atoms differ in power and potency, as the stars differ in magnitude. Nature's aim is for diversity. In spite of the apparent fact that all forces are ever striving for equilibrium. Nature's end, is the very opposite of equality; for the grand ultimate aim of every force is the production of variety. The only real difference in any of her infinite number of parts is that of polarity. For instance, the only difference between the Hottentot and the intellectual genius of modern civilized society is that which marks off their souls' respective polarity. It is only a question of personal opinion as to which of the two is the best and wisest. The civilized shams and personal adornments of society may more than counterbalance the crude decorations of the savage. The false Theology and cant of orthodox religion, combined with the many erroneous theories of so-called science, may more than make up for barbarian ignorance; for many savages are more learned in the real laws of Nature than some of our college professors. But be that as it may, the savage will be the real gainer of the two in most cases, for he will not have false dogmatic opinions to unlearn and forget. And, lastly, we would add, that the moral character of any savage will compare very favorably with the morality of our populous cities. In fact; making allowance for the planes of life occupied by each, the external differences between the two are only appearances, evolved chiefly by our own thoroughly biased and artificial educations. Another factor in these secondary causes of human suffering is the human will, or rather, man's capacity for utilizing the great will-force of the cosmos. Ignorance alone limits human possibilities in this direction. It is man's place in Nature to sway the mighty pendulum of force between the higher and the lower states of life (the super-mundane and sub-mundane realms of being) and in so doing his mission consists in evolving the attributes of his soul, and gaining all the experience possible. If suffering is necessary to enable him to accomplish this, then he will suffer. But, be the causes and consequences what they may in this life, depend upon it that what the soul suffers from discord it will be justly compensated for by the sum total of results when the cycle of its purification is over, and the past can be measured at its true worth.

We have now presented, as concisely as possible, the Hermetic explanation of karma, and shown that it is not the all-ruling force that Buddhism would make us believe.

Now we will expose the oriental delusion, and reveal its priestly origin. To begin with, we must carefully bear in mind a few all important facts regarding the esoteric philosophy of the dreamy Orient.

I. Anciently the real truths of all religion, especially those relating to the soul, its nature, incarnations and karma, were rigidly concealed from the people by a jealous priesthood with approval of the ruling monarch.

II. Fiction was substituted in the place of truth, or, in other words, the real truth was veiled and the appearances of truth was taught instead. And in order to obtain absolute power for the monarch and the church, it became necessary to formulate the dogma that their high priest, the pontiff or hierophant as he was called, was a direct incarnation of the Deity, or a re-incarnation of that being.

III. In process of time the priests themselves became corrupt and worldly, consequently, their spiritual perception sank into mental reflection. They not only lost the secrets of their religion and mythology, which were never committed to writing, but became themselves the dupes of their own theology, and accepted their formulated husks as divine truth.

Edward Gibbon, in his historical classic, "The Decline and Fall of the Roman Empire," published in 1776, records a thousand years of wars, frauds and persecutions. Emperors and bishops fought to control; religious dogma was forced on the people, they had no choice; the Athenian Philosophers were exiled or killed and their schools closed and teachings forbidden. We have a similar example in the christian clergy of today, as they seem determined every one must accept their faith.

The researches of all genuine Occultists support the above assertions. The book "Isis Unveiled", teems with facts corroborating our statements on karma and re-incarnation. And Hermetic initiates assert most emphatically that both karma and re-incarnation are nothing more than theological dogmas of an interested sacerdotal system. That is to say, the teachings based upon these doctrines by the Buddhist and other religious systems are false because the real facts of re-incarnation and karma were originally concealed, and then forgotten in the lapse of time. It is very easy indeed to prove that the accepted theories of the Theosophical Buddhists of the present day are the popular external dogmas taught to the ignorant masses ten thousand years ago. In support of this, the student should read "Illuminated Brahminism, the true theosophy" by Ranga Hilyod, an ancient sage of India.

The oldest records we possess show that human re-incarnation and karma were the popular doctrines of the people. Upon this matter A. P. Sinnet says; "This doctrine of karma is one of the most interesting features of Buddhist philosophy. There has been no secret about it at any time." Certainly, this is exactly what Hermetic initiates claim. It is a dogma of the Buddhist church, and was never concealed because, being false, it was not worth concealing. On the contrary it was always taught to the suffering masses groaning beneath despotic rule. It was exceedingly potent as a means of making the people submit quietly to the authority of the church and the tyranny of the king, who always went hand and glove with the priest. The masses were taught to believe that by submitting to the yoke they were thus working off previous bad karma; a very convenient doctrine we admit.

The chief Hierophant of Buddhism and the Thibetan adepts is the Taley Lama of Lhassa. "Every Lama," says Madam Blavatsky, "is subject to the grand Taley Lama, the Buddhist pope of Thibet, who holds his residence at Lhassa and is a re-incarnation of Buddha." This assertion fully corroborates what we said previously. Note well the last sentence, "and is a re-incarnation of Buddha." Compare this with the fact II on a preceding page, and you will see once more that we find the leaders of Theosophic Buddhism re-asserting the theological dogmas of a church and teaching them for truth. Buddhists would have us really believe that Buddha continues to incarnate and re-incarnate age after age. We can only say that no soul who has passed through the trials of material incarnation and the fires of spiritual purification would submit to continually exist within a material organism, and endure from age to age the hell of a Grand Lama's life. For the formulas, ceremonies and usages of a religious potentate are indeed a hell to the pure in heart.

We shall be met face to face with the assertion that with very high adepts and other exalted souls these things are different, that Nature's laws are either reversed or transcended. To this we would say that such statements are false; they are of the same stamp as the

Roman Catholic Bulls of the past, nothing but priestly word-juggling. Nature is no respecter of persons, and neither Buddha nor any other soul can continue to re-incarnate from age to age. The most that such a dominant mind could do would be to obsess and mould an unborn foetus to suit its purpose and then, by virtue of such obsession, partially inhabit the same. Under these circumstances the physical body is but the helpless machine of a dominant foreign mind, and we need scarcely say that no purified soul would sink to such a plane of existence. This question of obsession brings us to the subject of our next chapter, therefore, we must bring the present one to a close.

The whole teaching of Re-incarnation and Karma as taught by Buddhism, esoteric (?) or otherwise, is purely dogma; it is materialism run to seed, combined with oriental speculations. It is a huge system of selfishness, to work out good here for the sake of greater good hereafter. Such motives of exchange are corrupt. As Socrates says; "We give up some small pleasures for still greater pleasures." This, instead of being truly good, is the polar opposite. MOTIVE ALONE is the proper cause of action, according to the Hermetic doctrine. Do good for the sake of simple goodness and virtue alone, not for the sake of gaining favor. There is too much of this "I am holier than thou" about the oriental teachings of karma. A prosperous, self-righteous Pharisee gloats over his previous good karma when he sees his downtrodden brother and when he aids it is because he thinks the karma of the action will well repay him. Then again, when any serious case of suffering is presented to these great Buddhist souls for their magical intervention and psychological aid, we are piously told that karma cannot be interfered with. If, instead, they said that to aid was beyond their reach of power, they would probably speak the real truth. Lastly, let us say distinctly that the author has put the assertion of old Socrates (at the head of this chapter) to the test. The whole of these Hermetic teachings have been personally verified within the realms of spirit when free from the control of the body, and therefore, we know whereof we write.

In our next chapter we shall deal with some of the so-called evidences of re-incarnation and karma, and show them to be nothing of the kind.

CHAPTER IV

"All are but parts of one stupendous whole,
Whose body Nature is, and God the soul."

"What is mediumship, and who are the mediums?" was the question we once asked of the initiated masters of Occult science. The answer received was as broad in its application as the universe itself. "Everything is mediumistic, and every atom is a medium for the expression of spiritual force. God, alone, is the great central controlling spirit," said the master. Long years of spiritual research have verified the truth of the answer received and have established in the mind of the author the certainty that every word is an absolute fact.

We find throughout the vast infinitude of our universe that the spiritual and the material are so intimate that any attempt to classify and separate them, or to account for phenomena on the basis of either alone, would be like erecting an edifice without a foundation, or building upon ground as unstable and infirm as quicksand.

Modern science commences with matter, and confines its researches strictly to the domain of material forces and forms, the plane of manifestation. It terminates at the very moment its path impinges on the border of the imponderable, "the unknowable," whereas the real starting point of all true science is within the spiritual spaces, the cause plane. From this state its vast orbit sweeps downward throughout the whole universe of matter. In matter it recognizes all the different attributes and manifestations of the one Divine Force in every form of creation. From here its decisions return to and again ultimate in the realm of spirit. Divinity is unity, and the two great attributes of the divine soul coalesce as matter and spirit in the universe of manifested being. This is the duality of life. Matter is visible, it is solidified spirit, the passive or negative principle in a concrete, condensed or material form. Spirit is the movable, ever active, positive principle in motion, and between these two states there ramifies every grade of being.

Matter ranges and transforms itself from the lowest dense state of the mineral upward to the aerial and invisible gases, terminating in the "universal ether" of science. In this refined condition, the active and positive principles of Divinity, again, become united and are transformed into creative force. Hence it must be apparent to the thoughtful reader that, the universal ether contains within itself all that is, that was, or that ever will be. Such being the actual facts of the case, what are the logical conclusions that the student of spiritual philosophy may draw therefrom?

They are briefly as follows;—

I. That the universe is one mighty, inconceivable medium, and Deity the controlling and omnipotent spirit.

II. That Love becomes the medium of Wisdom, or, in other words, the passive becomes the medium of the active, state; consequently, matter is and must be the absolute medium of mind.

III. That the passive nature of the divine soul is the only means whereby the active spirit of Divinity can manifest itself, and upon this basis rests all the mysteries of the cosmos. This is Divine Love.

IV. In view of these facts, we find that the universal will, utilized by the imperial soul of man, is the one true center of all magical and spiritual power manifested upon our earth. Man is the great pivot around which revolves every phase of magical, magnetic and mental phenomena embraced within the realms of mundane psychology.

It has seemed necessary to the writer to re-impress all of the above facts upon the mind of the reader, notwithstanding the fact, that they have been very fully elaborated upon in the previous chapters, because they constitute the very fundamental verities,—the actual principles, which underlie the realities of mediumship, and therefore, are of primary importance here.

Mediumship is a well-known term to the present generation. It is applied to that state of sensibility which, though found pure and natural in some individuals, has been artificially developed in others. In this state they are enabled to come en rapport with invisible intelligences, and other powers, both physical and mental, because their odylic sphere (magnetic aura) has received a degree of sensitiveness compatible with their becoming mediums of communication for said forces. A medium, properly speaking, is a person or object in whom the capacity of reception and transmission is so fully evolved as to become of practical value in eliciting phenomena. After what has been stated, it should appear perfectly plain, that all human beings in their natural state are mediumistic; some in excess of others. This is especially so when we comprehend the different types of men and the relation of humanity to Deity. In a similar manner all material substances are "mediumistic" in this sense of being capable of receiving and transmitting force. Therefore, when considering the various forms and phases of mediumship, instead of viewing them in the light of "spiritual gifts," they must be viewed as the natural attributes of our internal nature, as the positive potentialities of the human soul. The various forms and degrees of mediumship are not spiritual gifts in any sense whatever. They are, when viewed from the interior plane, the awakened and active senses of the soul, and hold the same relation to the spirit as our five external senses do to the physical body. Just as our objective organism is governed and controlled by absolute and eternal laws, strictly applicable to its external nature, so is the internal, imponderable constitution under the government of correspondingly transcendental laws equally in harmony with its purely subjective nature. These laws constitute the "Science of the soul," and it is only by a thorough knowledge of this science that we can see the true realities of mediumship, understand them, guard ourselves from its terrible dangers and enjoy without fear its countless and unlimited blessings. By the aid of this glorious knowledge we are enabled to perceive the action and interaction of the two great planes of existence, and each coming day, observe with renewed delight the marvelous transformations of mediumistic adaptability. The flower that blooms in beauty, breathing forth to the air its fragrance which is at once grateful to the higher senses, and stimulating to the nerves, is a perfect emblem of Nature's faultless mediumship.

The flower is a medium for the transmission of those finer essences, to the human body, and of their spiritual portion to the soul; for the aroma of the flower is spiritualized to such a degree as to act upon the life currents of the human system, imparting to the spiritual body a nutriment of the finest quality that physical substance can afford. Herein may be seen some of the mysteries of incense, and the great value of its use, especially in religious ceremonies.

In this study of mediumship it must ever be remembered that spirit inheres in every grade of matter as the instigator of life, force and motion. It is attendant upon the ethereal currents that permeate all worlds and bind the universe together as a complete whole. And, in exact proportion to the refinement of substance, is the sphere vitalized by spirit. In the brain and nervous system of the human being the climax of material vitalization is reached. Here, spirit blends with matter in such requisite force and grade as are sufficient to form the astro-magnetic link of connection between the two worlds of cause and effect. It is the same with mental powers; intelligence is ever vitalized from the great Deific fountain of Wisdom; Sympathy and Affection are derived from the same Deific fountain, the soul of Love. No matter what the grade may be, whether that of the seraph basking in the very sunlight of divine purity, of man in his lowest estate, or of the brute raised but one degree above the planes of inanimate Nature;—the spark which vivifies the brute, the brilliant luminosity that lights up the brain of the perfectly developed human being, and that radiant glory flashing from the brow of the seraph, are alike kindled from the same eternal flame, for it is the grand prerogative of each grade of being, differing in degree of evolution, to transmit that which it receives from the realms above to the planes immediately below, thus, is each one faithfully fulfilling its duty as a medium in the scheme of life.

From the glorious pulsating soul of the central spiritual Sun, descending through every sphere of creation, deep down into the very bowels of matter, midst stratas of cold granite rock to the mineral lodes of dense metal, one eternal and harmonious chain of spirit mediumship prevails. Each plane depends upon the next plane above, and each, in its grandly sequent rotation, transmits the grosser portions to the planes below for their sustenance.

When the whole of this mighty scheme is taken into consideration, Occult students will see how necessary it is for those who wish to develop their spiritual possibilities to live upon a purely vegetable diet, because the eating of flesh attracts the soul to the animal kingdom and degrades the higher senses. A life spent amid the flowery fields and pine clad mountains, is the only existence that can fit the mind and educate the soul to the highest point compatible with material existence. Upon the contrary, the thinking mind will not fail to see that those who live in close, unhealthy, and densely populated towns, and are surrounded by a group of sickly or selfish minded neighbors and relatives, become subject to the very lowest planes of spiritual activity. These conditions often form the very hotbeds of error, spiritual and mental, and evolve the means of elementary obsession and wickedness. Under such antagonistic conditions progress is absolutely impossible, and those laboring under such adverse circumstances should avoid all contact with magic, spiritual phenomena and mediumship, as they would avoid coming in contact with a deadly pestilence.

It is to be hoped that these words of warning will be heeded and thus save much suffering and useless waste of vitality.

Having given a general outline of the nature of mediumship, it now becomes our duty to elucidate its laws and mysteries, and here we are met with the mightiest subject within the whole range of Occultism. No branch of study is of greater importance in the search of truth, or is more completely unknown and misunderstood by that large body of modern mystics and thinkers of the present day, who proclaim the doctrines of an esoteric Buddhism to the world as the essence of truth and wisdom. They must not understand, for such as these show their lack of esoteric illumination on the little known subject of mediumship.

Mediumship, though governed by well defined laws, so far as its general principles are concerned, is so subtle and intricate in its different degrees, forms and phases, as to be absolutely beyond the grasp of the ordinary mind. In fact, its ramifications and the results of its actions are as unlimited as the infinite. Therefore, it is only the more prominent and apparent forms that we shall attempt to outline. To do the subject justice more than one large volume would be required. As a matter of convenience, we shall divide the general laws of mediumship into two general classes; that of the controlling force, and that of the mediumistic instrument, known to initiates as the laws of Transmission and Reception.

The laws of Transmission.	The laws of Reception.
I. Activity.	I. Passivity.
II. Positiveness.	II. Sensitiveness.
III. Attraction.	III. Affinity.

The trinity on the left belongs to the controlling force; the trinity on the right belongs to the medium. In order to grasp the full significance of the above laws and of their inter-relationship, it must be borne in mind that the lower states of life are always the mediums of and consequently subject to the higher states. Therefore, every realm, from Deity down to the crystallized mineral, must not only possess the quality of mediumship, but also exercise the power of spirit control; the two extreme poles being God and crystallized matter. To illustrate this idea let us take the organism of man. Man, as we know him, is the mediumistic instrument through which higher states manifest their wisdom and power. This mediumship, on general lines, extends from the lowest specimen in the scale of humanity upwards to the highest initiated adept; the only difference between the two is that of development. This is an absolute fact. The exalted adept is actually a medium, in one sense, for the expression of still higher states of life than his own. No real adept denies this, though mere mystical pretenders always do. In other words, the difference is one of quality and degree, corresponding to their respective states. Man, according to his state, assimilates the specific grade of life essence from the universal force which corresponds exactly to the quality and development of his soul. As man ascends higher in the scale of spiritual development he becomes the recipient of finer essences, the coarser atoms are repelled and transmitted to less perfect organisms. This transmission goes on until the lowest state of humanity is reached, and from thence the life essence is transmitted to the sub-mundane realms of life, which thus, become the mediums for the expression of the surplus spiritual force rejected by man. This primal life force, in its original purity, contains all the requisite grades of spiritual nutriment for every form of existence in the universe, from God to the mineral. The mineral is the terminus, so to say, from which all phenomena react. There is no medium below this state. It is not the end of creation by any means, but only the turning point in the scheme of creation, where force comes to a focus and from which it reacts in both directions. Within each realm the same laws are also in force. Those forms of life which, by comparison, are passive, become the mediums for those which are active. Ascending to the mental plane we find it precisely the same with knowledge. The active research of powerful penetrating minds accumulates this knowledge, and then formulates the same into systems composed of more or less truth and error. This combination of wisdom and ignorance constitutes a religious sect or school of philosophy, which, in turn, impresses its force upon the less positive minds of the masses. The ignorant, therefore, become the mediums of the wise. This wisdom may only merit such a name, however, by comparing it with the ignorance by which it is surrounded. The sum total of a nation's wisdom or ignorance may always be found by examining its, laws, constitution and religion. We find the same law in force in politics. A great political leader, a giant mind, impresses its force upon a circle of kindred but less positive minds. These, in turn, react upon others, transmitting the same power of thought to them, and so on until that central mind;—like a sun, sways the destiny of millions of its fellow-creatures. These millions are simply the mediums for the expression of mental force. Again, the visible head or center of this force may, in its turn, be the medium of some other invisible head, whether such invisible power be mortal or spiritual, embodied or disembodied, makes no difference to the law. This might be termed a form of mass psychology if on the mental plane. All of these forms and phases, however, are to be classed as unconscious mediumship; because it seldom transpires that the operator is conscious of the magical powers he is using, or that the mediums are conscious of their mediumistic subjection. We think these brief illustrations will convey to the reader's mind something of the magnitude of the present subject.

We will now briefly notice a few of the most prominent forms of mediumship recognized as having a more direct connection with practical Occultism at the present time; the mediumship of spiritualism, and then conclude with some of its more recondite phases.

The sine qua non of all trance, or physical mediumship, is embraced in the term "passivity," and exactly in proportion to the degree of passivity attained is the power or strength of a person's mediumship increased. The question as to whether a given person may develop into a trance speaker or into a physical medium depends first, upon the brain conformation, and secondly, upon the magnetic temperament of the body. Some individuals are so complex that they may become either one or the other, according to the prevailing will of the developing circle. The chief point to be observed in these forms of mediumship, is that they tend toward the destruction of individuality, the medium becomes a slave to those in control. They can only be attained in the passive state, and the developing process is a means toward destroying whatever amount of will power the poor medium might have originally possessed. This destruction of the human will (subjection to spiritual intelligences as spiritualists ignorantly call it), is the greatest curse of mediumship. The controlling forces of such willless creatures may be anything and everything, according to "conditions" and circumstances. A medium that is said to be "developed"? stands upon the public platform, and is supposed to be controlled by some disembodied intelligence. But in nine cases out of every ten it is the psychological influx of the audience which, centering upon the sensitive organism of the medium, produces that peculiar semi-mesmeric state known as trance. Under such conditions the inspired oration will harmonize with the majority of the minds present, and, in numberless cases, the exact thoughts of individuals in the audience are reproduced. To the orthodox spiritualist, the oration will be received as an actual inspiration received from the "Spirit World" of translated humanity. Spiritualists should learn the fact, that mediums who can be controlled by a spirit can be equally controlled by a living person, and further, that of all places, the public platform is the least likely spot to be the center of high spiritual inspiration which emanates from ascended human souls.

Those forms of mediumship, known as Psychometry and Clairvoyance, depend chiefly upon the degree of sensitiveness attained; as brain formation and magnetic temperament possess only secondary influence in their evolution. Consequently, animals as well as human beings may possess these phases. Their characteristics are too well known to require further notice.

We must now notice two of the most subtle, and so far almost entirely unsuspected forms of this type of spirit mediumship. The first we will designate as "semi-transfer of identity," and the second as "thought diffusion."

In a previous chapter we have shown how a person, during his life, possessing an active, potent mind, will leave within the spaces of the astral light powerful thought forms or psychic thought embryos. These thought forms are the earth karma of the human soul. Now, under certain conditions, this earth karma of disembodied souls can be, and is contacted by those still in the flesh. Thus, for example, a person of strong positive mind, having rendered his soul sphere sensitive to contact by a partial development while his brain still remains positive, becomes a true medium, so far as the soul sphere is concerned, and always without knowing it (unless properly initiated).

Being self-conscious, as far as the mind and brain are concerned, he scorns the idea of mediumship, but in real truth he is as much a medium as a trance speaker. In this state he comes into magnetic rapport with certain thought forms within the astral karmas of the disembodied, and in this condition a semi-transfer of identity takes place, and he seems to exist in some previous age. He becomes identified with the karmic form controlling his sensitive sphere, and under these circumstances he becomes deceived by his ignorance, and imagines that he is recalling some incarnation of the past, if he is acquainted with the dogmas of the re-incarnation school. If ignorant of these doctrines, then he simply puts the whole matter down as a sort of day dreaming. Esoteric Buddhists, and others of the same school of thought, because of their benighted ignorance and unable to account for such phenomena, have invented their "re-awakened memory" theories. They consider these phenomena as veritable recollections of their past experiences, whereas they are nothing of the kind. They are indeed past experiences, but not theirs. They come into contact with this karma because of their magnetic mediumship. The forms they thus contact are those of individuals who belong to the same spiritual state of life, and who possessed, when upon the earth, a similar mental and magnetic temperament. All such evidences of re-incarnation are due to the simple action of mediumship. When the soul receives its true spiritual initiation, all these earthly errors vanish, and the fleeting phantoms of the astral world appear in their true light. The author once believed in such images as evidences of his past earth lives. Further development, under strict discipline, revealed the whole delusion. There is no true evidence to be obtained in support of that which is fundamentally false, neither is there any experience that appears to favor or sustain a re-incarnation theory which cannot be explained by the laws of mediumship.

Another form of this recondite phase of mediumship is that of thought diffusion. It is by this means that the potent, self-willed minds, behind this veil of outward Buddhism, are silently subjecting certain sensitive minds, in order to regain their lost sacerdotal power upon humanity. Thought diffusion is the power of diffusing certain thought forms containing certain positive ideas. These currents of thought circulate around the various mental chambers of the human mind, and, wherever they contact a sensitive sphere possessing any magnetic affinity to the center of such thought, they gradually impress their force and ultimately (in the majority of cases) subject that soul to their dominant ideas, and so prepare the way for the reception of the doctrines they want to teach. In this way, by the subtle mental magic of its devotees, religious theology obtained its first foothold upon the human mind. Though the action of this mediumship is sure, as long as the positive ideas have sufficient force to conquer, the reaction is equally certain, and it is this re-action that ultimately destroys the Theology. The magical offspring destroys its magical progenitor.

This diffusion of ideas is in active operation upon every mental plane; thus one potent mind evolving thought forms in Boston may suddenly set in vibration hundreds of sympathetic but less positive minds upon the other side of the Atlantic. They begin to think similar ideas, and to form similar conclusions. These ideas may become universal and constitute public opinion, if the projecting minds are potent enough. But few, very few indeed, are conscious of such ramifications of mental magic. Esoteric Buddhism owes its origin to such magic, and depends absolutely upon such Occult processes for its continued existence, but re-action is already apparent. Its followers never dream that instead of being independent, self-conscious thinkers, they are the mediumistic sensitives of Oriental control. The reader should never forget that upon the external plane there is nothing so potent as the magic of the human mind.

The conflicting theories of Buddhistic Theosophy on the one hand, and Spiritualism on the other, regarding the nature and source of those invisible forces which produce the various kinds of phenomena known to modern spiritualism, have given rise to much perplexity in the minds of many earnest truth seekers. The spiritualist, as a rule, affirms that such phenomena are due wholly to the action of disembodied human souls (many advanced spiritualists now freely admit the possibility of other intelligences than those of humanity controlling mediums); while the Theosophist utterly denies the possibility of such a course (except in the case of his Mahatmas, or with vicious human elementaries), and asserts that all the various forms and phases of spiritualistic phenomena are produced by one or more of the following agencies, either singly or combined:

    I. Elemental spirits, termed spooks.

    II. Human elementaries (the lost souls of depraved mortals).

III. Disembodied shells (the lifeless forms of disembodied mortals).

IV. The mesmeric influence of living individuals.

The actual truth is midway between these two extremes.

It is, indeed, a most glorious fact that disembodied human souls can and do return and commune through various mediumistic natures with embodied humanity. Still, the action of these souls is chiefly confined to, and manifested upon, the impressional and inspirational planes of mediumship. In so far the spiritualist is correct. There is, however, much truth, together with much that is false, in the Theosophist's theory. Let us, therefore, consider the agencies just mentioned, and in the order given.

I. Elemental spirits, termed spooks. There are innumerable classes and species of impersonal elementals in the various rounds and spaces, but only three classes have any influence upon mediums and spiritualistic phenomena. The first and lowest in the scale of intelligence, is the class of cosmic elementals, generated in the four realms of Occultism;—Fire, Earth, Air and Water. These creatures cannot deceive the medium. They are incapable of personating or imitating anything beyond themselves, unless they are impelled to do so by the medium's internal desire for such deception. In this case they may obey the impulse of the medium's mind. As they are completely subjective to the human will, they possess no real individuality of their own. When psychically directed, they simply are the blind forces of Nature, either active or latent according to magnetic conditions, and, therefore, would be correctly designated as the undeveloped mind of matter. The second class in the scale of intelligence is the Animal Elementals. These beings are the souls of animal forms of life undergoing the magnetic cycle of their impersonal existence within the astral spaces of the "Anima Animalis." When any animal dies upon the earth, it undergoes another cycle of life within the karmic spaces of its kind in the astral world. Here it evolves the forces and conditions to be utilized for its next incarnation. These souls, if we may call them such, especially those of domesticated animals, frequently become attached to human beings on earth with whom they have some peculiar magnetic affinity, or to whom they become attached during their external life. It is these beings that become the innocent instruments of fraud. They respond to the desires of the medium or to the secret wish of the circle or those who consult the medium. Under these circumstances it will invariably transpire that when a person, who possesses a positive opinion, consults a medium upon any given subject, the answer he receives will correspond to his thoughts, whether it be correct or otherwise. The same thing will happen when the client asks the advice or the opinion of a medium upon worldly matters. The answer will always respond to the secret desire which the animal elemental perceives in the mental sphere of the inquirer. This "control" cannot be charged with fraud any more than a pet dog can be charged who fulfils his master's desire. The benighted ignorance of both medium and client is the only cause for the apparent fraud. Mediums who become the instruments of this class of intelligences are generally those of unbounded personal egotism. They formulate the idea that their spirit guides cannot be any other than the most exalted personages. Abraham, Isaac, Jacob, Moses, Aaron and the whole of the prophets have in turn been claimed as their inspiring guides by this class of mediums. Such is not the case, except in the most rare instances. The obliging imitative soul of the animal elemental feels the full force of the medium's egotistical thought desire and immediately responds thereto and fulfils this mental idea. Even Jesus Christ and Buddha have been thus personated by impersonal controls who easily deceive the medium. But no matter who they claim to be they will always correspond to the ideal image of the personage existing in the medium's mind. If the medium be ignorant of the life, times and circumstantial surroundings of their ideal guide, when he lived on earth, then their ideal guide will be equally ignorant of himself. The writer has frequently met with spirits claiming to be Pythagoras who did not comprehend the first principles of Occultism, and who had entirely forgotten the order he instituted or the country he belonged to. We have met with Roger Bacon spooks who had never heard of alchemy and knew nothing of monastic life; with Ben Jonsons, who knew nothing of the times in which he lived on earth; with Shakespeares, who had forgotten their own plays, and the humble circumstances of the poet's early life. Nearly all these instances occurred where the mediums were actually controlled by the astral souls of domestic animals, chiefly dogs. This class, and also the cosmic elementals, are the chief agencies in all physical phenomena as they act under the control of human souls. The reason we assert that they were dogs is because, having evolved the lucid state, we ourselves could see the thoughtless impersonal creature responding to every latent thought in their medium's mind. When we formulated the positive thought that the control was not what he represented himself to be, he would generally confess that he was not, whereupon the medium would commence blaming "the conditions" for the poor report. Our personal investigations, extending over a series of years in England, France, Germany, Austria and the United States, with various types and phases of mediums, prove most conclusively that nearly half of that class of mediums who style themselves "business clairvoyants" and "test mediums" are controlled by various kinds of animal elementals, or "spooks." The third class in the scale of intelligence is the magnetic elementals, corresponding to the seven planetary divisions of Nature. These intelligent creatures are too bright and ethereal to be guilty of fraud. They are generated by the life forces of the planetary chain existing within each orb, and are the intermediate agents of the physical results of planetary influences manifested on the earth. They are the attendant familiars of certain classes of mystical students, especially those devoted to alchemy and astrology. It is these beings that usually produce the visions in crystals, magic mirrors, or vases of water, and in consequence of this they have often been wrongly termed planetary angels by certain schools of magical research. They are indeed planetary in nature, but they do not belong to the physical planet to whose nature they correspond except by affinity. They pertain to our own orb equally as much as man himself, and can give much information regarding the orb under whose dominion they act. If any deception transpires through them, it is but the reflection of deception (misunderstanding) existing in the minds of those who use them. They do not and cannot control mediums by mesmerism or by trance. Their sole influence is manifested in the impressional and clairvoyant phases of mediumship.

II. Disembodied Human Elementaries. This class is made up of the animal souls of depraved, wicked mortals who have sunk beneath the human plane and thus caused the separation of their divine soul from their conscious individuality. Those who fall so low as this are generally evil magicians and sorceresses, who are far more numerous than civilized society has any conception of.

This class are really magnetic vampires who prolong their vicious existence by sapping the life blood of their mediumistic victims. They will personate anything and everything. Their only aim is to completely demoralize the mediums and plunge them into all kinds of depravity. The chief characteristic of the Human Elementary is obsession, and nearly all those who go insane through religious excitement are the victims of elementary obsession. It is needless to add that these vampires are lost to all that is redemptive and good; they have gravitated to the lowest realms of brute animality in Nature upon the descending arc, and ultimately they become indrawn within the death whirl of that magnetic orb known as the dark satellite, and are swept to their final doom, extinction.

III. Disembodied shells. These are the magnetic forms of those who have lived, died and been buried upon the earth. They are perfectly lifeless; they hover around the grave which conceals the corpse to which they are bound, and as this decomposes the magnetic shell or phantom also dissolves. They cannot be drawn away from the grave. They cannot, in fact, be made to answer any mediumistic purpose whatsoever, and those who assert, as some Theosophists do, that they can be regalvanized into a temporary life and made to simulate the deceased individual, are sadly in error, and know not whereof they speak. The Buddhistical theory of disembodied shells and their influence upon the mediums of modern spiritualism is only another of the oriental delusions, disseminated to poison the budding spirituality of the western race.

IV. The Mesmeric influence of living individuals. Of this potent factor we need not speak, as it is evident that any spirit medium will feel, and to some extent respond to, the mesmeric will of a potent, positive, magnetic mind.

CHAPTER V

LA CLEF HERMETIQUE

THE HERMETIC KEY OF URANIA'S MYSTERIES

Written in the year 1880

PREFACE

Esteemed Brother Students of the Occult;

In preparing this peculiar work, I have been requested by those in authority over me to avoid all superfluous matter, and present the facts and teachings of the Hermetic Initiates as concisely as possible in the form most suitable for private meditation and study. But for this request, I could probably have made the work much more readable and interesting to many who dislike the dry facts and figures of original research. As it is, each one must supplement the scenery and sentiment for him or herself, and thus gain the credit of intensifying their own special pleasure, knowledge and Spiritual Advancement.

It is most important to remember that the Original Manuscript of the first portion of this work was written and issued to several in the month of January, 1881, before "Esoteric Buddhism" ever saw the light, and that the supposed "marvelous and original doctrines," issued by A. P. Sinnet, Esq., as from India, were all in black and white in England at the time. We have not copied from "Theosophy," but it is they who have stolen their jewels from us. In corroboration of this fact, read "Coleman's Review" of "The Secret Doctrine."

In trying to explain the Esoteric Numbers of the ancients, there is one great difficulty to be met with, namely, to be esoterically understood. Therefore, those who cannot understand or appreciate the sublime significance of the mighty Cycles and Periods we are about to reveal, had better, by far, leave all studies tending in the direction of the occult alone, seeing that it is not their sphere of thought. Their souls are not sufficiently etherealized for their humanly-divine attributes to come into action, and in spite of any ephemeral curiosity towards mystical research, they will never advance further than the gates of the outer court; they cannot, as yet, pass the fearful Dweller on the Threshold and enter the Holy Place. Therefore, they must be content to await their time, until the conditions are evolved by succeeding races of the human gamut that will admit of their soul's latent attributes unfolding themselves. There are, also, many who, while being in a condition to see the truth and grasp the real significance of the Mysteries of Nature, are totally unfit to receive such knowledge, because of their natural, but terrible elemental affinity. This fearful physical condition would lead them to devote all the occult powers at their command to worldly purposes. It is quite unnecessary to say that these individuals would become a scourge to mankind. Happily, only a very few of this class can grasp any real power, but become themselves the dupes and slaves of the powers they seek to control. To all such we earnestly and solemnly say;—abandon all thought of spirit intercourse, flee from occultism and spiritualism as you would from a pestilence, and may the Divine Guardians of the human race preserve your souls from the bottomless chasm upon whose brink they may possibly have been unconsciously reposing. For those who merely pry into the occult out of mere curiosity, we have nothing to say; they will obtain as much as they deserve and no more. "Ask and ye shall receive; knock and it shall be opened unto you," is just as true to-day in reference to esoteric knowledge as it was 1900 years ago; but it always presupposes that the one who asks or the one who knocks is in real earnest and seeks only to satisfy the deep yearnings of an immortal soul. The doorkeeper of the Temple of Truth is as deaf as the granite rocks to all others. You may ask and shout until you are hoarse, and knock and becudgel the door until you rouse up the furies with the din, it is all to no purpose; you can never take the Kingdom of Heaven by storm. It is fabled in the Holy Scriptures that Satan tried this means of obtaining power once upon a time and got hurled, with all of his assistants, into the flames of hell for such daring presumption, and that instead of the Kingdom of Heaven he obtained the bottomless pit as a fitting reward for his misdirected ambition and labor. There is more real truth in this religious fable than spiritualists ever dreamed of. But to the true student of Nature's inner laws we say, rest assured that you will receive a full measure of reward for all and every earnest endeavor. Urania's lamp will ultimately shine upon your dark and difficult path, and you shall indeed see the "saving light of the world," which will enable you to draw aside the veil of the mystic Isis, and behind this magic curtain, read the ever-burning truths of Nature inscribed upon the scrolls of time.

It is to you, my faithful and eternal brethren, that I present the Esoteric Cycles, the Golden Key, and the Silver Locks that guard our island Universe, viz.: the planet upon which we exist, which in itself, is a miniature Universe; so, also, is the human organism. In your possession, I know, they will be valued according to their true worth, and utilized for their proper purpose. Therefore, trusting that you may use your psychic powers wisely, worthily and well, and wishing you God-speed upon the upward path of your soul's eternal destiny, I remain with fraternal sympathies and brotherly love,

Most faithfully yours,

T. H. Burgoyne. №.

Private Secretary to The Hermetic Brotherhood of Luxor.

CHAPTER V

LA CLEF HERMETIQUE

SECTION I

THE CYCLES AND FORCES OF CREATIVE LIFE

In attempting to explain the sublime system of Esoteric Cycles, as taught in the Occult schools of the Egyptian Magi, we shall notice their great Cycles first, which relate to Human and Planetary Evolution, then compare, or rather introduce, for the student's comparison, the Sacred Cycles of Hindoo Initiates, and show some of their striking relationships to the well known facts of geological research, and, lastly, attempt to show how these natural periods of action and reaction of the Cosmic life forces have formed the truthful foundation upon which the Astrological Mystics have elaborated their planetary periods and sub-cycles of celestial influence over nations, and which is further and more fully elaborated by Kabbalistical lore, in the rule of the Seven Arch Angels as the seven Governors of the world, which they say "after God actuate the Universe."

NATURE'S TRIUNE INDEX

Nature has furnished her students with the means of reaching her mysteries, in the dual form of intuition and intellect, and of measuring her mighty forces in the forms of time and space. The first index of time is the rotation of the Earth upon her axis, the second by her annual motion about the Sun. These are broadly converted into days, months and years. The third index is that of the motion of the Earth's center (the Sun) through space, around a still greater center; this is broadly divided into two measures, viz.; first, through one sign of the Zodiac, a period of 2,160 years, and secondly, through the entire twelve signs, which complete his grand revolution, or great Solar Year, in 25,920 years of Earthly time. The third and last face of the triune index is our Earth's Pole. This magnetic point is the great finger of Nature's Cyclic Timepiece, which governs and registers all the great Cosmic cycles of our planet and its circuit.

Remember this significant fact, then, that the motions of the Earth's Pole is the motion of her Evolutionary forces, both Human and Physical.

POLAR MOTION

When this beautiful motion of the Earth's Pole has become familiar, the student will begin to see the divine harmony of Nature's grandest law, which law causes every portion of our Earth's surface to become alternately a fruitful plain or barren waste; dry land or ocean bed.

The Earth's Pole moves in one uniform direction, with a slow, imperceptible motion that forms a spiral path in the heavens, consisting of a number of small spiral orbits, or circles, one overlapping the other. These small spiral circles are termed Volutes, their true value in space being three degrees, thirty-six minutes, no seconds. 3° 36′ 00″.

The motion of inclination of the Pole is at the rate of fifty seconds of space per century, or one second in every two years. At this rate, it requires 7,200 years to move over one degree, and as there are 360 degrees in a circle, or the Pole's orbit, it takes 360 times 7,200 years, equal to 2,592,000 years, to make a complete revolution of its orbit, or one hundred Solar Years.

Each Volute being three degrees, thirty-six minutes, no seconds in true value, 25,920 years are required for the Pole to complete one small spiral orbit, and as there are exactly one hundred of these Spiral Orbits in the complete orbit, therefore 100 times 25,920 years equals 2,592,000 years, which period is termed, by Initiates, one Polar Day. One Polar Day equals one hundred Solar Years.

We will now give a few brief examples of Polar Motion:

If the student will, for a moment, imagine our Earth's Pole to be perpendicular to the plane of its orbit, and consequently coinciding with the Pole of the ecliptic; then the signs of the zodiac, and the apparent yearly path of the Sun will always be vertical at our Earth's equator; hence universal spring will reign in the Temperate Zones and a gentle, continuous summer in all sub-tropical latitudes; it will cause the equatorial regions of the Earth to become blazing, scorching deserts. The great plains will be unfit for habitation, owing to the fierce rays of a vertical Sun, continuing for long ages. Only the mountainous portions will be the seat of human life. This condition will also cause equal day and night all over the globe, but as we recede from the Equator, north or south, the sunlight becomes less and less, owing to the Sun attaining a lesser degree of altitude with every degree of latitude; until, at the Poles, the Sun will only appear as a dull red ball of fire, moving along the horizon, from east to west, in the twelve hours from 6 a.m. to 6 p.m., hence, darkness and universal winter reign supreme; and the Arctic Circle is an ever-lasting belt of ice and snow, whose frozen breath forms a complete barrier against the existence of human life.

Again, imagine the Earth's Pole, after a lapse of 648,000 years, and we shall now find that it is inclined at an angle of exactly 90 degrees, for, during this Period, it has been slowly, but imperceptibly to the Earth's inhabitants, moving or inclining away from the pole of the ecliptic. The twelve signs of the zodiac and the apparent yearly path of the Sun, are now vertical to the Pole of the Earth. What will be the fearful geological results? Why, that our polar regions will have a tropical summer. Each year the Sun will be vertical on the 21st of June to the North Pole, and on the 21st of December to the South Pole, and also that every portion of the globe, with the Sun and Earth's Pole in this position, will witness a tropical summer and an arctic winter. This accounts for and fully explains the existence of fossil remains of the seal, walrus and polar bear in the burning plains of Africa and Hindustan, and of the tropical remains now being discovered in the Arctic regions. No human being now living can conceive the fearful natural phenomena yearly transpiring during this period. For instance, all latitudes below the Poles had two midsummers each year; namely, when the Sun ascended north, and when it returned south again. The rapid rate at which the Sun rose into the polar circles, and the terrific heat of a vertical Sun upon the ice and snow, must have caused the most frightful inundations upon all the plains and lowlands. No wonder that it was called the Age of Horror by the Hindoos and Egyptian Magi.

The walls of the mighty Babylon and the eight-volved Tower of Babel or cloud-encompassed Bel were never constructed to resist any mortal foe. NO. Those city walls, which were 60 miles in circumference, 200 feet high, 578 feet thick, were not made to defy the strength of armies, but to resist the fearful forces of Nature, the floods that swept the plains of Shinar, from the mountains of Armenia, every spring during this Age of Horror. The tremendous embankments and river walls constructed by the Ancients are monuments of human skill and enterprise belonging to an epoch that antedates by thousands of years the Age of their supposed builders.

These mighty monuments of old are indeed the sacred relics of our early forefathers; but modern historians are so nosebound by Biblical chronology that they cannot yet see the light. Like young puppets, their eyes will not open to the light until they are nine days old. The student is here requested to notice that all the great solar and lunar observatories were constructed for a two-fold purpose. Their religion, unlike that of their degenerated descendants, was a pure, scientific theology, or "the Wisdom Religion." Those nations and peoples whom our historians denominate "ancient" were but degenerated castes, and, in comparison with the nations who built "the cloud-encompassed Bel," are quite modern. The grand, scientific Temples of the Sun and Moon, then, were erected at a period when the Sun was vertical to the latitude of the place, and their ages can be easily computed by the following simple formula. Our Earth's equator is the zero, or starting point, of all computations; and was taken into consideration by the ancient artists, who always built with some significant occult purpose. Each zone was constituted by the Great Solar Cycle of 25,920 years, during which period the Poles moved over one volute, which they, in round numbers, reconed at 4 degrees; and all those buildings will be found, when constructed on this plan, to point exactly to the time they were built, if their latitude corresponds with their symbol. For instance, the Tower of Babel was eight-volved; that is, with a spiral staircase winding eight times round it. This means that is was built when the sun was vertical in the latitude of 32 degrees; 4 times 8 are 32, or, as an initiate of our Noble Order, 63 years ago (1822), speaking of the awful Iron Age, says;

> "In this dread time Chimera had her birth;
> In this dread time the Cyclops cursed the earth.
> And Giants huge, of horrid, monstrous form,
> Who ravaged Earth, and strove e'en Heaven to storm.
> This was the Iron Age; 'twas Python's reign,
> When Polar-suns burnt up the golden grain,
> And sudden thaws inundate every plain.
> Hence Towers and Walls and Pryamids arose,
> Whose ponderous bulk might all their rage oppose.

"Assyrian chiefs bade Babel's tower arise,
   On Shinar's plain, aspiring to the skies,
   Whose eight-volved dragon, turning round the whole,
   Shows that eight cycles round the northern pole
   At four degrees asunder, closed their view,
   Which proves latitude was thirty-two.
   And still in thirty-two, beneath the starry host,
   The eight-coiled Dragon moulders in the dust,
   By Cyrus overthrown, who raised the pile
   Round which the Stars and Dragon used to coil;
   But still its form, its history declares,
   An hoary age of twice two hundred thousand years."

It may be noted that the very ancient sacred towers in the Pagodas of China always (unless they are of modern construction) faithfully indicate their latitude and date of their first foundation by the number of stories or terraces. Of course it is not supposed that these towers, like our ancient cathedrals, are not periodically restored as they fall into decay, but always on the same principle.

A great deal more might be said as to the different climates that ensued under different inclinations of our Earth's Pole, but these few illustrations will give the student a few ideas as to the actual cause of the various geological changes that are brought about by Polar Motion. Remember that the great Polar Day (2,592,000 years, moving once around, like the index of the clock) determines the duration upon our planet of that vital spiritual impulse of evolution, known among students and Initiates as the Great Life Wave. This Life Wave passes around the septenary chain, or circuit, of the seven planets, not in an even, regular, continuous action, but in waves or impulses. For instance, suppose the Life Wave of the mineral evolution commences, upon planet number 1; it will here go through its active evolution, and then, having reached its culminating point, it commences to flow, or pass on to planet number 2, and the vegetable, or next life impulse, begins upon planet number 1, and so on with the rest. Upon this point we would refer the student to Mr. Sinnett's valuable book, Esoteric Buddhism, but reminding you that, although there are many outlines in the work similar to these teachings, they are, in reality, widely different, as will be seen when you read his conclusions and those of this revelation.

In order to better illustrate the evolution of matter and the involution of spirit, we will briefly describe in outline the systematic and harmonious process followed by Nature in the complete evolution of a planet, similar in construction to our earth.

In the first place, it must be borne in mind that there are Seven Kingdoms, Seven Principles and Seven Ruling Powers in Nature, a trinity of sevens, and also that matter, so called, is but the most remote expression of spirit. The further a state is removed from its source, the more dense it becomes, until spirit can express itself in metallic form and become materialized as veins and lodes of mineral ore in the body of a planet, and tower itself upon that planet's surface in granite mountains, limestone hills or chalky dells; and that the boundless space is filled with a fine, invisible form of condensed spirit, known to scientists as cosmic dust; and, lastly, that Nature's operations are performed in an endless series of waves, which, in their motion, form graceful curves, the rise and fall of the arc of the curve forming its cycle of duration.

The Seven Kingdoms are the Three Elemental and invisible, and the Four Objective and visible planes of Nature, while the order of the Seven Principles, or forms of evolution, is as follows; 1, the Spiritual; 2, the Astral; 3, the Gaseous; 4, the Mineral; 5, the Vegetable; 6, the Animal; 7, the Human; see chapter II of section I.

The Seven Governors, or Powers ruling a planet, are the Seven Angelic States, mentioned more fully in LaClef chapter VI.

Having explained the rudiments, it will better express our meaning to use a Biblical illustration, so we will now esoterically explain

THE SIX DAYS OF CREATION,

mentioned in Genesis, each Day being one Polar Day, as before stated, or 2,592,000 years of Earthly time.

The words "the evening and the morning" signify the two halves of the Polar Cycle. You will notice that "the evening" is mentioned first, and "the morning" last. This is correct. The dark or undeveloped portion of each wave is the first half, and signifies, symbolically, Night, and vice versa. Further, it must be remembered that the spiritual impulse, or wave, must of necessity pass round the orbit that has ultimately to be traversed by the future planet before anything can transpire. It is the Divine Will sent forth by the spirit-state that is equivalent to the Word or Divine Idea of certain ancient writers. This Fiat attracts within its orbit the latent cosmic matter of space, and transforms it into the embryonic, nebulous light, the star dust or radiant fire mist, which is the form, or primitive matter, of all creation. The student must strictly remember that there is no specific duration of this state. It may last for millions of ages before the actual evolution of a planet, and that previous to the symbolical Six Days of Creation this planet exists for untold cycles in a nebulous condition, the exact size of its orbital ring, This being understood, we will describe

The First Day of Creation. The Supreme Angelic Governors project into active evolution the astral tide-wave, viz., the currents of astral light, and the nebulous matter is, at once, transformed into a rapidly revolving globe of fire, which solidifies and cools under the intense concentration of the Deific Will of the Governors in a wonderfully less space of time than any of our transcendental or spiritual writers can imagine. Fire was dominant for the first half of the Polar Day;—when its surface had become so far cooled as to allow the heated vapors of its immense atmosphere to condense and form water, which element was rapidly produced during the next half of the cycle. Thus, we see, that a rude globe was formed during the first day of creation; the first half, the evening, was given to the dominion of fire alone, and the latter half, or morning, was one ceaseless war between those opposing elements, fire and water. "And the evening and the morning were the first day." These two periods of the Polar Cycle are each 1,296,000 years, and were called by the Hindoos the Treta Yug.

The Second Day of Creation. The Supreme Angelic Governors now caused the first evolution of the gaseous or chemical tide-wave, and the evolution of a complete but dense atmosphere was the result. That is to say, the various constituents of the atmosphere were, by this wave, adjusted, and our planet's chemical affinities duly balanced. This caused the whole of the superabundant gross matter, such as carbon, etc., to condense and fall to the surface of the planet. During this day, also, our planet's surface was the scene of a continual conflict between heat and water; all was the scene of mighty volcanic action; mountain ranges continually rose and fell, and the ocean beds were always shifting.

The Third Day of Creation. After the gaseous, the great mineral tide-wave commenced, and the spirit atoms of future egos became incarnated in dense matter for the first time, namely, in the stratas of rocks and mineral lodes which constitute the stony ribs and metallic veins of our planet. Mountains, valleys, islands and continents were formed; the land above the ocean level sank, and the bed of the ocean became dry land. Now, for the first time, the seas and oceans occupy their proper beds. "And the evening and the morning were the third day." It must be added that during this period, also, the planet's surface was the scene of continual volcanic action; as was each and every period. At the close of this, the third Polar Cycle, we see that the evolution of the astral, chemical and mineral waves have now prepared our Earth for the first vegetable forms of life. And here, be it noted, that the first forms of all things were born (that is, had their origin) in water.

The Fourth Day of Creation. The vegetable tide-wave now reaches the barren shores of our planet, and produces the first rudimental forms of vegetable life, which develop into the most gross, gigantic shapes, rude and imperfect as the earth upon which they grow. But, as time progresses, so does the vegetable kingdom; each age giving more perfect forms. "And the evening and the morning were the fourth day."

The Fifth Day of Creation. The previous tide-waves having run their course, the animal life-wave now sets in, and from the lowest rudimental forms of life successively evolve the various orders of animal life, race after race appearing, running its course and becoming extinct, giving place to more complete organisms. "And the evening and the morning were the fifth day."

The Sixth Day of Creation. The preceding five tide-waves of evolution have now prepared our Earth for Nature's grandest climax; the evolution of the human form, Man, for at this age we read; "And the Lord made man out of the dust of the ground, and breathed into his nostrils the breath of life, and he became a living soul; and the Lord created man in His own image, male and female created He them."

During the five days of creation the vegetable and animal have been evolved, and, when man appears upon the scene, everything is in a vastly improved and highly developed condition, compared with the condition of the early monstrous forms. "And the evening and the morning were the sixth day." And here we must digress.

Some students of the occult imagine (for certainly they are not properly initiated and trained in the schools of occultism) that the missing link, or first human form, the connection between the animal and human, was caused by a spiritual impulse union, which, acting upon the highest form of animal, an ape, for example, produced an entirely different species, quite human in their organism, but hairy, etc., and that from this missing link the human race, as at present, has been evolved. But this is erroneous, and void of truth. While the spirit atoms have been evolving upward from the mineral, the spiritual form has been involving downward until it became tangible and objective, possessing at first a vast but loosely organized body. Each age saw it smaller and more compact, until, at the end of the Third Race of the First Human Round, the spiritual man had a compact, well-organized body, and the commencement of the Fourth Race, (the center of the seven) was the first point of contact, the focus of the spirit downwards and the apex of the material upwards. (see note below) Matter and spirit met and formed the first real physical man of the human race. This is the great mystery;—the lowest point in the arc of spiritual involution impinges upon the highest arc, or culminating point, of material evolution, and forms the origin of man. The evolution of the remaining root races having taken place, the life impulse begins to ebb and slowly quits our shores, and our Earth for the first time enjoys a rest. The six days of creation are at an end, and the seventh is The Day of Rest.

NOTE: This needs a little explanation. The first race of human beings who existed upon this planet were really spiritual. Their bodies were quite ethereal, when compared with our gross organisms, but were sufficiently material to be objective and tangible. They were pure and innocent, true Adams and Eves, and their country was indeed a garden of Paradise. They were natural born adepts of the highest order. They played with the Akasa and the magnetic currents of our globe as the boys in Bulwer Lytton's "Coming Race" played with the tremendous Vril. The elementals and nature spirits were, by their art, rendered objective, and performed the duties of servants to them. This was the true Golden Age. It was the first spiritual race of human beings; the progenitors of humanity upon our Earth. The race which followed them was termed the Silver Age in the arcane doctrine of the occult. Their descendants, altho pure and able to control the psychic currents, and Gods in comparison to ourselves, were far inferior to their forefathers of the Golden Age. Both these races, and also the third, viz., the people of the Copper Age, when they wished to die passed peacefully away, and their bodies were immediately disintegrated by the currents of vril. There were neither shades, shells nor phantoms in our atmosphere in those days. The third, or Copper Age, people were as inferior to those of the Silver Age as were the Silver to the Golden. Mankind was on the downward cycle; lies, deceit and selfishness began to be engendered, and consequently there arose a school of Black Magic. In this age the first elements of that curse, Caste, arose.

This, the Copper Age, was the last remnant of those who inherited the Divine Wisdom of the Gods of the Golden Age. The spiritual races had now reached the lowest possible point in the arc of spiritual involution, and the Fourth race, or Iron Age people, were the first of the gross physical races, who became mighty hunters, and ate flesh meat, and whose animal passions alone ruled their enjoyments. From this date the nations became migratory nomads, and soon lost all traces of that high civilization which belonged to the early Copper Age races. This is, then, the esoteric explanation of the Four Ages of antiquity, and refers only to the first round of mankind upon any newly created planet, and also to the highest and two succeeding races previous to the life-wave leaving the planet, viz., the three highest states possible in any given round. The others cycles of years, termed Golden, Silver, etc., refer solely to polar motion and the change of our Earth's climate.

The Day of Rest. The Sabbath of the Lord. The Earth slumbers and enjoys the peace of Nirvana. After this Sabbath, the first day of a new week commences, for the gaseous tide-wave, having gone the circuit of the planetary chain, once more reaches our globe. The atmosphere is again reorganized, purified, and galvanized with new life to make it fit to receive and sustain a higher phase of evolution. It breathes the breath of a new life upon our awakening planet. The life impulse that has been passive during the Sabbath of the Lord becomes again active.

After the expiration of the gaseous wave, and another Polar Day, the beds of the oceans have risen and become dry land, and the old continents are now at the bottom of the ocean, and, as this takes place slowly, the leading types of flora, fauna and surviving types of the seven human families retreat from the sinking continents and occupy the new-made land and mountains which are waiting to liberate their long-imprisoned spirit atoms, and this is affected, directly the mineral wave arrives, at the commencement of the Second Polar Day. The old mineral elements are now liberated, and the incoming mineral wave becomes incarnated in their place. By the time this tide has attained its climax the newly liberated spirit atoms of this planet form a new mineral wave, which, seeking reincarnation, begins to flow on to the next planet, which has already been prepared for it by the preceding gaseous wave. Then, in succession, comes the vegatable, animal, etc., to prepare a "New Heaven and a New Earth" for the incoming life-wave that shall evolve the Second Round of humanity, which, having again evolved its seven root races and their innumerable sub and offshoot races, again passes on its journey round the chain, leaving only a remnant of its seven leading types to survive the long ages of slumber, to give the struggling monads that Nature has left behind a chance of incarnating themselves to form the connecting links for the next round. And so does evolution proceed until each planet of the chain has evolved seven complete rounds of humanity, and then the Great Jubilee of the Earth takes place. Seven times 7 rounds equal 49; and 7 races of human beings on 7 planets is also 49; and the 50th. is the year of Jubilee, symbolized by the Jews every 50th. year, when no work was done and the land rested. "As it is below, so it is above, as on the earth, so in the sky." Remember this.

And now, as a conclusion to this part of La Clef Hermetique, we give the Cycles and Periods in full, tabulated, so as to enable the student to comprehend them at a glance. It only remains to say that at the end of every Great Period, of 1,016,064,000 years, the Sun of our system passes into a passive state of sleep, and remains so for 127,008,000 years. It is, in fact, the Solar Nirvana (just as the Earth enters Nirvana at the end of every complete evolution). All the planetary chains of the solar system are disintegrated during the great solar Nirvana, and recreated upon the awakening of our Sun from its cycle of rest. The alternate states of activity and rest are by the Hindoo Initiates termed the days and nights of Brahma.

THE CYCLE PERIODS OF THE GREAT LIFE-WAVE
OF MATERIAL AND SPIRITUAL EVOLUTION

One Polar Day, which is also the cycle of duration of any life-wave on our planet, is, when measured by the common years of our Earth's time, exactly 2,592,000 years.

And, although the 7 planets of our chain vary in the length of their respective life-waves, some a few thousand years more and some a few thousand less, they are, on the average, all of the same duration. Hence the great period of the life-wave, traveling once round our septenary chain of worlds, is 2,592,000 multiplied by 7, or 18,144,000 years. This is for the complete circuit of 7 orbs, but the cycle, or period, of the life-wave, from its leaving the Earth to its reappearance or commencement is 2,592,000 less than the above, or, in other words, exactly 15,552,000 years.

The period of evolution of the 7 great rounds of humanity, and producing 7 times 7, equaling 49, root races of immortal beings (for each race contains its own immortals), is the period of the life-wave passing seven times round the chain, or 127,008,000 years.

There are now say seven great planetary families, each family containing within itself seven root races, and each root race containing within itself, its numerous offshoot races. The perfected humanity, then, rests in the enjoyment of a blissful Nirvana, or "The peace of God, which passeth all understanding," for the 50th Period, that is to say, the 7 planetary families of our Earth have occupied 7 complete circuits of the life-wave round the chain, or 49 Polar Days. The 50th day is the day when those purified souls enter Nirvana, as a family, and this Nirvana lasts until the human life-wave has passed round the chain in a passive state and reached the shores of our planet again, or 18,144,000 years.

After the Jubilee of Nirvana, this vast, and now exalted, host of the 7 planetary families' perfected souls become, in their turn, the originators and guardians of a new and fresh race of humanity, each planetary family, or state, becoming the especial rulers of their own sphere, while their own late Angelic Guardians, the 7 spirits (families of spirits) that stand before the Lord, termed Dhyan Chohans in Esoteric Buddhism, ascend still higher into more perfect spheres of creation. You will take note that each family, or new angelic planetary state of lately exalted human souls, rules the corresponding family upon Earth. Thus the first family, or that which formed the first 7 root races after their cycle, rules the first seven root races of their new creation, and so on with the others. These new races of human beings evolve and pass through the same harmonious process of evolution, from spirit to matter and back again to spirit, thus completing the great cycle of necessity. The planet itself is not recreated after each earthly Nirvana, but re-awakened into activity and life to pass through 7 times 7 races, or circuits of the life wave, or 127,008,000 years.

After the period has again expired, this race of guardians also ascend to higher planes, and the second planetary family enjoys Nirvana for 18,144,000 years, and then in their turn become guardians of the third's 7 families (termed one planetary family). Then the third family originate, rule and guard the fourth, the fourth the fifth, and so on until our Earth (and the planetary chain in its turn) has evolved 7 great planetary families, each family consisting of 7 rounds, and each round of 7 root races, and has also enjoyed 7 Nirvanas. This makes up the grand period of 8 times 127,008,000 years, which, in its grand and complete total, equals 1,016,064,000 years of earthly time.

This period is obtained as follows; 7 periods of 127,008,000 for the 7 great planetary families, and 7 Nirvanas of 18,144,000, which make the eighth; the total eighth. This great cycle, 1,016,064,000 years, is the exact term of our planet's physical existence.

The 7 great cycles and the 7 Nirvanas together constitute the eighth, and produce the sleep of death. Our sphere will then have completed the period of child-bearing; old age has gradually settled upon her; she has borne seven sons, and now sinks into the eighth period—sleep—the sleep of death and complete annihilation. Cohesion loosens its hold upon the molecules, and atom by atom the planet's particles are disintegrated and dispersed in space. The great solar sleep, or Nirvana, takes place, and our Sun ceases to be active for a period of 127,008,000 years, viz., a complete evolutionary cycle; and it is only when the first warm breath of new spiritual life pulsates through the spaces of Aeth that a recreation of the planetary chains commences anew. The disintegrated atoms of former worlds are reconstructed with new cosmic matter, and once more evolution; but upon a higher plane; begins its almost ceaseless round.

Note the terrible significance of the figure 8. The eighth sphere of our chain is not a visible orb, but a lifeless, dark, semi-spiritual one. (see note below) It is the sphere of death, and the temporary abode of those souls, or shades, who have, through their depraved lives, lost their connection with the Divine Parent, the spiritual ego that gave them birth. Yet they have bartered a glorious, divine birthright for a mess of pottage, and now must sink unconsciously into the sleep of oblivion, while the enfranchised souls of their nobler brethren are urging their resistless course through the sapphire vaults and starlit realms of the Milky Way. And yet, O most esteemed and eternal brother, in the face of our eternal progress, these vast Cycles and most awful, incomprehensible Periods are but a few fast-fleeting moments of planetary existence. The whole eras of past eternity cannot bring one second more near the end of our immortal, deathless reign.

NOTE: This eighth orb is known to Initiates of the highest interior degree as "the Dark Satellite," whose ruling spiritual hierophant is known by the name of Ob. From this name came that of Oberon and so evil and infernal is the power of this sphere that all cases of demonia, enchantment or possession came to be termed Obsession. The buried cities of the Gobi desert belong to races who were the devotees of this Ob. (This was after the Gobi had become a portion of the continent of old India and does not refer to the "Golden isle" of the sea, when the Gobi was a tropical ocean.) Hence its name, Gobi, that is, the followers of Ob, or the country of Ob. This is the reason for the awful traditions mentioned in "Isis Unveiled" as to the hidden treasures being guarded by a legion of infernal spirits. It is from this evil orb that the powers possessed by the Black Magi are derived, and, in fact, it is the Spiritual correspondence of those brothers on Earth. For, remember, there is not a class of people, or a society devoted to any subject on Earth, but what has a spiritual correspondence in the realm of spirit. The Hermetic Law is one grand truth, viz., "As it is above, so it is below, as on the Earth, so in the Sky." St. Paul mentions, or rather refers, to this "Dark Satellite" when he publicly declares: "We wrestle not against flesh and blood, but against powers and principalities, princes of the air," etc.

CHAPTER V

LA CLEF HERMETIQUE

SECTION II

THE SACRED CYCLES AND NUMBERS OF THE ANCIENT HINDOOS

" 'Tis but a moment from its first
evolution to its bier and shroud;
Then, O why should the spirit
of mortal be proud?"

It would be a waste of time upon our part, and a greater waste of the time of the student of esoteric science, if we were to wade through and enumerate the whole system of these sacred cycles and numbers, or were he to attempt the task of remembering them. We shall supply the key to these numbers. This sacred mystical key will fit every cyclic lock, and only requires to be turned with a wise hand to enable the student to open every portal in the Oriental system of numbers.

The Five Great Yugas

Satya Yug	1,728,000 years,	4 periods,	units equal 18 and 9
Treta Yug	1,296,000 years,	3 periods,	units equal 18 and 9
Dvapara Yug	864,000 years,	2 periods,	units equal 18 and 9
Cali Yug	432,000 years,	1 period,	units equal 9
Maha Yug	4,320,000 years,	10 periods,	units equal 9

If the student goes over the above numbers, he will notice that they are all parts of the Divine Age, the Maha Yug, and that each is composed of the Cali Yug. For instance, Satya Yug, or 4 periods, is just 4 Cali Yugs, and so on; and the Cali Yug is the period of the Earth's Pole passing over 60 degrees of its orbit, and thus forming the sextile to its own true place. The Dvapara Yug is the period of the Earth's Pole forming the trine aspect to its true place, and passing over 120 degrees of its orbit. The Treta Yug is the period of the Earth's Pole passing over 180 degrees of its orbit, and forming the opposition to its own place. It is the Cycle that rules the day and the night, the evening and the morning of one Polar Day of Creation. The Satya Yug is the period of the Earth's Pole passing over 240 degrees of its orbit. It is the double trine, or twice 120 degrees. (see note below) It is also the Cycle that rules the great turning point of the life-wave of the planetary chain; that is, when the Earth has passed through a Satya Yug, the culminating point has been passed, and the life impulse begins to pass to the next planet. Again, you must observe the regular, harmonious progression of the terminating units of each Yug, 2, 4, 6, 8, and of the periods (Cali Yugs), 1, 2, 3, 4. These are the locks, and each one points esoterically to the mysterious, hidden number so carefully veiled from the rude gaze of the profane mind. This sacred, guarded number constitutes the Golden Key. It is the magical 9, the highest unit. It is a triune, or three times three, equal 333 (3 times 3 equals 9); this is 360, less 3 times 9, equals 27 degrees, and in its second aspect shows the magical number of Abracadabra, or 666 (18 equals 9). This sacred number is the perfect symbol of Deity. Multiply it as you like by any number and it resolves itself into 9; and just as all the different aspects of the Eternal and Divine Essence eventually return into the one primordial source, so does this number. No matter to what power it is raised, its ultimate is 9. Hence it is the Divine Figure that can alone unlock the Cycles of the Great First Cause.

NOTE: The Pole passing over 60 degrees of its orbit is, in the occult, symbolized by the Sun within a six-pointed star; or Draco, the Serpent, enfolding a six-pointed star in its coils. The trine aspect is likewise a trine, but also as a three-pointed star; i.e., having three rays.

The Pole in opposition, or passing 180 degrees, is in one of the aspects of the eight-pointed star, in which each ray is opposite another. The period of 240 degrees polar motion is symbolized by the Sun being enclosed in Solomon's Seal or the double trine, viz., 120 degrees added to 120 degrees is 240 degrees.

Having explained the preliminary details of the Hindoo system, we must now enter upon a more beautiful series of calculations of esoteric cycles; and it is necessary, in order to comprehend this, to reveal the Secret Period of the Hindoos, termed a Divine Year. This Divine Year consists of exactly 360 (9) common years, or the number of degrees in the Zodiac. With this year the ancients used to veil their more treasured Cycles.

We will now compare, side by side, the Five Great Yugas, with their esoteric periods when expressed by Divine Years;

	Common Years		Divine Years
Satya Yug	1,728,000, equal	4 periods, equal	4,800
Treta Yug	1,296,000, equal	3 periods, equal	3,600
Dvapara Yug	864,000, equal	2 periods, equal	2,400
Cali Yug	432,000, equal	1 period, equals	1,200
Maha Yug	4,320,000, equal	10 periods, equal	12,000

In the first place, we see that the Divine Maha Yug is composed of 12,000 Divine Years, which constitute the 10 Great Ages, (see note below) or Cali Yugs, and, in the second, place, that the Divine Years run thus; 4, 3, 2, 1 and 8, 6, 4, 2, and taken by themselves are 1,200 or 1 and 2 equal 3; and 2,400 or 2 and 4 equal 6; and 3,600 or 3 and 6 equal 9; and lastly, 4,800 or 4 and 8 equal 12; which are briefly 3, 6, 9, 12. We explain all these simple matters to show that all the sacred numbers of the Hindoos are one complete and harmonious progression of the 9 units. The student may, if he chooses, go into the Manwatares and Yugs at his leisure and as his inclination prompts. The Manwatares are portions of the Great Kalpa, which is 1,000 Maha Yugs of 4,320,000 common years. This is almost too much for human comprehension, and so we leave it, retiring content with the knowledge that it was but a method adopted by the ancient sages to express their ideas of the sublime majesty of Aum, and to show the utter fallacy of the finite ever being able to comprehend the Infinite, Divine, First Cause or the extent of His attributes.

NOTE: The Ten Ages, or Cali Yugs, are also, in the East, shown under the symbol of the Ten Avaters; the Goddess Cali, of the old Hindoos, being a kind of geological Isis, or Queen of geological formations. And lastly, while the whole of this is strictly true, so far as this; the physical or material plane is concerned; yet it must, by the laws of correspondence, be considered in its truly occult sense. The four ages are the four Great Cycles of human evolution; First, the Golden, the classical, Saturnian age; then the less spiritual or Silver Age; then the Copper; and lastly the Iron Age; the dense or material barbarian age or state, spirit in its descent, becoming more and more gross, until the lowest point of the age of Earth, or the Iron Age, was reached, and man entered upon the first human cycle. This, of course, teaches that our first progenitors were truly spiritual, or angelic, and that each age in the scale of involution made them more material; and directly the lowest point of the arc was reached, then material evolution commenced. But, of course, all these spiritual verities will open out to your mind as you carefully think over this brief paper.

We will now turn from the theoretical to the practical Cycles of the old Hindoos and esoterically explain

THE FOUR CELEBRATED AGES OF ANTIQUITY

In the first place, we have taught that the Hindoos' esoteric, or Divine, year consisted of 360 common years, and that the whole of their cycles bear a direct relation to arithmetical progression and proportion, such as 1, 2, 3, 4 and 4, 3, 2, 1; also 2, 4, 6, 8 etc. We have thoroughly explained Polar Motion, etc., therefore, if we calculate the motion of the North Pole from the period of its being perpendicular to, and coinciding with, the North Pole of the Ecliptic, over a distance of 90 degrees, when it would be horizontal, or in the plane of its orbit, we shall obtain four distinct periods, bearing the mystical relation of 4, 3, 2, 1, which will be found to have a remarkable character in the country round Benares, or latitude 27 degrees North (2 and 7 equal 9). Benares is the ancient seat of learning in India, and at one time was the center of their occult schools; but their sacred place, or temple of observation, was termed the Mountain of Light in latitude 27 degrees. By using the Divine Year as a Key, we find the meaning of the following periods or ages;

	Common Years	Polar Motion	Divine Years
Golden Age	259,200,	4 times 9 equals 36 degrees and	720
Silver Age	194,400,	3 times 9 equals 27 degrees and	540
Copper Age	129,600,	2 times 9 equals 18 degrees and	360
Iron Age	64,800,	1 times 9 equals 9 degrees and	180
	648,000,	10 times 9 equals 90 degrees and	1,800

Thus, during the passage of the Pole from one point of the quadrant to the other, occurred the mystical ages, which also correspond to fire, air, water and earth. These Periods will be found to differ by 64,800 years, or 180 Divine Years, from one another, and each portion of the angle moved over consists of the mysterious number 9, multiplied by 4, 3, 2, 1; thus, 4 times 9 degrees equals 36 degrees; 3 times 9 degrees equals 27 degrees; 2 times 9 degrees equals 18 degrees; and 1 times 9 degrees equals 9 degrees; and bearing in mind that our place of observation is Benares, or 27 degrees North latitude, we find that during 720 Divine Years the Tropics passed from the equator to 36 degrees latitude, North and South; and from this point during 540 more the Tropics passed up to 63 degrees latitude, North and South; and also from this position, during a further 360 Divine Years, it reached up to 81 degrees North latitude; and lastly, during a period of 180 Divine Years from this era, the Tropics reached the Pole, when every portion of the globe had a Tropical summer and an Arctic winter. But, to better express our meaning, we will briefly describe these four ages.

The first is the Golden Age, which began with a most delightful climate, a gentle, fruitful, universal summer. This ancient seat of science was indeed divinely favored by the laws of Nature throughout long ages, and no wonder it was christened the Golden Age, which corresponds to Fire. But the Poles gradually moved on, though at no time during this age was the meridian altitude of the Sun, on the shortest day, less than 27 degrees; the latitude of the observatory.

Then came the Silver Age, which corresponds to the element of Air. This period lasted for 540 Divine Years, and was a variable period. The summers were hot and the days long; the winters were cold and the days short, but the Sun was always visible above the horizon at noon on the shortest day, and the Tropics reached an angle of 63 degrees.

Next in rotation we have the Copper Age, corresponding to the element of Water, which lasted for 360 Divine Years. It was indeed a dull, watery, lifeless period. A Tropical summer and an Arctic winter, the spring deluging the plains and lowlands with frightful floods, etc. The Tropics moved another 18 degrees nearer the Pole, and on the shortest day at noon the Sun never rose, but was 18 degrees below the horizon. As, however, 18 degrees is within the angle of twilight, they had no absolute darkness.

Lastly comes the Iron Age, corresponding to the Earth; the Age of Horror, which lasted 180 Divine Years, and at noon on the shortest day the Sun was 27 degrees below the horizon, and never rose for weeks together in midwinter. It was cold, dark, frozen and death-like, and a period when the extremes of heat and cold waged incessant war, neither obtaining the victory.

In closing this chapter, we will reproduce, for notice, that the Pole passed over 90 degrees, or one-fourth of the circle, in 1,800 Divine Years, or 648,000 common years. Therefore, it passed its complete orbit of 360 degrees in 7,200 Divine Years, or 2,592,000 common years, from which take the Prajanatha Yug of 2,160,000 common years, and the remainder is the Cali Yug of 432,000 common years, or the Age of Heat. The Cali Yug is one-sixth of the polar orbit, and five Cali Yugs make the Prajanatha Yug.

The 70 Elders initiated by Moses and Aaron were symbolical of the 72 Divine Years; that is, 70 Elders and Moses and Aaron, making the total 72, or the magic 9; which is the period of the Sun passing the 12 signs of the Zodiac, or 25,920 years. It states in the Holy Writ that they (the 70 Elders and Moses and Aaron) saw the God of Israel, which, of course, was the Sun; and the 72 Elders represented its Great Cycle, or 72 times 360 common years equals 25,920 years.

A COMPARISON OF THE HARMONY OF
ESOTERIC NUMBERS AND ESOTERIC CYCLES IN
REFERENCE TO TIME AND MOTION

The Earth's Pole moves 1 degree in...........7,200 common years

And also moves once round in....................7,200 Divine years

The Sun moves thro' space at rate of.........108,000 Miles per hour

In one hour the Earth, by its revolution on its axis, causes 15 degrees of the Zodiac to rise, culminate and set; while the Pole moves 15 degrees of its orbit in......108,000 common years

The Earth, by its diurnal motion, causes the 360 degrees of the Zodiac to rise and set in 24 hours, and in this time the Sun travels thro' space.....................2,592,000 Miles

While a Polar Day of 360 degrees is..........2,592,000 Years

And the Sun moves round its orbit in........25,920 Years

Note that the sum of the digits in each number is the magic 9

CHAPTER VI

LA CLEF

A Key to the Work of Abbot Trithemius, entitled—
"The Secondaries, or Ruling Intelligences Who,
After God, Actuate the Universe."

The periods of the ruling Principles, or Intelligences, and their order of succession in the government of the world is incorrectly stated by the Abbot Trithemius, although there is every reason to believe that this wise and truly learned Abbot knew perfectly well what the true period and order of succession was.

And it was doubtless from reasons of policy that he thought well to conceal this knowledge from the ignorant and profane; knowing, as he must have done, that all worthy and accepted Neophytes would be taught the actual truth during the process of their Initiation.

The correct Cycle, or Period, during which each of the Seven Intelligences has chief rule over all worldly concerns, is an 84th. part of the Great Solar Period of 25,920 years, or a seventh part of the Sub-Solar Period of 2,160 years, and is equal to about 308 years and 208½ days. It will be seen that as the Sun's period, or Revolution, round his immense orbit is 25,920 years, he moves or passes through one Zodiacal Sign in exactly 2,160 years, and that a seventh part of this gives each of the Seven Principles one term of power in each of the 12 signs; and in one complete period of 25,920 years each of the Seven Intelligences has 12 times been the chief governor of this sublunary sphere.

The correct order, or rotation of succession, is the natural order of planetary application; thus, in the first order of the Seven Governors, Cassiel, (see note below) the Angel or Intelligence of Saturn, receives power, and after ruling the world for 308 years, 208½ days, resigns the reins of government to Zachariel, the Angel of Jupiter, who stands second in the order of the Ruling Powers, and after another term of 308 years, 208½ days, hands over the control of the world to Samael, the Angel of Mars, who for the same period subjects the world and its inhabitants to the influence of Martial force; then in the fourth order of the Seven Governors comes the Archangel Michael, the center, and also the chief, of the Seven Great Principles, who, having

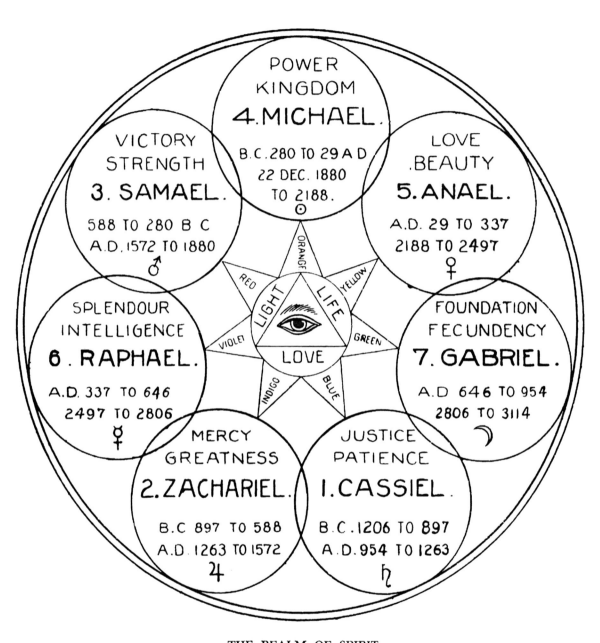

THE REALM OF SPIRIT

Symbolical Illustration
of the
Divine Harmony of Nature's Laws

ruled the world for 308 years, 208½ days, retires in favor of the next succession, and fifth in the order, whose name is Anael, Prince of the Astral Light and Chief Angel of the planet Venus, who, after ruling the world for 308 years, 208½ days, retires in favor of Raphael, who receives the scepter of earthly rule. Bright Raphael, the swift messenger of the Gods, and presiding Intelligence of the planet Mercury, rules for 308 years, 208½ days, when Gabriel, the negative, receives the Ruling Powers. This Intelligence, who is the Angel of the Moon, governs the Earth for 308 years, 208½ days, is the Seventh, and last, of the order and this completes the Sub-Solar Cycle of 2,160 years, when Cassiel once more takes command, and so on, Cycle after Cycle, "ad infinitum."

NOTE: Cassiel is the usual name given to the Saturnine principle. The Abbot Trithemius calls it Orifiel, as do several other writers. Hence, it is well to note, that many names are used Kabbalistically; each name expressing the nature, or qualities, symbolically, by the different Hebrew characters of which it is composed, each different name belonging to the same state or intelligence; denoting different aspects of its power or influence. All the active Principles, or positive angelic Intelligences, as a rule terminate with El, while the negative or evil powers terminate with On; one is solar, the other is lunar. This hint will be sufficient for the student of the Occult, who must ever remember that he must not measure good and evil by any modern conception of these terms.

Every power of Nature, whether it be an intelligent, or a non-intelligent power, is ever striving to obtain an equilibrium; that which we call evil is but a more intense expression of that which we call good; for instance, Pride, Love, Ambition, love of Self and Combativeness, are good, when combined in their true proportion, and any human being without any one of these, would be imperfect; but, carry one or two of these, otherwise good qualities, to a great extreme, and we should witness the greatest evil results. Then remember the Hermetic Law; "As it is below, so it is above, as on the Earth, so in the sky."

A brief glance into past History will be instructive to the student of Psychology, and to enable him to do this, and assist his researches, we supply the following correct data terminating a Sub-Solar Cycle with Michael receiving the Government of the world in the beginning of the year 1881, (see note below) when the sub-races of the West reach the Equator of Human progress, and carrying our researches forward from this date up to the culminating point of the arc; from which point Western Races descend the descending Cycle, and once more relapse into ignorance.

NOTE: The student must bear in mind that there are three different kinds of Cycles spoken of in La Clef. The first are Solar Cycles. Thus, 25,920 years form the Great Solar Cycle, and is the period of the Sun passing through the twelve signs of the Zodiac, and, consequently, completing one revolution of his orbit, round his center; but 2,160 years is a sub-cycle, a twelfth part of the Great Cycle, and the period of the Sun passing through one sign of the Zodiac and equal to 30 degrees of space. When the Sun has passed thro one sign he has completed one sub-cycle, and the new sub-cycle dates from his entry into a fresh sign. For example, the Sun, at the end of the year 1880 A.D., left the sign Pisces and entered Aquarius. (It must be borne in mind that the Sun's motion thro space is exactly the reverse of the natural order of the Zodiacal signs, as from Aries to Taurus, etc.) From this it will be seen that the Sun in 1881 began a new sub-cycle, and that the order of succession of the Seven Governors is such that Michael governs the first term of each sign, so that by the time Michael's rule works round again the Sun will be entering Capricorn, etc.

The second kind of Cycle is the period of the Seven Governors, which, although of exactly the same duration as the Solar sub-cycle of 2,160 years, yet it is not measured by signs or constellations, and, consequently, neither begins nor terminates with the sub-cycle, but is measured thus; From the commencement of Cassiel's rule to the termination of Gabriel's is one complete period or Cycle.

The third kind of a Cycle is the Arc of Human Progress, Mental and Physical, and which alternately carries a race of people or an empire to the summit of power and civilization and down again, in spite of itself, to the greatest depths of ignorance.

The duration of this Cycle varies considerably, according to the kind of race it effects. The greatest period is the duration, or reign, of the Seven root races of each round. The next, the duration of a single root race. Lastly, the duration of each of the numerous off-shoot races belonging to the seven branches and their minor sub-races. But, in any case, the Arc moves in the same harmonious order, obeying the Divine impulse of the Seven Eternal Principles of Nature, evolving its energies in great, mighty waves, when ruling the earliest root races, and comprising hundreds of thousands of years in a single period, in smaller waves that can be measured by tens of thousands of years when controlling the great branch races, and in gentler ripples of tiny wavelets of cosmic energy when directing the minor sub-races, measuring at the most but a few thousand years of Earth's time.

The year 1881 may appear incorrect to any one conversant with modern astronomy, which maintains that our Sun will not enter the Sign Aquarius until the year 1897 A.D. This is a difference of sixteen years, but modern astronomers are wrong. The Sun entered Aquarius in February of 1881. This is not the only mistake they have to discover.

The present Great Western Race is one of the seven branches of the Fifth root race, belonging to the fourth round of evolution, and the sub-races mentioned in La Clef, when speaking of the future glory and fall, do not by any means comprise or include the whole of the Great Western Race. It will be sufficient to say that France, England (Great Britain) and the United States may be taken as typical examples of the sub-races therein referred to. Several other European races are also included.

In carrying our investigations into the past ages, it will suffice if we begin in the year B.C. 1200, when Cassiel, the Angel of Saturn, resumed the Government of the world.

From the year B.C. 1200 to the year B.C. 897, the earth was under the melancholy influence of Cassiel's Rule; and in the very first year of his reign, Troy, the famous Trojan City was taken and destroyed by the Greeks, and many other events faithfully indicate the nature and power of Saturine influence. It will well repay those who will study Ancient History.

After Cassiel, the benevolent Zachariel, Chief Agent of Jupiter, became Regent of the world, and here we note the remarkable difference between the two Governors. In the beginning of this Angel's reign, Rome, the Mistress of the world, was built, and the foundation of a mighty Empire substantially laid. All Nations began to progress rapidly into a more advanced state of civilization, and to cultivate the Arts and Sciences, and lastly, but by no means the least of the benefits conferred by Zachariel, was the production, toward the close of his reign, of two of the most extraordinary men our era has ever seen, viz., Gautama Buddha in India and Pythagoras in Europe.

The Angel Zachariel, was in power from the year B.C. 897 to the year B.C. 588. Then came Samael, the Angel of Mars, who reigned from the year B.C. 588 to the year B.C. 280. This period is one of war, Martial Heroes and brilliant achievements on the field of battle. A glance at the history of Greece and Rome will suffice to show how true this is.

After Samael, came Michael, the Sun God, the shining chief of the Seven Intelligences, and ruled the world from the year B.C. 280 to the year A.D. 29. During this period most Nations attained the Climax of power and civilization. Toward the close of his reign, this bright Angel presented the Nations of the West with a teacher, who rivaled, in moral teachings and excelled in practical benevolence, Gautama Buddha, the greatest moral reformer the East has ever seen. This Teacher was styled by His followers, the Son of God, and was called by name Jesus, the son of Joseph and Mary.

He was called the Son of God Astrologically, because He was born into the world during the reign of Michael, the Sun God. And esoterically because he was at-one with the Universal Father.

And it is remarkably strange, that, no sooner did Michael's Rule end, than the numerous priestly enemies of this noble reformer became triumphant, and brutally murdered Him, as they have done thousands of others in all ages of the world.

The great religious symbol of all exoteric religious systems and dogmatic sacerdotal castes has been the Cross; inverted, it is a bloody weapon, the sword, and past history can prove how well its devoted priesthood knew its fearful use.

After Michael comes Anael, "Prince of the Astral Light," the Angel of Venus and Love, who ruled from the year A.D. 29 to the year A.D. 337. These were the days of religious persecution; the days, also, of faith and love among the Christians for the doctrine of their noble Chief. It was in these days when it was said, "How these Christians love one another;" but, alas, it was also a time of great licentiousness in Rome, when women, love, lust and debauchery were the order of the day. This period will show the occult student the two opposite powers or forces of Anael's influence. When exerted for evil, it is all that is obscene and disgusting, but, when exerted for good, it evolves that which is noble, elegant and true.

After Anael's rule terminated, the Angel of Mercury, or Raphael, commenced to rule, and was Governor from the year A.D. 337 to the year A.D. 646. It was during this period that the Gospels of the New Testament were forged. Christianity, under the rule of the Brain instead of simple faith and brotherly love, became proud. From being persecuted, she became the persecutor. The church became dogmatic, cunning, and thoroughly determined to succeed at all hazards. The most transparent forgeries were accepted as absolute truth. The mutilation of the works of the contemporary authors of the Apostles and the earliest Christian Fathers, and interpolating suitable passages of their own, were considered meritorious actions. It was during this reign that the celebrated Council of Nice was held, and the divinity of Jesus established—by vote.

At the end of the year A.D. 646 Gabriel, the Angel of the Moon, became the Supreme Ruler, and reigned until the year A.D. 954.

This period, like all Lunar periods, was one of intellectual slumber. The Dark Ages had set in, and gradually increased until Cassiel, the Angel of Saturn, took command, and goverened from the year A.D. 954 to the year A.D. 1263, and made things worse.

Pagan darkness and gross superstition held the sway, and reigned supreme, until the year A.D. 1263. The lowest point in the mental arc was reached, and Western nations were in the most dense condition. But a change was at hand, for the benevolent Zachariel, the genius of Jupiter, again resumed the management of the world, and reigned until the year A.D. 1572. This period is one of almost uninterrupted intellectual progress. During this Rule of Power, the despotic power of Rome received its death-blow.

Parliaments were instituted for the people, the days of Good Queen Bess came to an end. Protestantism flourished, and so prepared the way for Free Thought.

After the good reign of Zachariel, Samael, the Angel of Mars, came into power and reigned from the year A.D. 1572 to the year A.D. 1880 (until December 21st. 1880, when the Sun reached the Tropic of Capricorn. Michael began to reign on December 23rd.) This rule was the Age of Iron, and just as Rome conquered all before her over 2,000 years before, and achieved imperial greatness, so did Great Britain, the second Rome. It was again a period of war, mechanical inventions and martial glory, and, at times, the whole of Europe was one great battlefield, and resounded with the din of arms "and all the circumstances of war." In the future this will be called the age of war-like inventions, and noted for its huge ironclads, great guns, and other fearful engines of destruction.

Mars rules iron and all martial arts and sciences; hence the wonderful inventions of this age-period in steam engines, iron ships and elaborate machinery.

At the end of the year A.D. 1880, the Great Archangel Michael comes into power and once more has the government of the world until the year A.D. 2188. This will be a period of Imperial Greatness. Empires will shine full of glory, the Human intellect will have full play and all Churchés, Religious Creeds and Ecclesiastical Dogmas will fall to the ground and become things of the past. Parsons, Vicars and Bishops will have to work in different fields if they mean to obtain an honest livelihood. Yes, I repeat this prophecy. The Churches and Chapels will fall with a terrible crash, and be destroyed. But from their ashes, Phoenix-like, shall arise a new Religion, whose shining Motto will be; Veritas Excelsior, Truth Above. This era shall proclaim the rights of man. It is essentially the age of reason dreamed of by Bruno and Thomas Paine. During the reign of this Angelic Intelligence, the Masculine Element will receive the Solar influx and obtain its highest development. Intellect and Reason will remove most of our Social disorders and women receive more attention in worldly affairs; but at the same time, it is not a feminine period by any means.

Mankind under this rule, will become physically and intellectually immensely superior to what they are now. Startling discoveries in Chemistry, Electricity and all the physical sciences will be brought to light. Steam will be superseded by Compressed Air (gas), Electro-Magnetism (atomic power) as a motive power. In fact a new era of progress will dawn upon the world, as time and space will be annihilated by new transportation and communication; and, last, but not least, Science and Religion will become blended, spiritual intercourse an acknowledged fact, and Psychology the special study of the greatest Scientists of the day.

After the rule of Michael, Anael, Prince of the Astral Light, will receive the Guardianship of the world, and reign from the year A.D. 2188 to the year A.D. 2497. This is the feminine period, and woman will, during Anael's reign, become man's just and lawful equal, socially and politically. Intuition will show itself the superior of mere intellect, and the human form, physically, attain its greatest degree of perfection. Occultism will be taught in our Universities, Astronomers become Astrologers, and drugs for the treatment of disease be consigned to the limbo of oblivion, to keep company with the Religious Dogmas and Scientific Noodleisms of today. It is at this point that I would warn all Western Nations. Remember that this is the period of feminine force and love. Therefore, see to it that you form not those magnetic conditions that would attract into your midst the dark legionaries of Anael. If you do, Woe be unto you; as pride and luxury, licentiousness and debauchery will result, and the fate of Nineveh, Babylon and Rome will be yours; but if, on the other hand, virtue, morality and pure affectional love, stand paramount amongst you; then, all that is noble, elegant and true shall reign in your midst. Then shall Nations abolish fleets and standing armies, kings lay aside their scepters, and a Universal Human Brotherhood begin to comprehend their common origin and Divine relationship with the GREAT FIRST CAUSE.

After Anael, in the order of the seven Governors, Raphael will receive the Scepter of earthly rule—Bright Raphael, the swift messenger of the gods and presiding Intelligence of the Planet Mercury. This will be the grand era of the mind, the age of the Genius of Humanity, to assimilate all the stores of knowledge, treasured up by the past ages. This is the culminating point (see note below) of this sub-cycle of the sub-Western races. Raphael will govern from the year A.D. 2497 to the year A.D. 2806. During this period, the attainment of Adeptship will be the highest ambition of the noblest minds, though but few will attain unto this ideal height in any race of the present round. Science and the Arts will attain unto a degree of perfection unknown to any past age, and thus will close the Intellectual genius of the Western Race.

From the summit we begin to retrograde, for Gabriel, the seventh Governor, now takes up the reins of power, and rules from the year A.D. 2806 to the year A.D. 3114. This rule is again the stagnation of mind, and once more Humanity having attained the greatest height possible in this cycle, begins to travel on the downward arc and the nations again relapse gradually into ignorance, and spiritual truth will materialize itself into concrete sacerdotalism, nor will mankind of the West again reach its climax of civilization until about the year A.D. 7300.

NOTE: The culminating point of this Cycle is about the year A.D. 2800, or six years before the expiration of Raphael's Rule. The Sub-Western Races, then at their climax of development, will gradually decline, while certain other races of the West will be rapidly rising on their ascending arc, as will the nations of the Orient, who will culminate about the time of the Sub-Western Races reaching the lowest arc of the Cycle.

Flint glass can be made with a temper equal to that sustained by the finest steel, but the secret of its production is in the hands of the Adepts, and like all other secrets, will be accidentally discovered when the proper time arrives.

EXPLANATORY NOTE FOR CHAPTERS V AND VI

Throughout La Clef Hermetique and La Clef the terms, Powers, Intelligences, and Principles, have been used in a somewhat confused way. Hence, it is necessary to explain, that, when speaking of the seven Ruling Intelligences, the terms, Intelligences, Powers, and Principles are to be understood as meaning the same thing, each Angel being a Principle possessing both Power and Intelligence. But, when speaking in reference to Humanity, as follows in this note, the terms, Principle, Power and Force, are to be understood as referring to the attributes of the Human Soul.

By Feminine Powers or Principles, we mean the passive, receptive, intuitional qualities; and when speaking of the Masculine or Feminine Forces ruling in the world, as the case of Anael or Michael, we mean that the prevailing influence of the period is such as to evolve these qualities in the Races under its influence.

Students of the Occult will know that these seven Angels, exoterically called Cassiel, Zachariel, Samael, etc., are not single individual or Angelic or Spiritual Intelligences, but Angelic States, each state comprising innumerable hosts of purified Angelic Beings. The reason why these seven states are termed the Seven Planetary Angels, is, because their special force or power in its effects upon the earth's inhabitants, corresponds magnetically with the force exerted by the Seven Principle or Primary Planets whose names they bear; each state named after its corresponding Planetary Nature.

These Seven ruling Principles in their combined total constitute ONE RAY of the PRIMAL ESSENCE; and it is this ESSENCE whom we call GOD, just as the seven varied tints in the rays of the Solar Spectrum, constitute the pure white Light of the Glorious Sun.

There is, at the present day, a certain sect of Esoteric Christians, or more properly students of Esoteric Christianity, who have very mistaken ideas and opinions of what they call the new era, or the reign of Michael, which commenced A.D. 1881. Without in the least wishing to disparage the efforts of the students who are working with what light they possess, in the cause of Truth, we must warn the student of Occult Science against these erroneous theories, and say at once, that the Grand Galleries of the Great Pyramid have nothing whatever to do with "Anno Domini," 1881. These Esoteric Christians are in possession of a certain book entitled "The Perfect Way," or the "Finding of Christ." Against this work we have not one single word to say, because it contains a vast amount of truth, but, like all works upon the Occult, the truths are hidden from the unitiated. Failing to perceive this fundamental fact, and taking the literal point of view, a vast number of Esoteric Christians, who completely misunderstand the sublime truths contained in the book, joyfully imagine and proclaim to the public that this new Era begins the Love Element and the Feminine Forces of Nature; and Woman shall become triumphant during this era. That they are grossly in error "La Clef" will show. They further proclaim that "Woman" shall become the grand central figure of Humanity, the sublime Intuition of the Age. How these exponents of Esoteric Christianity can reconcile this theory, we cannot understand. The feminine can never rule the masculine. As well say the positive can be controlled by the negative, or a passive resist an active force. Woman is in possession of a major portion of the

Intuitional, or feminine principles or powers, and only a minor portion of the masculine. Man is just the reverse. Hence it will be seen that both sexes possess both qualities. When a race of Human beings is dominated chiefly by the feminine principle, as in most of the Oriental races of Humanity on every Planet, during the descent of spirit into matter, the people are by far the most spiritual, but at the same time they are vastly more dreamy, impracticable and simple, than they would be if governed by the masculine force chiefly. Hence it is that Humanity requires to undergo material incarnation; not to develop the feminine, but to evolve the masculine attributes of the Human Soul, and thus round out the positive individuality that will enable the perfected Monad to say I Am. Again, many of the Esoteric Christians are possessed with a species of prophetic mania, and almost go into hysterics of enthusiasm when they contemplate what they allegorically term the second coming of the Lord, i.e., the era of Michael, the Sun God, which, as they are well aware, commences in 1881. This class of Esoteric Christians triumphantly point to the Grand Gallery of the Great Pyramid, as indicating, by means of the Pyramidal inch, this Era, but, unfortunately for these individuals, the whole of their Esoteric Cycles, and a great part of their teachings, are not based upon the immutable laws of Nature, but upon the unsatisfactory foundation of mere assumption. To begin with, they assert that the index measurements of the Galleries of the Great Pyramid, consisting of 628, 1542, and 1881, point out certain periods of early Jewish. and later Christian history, and include the date, or time it was built, up to the present day, or A.D. 1881. These assertions, for they are nothing else, have no foundation in truth, and consequently are not worth the paper they are written on. This theory really amounts to saying that this grand monument of Ancient Egypt was built for the special purpose of recording the prophetical data of a nation of Israelitish Brigands, culminating with a Saviour sent to a nation of degraded vagabond Jews, to get murdered for his pains; and this Saviour's second rule, or advent, as a spiritual power to a few sub-races or Western people who value little else but money and position, whose motto is, "All sink if I swim," and whose only real God is Gold; this second advent is esoterically, they say, the true conception of Christ within, instead of without the Human Soul, of the people; but this theory is absurd upon the face of it, because the acknowledgement of this Divine inner principle has been accepted before by various peoples since the Pyramids were erected. But granting, for the sake of argument, that the galleries do point to some modern date, why not say they refer to 1881? after the birth, of Guatama Buddha, equally as well as the orthodox Jesus. Buddha's doctrines have found far more followers and accomplished infinitely more moral purity and brotherly love than Christianity, besides being free; absolutely free; from the foulest blot of every other creed;—Human Blood. Buddha's teachings, or words of Guatama Buddha (not the false doctrines and interpolations falsely denominated as Esoteric Buddhism, but I mean the original teachings of Buddha himself) ever tend to scientific free thought and self spiritual culture, but orthodox Christianity just the reverse in every particular. Orthodox Christian theology has always, in every age, opposed with all its colossal might, the least step toward progress and reformation; it has deluged every country under its baneful rule in torrents of Human Blood and exterminated, with fire and sword, every opposing school of thought. It stands pre-eminent as the only religious creed on the earth that proclaims a free salvation to the crime-stained soul, and the Divine efficacy of the atoning blood of the murdered Prophet. It is the only religion the world has seen that preaches the comfortable doctrine of eternal damnation mid flames of hell fire for the noble free-thinkers, who refuse to credit the infamous pretensions of its priesthood. This religion began with the blood of the innocents, and its history through the ages is recorded on every page in the eternal crimson letters of Human gore, until, Human nature rebelled against this inhuman Christian monster, and bound the power of the Church for evil in chains of adamant. Those who say that our advanced western civilization, and superiority in Art, Science and Manufacture, is an incontrovertible proof of the superiority of the Christian over the Buddhist influence, know nothing of Occult Law. The eastern races, over which Buddhism holds sway, have been traveling in the descending arc of progress, while most of the western, or Christian nations, were ascending the arc of the cycle. Look at eastern Christians, if any proof be required, who were in possession of Christianity before the west, and ought to be superior, but are they? Just as it has been before, so will it be again. The Orientals will be a highly polished and civilized race, trying perhaps to instruct the west by means of missionaries, when our remote descendants are rude barbarians. Remember the "Hermetic Law." "That which has been will also be again," or, in other words, "History repeats itself." The names of Christ and Christianity ought to be banished forever from the minds of all students of Occult Science. Let us have the simple teachings attributed to the man Jesus, if you will, but never call anything divine by the name Christ or Christian, although Christ or Christos anciently referred to the inner light of man. We require a new name that shall express the coming influx of the age; a name quite unassociated with Christian Theology. But, to return to our former argument, Esoteric Christians do not truly comprehend the underlying principles of the Occult, or they would not refer the Pyramids to anything Christian. We could say why the Pyramid was designed, at what era of the world it was built, who its great architect was, and why the Grand Gallery measured 1881 pyramidial inches, or the double 9, but refrain; such things are not committed to writing. The builders of the Great Pyramid, though knowing that each Cycle produces its own great teachers, probably never for one moment contemplated the actual personal existence of Jesus.

The mythical Jesus of the Christian Gospels is composed or made up from three different sources;—Firstly, Egyptian Theology; Osiris, Isis, and Horus, have been converted into Father, Son, and Holy Ghost (or the Virgin Mary). Egyptian fables, in reference to the birth, death, descent into hades, etc., have become Christian truths in reference to Jesus; while his ultimate position as the final judge of Humanity is only that of the resurrected, glorified Osiris; who lived thousands of years before the Orthodox Adam was turned out of the Garden of Eden. The second element of this triune composition, is the traditions of the actual Jesus, the Jewish Adept of the Essenes, in reference to his ministry among the poor, down-trodden inhabitants of his country.

The third and most important element is the actual "Life" and Miracles (so called) of Appolonius of Tyanna. This man was born about the year of the popular A.D. 1, and is the central figure, around which has been draped the Egyptian Myths and traditions of a Jewish Adept, the whole combined and greatly assisted by the pious forgeries of the early Christian Fathers, constitute the well known Orthodox "Life of Christ." The Gospel Jesus, as taught by Christianity, never existed.

CHAPTER VII

NARONIA

THE MYSTICAL CYCLE OF THE SUN

The real secrets and the inner mysteries of the sacred "Naros" appear to have been entirely unknown to either medieval or modern writers. In fact, the most prominent writers upon occult and theosophical subjects generally avoid all mention of it; or, if they do express their ideas, it is only upon its cosmic, or external aspects, as it applies to the Macrocosm, of the sidereal heavens. But of its spiritual and mystical importance, as it applies to the human soul of the Microcosm, they are universally silent. Briefly stated, the "Naros," in its astronomical and physical aspects, is a Luni-Solar Cycle of the period of the Sun and Moon, and is completed in six hundred years; and, strangely enough, such a period also coincides with some remarkable revolution in the mental and theological affairs of humanity; hence a few extracts from prominent writers will not be out of place to prepare the student for that which is to follow.

Madam Blavatsky, speaking of the Naros in "Isis Unveiled," Vol. I, pages 31-33, remarks "that he (G. Higgins) fails to decipher it (the Cycle) is made apparent; for, as it pertains to the mysteries of creation, this Cycle was the most inviolable of all. It was repeated in symbolic figures only in the Chaldean Book of Numbers, the original book, which, if now extant, is not to be found in libraries."

To the foregoing we may also add, neither will this Chaldean Book be found in the crypts of Thibet, Madam B. to the contrary notwithstanding. She very pointedly tells her readers where they cannot find such a book, but very wisely maintains a discreet silence as to where this rare work can be found.

The learned Countess of Caithness, in her recent volume, "The Mystery of the Ages," mentions the Naros on page 361 viz. "To the Christian Theosophist, Jesus is a manifestation of 'Adonai', the Christ, or Christ Spirit, of whom there have been many incarnations on this Earth, and He the fullest and most perfect. They believe Him to be the guiding guardian protector of this planet during His particular cycle, and that in coming to it, He comes to His own, not only to instruct, but to give a fresh impulse at the end of certain periods of six hundred years, called Naroses, or Naronic Cycles, and if, therefore, it could be proven by those who assert that Jesus is only a mythical, and not an historical personality, the whole theory of the Naronic Cycles, founded on astronomical science, which is to be found in the doctrines of every ancient country, all over the civilized world, would fall to the ground, and prove after a million of ages to be but a vain delusion."

It is scarcely necessary for us to point out that, if the Naros is as the authoress asserts, "founded upon astronomical science," then the Cycle is an astronomical fact, and as such is capable of mathematical demonstration; consequently is, and always must be, totally independent of the existence of individuals. In fact, an astronomical cycle, if true, possesses no real relationship with any personality, human or Divine, and this being the case, the Naronic Cycle will remain just the same truth, upon the plane to which it naturally belongs, whether the Christian Jesus is proven to be either Myth, Man or God. Neither does the genuine student of Occultism care, very much, in which position the supposed Redeemer is placed by the masses.

Therefore, the statement of the authoress that without the actual physical incarnation of the personal Jesus this theory of "millions of ages" would prove to be a vain delusion is the very height of mystical absurdity, and the self-evident inanity of such an illogical argument must surely become apparent to all reflective minds.

The learned Dr. Kennealy, Q.C., etc., in his book "Book of God," makes mention of the Naros upon pages 52, 53 where, viewing the period as a Messianic Cycle, he remarks; "This Naros is the Luni-Solar Naros, or Sibylline year. It is composed of 31 periods of 19 years each and one of 11, and is the most perfect of astronomical cycles, and, although no chronologer has mentioned it at length, it is the most ancient of all. It consists of six hundred years, or 7200 Solar months, or 219,146½ days, and this same number of days, 219,146½, gives 600 years, consisting each of 365 days, 5 hours, 51 minutes and 36 seconds, which differs less than 3 minutes from what the length is observed to be at this day."

"If on the first of January, at noon, a new Moon took place in any part of the heavens, it would take place again in exactly six hundred years, at the same moment and under the same physical circumstances. The Sun, stars and planets would all be in the same relative position." And in corroboration of what this learned doctor says, Prof. Cassini, one of the great modern astronomers, declares "this Naros to be the most perfect of all periods."

From this, then, we see the utter nonsense of modern theosophical mystics trying to twist and warp the harmonies of natural laws to suit their dreamy, sentimental speculations. The Naros exists in spite of each and every attempt of hallucinated mystics to make it conform to their erroneous doctrines.

The Luni-Solar Cycle of 600 years is the absolute measurement of mental development, and the Luni-Solar conjunction, which commences and terminates this Cycle, evolves forth the embryonic conditions which shall, during its rule, become manifested in the physical world. It is not true, from an occult stand-point, that the Naros specially refers to the birth of some great Saviour or Reformer. It is only true, that the conditions which this Naronic conjunction evolve prepare the way and call forth the man or men, who shall act as the pioneers in the world's need of a higher and a more liberal teaching. At the same time it will always be found that some very prominent teacher or reformer is born into the world at about the same time, not definitely to any nation or country, or exactly on time, within a generation or two, but always near to the period of the Cycle; but such teachers and law-givers are not the cause of the Naros, neither do they become incarnated to fulfill the Cycle, as the Countess of Caithness very foolishly imagines, but they appear simply as the result of increased mental energies, or in the downward arc of the race they appear to crystallize the existing truths and veil those things which have ceased to be of use and which may become a source of evil.

A brief outline of this thread of mental evolution can be traced, by noting that Guatama Buddha appeared in 600 B.C. or thereabouts, and that 600 years later the Jewish Reformer, Appolonius of Tyanna, appeared upon the scene of the world's history, then in another 600 years Mahomet, with his warlike issues came upon the planes of human existence. Another Naros passes away when we have a complete host of inspired reformers, and the Reformation began, viz., 1200 A.D. to 1300 A.D. and lastly, we bridge yet another cycle of the Sun and Lo; we have 1881 A.D. and naturally all eyes are looking for another Saviour. The Adventists speak of the second coming of Christ. The Shakers claim that He has already come in the form of Mother Ann Lee. On the other hand the Mormons say that Joseph Smith is the modern Messiah.

It is not of course necessary to say that all of these earnest, and doubtless well meaning sects, are wrong, outrageously in error, because no such Messiah will appear, at least not to them. He will move in the world quite unsuspected as to His true and real greatness; He will do His work comparatively unknown to the world at large; He will be looked upon as an ordinary individual by those who know Him; He will suffer the vilest kind of persecution at the hands of the Inversive element who dread the force of the principles He will leave behind him. His greatest friends, though mystified as to His real nature, will never grasp His real reality until He is beyond their purview. The Messianic Messenger of the ages will not be fully known until He has passed through the valley of the shadow of death, and is beyond the power of the world to flatter or condemn.

The Jews were looking for a Monarch, and a sign from heaven; the sign came, but the Monarch materialized under a very different form from what they expected. He came as the son of a carpenter. So the Christians of to-day are looking for the pomp and glory of a Celestial King. They, too, are looking for a sign from heaven; the sign came with the great perihelion of the planet in 1880 and 1881, and we may depend upon it that the teacher was there, ready and willing, but the world knows Him not, nor will it; the time has passed and He can only be known by the generations which are to follow. Hope, Faith and Charity were the symbols of the Nazarene. They were needed in His day and time, but Life, Light and Love are the great requirements of to-day; they are the pressing needs of the hour.

Having given our students some brief insight into the purely material aspect of the Naros we will not speak of its infinite ramifications upon the physical plane, but reveal a hidden mystery, a mystery that many occult students have hinted at, spoken of, and even attempted to define, but so far they have failed to grasp either its philosophy, basis, or its potency.

The esoteric aspect of the Naros is known to the occult Initiates as the Mystery of Naronia, and refers to the expansion and contraction of the human constitution. As a sort of illustration let us take the motion of the tides, the ebb and the flow. When the Sun and the Moon occupy the same plane in reference to the Earth, we have the high spring tides, etc. It is the same upon the mental plane, with the human brain. The brain of man, magnetically, expands and becomes illuminated by the Luni-Solar influx, from the new to the full Moon, at which time this magnetic force is at its maximum. It is high tide, so to say, and those who have the care and experience of lunatics will verify the fact, that, they become perfect astronomical calendars of the Moon's increase and decrease of light.

Let us take a step further, and we then come to the real dominions of Naronia. SHE is the CYCLE of the SOUL and enacts upon the spiritual plane of human existence, a similar series of events to those of the Naros upon the mundane sphere of life. Hence, we can trace a perfect analogy between the motions of the luminaries in space and the revolution of purely psychic entities within the odylic sphere of man.

Each year of life, the Earth, in her orbit, transits the point in space which she occupied at a person's birth, or in other words, the Sun returns to the same sign and degree of the Zodiac that he occupied in the horoscope. In this transit, the Solar force renews the life energies of the Soul and regalvanizes them with additional force (we are speaking spiritually, understand). These germs of new forces are Virtues, Powers, Potencies and Deific attributes of the great Solar Orb. They are spiritual ovums, or seeds of human possibilities, and if consciously nourished and cherished will evolve powers and states within the Human Soul, which correspond in their action to our hidden spiritual attributes. If unnoticed, uncared for, they remain until other forces polarize them, and then pass onward down their cycle.

When the Moon, in the course of her motion, arrives at the same place during each month, she impregnates these seeds and endows them with magnetic life; therefore, in an occult sense, she confers upon humanity the powers and possibilities of magical forces. It is this Luni-Solar influx of Naronia within the human constitution, then, that controls the real foundation and basis of spiritual development and occult power.

Remember these most important facts, then, and, guided by your own spiritual intuitions in the matter, use this knowledge according to the light which Nature has already given you, or which you shall hereafter receive. We have revealed to you the mystery of Naronia; have given you an outline sketch of its basis in Nature, and its philosophy in human evolution, as near as it is possible without leading you out of your safe path, or bringing you nigh unto dangerous ground.

For those who are ready to utilize this mystery, what we have here said will be plain and easy of comprehension. For those who are not yet ready, rest assured, it is wiser to wait until your spiritual nature is more highly developed.

CHAPTER VIII

SOUL KNOWLEDGE

THE LOGOS, OR BOOK OF WISDOM

EXPLANATORY NOTE: The Atama Bodha or Book of Soul Knowledge, is copied from a free translation of a very Ancient Sanskrit Manuscript, written upon Palm Leaves, and cannot be obtained except in rare and isolated Buddhist convents in the remote parts of India and Tartary. It is therefore placed at the disposal of Neophytes as a valuable Manuscript, of an unique and exceedingly rare work of great merit.   T. H. Burgoyne, Private Secretary.

BOOK I

THE LOGOS, OR BOOK OF WISDOM

"The Qualities cannot know the soul (Divine Ego),
But the Soul knows all Qualities." Mokah.

"Know the Divinity that is within you,
That you may know the Divine One,
Of which your Soul is but a ray." Proclus.

"He who sees all things in the Soul, and the Soul in all things, does not slight anything. It is more refined than an atom, and cannot be approached by argumentation. The truly wise, knowing the ubiquitous Soul, which sees the wakeful and the profoundly sleeping states, do not mourn. The Soul is pure, because it does not participate in the Qualities; it is distinct from the Qualities, because it is, itself, wisdom." From the Sanskrit work, Katha.

"Know, then, that salvation is not attained by uttering Mantras, or by the burning of incense, or observing thousands of fasts. Until the incarnated Soul knows that he is divine, he cannot attain salvation." Mahanirvana Tantra.

"As in a deamond (Magic) mirrow, one cannot see forms reflected, so a Spirit with immature organs cannot attain knowledge. As in unripe fruit, sweet juice cannot be found, so is knowledge not found in an undeveloped organism. The knowledge of the Divine element being in us, is, therefore, the first requisite, and as we acquire that knowledge, we progress in the development of the inner life, and any protest against that knowledge shuts us out from the Spiritual Life." Yagnaval Kya.

ATAMA BODHA

I. This book of Soul Knowledge is composed for those who have effaced their sins by penitence, who have attained the perfect tranquillity, who have destroyed their passions, and who aspire to the final deliverance.

II. Of all means, there is but one, Knowledge, that is efficacious for the obtaining of deliverance, even as there is no cooking without fire, can one not arrive at final deliverance without Knowledge.

III. For want of being opposed to it, action knows not to repulse ignorance, but Knowledge dissipates ignorance, as light dissipates the darkness of heavy clouds.

IV. Fettered in some wise by ignorance, but again becoming free when she is destroyed (Atma, Atma, Spirit, or Human Soul and Brahma, divine Soul) becomes of itself resplendent of great light, as the sun upon disappearance of the clouds.

V. After the Divine Soul (Brahma), troubled by ignorance, has been purified by the exercise of knowledge, the knowledge itself vanishes (diffuses), even as the grain Kalaka in water.

NOTE: Kalaka is used in many parts of India to purify stagnant and brackish water. The natural purifiers are very valuable in the East, and the Kalaka here referred to dissolves immediately when placed in water, hence the passage, "Diffuses even as the Grain Kalaka in water." The student is also here referred to an interesting account of the sweetening of brackish waters in the 15th. Chapter of the Book of Exodus. "So Moses brought Israel from the Red Sea, and they went out in the wilderness of Shur, and they went three days in the wilderness and found no water, and when they came to Morah, they could not drink of the waters of Morah, for they were bitter, and the people murmured against Moses saying, what shall we drink? and he (Moses) cried unto the Lord, and the Lord showed him a tree, which, when he had cast it into the waters they were made sweet," etc. Many kinds of plants will clarify water and make it sweet, the same as the oak cullings used in the waters of the land of La Gronde.

VI. Similar to the image of a dream, the world is continually troubled by love, by hate, and other passions. As long as the dream lasts, it appears to be real, but on awakening, it passes on into non-reality.

VII. The phenomenal world appears as real, even as the oyster shell appears to be silver, as long as Brahma is not known, He that is above all things, indivisible.

VIII. All the varieties of being are comprised in the One Being, veritable and intelligent, who is bound up with all, eternal, all penetrating, even as gold is in all variety of ornaments.

IX. Even as the air, director of the organs of sense, the Master, susceptible of diverse attributes, appears as distinct, by reason of their distinctions, but when these attributes are destroyed (latent), it virtually becomes one.

X. By virtue of these diverse attributes, species, names and different states are communicated to the Spirit, in the same wise as different colors are to the water.

XI. The body, formed of the combination of the elements to the number of five; Fire, Earth, Air, Water and Vital Breath; produced by the effect of action (Energy), thus forms the seat of perception of pleasure and of pain.

XII. The subtle body (Astral Body), which is not the issue of the five grosser elements, but which is united with the five breaths of life, with the faculty of interior comprehension (Manas), with intelligence (Buddhi), and the ten organs, is the instrument of the perception of the interior senses.

XIII. The an-beginning (indefinite), ignorance without beginning (undefined), is called the casual attribute, but which differs essentially from that triplicity of attributes, which is to be understood as Spirit (Atmanam Avadhavy).

XIV. In union with the five envelopes (Five Rogas), the pure Spirit, or Soul, subsists as the nature of one or the other, absolutely in the same wise, as a crystal reflects the colors of the various matters that are brought near it.

XV. Strive by concentrating the thought (mind) to liberate the supreme Soul, pure and free of the envelopes (Elements) to which she is united, that the body and the other, in the same wise as is sifted the grain from the chaff.

NOTE: The elements here referred to are the same intelligent forces generated by the so-called four primary elements fire, earth, air and water, and may be appropriately designated the Elementals of the Astral Plane, who become active agents in the fiery circulus, or astral zone, of the third or fourth dimensions of space. They are soulless, semi-material, magnetic beings, and are the chief, and in a great majority of cases, the only causes of the physical phenomena known to modern spiritualism. It is these elementals, and in fact this Astral Plane that constitutes the well-known Dwellers on the threshold in Occultism.

XVI. The Soul, although it penetrates into all things, does not manifest itself in all places; but it becomes manifest in intelligence (thought), as the reflection on the surface of a mirror.

XVII. The Spirit must be distinguished from the body, the organs of sense, the interior sense and the intelligence, who has perfected its nature, in the same wise as a true King watches his attendants.

NOTE: The Divine Spirit, or Ego, as also the Divine Soul, must not, under any circumstances, be confounded with the reason (mind). Intelligent reason, etc., are but varied expressions of Soul on the external plane, and do not exist at all within the pure realm of Spirit proper.

XVIII. As long as the organs of sense are in action, the Spirit is apparently acting in the same wise, as the Moon appears to be in motion, when the clouds pass by.

XIX. Having recourse to the Vital force of the Spirit, the body, the organs of sense, the interior comprehension and the thoughts (Mind) accomplish their respective functions, as men do their daily work by the light of the Sun.

XX. It is through absence of discernment, that the living and intelligent Spirit is attributed, the qualities or actions of the body, and the organs of sense, as there is attributed a blue color to the firmament.

XXI. Action and other qualities that belong to the attributes of the Manus (interior comprehension), are placed in the Spirit, through ignorance only, even as the motion of the waves is supposed to be caused by the Moon's reflection on the water.

XXII. Passions, desires, pleasures, and pain, dwell in the human mind, in as long as it exists in reality. In the state of profound sleep, when it ceases to be, they, as will are no more, they belong, therefore, to the intelligence, not to Spirit (Soul).

XXIII. Even as clearness is the pre-eminent quality of the Sun, heat of fire, also following in nature, the Spirit, essentially is life, beatitude, eternity, purity.

XXIV. The living and the intelligent part of Spirit (Atman) and activity of intelligence are distinct things. When by ignorance they are identified, the people say "I know."

XXV. There is no change for Spirit, there is not even knowledge for the intelligence; the Soul, knowing all things in excess, is subject to illusions, so far as to say, "I act."

NOTE: The one great thing needful for all Neophytes is to thoroughly realize the vast difference between the appearances and the reality. There is much that could be impressed as to the state which will enable one to distinguish between truth and appearance of truth. Know, then, that all things possessing form and weight are not what they seem, but are only external representatives of a more interior Spiritual correspondence. The Human Ego, like the divine Soul, possesses neither form nor weight; they are the pure formless emanations of Brahma. That which we may term Soul is but the external expression of the interior Soul, in itself invisible.

XXVI. If he take himself for the individual Soul, as (by mistake) one takes a rope for a serpent, the Spirit contracts a great fright, but when he comes to understand, "I am not the Soul, but the sovereign Spirit," he is freed from all fear.

XXVII. The Spirit (Soul) of itself causes to appear the organs of sense, and at their head, intelligence (mind), as a lamp illuminates a vase and other objects. But the Spirit, in its real self, is not illuminated by these inert things.

XXVIII. The Spirit (Soul) whose condition of being is knowledge, desires not the knowledge of another on the subject of its own knowledge, in the same wise as a lamp giving its own light, has no need for another lamp, to be seen.

NOTE: Or in other words, having attained the absolute condition of the At-one-ment, it cannot possibly be aided by any outside or external help, seeing that it is one with the Father.

XXIX. One having recognized the Upadhis, or attributes, without exception, saying, "This is not, This is not," let him recognize the unity of the Supreme Spirit, and of the Soul, by virtue of the great words, having rejected all the attributes of things temporal with such terms as, "It is not, It is not," let him strive to discern the identity of God (Brahma) and of the Soul, but obsequied by the celebrated words of Holy Writ, "Thou art He," This Soul is Brahma (God), "I am He."

XXX. Whatever cleaves to the body is the product of ignorance, it is visible, it is perishable as a bubble, but in that, which has not such marks of distinction, let the pure Being be recognized, saying of himself, "I am Brahma."

XXXI. (Thus says the Soul): To contain any difference from the body, I experience neither birth nor death, nor age, nor decreptitude, nor extinction, and am disconnected from the organs of sense. I have no point of attachment to their objects, even like a circle, when one comes to know the Soul by the intelligence of Scripture, one arrives at the speculative science of the Soul, which is herein resumed in Five Slokas. The first step in the way of life is reading the Sacred Books; the second is meditation, wherein the language of the Soul is understood.

NOTE: The language of the Soul is not, in its strict sense, Intuition, but is that one sole attribute of the spiritual intelligence, viz., Divine Perception. Intuition can only be called the language of the Soul upon the more external planes of manifested Being.

XXXII. Being freed from the Manan, or mind's sentiments, I do not experience pain, passion, hate, fear, love, or other passions or affections. I am that which is established by the precept of revelation, without breath, without Manus, absolutely pure.

XXXIII. Of Brahma is born the breath of life (Prana), the mind; all the organs of sense are air, the wind, light, water and earth, nursing all that which exists.

XXXIV. I am without quality, without activity, eternal, without will, without impurity, without change, without form, forever liberated, perfectly pure.

XXXV. I am as the Ether, penetrating all things, without and within. I am without imperfections, ever the same in all, pure in passions, immaculate, immovable.

XXXVI. He who is eternal, pure, free, one, entirely happy (in the supreme happiness), without duality (undivided), veritable, real, existence, Science, the Infinite, the supreme One, (Brahma) I am He.

NOTE: There is no such thing as sentiment recognized within the pale of pure occultism; sentiment always creates for itself, some grand ideal of an apparent reality, which in itself is but Maya or illusion.

SOUL KNOWLEDGE—BOOK II

EXPLANATORY NOTE: It must be borne in mind by the reader that the second part of the Book of Wisdom is in reality a commentary, or explanation of the first Book, and herein is set forth the actual secrets of the Kosmos. The whole arcana of Hindu Occultism is here laid bare of its arcane terms and its metaphysics, so bewildering to Western minds. It means the Initiation of the Soul and as such, it must be considered wholly apart from any internal formula, or ceremonial rite, consequently, it corresponds mystically with the perfect at-one-ment of the early primitive Christians, who taught that the kingdom of heaven (the region of Brahma) was within. The full realization of this will surely bring unto the Neophyte that peace of God which passeth all understanding, or the true Nirvana of our Oriental Brethren.

T. H. Burgoyne.

BOOK OF WISDOM

I. Such a conception, "I am Brahma himself," incessantly maintained, dissipates the hallucinations born of ignorance even as a valuable medicine drives out disease.

NOTE: It is of great importance for Neophytes to fully realize that the constant formulation of any idea, will, in due time (other conditions being fulfilled), through a process of Psychic evolution, cause the subjective ideal to become an objective fact, or from the embryonic plane of the soul state, to exist as a real entity, a veritable spiritual reality. This is the true secret of the evolution of the Soul-powers evolved by Occult training, and which in due time produces the all potent, perfect man, the Adept.

II. Sitting in solitude, freed from the passions, having completely mastered his senses, let a man picture to himself this Spirit, the supreme One, the eternally Infinite, without allowing his thoughts to be diverted.

NOTE: Solitary meditation is one of the means of success in the soul's search for Brahma. He who submits himself to the severe discipline of the Ancient ritual of training, will be in the best condition to contemplate, directly and without trouble, the Infinite Being, "One," "Indivisible."

The philosopher will have no other thought. That is to say, his own intelligence will have a constant application to Brahma alone, but to nothing outside of that most Holy, interior plane;—read, work, learn, and inwardly digest the words in the New Testament; "retire to thy closet, secretly, when alone in thy chamber, etc. to pray." This is the solitary meditation referred to by this Ancient Hindu writing, and when alone in the secret communion with your own Soul, bow thy head in reverence and awe before the radiant visitors from the world beyond.

III. Considering the visible universe as annihilated in the Spirit; let the man, pure in intelligence, contemplate continually the one Spirit, (Soul), as he would the luminous Ether.

IV. This continual formation of the Soul's ideal, which, in its silent aspirations, associates itself with the divine universal Soul, enables it to attain the union with Brahma.

V. When such union is attained, the pure Soul can fully realize its previous conceptions and thus participates in all the attributes of the Infinite One.

VI. Then knowing the highest essence, he rejects all that is distinguished by name, by form, or otherwise, and he dwells firmly in the at-one-ment, with the self existent, perfect, intelligent and happy Being.

VII. There is not in the supreme Spirit (Soul) any distinction between the perceiver, the perception and the object perceived in his quality of the one being, intelligent and happy. He shines by his own light.

VIII. Thus when the friction of meditation, without cessation, is made upon the word of the Spirit, the flame which issues therefrom, consumes all the combustible matter of ignorance.

NOTE: The ancient Sages have defined the recompense awarded to him who has contemplated. They have recourse to a comparison which frequently presents itself to the imagination of Hindo writers. Atma, or the Spirit, is likened to the Arani, a hard wood used for friction, a second Arani, the Manas, or mind is applied to the first. The friction of these two woods being made (the mind and the Spirit) continually, by the exercise of silent meditation, the knowledge of true science, which proceeds from it after the manner of a flame (from friction) destroys completely the combustible portion of the wood of ignorance, even to its very roots, with all that which proceeds from it. Then the aspirant for perfect deliverance is confirmed in his royalty, and finds that he has accomplished his duty.

IX. When the previous ignorance has been dissipated by knowledge (comparable to the light of dawn), then the Spirit itself manifests itself in a manner, shining like the Sun.

X. The Spirit, always accessible, becomes as inaccessible, as the consequence of ignorance. This being dissipated, it shines as fully and as truly accessible, in the same wise as jewels on a maiden's neck, though she may have forgotten them.

XI. The Spirit of life (Principle of life) the undivided Soul, the living Soul, is attributed, by error, to the supreme Being, or Brahma, as in contempt we attribute, or liken the outward physical form of man to that of his Creator.

NOTE: Again it is necessary to say we must not confound the Soul with the great Spirit; neither must we disquiet ourselves by trying too soon to distinguish in one's self the Soul, the principal of individual life, but be content to know one's self to be identical with the universe, with Brahma Himself.

XII. But once having seen the true nature of the Spirit of life, this error disappears of itself.

XIII. The knowledge that is born of the comprehension of the being, having, of himself, his existence in reality, destroys completely the ignorance that causes us to say, "I am," "I am not," or "that appertains to me," in the same manner that the light of the Sun dissipates all darkness and uncertainty in the visible response of the sky.

XIV. The Yogi, the possessor of a perfect discernment, contemplates all things as subsisting within himself, and thus, by the eye of knowledge, he discovers that all is but the one and the same, Spirit or Soul.

NOTE: Our ancient Author wishes to say how the Yogi sees, without distinction in the Spirit, all that is perceived in the visible world, with the character of diversity. All the world is the Spirit, in fact there exists nothing but Spirit. It is similar to crockery plates, vessels and other utensils, which are made of clay, no matter what their shape, color, and size may be. At the bottom there is nothing but clay.

XV. He who is from the force of vitality the potent man rejects the qualities of the anterior attributes, viz., body, mind, etc., are, on a higher plane, only the conceptions of ignorance. He becomes Brahma by reason of the essential nature of his interior formative being, thus he is perfectly happy, even as the chrysalis becoming the butterfly.

XVI. After having traversed the great ocean of illusion; after having destroyed in himself the evil Genii of passion, of hate, and other vices, the Yogi shines intimately, collected in tranquility, and finds his joy in the Soul.

XVII. Renouncing all attachments to an external and fleeting happiness, satisfied with the happiness of the Soul, the wise man is forever resplendent in the interior light, and, similar to a lamp under a glass shade, does he himself protect.

XVIII. The Muni ascetic, although he submits to the attributes of the body, but comparable to the Ether, not being soiled by the natural properties, should, although he knows all comfort himself, as an ignorant man passing as the wind, detached from all things, yet material.

XIX. From the moment the attributes are destroyed, the Muni (Ascetic) enters immediately into that which penetrates all things as the water into water and air into air, the fire into the fire.

XX. The possession, after which there is none other to desire, the felicity, above which there is no greater felicity, the science, above which there is no greater science, let it be known—This is Brahma.

XXI. There is no being within, without, above, or beyond the One Being. All the interior, movable world, is the spirit of the One, and the external world is the same soul. Nothing exists apart from the One, and this One is Brahma.

XXII. The seen (object of vision), after which nothing more is desired to be seen, the existence in union of which there is no fresh birth possible, the knowledge above which there is no knowledge desired, let it be known,—This is Brahma.

XXIII. The Being that feels all in the intermediary, superior and inferior religions, living, intelligent, happy, without a second (duality), eternal and one, let it be known,—This is Brahma.

XXIV. That which is designated in the Books of the Vedanta under the mode of existence, rejecting all that is not for its own self, the imperishable, incessantly happy, the One, let it be known,—It is Brahma.

XXV. Admitted to a portion of happiness, belonging properly to the Being incessantly happy, Brahma; and the other Gods (Gods of the vulgar masses), because at various degrees, partially happy.

XXVI. All things belong to Him (the One), all activity depends on the One (Intelligent). This is why Brahma is everywhere diffused, as cream in the mass of milk.

XXVII. That which is neither bound, nor gross, nor short, nor long, nor subject to birth, nor perishable, that which is without form, without quality, without color, without name, let it be known,—It is Brahma.

XXVIII. He by whose splendor shines the Sun and the stars, but who is not enlightened by their lightness, He by whom all things are illuminated, let it be known,—It is Brahma.

XXIX. Penetrating all of himself, alone from within and from without, illuminating the entire universe, Brahma shines from afar, even as the light of radiant Suns.

XXX. Brahma has no similarity of appearance with the worlds, for in reality, there exists nothing else but Brahma. Shall something produce itself external to Him? It is nothing but a vain appearance, as a mirage, that figures on the wastes of the desert.

XXXI. All that is seen, all that is heard, is not different from Brahma, and by a knowledge of the truth, this Brahma is contemplated as the existent, intelligent, happy, indivisible Being.

XXXII. The eye of science contemplates this living, intelligent, happy, all-penetrating Being, but the eye of ignorance knows not how to contemplate it, in the same way as a blind man knows not how to contemplate the varied forms of external nature around him.

XXXIII. The soul, illuminated by the sacred lore and other means of knowledge, warmed by the fire of science and purified, shines of itself with the brilliancy of gold seven times purified in the furnace.

XXXIV. The Atman Spirit (or Divine Soul), the sum of all knowledge, resting in the ether of the heart, drives away darkness, penetrates all, shines, and all is illuminated.

XXXV. This is the great completion of existence; it is the great and final deliverance from sin, from pain, and also from death; and when compared with the vanities of this illusionary world, it is the Pearl of Great Price, and happy indeed is he who becomes its possessor.

XXXVI. He, therefore, who undertakes the pilgrimage of the soul that is within his own self, without considering the state of the heavens or the country, or the time, dissipates the cold and the heat, and attains unto a perpetual happiness, free from all impurity. This one, freed completely of works, becomes omniscient, all-penetrating, and immortal.

SOUL KNOWLEDGE—BOOK III

THE APHORESMATA OF THE LOGOS

I. Whatever exists, either exists as a whole, as God, or is a part, or an emanation from God.

II. In the Whole as an angel, unconscious of the Whole, is an undescended Spirit.

III. Parted from the Whole, yet a portion of the Whole, and unconscious of the Whole, is the law of differentiation.

IV. Parted from the Whole, with the Whole, yet external to the Whole, is a descended or fallen spirit.

V. Parted from the Whole, with the Whole, yet conscious of the Whole, and knowing it has fallen away from, and that it should, and can, return to the Whole, is the Law of Reascension.

VI. That which is parted from the Whole, and turns again to the Whole, is the Law of True Repentance.

VII. That which was parted from the Whole, and has again returned to the Whole, as a part of the Whole, remains so forever as a blest spirit, and is the Law of Perfect At-one-ment.

CONCLUDING NOTE

Materialistic Science demonstrates, beyond all disputes, the indestructibility of matter, and consequently aids, assists and verifies the teachings of our ancient Sages, who taught, as we still teach, that matter is but an objective phenomena, expressing form and weight, which in themselves, are but relative terms. Matter is but the condition of the external, expressing by its infinite correlations and forces, its exact correspondence with an internal cause. It is the same thing in a negative state, or the antipodes of Spirit. Matter and Spirit,— what are they? They do not exist, except as relative terms to express the ideal states of the one Primeval Force, viz., of Action and Repose.

T. H. Burgoyne.

CHAPTER I

THE SOUL—ITS NATURE AND ATTRIBUTES

"The divine spirit is to the soul what
the soul is to the body." — Plutarch.

First, we must speak of the soul. If it were possible for a duad to exist in which there was a distinction without a difference, we should say that such a combination was a perfect type of "soul" and "spirit." But as such is not in existence, we must try to express both the distinction and the difference by other types, albeit, in regard to soul and spirit, the one is not perceptible without the presence of the other.

The terms, "soul" and "spirit" have become interblended in such hopeless confusion, that it seems almost impossible to unravel the tangled skeins of definitions, and present a clear, comprehensive outline of the two and show them as they really are when viewed in the light of spiritual illumination.

The soul is not the spirit, but it is that by which the spirit is known, or, rather, that by which we understand the nature and powers of the spirit. In the first chapter of this work a complete definition of spirit is given, so far as human language can express or define an undefinable entity. When we come to define the soul, we are compelled to use illustrations that shall follow out the definition there given.

We have spoken of the spiritual Ego as an atom of divinity, a scintillating atomic point evolved from the divine soul of the Deity. Now, while this is quite true as regards the Ego, yet, when we desire to define the soul we must request the reader not to confuse the two, but, as a mere matter of mental convenience, consider them as the cause and effect, so to say, of spiritual evolution.

The soul is formless and intangible, and constitutes the attributes of the divine spirit; therefore, we can only conceive and know of the soul by learning the powers or attributes of the spirit. When we have learned them, we shall possess a clear conception of the soul and its real nature. In order to make ourselves better understood, let us illustrate the idea. Take a ray of light. What do we know concerning it?

Nothing, except by its action upon something else. This action we term the attributes of light. In themselves the attributes of light are formless, but they may easily be rendered visible, either by their colors when refracted by the prism, or by their effects when concentrated upon material objects. Here we have what may be correctly termed the soul of a ray of light. Another example may be taken as illustrative and expressive of the idea we wish to convey, viz.; the organism of man. Man, as at present constituted, possesses five external senses, viz.; seeing, feeling, hearing, tasting, and smelling. In reality, he has seven senses which may be used externally, but the two higher attributes of the sensuous gamut are still in embryo so far as the generality of mankind are concerned. The sixth race or atomic age children who are externalizing at the present time, will evolve the sixth sense (intuition or perception through spiritual sensation, and learn to use it in their daily lives); the seventh race will evolve the seventh sense; and then mankind will be physically perfect. But as these two higher senses need not interfere with our illustration, we will only notice man as he is, and be content with five. All our knowledge concerning external phenomena must come, at present, through the mediumship of one or more of these senses. The organs through which the functions of the senses become manifest are visible, but the senses themselves are invisible and formless. We know them only as the attributes of the body; while the mind, which is perfectly and absolutely dependent upon the senses for information, well represents the spiritual Ego in its relation to the soul.

The reader will observe from what is here stated, that the soul, itself is, as before said, formless and intangible, and therefore can only be defined as the attribute of spirit. The one cannot exist without the other, but at the same time they cannot be called one and the same, as there is the same difference between the two as there is between a ray of light and its action; and the same distinction as there is between the body and its physical senses. Without the one we cannot know the other, and vice versa.

A very large percentage of the readers of mystical literature have imagined that the human soul is some kind of a spiritual organism, similar in many respects to the body, and the means whereby the divine spirit manifests itself. But, as shown, this idea is radically erroneous. The spiritual body is the result or outcome of the soul's action, but is not the soul itself. It is an attribute of the soul, just as the soul is an attribute of the divine Ego, and this divine Ego, in its turn, is a crystallized attribute or expression of Deity. What then is Deity? the reader may ask. All that we are able to answer is, Absolute Potentiality; pure, formless spirit; unlimited, unconditioned intelligence. Definition can go no further in this direction.

Having attempted to define the soul as distinct and yet inseparable from the spirit, we will now try to give some idea concerning its attributes, and in this connection it will greatly aid us if we first point out the difference between the soul and the body, and also the correspondence.

The physical body is evolved by a reflex action of the interior soul during the process of evolving its spiritual organism. The medium between the two is the astral form or spiritual body. It is from the latter that the physical body receives its form and force. The spiritual organism protects itself, so to say, from the external plane by evolving an astral raiment. This raiment, or astral body, crystallizes a more or less distorted reflection of the spiritual form around itself and thus produces what is known as the human form divine, upon the external plane. This physical organism is constituted and evolved in such order as to render the most perfect expression (in unison) of the physical senses. No one sense is in excess of another, in a perfectly sound human organism; while the different animals generally typify the extreme expression of some one particular sense, as sight, scent, feeling, etc.

This human body, through the mediumship of the brain, which is the sounding board of the senses, communicates with the external world which is composed of various elements. The result is form, sound, color, etc. Our senses, then, constitute the only source of our external knowledge, and form the basis from which spring our ideas, thoughts and feelings. Our thoughts are thus moulded by the various phenomenal states through which we pass. This state is our external consciousness. It is purely an intellectual state, based upon, and depending upon the continuance of the physical senses while on earth. The sum total of human knowledge upon special subjects is tabulated and classified; this is reduced to a system and called science. We are thus able to see and appreciate the relation of the physical senses to the physical body, and grasp their importance to the still remoter mind which utilizes the knowledge so gained. The attributes of the spirit, which we term the soul, bear a perfect correspondence to the physical senses of the body. That is, the soul bears exactly the same relation to the spirit as the physical senses bear to the human brain. Thus we have the senses which are physical, and we have the senses which are spiritual. The physical are simply a reflection of the spiritual. The senses of the body and the senses of the soul are two halves of the same attribute, the external and the internal. We see the intelligence, the mind, which at the back of the senses utilizes and tabulates the impressions it receives of the outer world, the world which it, itself, is powerless to penetrate. The mind is something above and beyond the senses, though it is absolutely dependent upon them. It is the same with the soul, and the spirit. All knowledge from without or within the universe of external life is received by means of the soul. But at the back of this soul, there rests the eternal scintillating atom of Deity above and beyond any human conception. There it rests in serenity and peace, tabulating and utilizing all the knowledge and experience which the soul in its various cycles is continually receiving. "As it is below so it is above." This law of correspondences should ever be remembered. It is man's universal but infallible guide, and anything conflicting therewith should be rejected as erroneous.

The seven senses below correspond to the seven senses above, and the sum total of the results obtained in each case is the same, only upon different planes. These results may be fully expressed by the word PERCEPTION. Absolute perception implies absolute consciousness. Unlimited perception, therefore, is the grand goal toward which the universe of manifested being is eternally marching. It is the climax of evolution. But it is a goal that nothing below Deity can ever attain, because there is always before us the infinite beyond, the awful states of the infinite unknown. The more we learn, the more we learn the more there is to learn. Progressive life is eternal; thus we have a complete demonstration of the immortality of the spirit, and consequently, that of the soul, as the twain— Bride and Bridegroom—are one.

We have now arrived at the last part of our subject, viz.; the method of the soul's unfoldment or development. Of this we can only speak in general terms. There are certain fundamental laws applicable to all, but, to be successful, something more is requisite. It is necessary for each soul to follow a system specially adapted to its special state. Each person must find out for himself the special development required of him, unless he can come into contact with others capable of reading his soul's requirements aright. If they can give him the necessary information so much the better.

There is a trinity of laws to be observed; I. Physical harmony and cleanliness in one's surroundings. II. Mental peace with clean thoughts and freedom from worldly cares. III. Spiritual purity, and complete isolation from impure currents of thought. Evolve these states from within and the without will take care of itself. Honest desire (prayer) must be first. These are the methods of the soul's unfoldment. Purity is the great touch-stone, and as Jesus has truly observed, "Blessed are the pure in heart for they shall see God." How many can follow out such a code? "Not one in a million," comes the answer, vibrating across the spiritual spaces of Aether. And the saddening thought that such is indeed the truth in this age, compels us to indraw the spiritual forces which the present discourse has expended, and conclude with a few brief words of friendly advice.

To be pure in body, a pure diet must be the menu and the highest form of food possible to man must constitute his physical sustenance. The products of the soil are plenty; they are simple but sufficient. Purity of mind demands clean thoughts. We cannot be perfect, so let us be as perfect as our surroundings render possible. Learn to say I will and I will not, then see that your assertion is sacredly maintained. Be honest with yourself.

Let us remember that the material life of man is only one second of his existence, and that it is one of the most unprofitable things in the world to be selfish. Selfishness is the road to the Hells of the soul world. Evil on earth produces suffering in the next world as all accounts must be balanced.

And, lastly, if these things are followed with an earnest loving spirit, rest assured that the blossoms of the soul will expand into full-grown flowers, and for the labor and self-denial expended we shall reap the spiritual rewards which will repay us ten thousand fold. Remember, and realize, the words of the wise Proclus;—

"Know the Divinity that is within you that you may know the Divine One, of which your soul is a ray."

CHAPTER II

MORALITY AND IMMORALITY

"Every soul is immortal by virtue of
its community with God."—Albertus Magnus.

In attempting to elucidate the problems of "Mortality and Immortality," death and life, it must be understood that we are dealing with questions that depend, in a very great measure, upon the construction which is placed on the terms used. It is not our province to enter into the scientific minutia of these problems, nor to present the student with an abstract of learned nonsense concerning the various derivations from which the words are supposed to have reached us. Equally unimportant to our purpose is the sense in which our hoary ancestors may have used them, seeing that such questions must ever remain purely matters of speculation and opinion, and "when doctors disagree, who shall decide?"

At present we are concerned with the Occult side of the problems, and with laws which are so far removed from the realms of mere opinion as to constitute eternal realities; the manifestations of which can be realized and verified by each individual soul for itself.

Simply and briefly stated, immortality means life, continued life; mortality means death or the extinction of life, and therefore stands as the antithesis of life and immortality. At least, such is the generally accepted sense in which the words are now used. Mortality and immortality in their external relation towards each other stand as polar opposites, and as such they are the alpha and omega of cyclic existence. They represent "the evening and the morning" of every phase of God's infinite creation, upon the outer planes of manifested being, i.e., cosmic evolution. Life and death, then, form the grand spiral axis of time, and its resultants to the human mind are seen in the world of phenomena.

For the sake of convenience we will consider each problem by itself, and then, as a stimulant towards mental reflection, leave their relationship to each other, to be thought out by each reader, separately, for himself.

Mortality, as previously stated, means death and extinction upon the material plane. But when viewed from the higher and more interior standpoint, death simply means change of form and function. There can be no absolute extinction in the strict sense of the term. Atoms are immortal, eternal and indestructible; but a universe or an organism which is composed of an infinite number of atoms, may be dissolved, destroyed and forever lost, i.e., lost as an organic whole, but not lost as regards its separate atomic parts. The mental being which bound these atoms together loses its force during the process of change or death, consequently death is simply change of polarity. In order to see this, it must be understood that the moons, planets, suns and systems have their own special individuality, exactly like animals and men. On the contrary, an atom has no individuality, so far as its external form is concerned, but it possesses a cosmic individuality, an attraction and repulsion specially its own, by virtue of its differentiation from the universal One. It is the complex expression of the myriad atoms which compose the organism or the universe that constitutes its individuality. This individuality gives expression to a form suitable to its nature, and constitutes the personal or external appearance. These facts must be borne in mind, or the real meaning of this chapter will be misunderstood.

As a general principle of phenomenal expression, it may be said that Nature embodies, within some external form, every idea, thought and motive which mankind evolves. The only limit to her possibilities in this direction is the mental and magnetic condition of the race. In fact, every organic form that we see around us is Nature's expression of thoughts and ideas. These thoughts and ideas are representative of spiritual qualities which react upon the astral light, and these spiritual qualities emanate from Mind or mental being, either human or divine.

As an illustration of the process of death, and change, let us select two cases, one from the vegetable world, and one from the animal kingdom;—a tree and a tiger. The tree dies, decay sets in, and very soon it appears to be gone forever. But this disappearance is only an illusion, for the tree not only exists but exerts a very powerful influence upon the material plane. The tree, so far as its phenomenal outcome is concerned, has only been a means by which the progressive cycle of evolution works upward from the mineral state. It is composed of millions of atoms of life undergoing their various cyclic rounds within the vegetable circuit, and as a natural consequence of this internal spiritual activity the tree possesses a karmic sphere within the astral spaces of its life wave. The astral tree, if we may so call this karmic counterpart, is far more beautiful in its wonderful details, and more perfect in its symmetry and geometrical proportions than the physical tree of earth. When the material tree no longer exists as a living earthly organism, the arboreal image within Nature's wonderful laboratory becomes the means of reflecting the outlines of a still more perfect vegetable organism upon the outward planes of matter. These outlines of astral skeletons of future trees possess the attractive force which draws within them the living germs of the young seedlings growing upon the earth. This action feeds the physical tree, then goes to lower forms.

The greatest perfection of one tree becomes impressed within the astral light and becomes the means of developing a more perfect organism of its kind in the next generation. The ideal of the tree becomes externalized in its offspring.

The trained psychic, and those who naturally possess spiritual lucidity, can see this ethereal vegetation within the astral world. Therefore, proofs of the two planes of existence may be quickly obtained, should they ever be required. The internal plane is more alive than the external, but to resume. The physical tree disappears, but does not die as we suppose. When physical death transpires it undergoes a change; the sphere of its activities become translated, removed from the external to the internal, in strict obedience to the higher laws of its internal nature. Thus we see that the tree, having served its purpose on earth, vanishes from external sight, while its ethereal counterpart performs another cycle upon a higher plane. When each has fulfilled its purpose the various evolving atoms which constituted its life form, obeying the interior laws of their cyclic round, seek re-incarnation. They separate and the cycle is complete. The individual tree no longer exists as a tree. But there has been no death in any case; only a change of form; for the atomic forces of the tree re-appear upon a higher plane in a million varying forms throughout every department of Nature.

Having considered death in regard to the tree, let us now examine, in the animal kingdom, the case of the tiger. We have already stated that Nature ever strives to externalize ideas and thoughts in some form or other. This statement must be borne in mind. The tiger presents us with a fine illustration of this law of transformation upon the outward planes of existence.

We all know what the tiger is when endowed with physical life. His chief qualities are selfishness and destructiveness. He is, in fact, a complete expression of cruelty. When death transpires, the astral tiger, like the astral tree, becomes indrawn within the karmic sphere of its astral world. There it performs the higher evolutions of its special round until the life atoms, which constitute it, become "rounded out" and ready to externalize in some higher form. Thus the tiger, like the tree, is one of Nature's countless mediums for the expression of mental force. By the interior laws of its constitution, it forms a central vortex or focus for the materialization of the purely selfish and destructive elements of humanity. When death removes the physical tiger from earth, the ethereal tiger becomes the sphere of action until the tigerish qualities have run their cycle. But we cannot say that there has been any real extinction, or that death has come upon the tiger, any more than we can say that the caloric of the sunbeam is destroyed because the solar ray is no longer brought to a focus. The eye of the initiate can distinctly see the ferocity of the animal in the inhumanity of the man.

Mortality or death, then, can only exist and be a truth in reference to individual forms. It has no existence in reality when brought face to face with the spiritual qualities and mental force, which created these forms. Change of sphere and change of action are the only realities of death. Ever onward, ever upward, forever and ever more. Eternal progression is the anthem of evolution, and the cycles of action are but intervals of time measured out to the life forces by the pendulum of creation.

The second portion of our subject "Immortality" is the polar opposite of death and mortality. Individual forms and characteristics are the only things that change and die. Death, as we have shown, is not extinction of the life atoms in the literal sense of the term, but simply change of sphere and function. Death is the grand terminus of one cycle of existence, and the commencement of another. Mortality is the harbinger of a still higher state of life, and consequently the forerunner of immortality. There are exceptions to the general rule, though they are few. The most important of these exceptions we shall notice in our next chapter.

There are two distinct phases of immortal life, viz.: conscious immortality, and unconscious immortality. One relates to mind, and the other to matter; one to intelligence, and the other to substance.

There is only one grade of external life which can be said to inherit immortality in the Occult sense of the term. This grade includes those souls who are truly human who have soul qualities of such high degree that they can advance. Not as we know and recognize individuals, but, rather, an individuality consisting entirely of soul qualities, a purely spiritual state which can only be partially expressed by the use of words. All the states below the human plane are only so many radiating lines which converge to a point, and are brought to a focus within the human organism. Therefore, every quality and force upon the planet or within the system of which the organism forms a part must find expression within man, this uterus of Nature. If this were not so, man would not constitute a miscrocosm or universe in miniature. In the grades below the human state, we do not find complete organisms. They are mere temporary shapes of matter continually dying out of existence, when the forces they were evolved to express are exhausted, and thus give place to something more perfect. They are not souls in the true sense, but refracted attributes of souls. They are qualities and functions in the process of evolution; isolated parts and characteristics of a whole; organs, but not organisms.

Commencing at the very lowest point of animated existence, we shall discover only the most rudimentary expression of the simplest functions of organic life, viz.: a desire to live. As we ascend higher the organs become multiplied, and the desire to live increases. This gradual scale expands right up to the perfect human soul in man, where we find a miniature universe, absolute and complete within itself. The central Deific atom, controlling this universe, has traveled all the way up from the lowest crude fire rocks of cosmic evolution. It conquered every state through which it ascended upon its progressive, toilsome journey. And in each state evolved from within itself a complete attribute corresponding to the state, by virtue of which, it polarized and bound the atoms of life, and annexed them as a portion of its spiritual empire, thereby forming the means for their progression also. Until, at last, the Deific atom sits upon the spiritual throne as king of the microcosm, capable of thinking, creating and evolving from within itself the glorious states of the angel.

It is, therefore, an Occult truth to declare that all things below man are mortal, and all above immortal. Man, alone, of all God's marvelous creations, contains within himself the forces of life and death, of immortality and mortality. Man, then, contains "the promise and potency of life" and constitutes, upon the spiritual plane, what Tyndall's protoplasm does upon the physical, viz.: the possibilities of infinite progression.

To attain unto immortality it is necessary, as we have shown, for the central life atom to conquer every state below the human, and then to become externalized upon earth as an individual human being, to undergo the trials and become subjected to the responsibilities of a conscious, reasoning, individual struggle for life. The nature and quality of the soul, combined with the polarity of the organism, will launch the individual into the exact conditions and circumstances that are best adapted to arouse all the latent qualities within; both animal and human. It is not a previous karma that determines an individual's condition in life, but it is the nature and quality of the soul conflicting or harmonizing with external conditions. This turmoil of life, this ceaseless human warfare, is just as necessary for the soul's final development as are the earlier struggles through the states below. Man possesses the possibilities of immortal life in such a potent degree as to nearly always succeed. There are, however, a few solitary exceptions which will be noted in the next chapter.

After man has passed through the travail of human life he then meets the struggle of his karma in the realm of spirit. Here he may even sink forever, because he does not actually possess immortality, only the promise or possibility of it. After the four realms of the astral world are passed he enters the sixth state of the soul world, where he should become re-united with his soul mate, his missing half. Until this union is complete there is and can be no actual immortality. Previous to this he is but a part of himself, and has control only of half of his spiritual nature. It is the union of the two that forms the absolute one. "And they twain shall be one flesh," saith the old Jewish Scripture; "as it is above, so it is below."

From the foregoing it will be seen that it is the reunion of the twin souls in the realm of spirit that confers upon man the state of angelhood. He is human no longer, he is then Divine, and as a Deific being he possesses the attributes of eternal progression and immortal life.

CHAPTER III

THE DARK SATELLITE

When we look about us with the physical senses, Nature seems to be in continual warfare with herself. In fact, it seems utterly impossible to find anything not in deadly conflict with something else, either visible or invisible. Observing this, mankind has unconsciously, from time immemorial, formulated the idea of two great powers, viz., "good" and "evil". From this idea the grand dogma of theology—"God" and the "Devil" sprang into existence, and became the chief corner stone of every sacerdotalism which the world has witnessed. And while there is some basic truth in this idea, as in every popular conception, since mankind as a whole cannot formulate any idea that is wholly and absolutely false in every detail; yet, there is also much that is utterly false in it, owing to the fact that man, while existing upon the material plane, cannot grasp the divine idea of Absolute Truth, nor realize the logical absurdity of more than one Absolute. He, therefore, utterly fails to comprehend how that which is relative evil can be harmonized into absolute good. Accordingly, to the majority of mankind, this mighty problem of good and evil is still unsolved. Few, very few indeed, even of the profoundly learned students of Occult lore in the past, arrived at a true conception of the subject.

During the lapse of the ages, countless legends and allegories have been evolved, to embody the facts and the processes connected with this arcane mystery, but the metaphysics of these legends have never been revealed to the uninitiated. Especially has this been the case in regard to the Dark Satellite. However, the time has now come when certain facts in regard to this orb of evil are for the first time given out to the world "pro bono publico."

In the first place, certain misconceptions in regard to the dark orb need to be corrected. Many earnest students have thought it to be "The Lost Orb" of the Grecian mysteries, hence similar to the Egyptian conception of the spiritual "fall". But there is, in fact, no connection between the two. The lost orb, in its cosmological aspect, will be found noticed in the second part of this work. In its spiritual aspect it applies to the fallen human soul, not the lost soul. Herein consists the difference between the two orbs, the lost and the dark.

Another misconception has regarded the Moon, our Earth's visible satellite, as identical with the dark orb. Many Theosophists assert, in a very mysterious manner, that the Moon is not only the eighth sphere, or the orb of death and dissolution, but that it is "the dust bin of the universe," although Dr. Wyld, formerly president of the London T.S. fully exposed the absurdity of this mysterious Theosophical Secret in the columns of "Light." This conception is radically false as regards the Moon, although it approaches the realms of truth in some respects regarding the nature of the mysterious dark satellite itself.

With these brief introductory remarks it now remains to point out how to form a perfectly correct conception of what the dark satellite is, and its fearful importance at the present crisis of the world's history.

When the student brings before his mind the teachings of the preceding chapters, and the conclusions they lead up to, considering them as a whole, it will require but a brief and careful application of the laws of correspondences to enable him to gain a perfectly accurate idea of this hitherto concealed region and portion of the Earth's constitution.

By referring to the "Hermetic Constitution of Man" as elucidated in chapter II of section II of the present work, let the student review the seven divisions of man, then, bearing in mind the fact that the planet which man inhabits is also an individual, possessing a sevenfold constitution corresponding in every respect to the constitution of man, let him strictly apply the Hermetic law for himself,

"As it is below, so it is above,
As on the earth, so in the sky."

Then, he will know exactly how to go to work to comprehend the subject. But as the ordinary student, living wholly upon the external plane, is not in a position to verify his conceptions, he must content himself for the present to accept the revelations which will be made upon the authority of those who do know, and have verified the truth.

In chapter II of section II of this work "Hermetic Constitution of Man," occurs a description of the animal soul, as it is called. Now, that magnetic sphere of our planet which exactly corresponds to the animal soul of man, is what is Occultly termed "the Dark Satellite." Therefore, in order to comprehend this dusky sphere, its nature and functions, it is absolutely necessary to understand the nature and function of the animal soul of man, together with its relations to the other six divisions; and also, to clearly grasp man's relation to the planet of which he forms, as it were, an atomic part towards an organic whole.

When the above is understood, it will then be seen that this dark, magnetic orb constitutes the grand center or focus of the Earth's animal force; in other words, it is the realm of the undeveloped good in Nature, whose terrible motto is embraced in the word SELF.

During the "Golden" and "Silver" periods of our Earth's evolution, this dark satellite was in the aphelion portion of its orbit and its influence was scarcely felt; or else, its influence was seen and recognized only in its true relation of animal force and undeveloped good. As a factor of evil it was imperceptible. But during the Copper and Iron ages the dark satellite gradually approached the Earth, and its degrading forces became more and more bewildering and potent until the year 1881, when it passed its grand perihelion point. The year 1881 was to see the second coming of the Lord. Many sects expected Jesus to come in person, select their group as the chosen few, guide them to heaven and leave all others on earth to suffer their fate because of their sins and non-belief. This proved to be a real error. The ushering in of new spiritual thought and the new atomic age is actually the new dispensation, the second coming of Christ. Wars are necessary to bring about the change, the old must be uprooted before the new can take its place. The dark orb is now slowly but surely receding, and although the clouds are not lifted from the mental horizon; and though the fearful world-wide conflicts which occurred are not yet settled; and confusion and chaos seem more widespread and error more rampant than ever before in the world's history, yet the crisis is past its darkest culminating point. As it is often darkest just before break of day, so even now the dawn of a brighter morn is at hand, when the faithful, resolute truth-seeker shall be able to solve for himself this awful problem of good and evil, of light and shadow. Therefore, sustained by the knowledge of the ultimate victory of order and equilibrium over chaos and opposing forces; even though all mankind are enveloped in the darkness of battle and involved in the vortices of the defeated legions of error; let us turn our attention more closely to the satellite itself, which has been such a disturbing factor to our planet's mental equilibrium; and consider this sphere with special reference to the implications of responsibility forced upon every soul seeking light and immortality.

In the first place, this orb possesses a complete organization of its own; and is governed by well defined laws, the nature of which may be known only too well by patiently observing the merciless instincts of the lower animal nature as manifested in man; where the moral consciousness is absolutely wanting. Our daily news, continually, reports all sorts of vicious crimes against God and man. Throughout the whole of this loathsome sphere are numerous races of spiritual beings; many of them possessing the highest forms of cunning and intelligence possible to the animal plane. It is these creatures; who are neither elementals nor elementaries, but treacherous beings; who produce the greatest portion of the suffering and misery which afflicts humanity. They are the active Occult agents of that potent fraternity within the spiritual world which has its external expression and correspondence in the brotherhood known upon Earth as the "Black Magi," or "Inversive Brethren." These two fraternities, viz: the spiritual rulers and potentialities of the dark satellite upon the astral plane, and the schools of Black magic, vice and crime, upon the physical plane; constitute the two halves of the planet's evil desire.

From within the dark center of the astral realms of the former, the spirit of lies, murder, crime, fraud and religious imposture is first formulated, and then projected to the earthly fraternity as the means of its continued existence. From these centers it is re-formulated to suit the spirit and temper of the times; and then its psychological influence is projected into the mental whirl of the race, where its silent, subtle influx poisons the dimensional spaces which constitute the magnetic planes of human life. From thence, these unseen Occult currents penetrate the innermost recesses of the human mind, and possess the soul to such an extent, that deep down in the heart of man; no matter how pure and disinterested he may appear; there lurks the slimy reptile of selfishness, yea, even when he least suspects it. It is this grim monster, SELF, that each aspirant to Occult truth seeks to conquer. When this Goliath of the soul is struck dead by the smooth white pebble of the spirit, slung with the neophyte's will, the grand ordeal is over, the crown of immortality won. "To the victor belong the spoils."

We have pointed out the fact that it is the dark satellite from whence proceeds the spirit of lies, murder and frauds. This was well known to the initiates of the greater Hermetic mysteries, for

we find the idea very clearly defined in the mystical language of
the ancients, as the following extract from one of the supposed lost
magical works of Hermes Trismegistus will show. Speaking of the
magical rulers of the dark satellite as they sit in council, creating
delusion, we read:

> "So they called forth a form
> From the deep dark abyss
>   To embody their evil desire."
> "Obedient it came
> From the realms of the dead,
>   Arrayed in its magic attire."
> "As it passed o'er the earth
> The fair flowers fell dead,
>   From its breath of poisonous fire."

Indeed, so thoroughly has this poisonous fire of self-interest
permeated the world, that the fair flowers of disinterestedness have
become an almost entirely extinct species, and should the real state
of unselfish, unworldliness of a true mystic become known, he is
either regarded with pity as non compos mentis, or else looked
upon with suspicion as an imposter, acting from motives more subtle
than govern the ordinary mortal.

The manner in which this poisonous magnetic energy is projected from the dark satellite to the earth is wholly inversive, and
the rulers and magical hierophants make use of this inversive force
to distort and corrupt Truth in every form wherein it struggles to
become manifest upon earth. The powers and influences attributed
to certain races of astrals, by the authors of "The Perfect Way,"
belong in reality to the rulers and principalities of the dark satellite,
who mercilessly distort every arcane truth into theological dogma,
of partial error, causing it to assume to the human mind the delusive
form of the externals of truth and logic. But the delusive form is,
after all, only a very flimsy sophistry when subjected to the keen
searching eye of the soul. Consequently, it is always those who are
half informed of Nature's mysteries; the half-initiated, so to say;
who fall into the snare. Herein is seen the Occult truth in the
proverb, "A little learning is a dangerous thing."

Just as the dark satellite was at its perihelion, these inversive
brethren achieved the greatest apparent theological and metaphysical
success in the re-launching forth, throughout the world, of the doctrines of "Re-incarnation," "Karma," and "Disembodied Shells," as

formulated and taught by the decaying priesthoods of the dreamy Orient. Viewed in its true light, this gigantic movement of the inversive brethren was aimed as a death blow to the rapidly spreading spiritualism of the Occident; since, wherever accepted, these doctrines, as taught and interpreted by the Buddhist cult, destroy at once, all belief in the possibility of spirit communication between disembodied souls and external humanity. Such a movement, however, is doomed to ultimate failure, as there are certain absolute truths connected with spiritualism that will live, notwithstanding the ignorance of the expounders, its many errors and gross impostures. These truths can neither be suppressed by inversive magic, nor smothered by an oriental theory. Their misrepresentations are too patent to the candid mind, and reaction against the speculative mentality of the East, sooner or later, is sure to set in. The Western matter-of-fact mind, will tear the grim mask from these would-be brethren of the snow-clad Himalayas, and show to the world who are the denizens of the shadow, and who are the children of light.

At this point the question naturally arises, "of what personal or selfish benefit is the propagation of error to the inhabitants of the dark satellite?" The answer is simply this, it furnishes them with the means of prolonging their external existence while on earth, and supplies them with an additional lease of life in the world to come; as will be made manifest from the Hermetic laws of death given below. According to Hermetic laws, death is not what is known as physical dissolution, but is a failure on the part of the human being to polarize the atoms which constitute his soul so he may realize immortality. It is, therefore, a falling from the human plane to the animal plane, where conscious existence may be prolonged indefinitely by means of dark magical arts.

The following are an accurate rendering of the real ideas as taught by Hermes Trismegistus.

THE LAWS OF DEATH

I. "As it is below, so it is above; as on the earth, so in the sky."

II. "There are two states of being; one is mortal, the other is immortal."

III. "That which is mortal is dissolvable, and dissolvable bodies pass away like a mist in the morning."

IV. "An immortal body is an essence which is eternal and incorruptible."

V. "But the twain, the mortal and the immortal, cannot exist together forever, but each returneth to the place from whence it came."

VI. "The mortal body is sensible, but the immortal is reasonable."

VII. "The former contains nothing that is perfect, the latter nothing that is imperfect; for the one is the essence of the matter, and the other the essence of spirit, and man, the microcosm, holds the balance of the twain."

VIII. "And there is a fierce warfare for the victory, between the lower and the upper, as they both desire to obtain the body as their prize; for the state of man is envied by the lower and glorified as a noble state by the higher."

IX. "Now if the man inclines toward the lower nature which is mortal, he thereby aids the lower imperfect powers to oppose the higher which is immortal, and must suffer the pains of slavery for his disobedience to the Work-Man, his maker. But if he inclines to the higher, then he is truly wise and blest."

X. "Should man, after being attracted by the vanities of the world and then, after obtaining a knowledge of the things that are, return to the vanities of the world, he will be punished with torments and fire in the darkest states of disembodied souls."

XI. "Should a man after knowing the things that are become rebellious of restraint to that part which is immortal, and return to the vanities of the world, the higher essence will straightway depart from him, and he will become the slave of the lower essence which will seize upon him and drive him to all sorts of wicked arts and evil ways."

XII. "When man has thus impiously disobeyed his Creator and turned his face away from that which is immortal, behold, he is then disinherited from his birthright, and is no longer counted among the children of God, because he has become an evil, perverse thing, possessing only those things which are mortal, and he is punished with death."

XIII. "And so death is meted out to all those who rebel against their Creator impiously, because they know the things that are. But to those foolish souls who are ignorant, and who have not knowingly rejected their Creator, behold, they are purified after much suffering and are sent to the world again."

The teachings involved in the above laws are so clear, so simple, and we may also add so divinely just, that to attempt in any way to explain or annotate them would only be to sow the first seeds of error and misunderstanding. We will, therefore, leave them with the reader as they are, pure and free from the mental bias of any mortal being.

In a previous chapter we have shown that all realms of life above the human are immortal, and that those below this plane are mortal, or, they only possess the possibilities of immortality in a rudimentary form. Man, alone, possesses the elements of both life and death. The laws of life have also been fully elucidated, and the soul which even only imperfectly obeys them will, "after it has been purified by much suffering," ultimately reap the reward of eternal conscious existence. Consequently, the great majority of those souls who are really human beings, will inherit immortality as the natural consequence of their humanity. But there are exceptions, which though few in number, comparatively, require special notice. These exceptions may, for the sake of convenience, be divided into three distinct classes. The first and most numerous class consists of imperfectly organized, sensitive, weak-natured individuals, with little or no mental bias, who possess strong mediumistic magnetisms. Individuals of this class, though perfectly human to begin with, soon lose the actual control of the external organism, and in consequence, the body becomes the obedient instrument for any and every class of disembodied earth bound spirits, or, what is still worse, it may become the slave of some vicious elementary. In this case there was no real or true individuality to start with, therefore, no one can assert truthfully that he was actually acquainted with the true personage; for, most probably the real soul had departed in the **very early infancy of the organism's** physical existence, how, when, or where, none but the trained seer can tell. In every individual case the astral causes that produced the soul's abortion will differ widely.

The second class are those who fall victims to premeditated obsession, and are by no means so numerous as the former. In this case the organism is generally very fine, so far as the magnetic temperament is concerned, but the soul is utterly wanting in spiritual volition or will. That is to say, the magnetic polarity is of such a nature that the spiritual will of the soul is almost powerless to act upon it. The absence of this essential element of human life may be the result of mental conditions of the mother during pregnancy, or of a mental coma, so to say, of both parents at the moment of conception. This mental coma externalizes itself in the offspring as a lack of vim, nerve and fire. Hence, we often see this condition manifested in the children of kings, noblemen, and those of great wealth, who have the means to pander to and gratify a fashionable, sentimental lassitude. In addition to this lack of spiritual volition, the magnetic constitution is always strongly mediumistic and the individual, if left quite free from the control of others, naturally would be good, highly sensitive, and in the true sense of spiritual parlance, "a spirit medium," inspirational, physical, or clairvoyant, according to his peculiar magnetic grade. This is the reason why they often fall the victim of premeditated obsession. When obsession transpires it is generally found that some potent external mind, that of an evil sorceress, or black magician, (according to the sex,) requires the organism for the purpose of prolonging their own personal existence. When a suitable mediumistic body is found, they bring the whole of their powerful magnetic will to bear upon the almost willess brain of their victim, and slowly but surely eject the rightful occupant, and then, by virtue of their Occult powers and magic arts, inhabit the organism themselves, while the near friends and relatives of the victim are often surprised at the remarkable change which they notice has taken place, in temperament and disposition, but alas,—they seldom or never suspect the terrible truth which such a change implies, nor can they possibly be brought to fully understand that the individual moving among them as usual has nothing whatever in common with their silently departed friend.

The third and last, also the least in number, of these classes includes those who are born into the world under strangely conflicting conditions. They possess all the essential elements of manhood with a powerful current of the most potent and concentrated form of selfishness and pride. In addition to this undesirable quality they express the highest form of intellectuality combined with a powerful will and mediumistic temperament. These dominating conditions predispose them to the study of psychology and Occultism, hence they fall an easy prey to the members of the Black Magi and their inversive astral Brethren. Their selfishness, combined with their unbounded ambition and desire for power, precipitate them headlong into the most frightful practices, where, surrounded by the infernal rites of their diabolical seducers, they become the helpless slaves of the very powers they sought to control. Henceforward, they are lost. As the Hermetic law states, "They are punished with death," and they know it, and consequently are compelled, for their own safety, to remain faithful to the order which entrapped them. Their only motto is self, their only desire is to live, and this they will do at any cost. For their own single lives they would sacrifice the balance of God's creation, if such a thing were possible, simply because death to them is death in reality.

In the first and second classes of so-called lost souls, the true individual, as we have shown, does not become lost, he is "the foolish," ignorant soul, "sent to the world again." Not sent to the world again by means of re-incarnation in matter upon the outward planes of life, but by a sympathetic union with some kindred soul on earth, whose experiences they can experience, whose sorrows they can feel, and whose joys they can share. The writer has beheld numerous cases of this kind, where the soul of some unfortunate, mediumistic organism was sympathetically attached to the organism of a living individual, as a means of progress, and of completing this round of external experiences. In this class a person simply loses his physical organism. This personality, along with the animal and astral portion of it, becomes a lifeless shadow at death, and slowly disintegrates within the magnetic spaces of the astral light. It is a misty form, incapable of personating its original owner, or of being "galvanized into temporary life." While the counterfeiting, obsessing forces, after loss of the physical body run the cycle of the magnetic existence within the electro-vital spaces of the planet, then become attached to the eighth sphere, the Dark Satellite or orb of death. This attraction is brought into force by virtue of their affinity with the realms of elemental being. They have sunk beneath the plane of humanity, and consequently are no longer human, and when once they become enclosed within the fatal magnetic whirl of death, they lose the polarity over the feeble atoms which constitute their only being, and gradually dissolve, atom by atom, like the poisonous miasmatic mists before the rising sun. While the Deific Atoms themselves, which these lost personalities failed to realize, imperishable as ever, enter upon a new cycle of involution and evolution, thus slowly building up new individualities for themselves. Not on this planet, the scene of their failure and suffering, but on a higher plane, in worlds more ethereal than ours.

CHAPTER IV

THE TRIUMPH OF THE SOUL—ADEPTSHIP

Having considered the failure of what might be termed the human-animal soul, in the preceding chapter, we now come to the triumph of the human soul over the forces of matter, known as adeptship. This subject furnishes a fitting terminus to the first part of our mystical studies, in which we have included, though briefly, every important section of Occult science embraced within "the lesser mysteries" of Nature.

The triumph of the human soul over the forces of matter, termed adeptship, does not refer to the attainment of immortality; since, as previously stated, the vast majority of mankind inherit immortality as the result of their humanity; although this is not completely assured until they have passed through the sixth state of the soul world. In this chapter we refer to those rare embodied human beings who are so· organized and circumstanced as to be able to evolve the sixth and seventh states of consciousness; or, in other words, those who have the inborn ability to attain to the powers and blessings of their immortality, while yet living outwardly, upon the human plane of embodied existence.

The literary world has been flooded with descriptions and explanations of adeptship. Definitions have even been attempted of the various degrees and grades of this exalted state; but so far, nearly all of such would-be expounders of states higher than themselves have (with one or two exceptions) failed most completely; for the very simple reason that, no human being can describe the nature and condition of a higher spiritual state of life than that to which his own spiritual nature has attained. Only two grades of individuals, therefore, can really describe adeptship. One is the adept himself, and the other is his accepted neophyte, his future successor, who has passed the third initiation, and is, thenceforward, in perfect magnetic rapport with the master to whose state he is to succeed when that master ascends unto a still higher sphere of spiritual life and power.

To those real seekers of esoteric knowledge who aspire to know Truth, irrespective of the source, or claims of any literary or learned worldly authority, we offer the following elucidation of adeptship. It comes from one who has actually passed through the various realms and states of spiritual existence, necessary for the acquisition of such knowledge. Therefore, his statements are the result of personal experiences within the world of spirit. And should the writer be blindly charged with contradicting the previous teachings of the modern Theosophical authorities upon the subject; he desires to point out the fact that, very few (if any) of them are entitled to explain the lofty state they would set forth.

If they do not know of their own experience, their descriptions are mostly inference and surmise, rather than conscious knowledge.

In order to present the subject as clearly as possible to the student, we will consider first, the various grades of adeptship; second, the nature and functions of adeptship; and third, how adeptship is attainable.

I   THE VARIOUS GRADES OF ADEPTSHIP

In the first place, there are three distinct grades of this exalted state, each grade containing within itself three separate states or degrees of life and power, so that in the whole there are nine states of Wisdom. These principle grades may be designated, in general terms, as the natural, the spiritual and the celestial states, of the soul's progressive evolutions. The first, the most external state, relates to the world of physical phenomena, and deals exclusively with the elemental spheres of the planet, and the astro-magnetic currents which control them. The powers of the adept of this grade extend from the elemental zones of matter in the world of effects, up to the astro-magnetic spheres in the realm of cause. "Beyond this astral world they become powerless. Hence, their highest achievements are within the realms of external magnetic phenomena."

The second grade, which constitutes the interior or spiritual state of the first, relates to the realm of spirit, and deals exclusively with the spiritual and ethereal forces of the planet. The adepts of this grade are the translated souls of those who have graduated through the various degrees of the first. As such, they fulfill the duties of the master or teacher to those who are still graduating in the outer degrees of spiritual life. Their power extends from the magnetic zones of the astral world up to the ethereal and spiritual spheres of disembodied humanity. Beyond these states of spiritual life they cannot penetrate, hence, their highest achievements are within the spheres of disembodied existence. Occupying as they do, the interior degree of life, they are enabled to combat the hells, on the one hand, and to sustain the heavens, on the other. These spiritual adepts cannot descend to earth (as we understand the term) and manifest their power externally, without the aid of a properly trained instrument, whose odylic sphere they can temporarily occupy. Their chief means of communication with the external world are the adepts of the exterior grade, through whom they transmit such portions of spiritual truth as the world has need of.

The third grade constitutes the internal or celestial state of the second; and is the highest degree of spiritual life that the embodied human mind can comprehend; and relates to the higher states of purified souls. It is above and beyond what we know as the human. It is angelic and celestial in nature. Of its Deific powers and potentialities we can not speak. They are beyond the grasp of external life.

At this point, it is of the utmost importance that the student should clearly grasp the relation of these three grades to each other, in order to form a correct idea of the nature and functions of adeptship, **and also, in order to understand by what means it may be attained.**

The first grade and the three degrees included therein embrace all the possibilities of humanity under the external conditions of the present cycle; for, beyond the limited possibilities of the "Life Wave" not even the adept, heir elect of the angels, though he be, can transcend. The various astral spaces which mark off the limits of these human possibilities, constitute the boundary line of Nature drawn by the finger of Deity between the two worlds of human life, the natural and the spiritual. When the external life mission of an adept of the first grade is fulfilled, a process analogous to physical dissolution transpires; the physical atoms which constitute his organism are liberated and the exalted soul enters upon a higher state of evolution and life, and becomes the spiritual man or an adept of the second grade. The second grade is thus a continuation of the first, upon a higher and more interior plane, and the scene of the soul's activity is transferred from the astral and magnetic spheres to the realm of spirit. This state holds the grand key of life and death, wherein all the greater mysteries of external life are concealed. It also stands midway between the man and the angel, and thus presents to us the equipoise between the human and the divine.

From the lowest grade of the human being on the external planes of matter up to the highest grade, or the perfect man, there are seven states; so, also, in the realm of spiritual humanity, there are seven states from the perfect man up to the angel. The vast importance of this grade of life, or spiritual adeptship, is also manifest from the fact, that, it is upon the boundaries of the sixth and seventh state of this grade, that, the two halves of the divine soul become permanently and eternally united. The twin souls, male and female, when united, then constitute the complete whole of the divine Ego. This mystical union is "the marriage of the Lamb" of Saint John, wherein the man becomes the angel, the human becomes divine, and enters upon the unknown cycles of Deific life. He is the grand angelic hierophant of celestial mysteries; the nature, power and function of which, are too transcendent for the comprehension of embodied mankind.

II THE NATURE AND FUNCTION OF ADEPTSHIP

In passing to this branch of our subject we shall deal only with the first grade, or adeptship of the external degree; since, before it is possible for the student to fully comprehend the powers of the second, he must himself attain unto the first grade. Therefore, to avoid any misconception, let it be distinctly understood that the whole of what now follows pertains exclusively to that state of adeptship whose members live, move, and have their being, and launch forth their powers, either upon the external planes of physical life, or else within the spheres of the astral world immediately interior to it.

Since the adept is the perfect man, it is evidently necessary for us to comprehend what is the nature of his perfection, in what does it consist? We have already fully explained, that, in the Occult sense of the term, man is a composite being possessing a seven-fold constitution, having seven cyclic states of existence; that is to say, progressive states of evolution upon the physical plane. The perfect man, therefore, is he who evolves in full his composite being and attains unto the seven states, while yet existing in external physical conditions. While on the other hand, the ordinary human being is compelled to attain whatever he lacks of perfection after he leaves his physical body, within the purgatorial states of purification of the soul world. Ignorance and selfishness; or else, the jarring discords produced by the combination of the two; force the great majority of mankind out of the central line of march mapped out by progressive evolution. At the present time, mankind has evolved but five physical senses. A few sensitive souls are aware of the higher two, but are not able to make much use of them. The perfect composite man possesses not only seven physical senses, but also seven soul senses, related to each other as follows:

PHYSICAL SENSES	SOUL SENSES
1. Touch	1. The power to psychometrize
2. Taste	2. The power to absorb and enjoy the finer essence of the life wave
3. Smell	3. The power to distinguish the spiritual aromas of Nature
4. Sight	4. The lucid state called clairvoyance
5. Hearing	5. The ability to perceive the ethereal vibrations termed clairaudience
6. Intuition	6. The capacity to receive true inspiration
7. Thought transference	7. The power to converse with spiritual intelligences at will

When the human soul has attained unto these seven states, his divine right to rule follows as a natural sequence. The powers of the will increase as the attributes of the soul expand; therefore, it is perfectly useless to preach so much about cultivating the will, since, that is accomplished by evolving the soul qualities or senses. The magical powers of the adept, which enable him to partially control the elements and to produce various kinds of physical phenomena, at will, are not the outcome of that terrific will force, so pleasing as a sentiment to many drawing-room occultists, but, they are the mild expressions of a firm but gentle soul in the process of evolving forms, in the spiritual imagery of thought. There is nothing "tremendous," nothing of the "fearful intensity," about it, for the slightest tremor of the purified soul, when consciously placed en rapport with the astral light, will produce surprising results. And the higher the plane from which the embodied adept projects his thought desire, the more extensive and potential the phenomena in the sublunary world of effects.

Such, then, is adeptship; such are the glorious possibilities attainable by the human race, when the spiritual attributes of their being are allowed to grow and expand in the sunny atmosphere of a pure and unselfish life. It is a state that may well be regarded as the climax of our Earth's possibilities upon her outward plane. A victory of which the human race may justly feel proud, is the grand triumph of the Soul over the forces of matter.

III   HOW ADEPTSHIP IS ATTAINABLE

We will now proceed to explain, as far as permissible, "the modus operandi" by which adeptship is actually attained. But, first, it will be necessary to consider who may and who may not possess the necessary qualifications; since the adept is, of a truth, like the poet, "born and not made." The adept is a born king of his kind. He is a spiritual and mental giant of his race, and cannot be made without possessing these royal qualities, in a very highly developed state from his birth. External life is too short, and the antagonistic forces to be overcome too great, during the present cycle, for the adept to be manufactured out of the rudimentary forces and embryonic soul qualities of the average mortal. It has been asserted by one who claims the honor of adeptship, that "the adept is the rare efflorescence of an age." This is, however, only figuratively correct, as in real truth, there are several such flowers in each race during the course of a single generation. Each family plant or race of mankind ultimately produces the rare flower of its line, and then becomes exhausted for that cycle. "It has run to seed."

Not all of these rare flowers of the royal line may attain adeptship; since they often exhaust their forces in other directions for the good of humanity; but such souls alone possess the possibilities; or, in other words, they have the necessary primary inborn qualifications.

Therefore, when these primary qualifications exist in a person, the first course to be pursued is to devote as much time as possible to the study of spiritual subjects obtainable in the outside world, and to master each and every branch of Occultism. Simultaneously with this study, the body must be trained in regard to matters of diet and the sexual relations. In other words; the human soul must be evolved entirely above the animal soul; i.e., the sphere of undeveloped good in man's constitution must be developed. The animal forces, passions and appetites, must be gradually developed, and transformed or evolved, into human qualities, instead of being conquered and chained, like wild beasts, as taught by oriental mystics. The problem of good and evil must be solved by the student, in each individual case. And right here consists the vital point of failure or success, defeat or triumph. Can the student train his physical desires to work in harmony with his spiritual desires?

We have labored, over and over again, to impress upon the student, that man is a composite being, and that perfection consists in harmonious evolution. It ought by this time to be self-evident to any candid mind, that those fearful practices in the East, of asceticism, celibacy, self-multilations, etc., are criminally wrong. They simply starve and chain the animal into subjection, instead of developing it into a useful, obedient and most highly important factor of the perfect man's seven-fold nature.

In regard to the question of diet, the first aim should be to remove gradually and yet as rapidly as possible the desire for animal food. In the flesh of animals, the particles of vegetable matter have been completely polarized toward the animal soul, hence, when taken into the human system, they tend at once to build up and fortify that very portion which we wish to transform and eliminate. Fish, however, are sufficiently removed from the human to be allowed to the beginner, yet, as he progresses, vegetables, grains, and lastly, fruits, will furnish the requisite amount of physical nourishment.

The question of the sex relation and its various mysteries are covered in Chapter IV of section I, so we will only add a few words which seem demanded by the fearful danger arising from the illusive doctrines now freely circulated by the "inversive magi." Love, pure and divine, is the grand keynote according to which all the harmonies of the Infinite Universe are tuned. Love is life and immortality; while lust and the vicious teachings and practices which insidiously, or openly, produce a contempt for sex and love, all tend toward the dark satellite and death, in its awful and occult sense. Just in proportion as love is displaced, self rushes in to fill the vacuum with ruin. Therefore, to ignorantly follow any occult training which unbalances or crushes, ends as disastrously in self, as selfishness does to start with. The training must be harmonious to properly develop the sevenfold nature.

The ascetic, whether ignorant or selfish, who starts out to attain magical powers for himself, and who enters upon a cold, rigid use of the will to crush and annihilate his animal passions, may succeed in these regards; but, he will find out too late, that his powers over the elements and forces of Nature have been purchased at the awful expense of the destruction of the feminine portion of his own soul, by gradual absorption into himself of the being upon whose development, in harmony with his own, depends his immortality. He, therefore, can never realize that union with his twin soul which constitutes the divine Ego. He can only know self. Thenceforward, he denies there is aught in the universe beyond his state, except Nirvana to which he is drifting, which is practically a condition of annihilation, but which he fondly pictures, in as vague and pleasing terms as possible, as "absorption into the Infinite." He denies point blank (since they no longer exist for him) the angelic and celestial states, and devotes himself to a systematic dissemination of the dogmas of karma and re-incarnation. Karma and re-incarnation are the most subtle and enervating forms of fatality conceivable by the human mind, since they sap the soul of all true inspiration toward the higher self and perfect life. These subtle doctrines not only continually prompt man to leave undone many things until his next incarnation, but, generally, they leave mankind in that helpless, apathetic condition, exactly suited to render them an easy prey for the inversive magi, who exist upon their vitality.

We will now give a few directions for the evolution of the soul senses or qualities. In the first place, some special time in the morning and evening should be set apart for the evolution of the spiritual sight. This may be done by gazing into a crystal magic mirror, or magnetic disc, which is used, matters not, since spiritual lucidity (if the quality exists) will be developed. The spiritual sense of touch, or the powers of psychometry, should be evolved (as often as possible) by placing any object that comes handy, such as rocks, shells, letters, etc., to the forehead. If no particular perception transpires, try the sensorium or that part of the brain situated between the crown and the forehead. If this effort should fail, try the solar plexus, and note the impressions received, then test these as to their correctness or otherwise, by examination of the article. Remember, that, many efforts may be required to arouse the dormant sense into action; therefore, do not be discouraged at repeated failures. The sense of spiritual hearing or clairaudience will follow the senses of sight and touch as a natural sequence. When these senses are evolved the primary difficulties are over and that one who will thenceforward act as master and teacher will make himself known. How, when or where we cannot say, but, there will be no mistake; no fear of deception by the Black magi; the truth will be realized within; it will not require one single shadow of external phenomena to convince that soul which is fully prepared for the master's reception; neither will the student have long to wait in expectation. "At the very hour when the soul is ready, behold its guide will appear."

The student should fully realize by this time, that, the soul powers mentioned above, possess nothing in common with the so-called spiritual gifts, evolved during the development of spirit mediumship. The medium is under the partial or absolute control of some foreign mind, but the neophyte, in the course of his development, evolves powers which are the free, clear, conscious outcome of his own divine nature. Consequently, in self protection, when training our spiritual nature, we should isolate ourselves from contact with the discordant world as much as possible. A life among the wild mountain solitudes is especially potent in this respect, as it brings us at once in direct contact with Nature as she really is. In these surroundings, the senses of the soul become stimulated and quickened, the physical organism is removed from the contaminating pollution of city life, and is thus protected from the unseen snares and temptations of the world. And as the external mind, when alone, soon begins to explore the craggy mountain sides and examine their fauna and flora; so the soul, when removed from the chaining magnetism of large masses of men, soon begins to soar upwards towards its source on high, returning from each spiritual flight with some occult treasure for its owner, though he at first may not fully realize the precious jewels which he is accumulating.

As there may be many roads which will ultimately lead us to the same mountain top, so there are many systems of occult training. But the one best suited for the Western Races has been presented. The end in view of every system is the same, viz.; first to evolve conscious lucidity, then the rest will follow. When once the aspirant becomes the accepted neophyte, whether he personally sees the master or internally realizes him, makes no difference, his future progress depends upon his strict obedience to the commands received, unselfish motives, and a pure life.

To persons of negative temperaments, Yoga training will produce the desired results. But this system is more suitable for eastern organisms than Western. There is, however, a mine of Occult lore in "Yoga Philosophy."

With these remarks we bring the present course of occult study to a close. The studies presented here are probably as much as the ordinary human mind will be able to realize, during this age of the world. At every step we made in writing this book, we had to fight against the fierce, cruel legionaries of the Black Magi, whose terrible secrets we have been the means of revealing to the world. These inversive brethren pose before the world to-day as the harbingers of light and oriental wisdom, but, beneath this external delusive glamor, we can see the bloodthirsty forms of the shadow. Our task has been accomplished rather with the point of the sword than through the instrumentality of the pen. The mediumistic upholders and supporters of oriental magic, dogma and delusion, have also done their best to destroy our work; but it lives; and will survive long enough to crush them with its glittering force; for omnia vincit veritas, constitutes the motive force behind it. Charges of fraud, and accusations of Black magic, have been systematically tried without avail; and nothing now remains for them but calumny and slander; but, whatever these inversive opponents of truth may see fit to bring forth in the future in order to stem the swelling tide of Occult knowledge and spiritual progress, rest assured, they will ultimately fail; and the terrible agonies of their conscious defeat will discount a thousand times the benefits of an apparently temporary gain. Here we close this part of our work, casting our labors as bread upon the mental currents of life, and wait with patience, for it will be after many days ere the results will be known. In the meantime, we shall rest with the certain knowledge that whatever is, is good, undeveloped though it be.

Throughout the preceding chapters the author has repeatedly directed his criticism against Buddhistical Theosophy. In so doing he desires his readers to always bear in mind that, he does not include any true Theosophist, nor any really earnest seeker after the hidden light of Occult lore, be they theosophists, Jews of the orthodox faith, or Christians. In using the terms of Buddhistical Theosophy, Modern Theosophy, etc., he means only the hidden disseminators and public worshippers, of that peculiar phase of Buddhism wrongly called esoteric, which make re-incarnation and Karma an absolute dogma of faith; and the corner stone of Occult philosophy; as intimated by the real external founder of T. S. in the columns of "The Path," in an article professing to "explain" certain very inconvenient passages in "Isis Unveiled."

CHAPTER V

The following quotations are from letters of Thomas H. Burgoyne (Zanoni) addressed to one of his pupils. They are from letters that were lessons. Others may question and find these replies an answer. Only students of The Hermetic Brotherhood of Luxor will recognize Zanoni as the Messenger and so receive these elucidations of the Path as authentic.　　　　　　　　　　Belle M. Wagner.

Where is the Divine Ego? Ordinary language cannot convey anything but a most crude conception of spiritual things, and even at best the realities of the higher life can only be explained in parables by utilizing earthly things by way of illustration, so I will offer an illustration used some time ago.

Suppose we have a globe of glass or other material capable of absolutely confining everything within its own circumference, and further let us suppose that it is a vacuum inside. Now, let us fill this globe with steam (not air) which is, as we know, an ethereal form of water. After the globe is filled with this vapor, it is, of course, full and no more can be forced into it. Let us further suppose that the globe has a sufficient temperature to maintain the steam therein at its invisible thermal condition. The capacity of our globe is thus exhausted with the watery element, which we will say is one gallon. We can now put one gallon of volatile alcohol into the globe and the atoms of alcohol will find room amid the atoms of steam. We can also further take a still higher form of matter and insert one gallon of ether (not the ether we breathe but the kind distilled from alcohol) into our globe. We now have three elements filling a globe of which not an atom more of either could be inserted if it was a perfect vacuum. It is a case of one within the other yet being the same size of each other. Of course, we might go on almost indefinitely, so that it amounts to this; there are seven dimensions of matter, and we will suppose them to be cubes one foot square, thus—

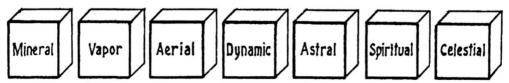

Mineral　Vapor　Aerial　Dynamic　Astral　Spiritual　Celestial

Now, within our cube of pure mineral all the other six can be absorbed, although all are exactly the same size, and there will remain visible the one cube of matter, and, to the physical senses, it will be just the same after as before this absorption, except that it will weigh a little more after the other six are a part of it. It is a STATE WITHIN A STATE, as the soul within the body, the Astral body, the Spiritual body, etc., and the Divine Ego is in the SEVENTH STATE, viz. the Celestial Heavens of our solar system; but we can no more precisely point where, as to a certain point in space, than you can locate the ether and the atmosphere; it is above and around us as well as within. Until the human mind is capable of understanding the terms WITHOUT and WITHIN apart from supposing that, a thing within must be smaller than the object enclosing it, and that the atoms of the one constitute a world totally free and apart from the atoms of the other, no real conception of a true spiritual reality can be formed. The very world in which we live, the houses we occupy, and the streets we frequent, are equally as crowded spiritually as materially. There are Astral Cities within Material Cities, and the inhabitants of the interior are as unconscious (generally) of the physical inhabitants of the exterior as the exterior masses are of the internal occupants. These lower cities and states are upon the first or earth sphere, and constitute the Hells of the soul world, and stimulate all the real Hells we see in every crowded city. You must not look upon the Divine Ego as some great angelic power. It is a simple Cherub of Innocence, lacking Wisdom and real intelligence, even as a babe. The two parts of itself are the soul monads projected from the little, pure Cherub Sun, like reflected rays; and its powers become crystallized in matter; the Man, the Wisdom or Intelligent and Positive force; and the Woman, the Love and Formative or Plastic power; finally the cycle is complete; the Man in his acquired Wisdom and conscious knowledge of Creation; and Woman, in all her matured Beauty and realized Love; then the Soul Ego becomes absorbed within their own Divine Form, and they become like two suns, which eternally revolve around each other, the CENTRAL INVISIBLE FOCUS of which is the atomic point of contact; and you can no more locate this invisible Deity than you can tell where the Red rays of the spectrum terminate, or where the Orange rays begin. It is a part of each. It is no more a part of one than of the other, and the two form one complete whole. This is as far as language can explain.

You ask whether it is right to appeal to the Divine Soul as within.

Yes it is. Woman should always locate her aspirations in the breast. Her bosom is the seat of her highest spiritual vibrations. The brain is the location in man.

Each planet prepares the zone for her own disembodied offspring. The souls of these zones have formed a grand inter-planetary zone. This is a fact which I have verified; but this zone is not in direct contact with our earth.

All of the visible stars; telescopic or otherwise, belong to our Universe and this universe has one mighty, inconceivable center; a glorious spiritual sun. Each one of the myriad suns of the first order are parents of countless secondary suns, and our own sun is one of these secondary suns. We cannot see any other Universe than our own, until we reach the solar sphere and become the angel; and then, not until we are prepared to ascend into other and brighter realms of being.

Mankind face a glorious destiny and the small sufferings of external life, fearful though they may seem to those still in the flesh, are as nothing compared with the endless possibilities of the human soul. And Oh, how my heart longs, at times, for the bright realms that I have so often trod; for the glorious vistas of the Infinite's bright creation; for that plane of life wherein the soul perceives the might and majesty of GOD in all the scintillating gems of His flashing, fiery crown. Each jewel is a glorious sun pulsating with creative life and carrying onward in the wild, whirling journey of evolution, its brood of planets with their countless races of intellectual beings, souls and Deific entities, brought forth as the manifestation of the Infinite Good (GOD).

The symbol upon the cover of this book The Light of Egypt is complex. It is the symbol of Spiritual Initiation, and means, literally, "I have pierced the illusions of matter. I am conscious that I am Divine." The seven stars represent the seven Principles of Nature. The serpent represents the objective phenomena, and the arrow piercing the serpent represents the human soul which is conscious of its origin, power and destiny.

It is when I read such articles as the one put forth by Huxley that my own eternal spirit rises in just indignation. Oh, that I could spread before the suffering world but one tithe even of the grand, glorious, eternal spheres of supernal existence that await the human souls after the change called death. Oh, that I were only able to reach each human heart, that must sink in despair when they read such soul-killing words of Atheism, and breathe into them the joys of the land that is beyond the sunset of this earthly life; of the land that is indeed fairer than day, where the spirits and angels dwell. Would that I could only reveal to them the marvelous beauties of super-mundane life that I and others have seen with our very eyes and recite the wonderous harmonies we have heard with our ears; speak to them of the unutterable beauties of celestial landscapes that our feet have trod, and tell them that life is ETERNAL and PROGRESSIVE; and that the soul's own bright individuality increases forever in Wisdom and Immortality. But, alas, it can not be. Men and woman must work out their own salvation and render unto themselves a just account of the deeds done while in the body. They would not accept the eternal food I spread before them, they would not understand. I am like a rich man, possessing in over-flowing abundance the fruits that are eternal, while thousands pass my door, starving; and yet they will not come in and be filled. But they continue on their way, seeking after dreary forms of belief that crucify them in Faith, Hope and Charity; they persist in flying from the light to become blind followers of blinded professors.

The soul at death enters the astral soul world immediately surrounding the planet. After purification, it passes on to the mighty zones in the orbital path of the earth. It is in these beautiful zones that the spirit homes, in the true sense, exist. Your higher aspirations, your sublimest ideals are there, beautiful, living realities entwined with the struggles, hopes, thoughts and victories of the Twin Souls.

My science and the religion I teach and worship is Nature's laws; my aim is the royal grandeur that surrounds the true perfected man. Thank God, I know, my teachings are not speculations. They are the living outcome of what I have seen with my eyes, found with my mind and heard with my ears.

If the emotion responds to the expression, it does serious harm; for the emotions are the reactions of the magnetic vibrations produced upon the Odylic Sphere; and, like a storm (it is really a storm) at sea, even after it is over and the sun shining again, etc., there is still an angry swell of the waves for some time; and the more frequent such emotions are brought into play, the more susceptible the actor becomes and the more readily they will respond in stern reality to the parts they have played. If we want harmony, love, truth and true brotherhood, we want as little of the contrary conditions as possible.

The true growth is to imitate love when hatred springs up; child-like innocence when jealousy would take full possession. There cannot be too much of this, if the motive be pure; if impure, then hypocrisy is the outcome, and this is wrong.

Never pantomime anyone except for some very important reason, because when so doing you penetrate the astral life forces of the person, and so very few are pure that you cannot help suffering to some extent from the contact. An angel is not pure enough to enter Hell and return without taint, except after a special preparation for the purpose, and besides this you contact magnetic currents that may react upon you for many years to come.

One word about facial expression; when a person has such complete control as to personate Hate, and, at the same time feel Love, they may carry such facial expression to any extent without danger. This is true art. It is, however, imitating Nature under false pretenses, so to say.

Twins in spirit are naturally a part of each other, and when the state of Angelhood is reached, there is but one Odylic sphere between the two. It is the Mystery of the Trinity; God the Father, God the Son, and God the Holy Ghost; yet there are not three Gods, but only One God.

It is the Male, the Female and the Divine Ego, or Crown, united in the grand triad of Angel that completes the Trinity. The Divine male, or Wisdom, which gives forth the idea of all action; the Divine female, which clothes the idea of her Lord with form from her creative nature, and the sexual vibrations of both which endow the idea with evolutionary life and motion; these constitute one of the arcane mysteries of life.

On such subjects as these I could write volume after volume and neither tire nor reach the end of experience and the things I have seen and heard in realms of brighter beings than on earth. Many marvels have been disclosed to me in my wanderings in the Occult world. I could tell you of the homes of the dead, of the damned, of the lost; of the homes of the blest, of the pure and virtuous in life; and of infinitely higher realms than these, where no mortal of earth hath trod, or even dreamed of; except he has passed through the fire of soul purification, a fire seven times hotter than the fiery furnace that purified Shadrach and his companions.

I put my body into the deep magnetic sleep and instantly leaped forth into the boundless ether. Oh, how gloriously Orion and the Pleiades were shining in the starry vault of night. The Moon lent her glory to the scene while all the living, pulsating, life of the astral spaces was joyous with the full vigor of creative life. I merely noticed these things as I sped with the swiftness of light itself, once more, to visit my far-off spirit home; once more, to see the treasures I had collected in the past; treasures I had fought for, suffered for; treasures that I had won for myself alone. Oh, how I drank in the melodies of the circulating stars and from the bottom of my soul sang forth, "We praise thee, O God."

This world is a preparatory place of probation, passion and pain, to expand the inner spiritual self and enable it to reach outward and upward toward that grander life that constitutes the goal of every purified soul after its final Initiation.

Our organisms are nothing more than the plastic molds of mediumistic matter; external vehicles of the soul; through which it may attract to and gather up the varied experiences of mundane life. They are forms, as transitory as the fleeting clouds above us, which become the sensitive plates, whereby the marvelous vibrations of creative and Deific life may express their wonderful transformations of sensations; and which, in turn, produce all the multitudinous delights of the physical senses; while the only living reality amid the Universe of moving, transitory and apparent realities, is the Divine Ego; God of each biune soul. Each one of us is but one of the reacting forces of a biune soul, and the immortal Ego; which binds together and forever the separated yet united identity of each. Each one's Ego is their own God; the only God; for Allah in His own image created He him; male and female created He them.

Woman was not the cause of the "fall". The real cause, per se, of descent into external conditions, was the necessity for conflict with the grosser forms of life and matter, whereby the soul could awaken the dormant atomic entities of its own being. The fall was a necessity of further progress, and the separation of the biune soul, the spiritual divorce, so to say, between Osiris and Isis; was because of the impossibility of the soul sinking beneath the forces of matter when united. It was only by separation and weakening their power that elemental conditions could subjugate them for a time. There is nothing impossible to the reunited souls. They become, by Divine Right, the King and Queen, co-equal and co-eternal rulers over all the elements in Nature. Their will, in the Astral world, is law; and the reason why the few souls who do become united, by the accident of marriage on Earth, are not more powerful, is because they are ignorant of their Divine relationship. They have the power but they do not know it. They are like a poor man dying of poverty with millions of dollars hidden under his hearthstone.

Each planet, moon or sun, evolves Karmic zones from the life principles of its own nature. They are the realms of astral life; and by reaction become the spaces of causation for every form and every manifestation of objective phenomena. When man appears upon the scene of action, the laws of his being form around the orb which evolved his race, a heavenly zone; a realm suitable to his condition and the mental evolution to which he corresponds. To say that the Earth, for instance throws off the substances generated from its own independent action is wrong; for, in a larger sense than we apprehend, worlds are cosmic individuals, of which, like human beings, no two are alike. They are bi-sexual organisms, however; and therefore, the ethereal zones or spirit worlds, they form in space for their offspring, constitute the Karma of their lives; just as the actions and motives of individuals form their Karma in the world to come.

The worlds of space breathe even as man breathes. "The breath of God" in man is only a miniature of "the breath of God" in worlds. The planet inbreathes to give its offspring life, and the planet's respirations constitute the material, so to say, from which the ethereal heavens are formed. These zones move with the Earth and the system of which she forms a part. Each orbit is fixed within certain limits, as is man's freedom of action, and these orbital paths, which constitute the center around which the zones of life are formed, move with the solar system; each system being, in one sense, an universe of its own, carrying with it both objective and subjective materials.

The sun of our system is surrounded by mighty sun spheres which extend all the inconceivable stretch of space represented by the vast orbit of our sun. Vast beyond belief as it takes 25,920 years of earth time for our sun to complete one round of its vast orbit.

The correspondence between the human form and the astral body is very close, so close, in fact, that no one could mistake the likeness; but it is, of course, more ethereal in its features. If the individual be one of active mind, noble qualities and high aspirations, the astral counterpart, while being a true likeness in many respects, gives a higher expression to each line in the countenance and features, which correspond to the qualities manifested. It is more Divine in its looks and lineaments; looks like an angelic brother or sister of the physical body. But, on the contrary, if the individual be gross, selfish, brutal and a slave to his lusts and passions, then the astral takes on a hideous countenance; is demoniac in its lines and features.

When the higher realms of the spirit spheres are reached and the true spiritual body manifests, there are the same differences, the form becoming more and more Divine and beautiful.

In all states the human form is maintained. It becomes, more and more, inconceivably beautiful as it progresses higher and higher. The internal organs of the body are simply the means by which certain functions are manifested and performed. Each organ, group of organs, function and set of functions, have an astral and spiritual correspondence; but, rid the mind of the gross, material part. The heart, lungs and liver are all there (not in the same form, however,) in the astral organism, and in the astral world disembodied souls eat and drink as we do, but their food is strictly subjective; it corresponds to their state.

In the spirit realm proper, life is continued by breathing and absorption. There is pregnancy and birth in the angelic world even as there is in this, but under very different conditions. The sexual organs on earth represent sacred functions in Heaven.

In the spiritual world, vivid formulation is an absolute necessity of possession. If you can vividly formulate the image of what you desire and bring it to you, it becomes as real, hard and firm as a table in the material world; that is, if the object possess such properties; but if you grasp after it, it will vanish from your sight. Most people who die live in a strange, dreamy, vanishing world.

If a spirit is not of my vibration, he cannot see me nor my surroundings.

You cannot understand now, but you will, the wonderful state of being where all are one and yet are individual. To become one with these legions of the blest is to give the soul to Ra.

In the spiritual world you will find great brotherhoods of music, medicine, astrology, etc., Each has a head supreme in the particular vocation represented by the brotherhood. Over all is a supreme, priestly power who does not dictate but counsels.

A tone arouses vast legions of life, when the particular vibration of their life is sounded. They take form and act as servants of the potency that can arouse them.

For a soul to be immortal, there must be something immortal and vital in his internal mind, for his atoms to revolve about; a principle of justice, and love. This is the axiom of immortality.

Only the angels of the sun return to the sun.

What you truly expect will be your destiny.

Curses are elliptical in their orbit, when the curse is heavier than the crime.

Render unto Caesar that which is Caesar's and unto God that which is God's. Only as you learn to do that, can you be just, and only when just, can curses or blessings be rightfully administered.

A soul is true when performing its functions.

All of the races that have thought of beauty have left the potency of their ideas in the astral light and become a fecund cause of its externalization.

Human beings on the earth plane can concentrate their minds on some definite thing and the results are sometimes astounding. Most people think idly, vaguely; then someone's strong mind can attract these wandering thought vibrations and, making his own brain the instrument for the display of the collected energy, launch his own idea on the sensitive camera of the astral light and produce a thought form that he can send with fearful potency to perform his will. This is to be a Black Magician; for the only form of power that the Adept should launch is his OWN IDEAL OF HIMSELF, in higher and better states than he has attained to. He receives that ideal by reflection from his Soul Mate.

At death, the soul enters its own soul images, and with relentless monotony, the panorama of all he has vitalized swings around him. He rests no more than a sleeping body in awful dreams; and these images continue for ages, aye, for thousands of years; until the soul can endure no more and falls asleep, to awaken; if it does awaken; only as a little child. It is to escape this that the Occultist toils and labors.

Relax and concentrate your soul on your solar plexus, saying the Mantram, "My soul is one with the Universe and my spirit an emanation from God," then ask yourself, who am I? what have I been? and what must I become?

The monad is incarnated in the brain. It may be asleep while the over-soul of the brain (animal soul) is awake; or the monad (human soul) may be awake and the animal soul asleep; or both may be awake; then the King rides in his chariot.

Truer than all, is the saying of Christ, "My Father and I are one." Nowhere can a creator be found. We ourselves are the outcome of life and effort. Effort is our immortality; always striving for that which we are not. The next existence is like this in essence, but more vivid. The human heart is the only moral life there is. Life is neither moral nor immoral; neither God nor Devil; and when the soul can penetrate and see and KNOW the Truth, the NAKED TRUTH, it says, "My Father and I are one."

The women are losing their feminity and thus are losing their conscious immortality.

Effort is immortality. When the soul sees an ideal beyond his own performance, then, at that very moment, he ceases to be immortal.

Again I would say, that, on man depends a woman's immortality, and on woman the man's, for no one can make an ideal of himself. He receives the image by reflection and then grows the power to become it through love; thus man, by his ideal, raises the woman of whom he is the expression, and woman, by her ideal, raises the man of whom she is the expression; thus they are the creators of each other. In soul matehood neither one nor the other can be greater than each one's inherent ideal of the other, and, unless that ideal is rounded out, they fail of their united immortality. This is a great and awful truth.

Ra is, and you reach him only by the deep conviction of his existence and the profound pleadings of the heart. He is the creator of this Earth and therefore never lived on it. He belongs to a previous evolution; is, as it were, the incarnation of the oversoul of the great sun-sphere. To give the soul to Ra is to become one with those legions of the blest.

The soul must never sleep or die without affirming its immortality.

Every immortal soul is the seed of a Universe; but millions have no immortality.

In life MEAN your sympathy with others; do not SUFFER it.

Nothing in life is worth while but moral effort. There you have the key, if you know how to use it.

Stand apart from life and look upon the acts of your own and other lives as a drama played by indifferent actors. I speak of the objective life. Only principle is vital.

Lie down, and, commencing with your feet, say, mentally, "my consciousness is not in my feet" and feel an indrawing therefrom. Then the hands, legs, arms, abdomen, solar plexus and brain, and finally rest in the monad alone. Then indraw the thought of your soul ideal to that center, the Divine half, your Soul Mate, and the blend will take place. Then redraw the love thought to the region of the heart and breasts and breathe your love in dynamic respirations.

For vital strength, be conscious of your vitality, and hold it in the solar plexus, never in the brain.

When women have their monthly periods, they lose a great deal of vitality. Draw your soul power up to your brain; then relax as nature needs. This is a secret of the Order.

Draw into your soul and relax your body.

You must continually indraw the thought of your love. Take it within yourself.

First lesson in control, the thought; the kiss the last. This in marriage.

Meditation;—1, I am. 2, The Universe is. 3, Consciousness. 4, Reflection from Consciousness. 5, Form from Reflection. 6, Temperament. 7, Environment.

Do you know these three? 1, Life after death. 2, Motive alone, as the responsible portion of action. 3, The astral, higher world, as distinct and apart from the soul world. If you can answer, YES, to these three, act on it. Live; find out the world you live in now. You shut away from yourself the subtle, psychic infiltration of the highest by searching into Spiritualism. Let it alone.

There are those in your life who must pass out of all life; for, know that, all are not immortal.

It is a great thing to be IMMORTAL.

When one has sinned against their own soul, that one loses his immortality. The Ego buds in the surviving half, in the monad of the Soul Mate, that has not so sinned; a new half, when the first has failed; and the journey is again to be made of Involution and Evolution, while the surviving half waits for the prodigal.

One must have keen repentance for past sins. Not to have it, is to be the Devil. Every atom of sin must be atoned for; every debt to Nature paid in full.

Give to your Divine Love the soul of your heart. Do you understand, "the soul of your heart," the ubiquitous sense of, I in You, and You in Me; as you read in the Gospel of the 1st. John?

I give you the key; Hold your love ideal in the morning; it gives the vibrations of the day.

Meditation; Draw into yourself what you would have your ideal be. Draw it into your soul.

But a narrow line separates the two worlds; do not try to live in both. Make that line NOT the boundry of this world but the platform of the next.

You have been walking on the river's bank long enough; you must cross the river.

You can live in Paradise now just as well as in five, ten or seventy years, for thoughts make Heaven or Hell.

Are you never conscious of a higher consciousness, a higher self? All the lower self must be raised into that higher consciousness, if we would be saved.

This is the Occult Catechism; Q. Who and what is Man? A. The answer comes like an echo; Thought. Q. What is God? A. Music, rhythm, melody, harmony. Of music is born thought, and thought makes Man.

There comes a time when the seeker becomes a fakir or a saint. A few, born to it, attain practical Occultism, but generally elsewhere and otherwise is the master attained, not here as you first dream.

Grace before Eating; only in the flesh can one enter into true relations of the spirits of the flesh. They become your servants or your masters, just as you treat them. Your body is related to all the kingdoms of matter and consequently to all ascending life spirits. So repeat this from your soul before each meal; "Eternal spirit in whom we live, breathe, move and have our being, consecrate this food we are about to partake of, to our bodies as well as our souls, and also to those ministers of thine who may be present. Peace be between us." Then throw some salt down to the spirit of earth.

When the soul calmly looks upon virtue and vice, as power and sin, and suffering as experience; then is the angel evolving; but make no mistake, vice must be conquered.

The Avatar, the Messenger, must be the harp whose notes vibrate in all the spheres. To be that harp, the physical body must be mediumistically sensitive, with a strong, dominant soul in control, allowing, however, the body to vibrate sympathetically to all forms of suffering. The Messenger must feel. It is feeling that creates. Figure the creation of a world first as vapor, which only FEELINGS and THOUGHTS can impregnate. The harp, the chord, the word, having felt with all; is the seed and Ra of a Universe.

Cosmic consciousness, like any other flash-light of spiritual inspiration and truth, is, on this plane, of very secondary importance so far as actual value is concerned. It is wholly worthless as a realization of any truth and at best, even in its highest manifestation it is purely personal, and means nothing to any one, outside of this one's personality. Whatever idea or set of ideas happens to possess the soul of the person, their cosmic consciousness will be colored by it. We have three notable instances, viz., Andrew Jackson Davis, Jakob Boehme and Emanuel Swedenborg; each of whose cosmic at-one-ments were true; but whose sub-consciousness's were possessed of different root ideas; hence they differed materially from each other, and all were wrong as to the real truth, per se. I, myself, have had this cosmic atonement at least a thousand times, in fact, it was a part of my daily life at one period; but unless you, yourself, be grounded in the very truth of things, these ecstatic trance-like experiences are about as valuable as those of St. Francis of Assisi; in other words, of no value whatever to any one but the personal experience of the person. One living, vital, clearly expressed thought is worth a thousand hazy spiritual dreams.

The Immortality of the human soul depends upon action. The man or woman who lives a purely ignorant, worldly life, who does not in any sense feed the interior spiritual nature, drifts into a sort of mental decay and spiritual rot; and at death, like the old tree, as it falls so it lies; but if the tree is cut during its vital life, when it is full of vigor, it instantly sends up a second growth far more powerful and vital than the first. It is the same with man; if he dies with spiritual vitality quickening his being, then he lives on after death, bridges the abyss of the two worlds, and has all the potentialities of a God within him.

Immortality depends upon mental and spiritual vitality, not physical energy. The physical body is merely the earth, so to say, whose main office is the evolution of spiritual life; but man mostly makes it nothing but the basis and center of purely material ends. Jesus of Nazereth was right, "Lay up treasures where neither moth nor rust doth corrupt, nor thieves break in and steal."

Thoughts, ideas and aspirations, become powers, To Be. These are re-incarnated into other lives after some human soul has given them material birth; but the monad, the Spiritual Soul, the thing that thinks, NEVER. Its only chance for immortal life is Here and Now, when incarnated as man on earth.

Man does Not return to earth a second or third time, to correct former errors and try anew. An acorn may become an oak tree but the tree never returns to an acorn.

Each spirit Ego sends forth its soul monad with its just share of its Divine patrimony, when it obeys the universal law of attraction to matter. With this fair equipment it begins its eternal round of being from a limitless state within the universe of external manifestation; and like everything else endowed with life, it attracts and repels, and in any state, it can only do the best it can. Its best is, when its own inherent force is dominant; its worst is, when it is weak by reaction. Its life at any point is only a mere transitory condition, a mere moment in the web of its eternal existence. At every stage it loses or gains something, and the sum total of such gain and loss comprises its Human possibilities, when it becomes incarnated as man, and constitutes his need for expression; be that expression what it may. But in assuming the responsibility of a Human soul, the monad must take its chances; so to say, regarding its environment before and after birth. It will be brought into the light of the intellectual day by powers over which it has no control; viz., Polarity; natural attraction and replusion of its Spiritual State of development. Money, rank and family, have no value in the spiritual world; because they are unreal, temporary, man made. The eternal verities only have power. The polarity is that which attracts it to the mother's womb; its Spiritual state determines its mental capacity; and these two, Polarity and Spiritual Degree of life; acting in harmony or conflict with its material environment, produce everything we know of life; and to these must be added another factor, an unknown quantity, the inherited tendencies or real qualities of the parents, to warp or expand the young soul. Some people are more animal than human and should not be parents. Some are dwarfed below their normal state, some are expanded beyond their real merits. Human destiny begins its harvest, only in this life; and as life becomes more advanced, so will destiny.

Today, we are forging the environment and fate of the millions of souls of the unborn generations to come. Fate can only act when conditions are ripe, remove vice and crime from the earth, and human destiny is powerless to reproduce them. Remove riches, poverty, drink, social rank, and disease, by just laws, moral education and pure living; and fate can not reproduce them. In this higher condition of man, destiny will act upon some thing higher than disease, poverty and crime. There are other things in the gamut of life, for there will be discord of some nature, and hereby destiny will become manifest. Where man WILLS, the fates themselves are powerless; but it must be the Will of Universal not Individual man.

Each soul is and ever must be the arbiter of its own destiny, and whatever our fate here, in this our earthly environment, WE have WILLED it so. We, without knowing it, have given the Nod of Jove to every great crisis in our lives; for every crime; for every grace; and we alone, must be the judge, and bear the judgment too. Only be sure that you attain the one vital reason for you being here upon earth; be sure that you gain the crown of Conscious life; for this also rests upon the same laws as destiny; it is NOT certain, unless WE MAKE IT SO; for "many come but few are chosen", and those, whose names are written in the Book of Life, can in no wise remove the self inflicted curse from those whose names are not, therein.

Who then, can for a moment question Fate, or asking fate, who can say why this evil, why this good, seeing, that in either case, the moment of its existence is past and gone, before an answer could be given; and new actions have taken their place. So it is with earthly life, it is one moment only, a single breath in the scale of being, a half conscious dream of the senses from which we shall awake, thankful in any case to find that after all; it was but a dream, and that the crown of life, the Sacred Jewel of the Lotus, lies beyond—

> Beyond the distant blue,
> Beyond the vaults of heaven, where the
>   starland shimmers bright,
> Beyond the blazing morning suns.
>   Beyond the orbs of night.
> Beyond all things that man has thought,
>   Beyond what Saint has seen,
> There lies the Crown, ETERNAL LIFE,
>   SELF WROUGHT BY SELF MADE BEING.

These things I KNOW, and in view thereof, can I not ask like the inspired apostle, "O death where is thy sting, O Grave where is thy victory?"

The physical body cannot always be controlled or made to express the real state of the spiritual ideal. In fact, very rarely can this be done; because it is not possible under present earthly conditions, race conditions, for one person to completely subdue his environment. Rare, very rare organisms are capable of doing this, but then such rara-avis, are as infrequent as the giants of genius. The ideal life may be lived, however, by all who can grasp the idea of I AM; as long as they can hold on to the central know; so to say, hold on to a chain whose link is the Illuminated I, the EGO.

We all can make the body more expressive of the spirit, than it is; but most of all depends on prenatal conditions, over which we have very little control.

It is little better than nonsense to say that selfishness manifests itself as constipation, and vanity as dispepsia, etc. pure nonsense. That is going crazy after correspondences and like the blind man of Bunyan's jury saying, I see, when he had no sight.

That mental states and characteristics have their reflex action there can be no doubt, because the one implies the other, but selfishness in one man may cause anything from indigestion to syphilis, while in another it might only hurt his liver, his lungs or his spleen; in other words, the same mental trait will afflict differently, different organisms; all depending on race, heredity, and astral influx, and this last is the most potent of all others.

The great altruistic thoughts and ideas people give birth to, will live; yea, and mature; bringing forth as the scriptures say, "some forty, some sixty, some an hundred fold." It is right here that re-incarnation is a Divine truth; for thoughts and ideas are re-incarnated, but not man. Also right here, that we explain the paradox of what Plato said, "Ideas rule the world," and in the next breath, "Spiritual ideas are impotent against purely material forces." But, let those spiritual ideas become incarnated in material forms, then they are potent; they rule the world; then they become the power of mind behind the human throne.

You and I, and, to a greater or less extent, every embodied soul, are the centers of ideas incarnated in us, and controlled by the monad; like the Sun sways his satellites. Certain groups of ideas will externalize as things, being in a certain stage of gestation, so to say; and from the knowledge and power of seeing this clearly, an event can be estimated with the same precision as the birth of a child can be foretold by a trained physician; consequently, those who are psychic, may not know WHEN the birth of an event will occur, but they Feel that it will, hence prophecy.

The primal foundation of all thought is right here, for instance, M. Theon may wish a certain result; if I am receptive, the idea may become incarnated in me, and under an extra spiritual stimulus it may grow and mature and become a material fact.

Who shall say, with any actual knowledge, what or whence, of the power behind the Great White Throne of Deity, the Infinite Creator, or where or in what manner, began the very dawn of primeval creation. It cannot be. The mind becomes dazed at the thought, and the soul itself would become insane in any attempt to penetrate within this infinite force, the impregnable mystery of the Infinite Universe of Being.

You are quite right in saying that others must have asked the same question. Yea, truly this is so; for in the fathomless past, millions of eons before our Sun had an existence, even; this question arose in the minds of those who, in other worlds, began to feel the promptings of an immortal soul. But it is, after all, but the query of a child in spiritual experience; and by correspondence, upon the same plane as the child of today; who asks about the man in the Moon, "how did he get up there." Also, as the first scientific mind began to speculate of things beyond the limited vision of his fellow beings, in their dimly lighted cave asked, "What is Life?"

Today, with all our marvelous advancement in the realm of physics, chemistry, the revelations of the Spectroscope, we are not one iota nearer the actual solution of the cause. As Hermes says, "All is living, Life is one, God is Life", and therefore, "the origin of life is in God." Your question, therefore, resolves itself into knowing God. You can, as you already know, only attain this knowledge yourself; as you realize, you are a part of God.

There is an old myth, or perhaps it had better be called a symbol of The Beginning; the Winged Egg of Deity, floating, unconscious, upon the unmanifested void, an universal ocean of formless Aeth. After millions of ages had passed, the primordial cell, the origin of all things, began to move with life, and The Universe began; but, "how came the egg there?" To answer that is beyond my power.

As to intelligence, yes, emphatically so; listen to me; In the lowest stratas of unmanifested life, organic or inorganic, there exists mind in some degree. Back of this; back, conscious mind reaches into the great unknown, infinite void of all manifestation. It lives, unseen; and to us, unmanifested being. It is there, that life and being first flow outward; brought out; so far as the organic worlds are concerned; by the cyclic pulsations, of all the outward towards the inward being, of the Universe; the great unknown; the very Arch Deity of All is there; not as a being with parts, but as an ocean of living mind, of unmanifested seed; The Great All Father of All Being; the biune Father-Mother, life of everything that is, was, or, shall be; and from HIM flow the infinite rivers of living force, to become manifest. This state is the Isis, of the Soul of the Universe. Biogenesis is the Divine Law; life from life, God is life, and life is thought.

There are only certain fundamental truths that are true, per se, which possess definite reality. They are nine in number and I suppose, can be finally reduced to one, a Trinity of Trinities. The First Trinity is the primary concept of all things which has neither beginning nor end, unconditioned, therefore, boundless. For all speculative purposes; 1, MIND. 2, SUBSTANCE. 3, MOTION. may be considered as; Intelligence or Mind; Ether or Substance; and Force or Motion; and the outcome of this triune concept is the evolution of the grand something upon which the entire fabric of the universe depends, and this is; CONSCIOUSNESS. The impersonal becomes, as it were, personal, and there comes into being "THE THING THAT THINKS" apart from the universal thought. From this comes the next or Second Trinity; 1, I am. 2, God is. 3, The Universe exists. This is very different from the first Trinity; because it contains only One indisputable fact, which is, I Am, this it knows. It believes that God is and that the Universe exists. It thinks because it sees. It can see the universe but cannot see God.

You see, we are now getting into the realm of appearances, and this is because the Thing That Thinks, i.e., CONSCIOUSNESS, not being the universal mind, but an entity or differentiated atom of it, is not the universe; therefore, reduced, as it were, from knowing the unknowable; it can only see and think, and the consequent ideas must always depend on What it does See.

The God Idea, is simply the over-whelming conviction, the consciousness of the awful powers by which it finds itself surrounded, tremendously greater than itself.

The last Trinity is; 1, Life. 2, Change. 3, Creation, and this is at last on earth. Everything is alive, there is no death; only change, eternal change; and the idea, the Thing that Thinks, Creates; and is thus a conscious microcosm patterned after the boundless, unconscious MACROCOSM.

This is a very simple little primer of spiritual and material truth, in which great truths, that would require big books to explain, are reduced to their simplest, primal concepts; and while there is nothing, beyond which, the mind of man can conceive, there is infinite space for theories and isms to grow between the lines; but, remember, that man has no friend but humanity; his Gods and Devils are found useless and powerless against the genius of man. The live, green earth, is man's mother; and the earth and all that dwells therein are his by the Divine right of possession. The stars of heaven look down upon him, but there is no sympathy in their light; no companionship, in the real sense; but the earth looks up and bids him rest. She supports him and gives him of all she possesses of life and beauty. She produces the flowers that gladden the heart of his childhood, and the rich harvest that gives strength to his manhood, and later she will cover up the useless mortal part of him, beneath the green, grassy mound of her bosom, down upon which, the distant stars, all unconscious of him or his destiny, will look without pity. So, Thank God; the great inconceivable Universal God of the Infinite Creation; that man exists; that he lives and moves and has his being in every stage of existence; from the living granite foundations of our mother earth to the angelic glory that surrounds the soul and sways the Sceptre of Ra.

God, Man and the Universe; and these three resolve into two; as eternal mind and eternal substance or Ether. Motion itself, is only the inter-action of these two. The great Arcana being; that, Spirit and Matter are at last One, under different forms of expression. Mind, alone, being eternal, and Consciousness Immortal. There is a difference between these two. Mind is God without beginning and without end. The universe of mind is the sub-consciousness of Deity. And differentiated consciousness is an individualized atom of God. It is an evolution, per se, to which the whole universe is progressing, but to which it can never attain the end; because, it is both illimitable in bounds and inconceivable in results. Hence, to come back nearer to ourselves, we see that it is in order and quite natural; that, if the measure of consciousness attained by the evolving monad, when the state of man is reached, does not or cannot awaken Itself to Itself, but is only a reflection of the earthly maya; then it can have no vitality left at death of the body to keep its grip upon the spiritual attraction of its Ego. Its failure to realize itself, is the signature which it has affixed to its own spiritual death warrant; and, unless, the monad can hold on its way and finally coalesce with its Ego, it goes, like the body, back into the universal womb and tomb of the Universe.

Life is the final mystery of God. The old philosopher who wrote those lines knew more than appears upon the surface. It means that, to solve the problem of life is to exhaust the mysteries of God; i.e., to be equal to Him or It; and as this is impossible, the answer is clear, the problem cannot be solved.

Life is motion, says science; well, so is thought; for thinking implies action, mental or spiritual. All action is motion; and without mind, existence becomes a blank. Life may be consciously or unconsciously, active; but in any state it is still action; and it is only a difference of degree, between the active man and the apparently passive rock; for life is in both. So that, to say that life is motion simply begs the question. So likewise does the answer of the theologian; who, dogmatically says, it is the Breath of God; since, neither he nor any one else knows what the Breath of God is. In each and every answer, we find the same sorry attempt to conceal ignorance by the jugglery of words. But in spite of this, and in spite of the experiences of the ages, in every generation, man thinks the problem capable of solution, and sets out to solve the Riddle of the Sphinx. The fully developed soul knows that the problem is and will remain, unsolved.

As I look back over the mental excursions and spiritual explorations, I made into the mystical regions of the unknown, I can see rung after rung of my spiritual ladder, still there, clear and distinct, each stone built upon solid fact and scintillating with the light of truth as it spans the two worlds, like stepping stones to the Infinite, until they reach the Mystery of Life and God, or the Origin of the Vast Universe of Being. Mind and Soul fail to go farther, and beyond this point, not even God, He, She, or It can go; because of the ever eternal beyond.

It is right at this point where science has the advantage of religion and scores a grand truth. "There is no possible point in this universe," says Tyndall, "nor any conceivable state of existence where it can be said, This is the End; This is the Ultimate; for there is always something beyond." The scientist, laboriously seeking the origin of life; the theologian, attempting to define the nature of God; and the transcendental mystic, seeking the Philosopher's Stone; comprise a trinity of thinking idiots, that the world could very well do without. Each, in his own special sphere, looks with contempt upon the other; and each spends his time fruitlessly chasing a "Will o' the Wisp."

Man we know; from whence he came, we know not; that is, not in the abstract; his purpose here, we also know and we know whither he is going; and to know all this is quite enough; but, the Why and the Wherefore of Life, we can never know; neither here or hereafter.

The sixth Race will ray out into seven branches. The Fifth Race was comprised of Aryan, Semetic, Slavonic, Greek, Latin, Celt and Teutonic. The Japanese belong to the first group of the Aryan branch, composed of a blend of the Macayan and the Mongolian families. The Teutonic; the last blend of and of course, the highest form or 'ower of the Fifth Race; embraces all Goths, Danes, Vandals, Saxons, Norsemen; and the finest product of the blend of Scandinavian and so-called Germanic peoples, is the Anglo-Saxon; the very flower of the

Fifth Race and that which will be the main matrix for the birth of the Sixth Race.

Zanoni means; Zan, a Star; oni meaning, child of or son of; thus Zanoni, Son of the Star. The double Ze ( ) means completion.

The chasm between the soul world and the astral is just the idea of God. God, spirit, per se, is unconscious as the spinal cord is unconscious. God, Ra, is the brain and at the acme of consciousness. God, like spirituality, retreats, as it were, toward the ocean of unconsciousness. Ra is the acme of grand intellectual consciousness; but He has a greater than Himself; aye, many, greater than Himself; more spiritual but less intellectual and less conscious. They too, have greater than themselves; less in consciousness, and so on, and on, until the great unconsciousness, the spinal cord, as it were, of the universe is reached; but, that spinal cord is not a center, for, it is a nervous system, penetrating everywhere. Our God is Ra, for, we would not be, without Him. His soul's vibrations (the Sun Angels are One in vibration with Him) called us from the great unconscious; gave us the Breath of Life; and we are, in our inmost possibility, but images of His; expressions of His Soul. His higher evolution depends upon the souls, which He has drawn into Being. He is like a peak, only to be lifted higher through the upheaval from beneath. As the souls, that He has quickened, gain the Great Immortal vibration, I AM; as they gain the centripetal force, that holds them in identity; as against, the great centrifugal power that would call them back into the unconscious; they form with Him, the Over-Soul vibrations, of a conscious God-Head.

Yes, Ra may fail. The world of souls that He has launched forth, may not return in sufficient numbers; and then again, would a new Solar Sphere be launched. So now; it is a fight for Ra, as well as for yourself. Every spiritual conquest you make for yourself, you make also for Ra. He is dependent on you, and you on Him. Consciousness against unconsciousness. Ra is thus, Jehovah, the Lord of Hosts; the manifest, visible God of this Solar System.

At a certain height from Earth all discordant vibrations unite and concentrate with the accordant ones into one hum, one note. Each planet, thus, has its note; and the great chord of our solar system sounds. The Sun is the sounding board. Each Solar System is capable of that amount of evolution, that is involved in it. Involution is the coil, the spring; so the next universe may be in a larger vibration or it may go higher, than its own impulse, from the latent energy, not used in the first; carried over, as it were, as capital, unused energy.

All immortal souls blend with Ra, the Supreme Seed, in becoming Creators, with Him.

In that Angelic Sun World are found our Divine Parents.

The spirit is the Master's imagination; the tool; and the body is the plastic material. Imagination is not fancy. Imagination is the foundation of the creative faculties; while fancy is the cornerstone of superstitution and foolishness. The imagination of man becomes pregnant through desire, and gives birth to deeds. We all, can educate and regulate our imagination, and thus, contact spirits; and be taught by them. And by living an unselfish and pure life, we can become the mediums of good cheer to those around us. Just as the sun continually shines in the heavens, though often obscured by a veil of clouds. Whoever fails in getting the lessons out of their experiences in this world, just so much, will they be at a disadvantage in the next sphere. Man's aspirations are the spiritual essences that awaken eternal emotions. Thus proving, that, mind is universal; while will is the attribute or faculty of the mind, for effort. It is not distinct from the mind, but a name for a certain power which the mind possesses.

Every man, plant and animal, bears external and internal evidences of the influences dominant at the moment of germinal development. Thus proving, that, every form of life is a medium for the manifestation (expression) of natural forces.

We cannot cultivate Will, without Faith. They are as light and shade, inseparable. We can accomplish a little without much Will, but, without Faith, nothing.

Mind sleeps in the plant, dreams in the animal, and awakes in man. In man, it becomes conscious of itself, and capable of a relatively independent existence.

Thrifty Nature, surely; no prodigal, the most notable house keeper, nothing wasted; everything utilized.

Involution and Evolution. The over-shadowing presence of the Ideal Form is progressively Involved, as the outer structure is Evolved.

QUOTATIONS FROM LETTERS

SUMMARY

1. There is one unknown state, which, in its ultimates, is and must forever be unknowable to either Man or the Angels, and this state is the Great First Cause; THE UNCREATED, THE ETERNAL, ALONE.

2. From this we receive the biune spirit called GOD, manifesting itself as ONE LAW, ONE TRUTH, ONE PRINCIPLE, ONE WORD.

3. And the beginning of all things is the differentiation of sex. The ultimate of all things is the perfection of sex.

4. The potential germs and ideas of all creation to be, lie within the forces of Involution; while all creative manifestations in matter, in spirit, and in forces that play between, are the product of Evolution.

5. Involution is the Father of All, and Evolution is the Mother of All Existing Things, conceivable or inconceivable.

6. There is a Trinity within all things in which there is life, whether it be spirit or matter.

7. And the language of Nature is Symbolism, and the key to Symbolism is the Law of Correspondences.

8. When, through study, you have penetrated into the Sanctorum, you have gained the right to demand and learn the mysteries there. You have opened the door, the treasures lie before you. By your own work, only, will you be able to take possession of them. Eternal vigilance and work is the law of progression.

9. Remember, O Neophyte, that Goodness alone is Power.

10. Divine Humanity! Learn, O man to know thyself, and walk with the knowledge of the Spirit within thee.

PART II

THE SCIENCE OF THE STARS

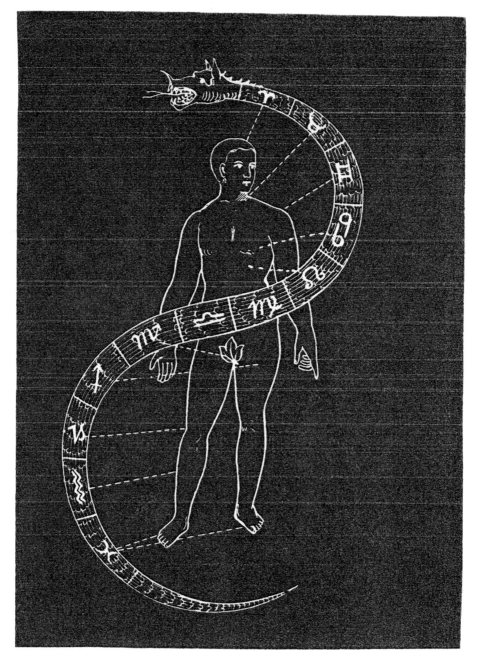

FIGURE I SHOWING
WHAT PART OF THE HUMAN FRAME
IS RULED RY EACH SIGN OF THE ZODIAC.

THE SCIENCE OF THE STARS

INTRODUCTION

In commencing this brief elucidation of the Astro-logos of the Ancients it is necessary, perhaps, to inform the reader that the system about to be elaborated is purely astro-masonic and constitutes that special branch of the primeval "Wisdom Religion" which made the ancient Occult Schools of Egypt and Chaldea so justly famous for their Esoteric learning.

Astrology, per se, is a combination of two sciences, viz.: astronomy and correspondences. These two are related to each other as hand and glove; the former deals with suns, moons, planets and stars, and strictly confines its researches to a knowledge of their size, distance and motion, while the latter deals with the spiritual and physical influences of the same bodies; first upon each other, then upon the earth, and lastly upon the organism of man. Astronomy is the external lifeless glove; correspondences is the living hand within.

It was from the mystical land of Chaldea that our Egyptian ancestors derived their knowledge of Astronomy and Astrology. This knowledge was, fortunately, transplanted into good soil and flourished for untold ages under the fostering care of her mighty priesthood and colossal sacerdotalism.

From the fertile valley of the Nile, long ages before Abraham and his herdsmen wandered over the desert of Arabia, this sublime science of the starry heavens, with its priestly devotees, was carried by tidal emigration over the Caucasus, across the arid steppes of Asia, through the wild mountain passes of Afghanistan and Thibet to the burning plains of Hindustan, and from thence was spread by India's dusky sons among the Mongol and Tartar races of the still remoter East.

Knowledge, we are told, travels westward, and, so far as Europe and America are concerned, this is true in the present cycle. But the time once was when this mental and intellectual current was reversed, and knowledge traveled eastward.

From the magical schools of the lost Atlantis, the sacred stream of learning flowed towards the rising sun into the regions of Central

Africa, and from thence to the coast, up the Persian gulf to Chaldea, then from the banks of the sacred Euphrates and the plains of Shinar the stream flowed backward (as though weary and seeking rest) toward its native home in the Western seas, only to be detained upon its journey and to find a temporary resting place in the wondrous valley of the Nile; when, after changing its personal appearance somewhat and adopting the dress of its gifted patrons, it was again projected onward by the restless impulse of Egyptian enterprise, along the shores of the Mediterranean and Black seas to the Caucasus, and thence eastward, as before mentioned, to the dreamy skies of India.

When we come to think of the awful vastness and inconceivable beauty of the glittering worlds which stud, like jewels, the dark canopy of our midnight skies, undoubtedly, we must admit that the contemplation of the shining heavens, with its myriad galaxies of starry systems and stretch of fathomless eternities, forms a sublime study for the thinking astronomical mind. There, alone, can he see something of the boundless affinity of the universe. But to the Occult student of Urania's blazing firmament, the shining constellations, with their cabalistic names and weird mythological histories; the glittering suns of these far off astral systems; and the shining planets which belong to the same solar family as ourselves; possess a deeper interest. Everything around us, save this blazing firmament, is in a state of transition. Besides the fleeting changes, which the return of the seasons bring; the landscape around us is changing its aspect every year. In fact, all around us is change. There is nothing but one eternal change of form. But the gorgeous creations in the sky are still there; undimmed in brightness, unchanged in grandeur; performing, with unflagging pace and unvarying precision, their daily, their annual, and their mighty cyclic rounds. Upon the same heavens, just as we see them now; bespangled with the same planets and with the same familiar stars; gazed the first parents of our race, when they began and also when they ended their pilgrimage upon this mundane sphere of life. The same constellations; Arcturus, Orion, and the Pleiades, sang together with the morning stars when the fiery foundations of our earth were laid; and they rolled in the fabled darkness over Calvary when the gentle Nazarine was slain. These wonders in the sky, are truly the only objects which all nations have witnessed, and all people have admired. They are truly the only objects in the universe which have remained unpolluted by the finger of man. They presided at the Horoscope of our birth; they will sing the funeral requiem when we die; and cast their pale radiance over the cold, silent tomb beneath which we are ultimately destined to repose.

Before the aspiring student can become the astrologer, he must make himself familiar with the general principles of astronomy, and learn how to trace the external symbols of physical life, which are the phenomenal results, back into the stellar worlds of cause. The whole mystery of this system, therefore, may be designated in general terms as the science of cause and effect. The text book of Astrology by A. J. Pierce and Wilson's Dictionary of Astrology should be closely studied as aids to obtain this knowledge.

From the foregoing remarks it will be seen that the reader must not expect the revelation of some divine, mysterious secret that will instantly convey the power of reading the past, realizing the influences of the present, and foreseeing the momentous events within the womb of the future; on the contrary, he must expect nothing but a clear and concise statement of Nature's immutable laws, which require both study and application to master. He will, however, find in this series of lessons a complete exposition of the Occult principles of Nature, in so far as they mold and guide the physical destiny of embodied humanity. But, the principles involved and the ultimates evolved as the natural outcome of cause and effect, can only be mastered and understood by devoting time, unprejudiced thought, and deep study; first, in learning the theory, and then in reducing that theory to practice. Astrology does not imply fatality. On the contrary, probably two thirds of man's so-called misfortunes are the result of his benighted ignorance. Man, when ignorant of the laws of Nature which control his existence and destiny, is somewhat like a lifeless log floating with the stream. It may be that the various currents of the river will carry him safely to the river's mouth, and launch him uninjured upon the great Ocean of Eternity. But it is far more likely that the winding course of the river of life will land him into a mud bank of trouble where he may stick fast for the remainder of his days; or, liberated by some stronger current, may again take his chances, either of future safety or of floating into some whirlpool of destruction. But when man understands the laws of his being, he is then safe on board a strong boat. He sees the whirlpools and mud banks of life ahead, and skillfully, by the use of his steering apparatus (the will) avoids collision. But it often happens that with all his knowledge and skill he cannot successfully battle against the mighty currents that oppose his way, simply because there are, in these days, too many lifeless logs of human lumber that are constantly throwing themselves with the swell of the current athwart his path. But it must be at once apparent to the student how infinitely superior the one is to the other, and how enormous the chances of success are upon the side of the one who hath attained unto wisdom; who by study, knows himself and the laws of Nature.

The heavenly bodies urge, predispose and influence to a great extent, but they do not compel. When we are ignorant of their power, we decide our actions to the best of our worldly knowledge, and we think we have free will in the matter; but, if we could only see the influences at work moulding our actions, we should see that we were obeying the stellar powers with slave-like servility; not always wisely, indeed, but blindly and too well. Under such a state of bondage the planetary influence would, indeed, be fatality. Knowledge alone is the great liberator of human suffering, and social inharmony. Our delivery from pain, our freedom from bondage, in other words, our free will, increases exactly in proportion to the extent of our knowledge, if used properly. It is the Wise Man who rules his stars, and the fool who blindly obeys them. Consequently, this Chaldean science of the stars, in order to be practically utilized, must be thoroughly realized; but when realized, it will repay the student a hundred-fold for the time and labor bestowed in learning the way. It will give him a tangible foundation, whereon he may safely stand amid the wild and conflicting opinions of unbalanced mystics. In it, he will find the key of the sacred sanctuary, wherewith he may eventually unlock the doors of the temple and penetrate the mystic veil of Isis, there, to behold the lovely form of the Goddess and to read the glowing verities of Nature inscribed upon the imperishable scrolls of time, and, if he have the will to seek further and deeper, the truths of eternity itself.

Astrology, in its purity, though forming a system of divination, is totally unconnected with either fortune-telling or sensitive, irresponsible mediumship. It is a divine science of correspondences, in the study and application of which the intellect and intuition become blended in a natural, harmonious manner. They commence to vibrate in unison. When this union becomes complete, the ignorant man becomes the prophetic sage.

Therefore, we would earnestly request the student of the system herein about to be taught, to thoroughly master each principle and detail laid down; commit them to memory so as to be able, instantly, to recall and repeat them when necessary. Study well the Occult principles of the science before attempting to master the external mathematical formula; and never lose sight of the fact that no one principle is of itself absolute, but, to become potent, requires the active cooperation of the other forces. If these oppose with their influence, instead of assisting, then it at once becomes a question of power against power; if they equal each other, the influence of both becomes nil, and the effects, instead of evolving into the realm of external life, become crystallized within the realm of force, and die within the womb of Nature. And lastly, remember that this ancient system of the hoary sages, who first discovered the starry truths of the Chaldean lore, constitutes the basic principle from which all doctrines, Occult theories, and sacerdotal systems have radiated. Every religion under the sun has an astrological foundation, and every science the human mind is capable of elaborating, springs from, returns to, and ultimately becomes lost within the starry realms of Urania.

In conclusion, therefore, we hope that our efforts to instruct the student in these sublime mysteries will assist him to store up a supply of precious food which will enable him to receive mental pleasure and spiritual profit, thus proving a blessing to the body as well as the soul.

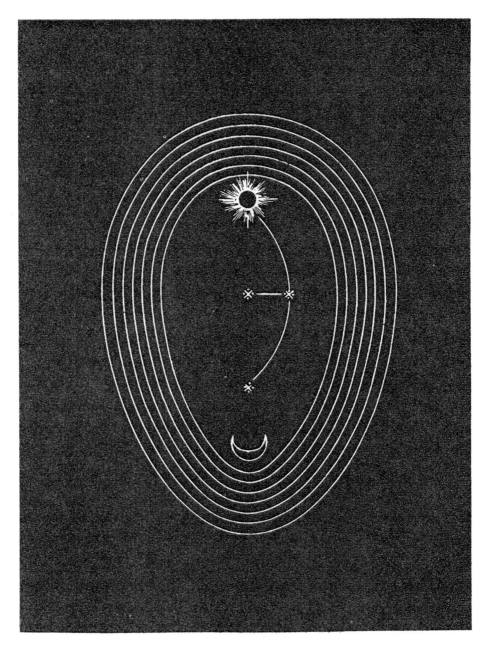

FIGURE II SHOWING
THE ODYLIC SPHERE OF MAN.

CHAPTER I

THE PRINCIPLES OF CELESTIAL SCIENCE

"So God created man in his own image,
in his own image created he him."
Genesis, Chap. I

Man is a microcosm, a universe within himself, and as such he is a perfect epitome of the infinite Universe, the Macrocosm. The Chaldean sages, therefore, when constructing their mighty system of sidereal astrology, held to this idea throughout the whole of their philosophy. In order to penetrate the mysteries of God, they first sought out the mysteries of man, and then, formulated a complete science of correspondences. The Human organism, so complex in its wonderful mechanism and so beautifully harmonious in all its parts, became their architectural design upon which they constructed the Grand Man of the starry heavens. The twelve signs of the celestial zodiac were divided into sections of the human frame, so that the entire zodiacal belt was symbolized as a man bent round in the form of a circle, the soles of the feet placed against the back of the head. Each of the twelve signs contain 30 degrees of space, the whole making the 360 degrees of a circle. This 360 is the symbol of completion. When the 3 and 6 are added together they make 9, which is the highest unit we possess, and as such is held to be the sacred number of Deity. It is a triune trinity, 3 times 3.

The mystical symbolism relating to the 12 signs of the zodiac and the human organism holds an important position in our system. In this connection, they form the body of a musical instrument as it were, while the sun, moon and planets constitute the strings. Our bodies then, when astrologically considered, are merely sounding boards for the celestial notes, struck by the starry musicians during the performance of their celestial opera, "The Music of the Spheres." Figure I shows what part of the human frame is ruled by each sign. It will be noticed that the sun and moon, through the mediumship of their signs, Leo (Ω) and Cancer ($\mathfrak{S}$), govern the two principal organs, viz., the heart and the lungs. When these are in an harmonious condition within the body the whole system is healthy; this is also correspondingly true regarding the Grand Man of the skies, or, in other words, the natal horoscope of the person.

More depends upon the position, aspect and power of the sun and moon at birth, than upon all the planets of our solar system combined. For this reason, the sun and moon are, to us, the transmitters of the stellar forces. They act in the capacity of astral mediums and cast their gathered or reflected potencies into our magnetic atmosphere, harmoniously or discordantly, according as they are aspected by the benefic or malefic rays of the major planets. The only difference between the two being, the sun is electric in its action, hence positive; and the moon is magnetic and negative. In themselves, alone, they are neither fortunate nor unfortunate. If these facts are remembered, we cannot go very far wrong in our astral studies.

Man has five positive points of projection and four positive centers of energy, thus making up the mystical nine, the symbol of Deity. In addition to these, he has one great receptive center, which completes the number of the Ten Sephiroth. The head, hands and feet, are the five points of projection from which, streams of vital force are constantly radiating. These five are symbolized by the five pointed star and the five sided figure. This quintile, the Grecian symbol hygeia, was the Pythagorean symbol of health, and when these five points radiate their forces in straight lines from their various centers, the result is perfect health.

The positive centers of energy within the odylic sphere are the brain, the spleen, the heart and the generative organs, while the great center of reception is the Solar Plexus.

When trouble or anxiety of mind crosses our path the first place where we feel its influence is that part of the body called the pit of the stomach. This sensitive region is within the solar plexus. How many times do forebodings of coming trouble impress themselves upon this delicate center? As a rule, when we are in trouble we have no appetite; this calls forth inharmony in the various secretions of the body. When sickness and its disagreeable correlations threaten to take possession, keep this mighty center protected, and you have the true secret of absolutely perfect physical health, providing you possess, to begin with, an organism whose mental and physical forces are evenly balanced.

The solar plexus is our grand contacting point whereby we are placed en rapport with all things external to us. Therefore, we can see that the true psychical basis of physical health rests with this center; for it is taken for granted that man is, by lawful superiority, the natural ruler of those powers which live, move and have their being within his own magnetic dominions. To possess true psychological power which shall be subject to the imperial will and thus be able to assume perfect control of the odylic sphere; to concentrate all our loyal forces, at a moment's notice, upon any particular section of this magnetic kingdom, and thus instantly subdue any revolt of the reactionary powers;—it is absolutely imperative that our physical bodies be kept free and uncramped by any article of dress which restrains us from developing our true natural forms. Mental and magnetic liberty depends, to an extent hitherto undreamed of, upon the perfect freedom of the physical organism. Therefore, that which cramps, binds and warps the body out of its natural proportions, is fatal to any real spiritual progress; because it correspondingly inharmonizes the action of the odylic sphere. For this reason alone, India, Chaldea and Egypt adopted the loose flowing robe; for this reason alone, is the dress of all priesthoods loose and ample; to give them the very fullest measure of magnetic power. Corsets and small pinching shoes have done more to destroy the true spirituality of the present generation than all the other causes of ignorance combined.

Anything to be truly beautiful must be truly natural. It is our utterly false idea of so-called female beauty that is doing an inconceivable amount of spiritual mischief at the present day. If our fairer sex could only see one degree further than the limits of a depraved, artificial fashion they would soon realize that small waists, pinched up with corsets, make them look more like wasps than intelligent human beings, and that small, pinched feet, with their cramped, ill-formed toes are as much of a real deformity as a shrivelled hand or crooked back, the only difference being, that the latter are apparent to the external eye, and the former concealed by dress and a pair of dainty shoes. Upon the plane of reality, our true selves, the deformity is there and is as much the result of ignorant superstition as the maimed limbs of Hindoo fanatics who place themselves beneath the wheels of the car of Jagannatha. Therefore, let us impress upon each student the absolute necessity of perfect freedom in dress. Remember that a cramped waist means an almost useless solar plexus, and a useless solar plexus means spiritual incapacity; spiritual incapacity means bondage to the forces of Nature, and this slavery means becoming the helpless medium of Nature, upon which the discordant rays of the planetary forces can act and re-act uncontrolled. It is for this latter reason alone that this apparent digression has been made; because the greatest value of astrological science consists in controlling the stellar powers, or rather, let us say, evading their malefic influences. A few more words upon this important subject, and then we are done with it, for "verbum sat Sapienti." The physician, the priest, and the scientist are equally loud in their assertions that they are perfectly unbiased and open to reason; and they are equally prejudiced and dogmatic should any one be so foolish as to accept their invitation, and attempt to reason with them. We are sorry to say that the fair sex are somewhat similar in regard to their tight lacing. They will, almost without exception, assert that they, individually, do not pinch themselves, but they will readily admit that others do. It is really surprising how blindly foolish we can be when we ourselves are concerned. They little dream that the constant use of corsets retards their natural development, and, though they may have become used to them so that they do not hurt, but on the contrary feel comfortable; yet in real truth they are held in a grip of iron, and are magnetically ruined. One glance at the form around the solar plexus of a female who wears corsets, and one who has never worn them, ought to convince the most sceptical.

When we regard the astral structure of man and closely examine his magnetic organism, we see that he forms a beautiful oval or egg shaped figure; the narrow end being the feet, the broad end being the brain. This oval form constitutes the magnetic atmosphere, or, in other words, the odylic sphere of the person, and consists of seven concentric rays of force, each of which has a direct affinity with the seven creative principles of Nature, and therefore, corresponds in color to the seven prismatic rays of the solar spectrum. Each zone or ring exercises a peculiar power of its own, and is pure or impure, according to its state of luminosity. When mediumistic clairvoyants assert that such and such a particular color denotes a pure and benevolent person, or one who is depraved and sinful, they assert that which is untrue, for each color has a special purity of its own; purity and impurity depending entirely upon the brightness of its tint. For this reason the animal passions, when exercised, dull and becloud the soul sphere, while the exercise of the spiritual faculties illuminate. To better understand these facts, see Fig. II. The brain center is represented by a sun, the feet by a crescent moon, and the three secondary centers of force by stars. The ingenious student can easily make this figure complete by mentally inserting within the oval odylic sphere, the seven prismatic color rings.

From these seven colors are formed every conceivable shade and tint in the infinite variety of combinations, found in the infinite variety of human beings; each and all depending upon the ever changing positions of the stars, and also upon the corresponding magnetic states of our atmosphere at their respective moments of birth. The color and magnetic polarity of this odylic sphere are fixed, quick as lightning's flash, at the first moment of our separate material existence. This true moment is, generally, when the umbilical cord is severed, and the child exists as a separate being, independent of its mother. Until that time the body is polarized by the soul force of its parent, and the planets can only influence it by reflex action from the mother's organism. But when the tie is severed, the lungs become inflated with the magnetic atmosphere, charged with the stellar influx, and in an instant the whole organism thrills with the vibrations of celestial power. These vibrations produce, in each of the concentric rings of the sphere, the exact tint and shade of color corresponding to the harmonious or discordant rays of the heavens at the time.

These vibrations, once in action, retain their special polarity for the whole tenor of earthly existence. They form the key note of the musical instrument which is ever sounding forth the harmony or discord of its material destiny. This key note is either high or low according to the particular influences which may be operating upon it at the time. At one time the life forces may be so low that the note will be too faint for the most sensitive clairaudient to detect; at other times the throbbing pulsations of life will be so strong with physical vitality that it will swell into the highest octave, and launch forth such potent health giving vibrations as to affect other bodies near it, and draw therefrom responsive vibrations, thus giving life and health to others, in harmony with but weaker than itself. But, should the bodies with which it comes in contact be naturally antagonistic to it, in temperament and magnetic polarity, then, instead of responsive harmony, their contact will produce fierce jarring commotions of discord to the detriment of both, the weaker being the greater sufferer.

The action and inter-action of planetary influx upon the human being after birth is determined upon the same lines. When a planet, by its progressive motion reaches a point on the sphere where it forms an inharmonious angle with the angular vibrations set in motion at birth, magnetic discord is produced. This magnetic storm, so to say, awakens and sets in motion the cosmic and other elementals corresponding in their nature to the primary cause, and external misfortune and trouble are the material results; and vice versa, should the planets form benefic rays, etc. This is the true secret of planetary influence so far as what is termed good and bad luck. It is magnetic harmony or discord.

From the above, the student will see what a fearful mistake so called "Christian Scientists" and metaphysical healers make, unless they truly understand the Occult principles of Nature. It is utterly impossible for antagonistic natures to benefit each other mentally, no matter how good or pure they, as individuals, may be. To attempt to do this is like trying to make oil and water harmonize; this is the true secret of the mental healer's lack of success with certain individuals.

For example, any person born under and controlled by the Martial electricity, which corresponds to the element of fire, will prove antagonistic ·by nature to anybody and everybody who is governed by the Saturine principle. They will not blend and mingle. The most gentle and loving spirit that it is possible for the healer to exercise under such circumstances will recoil from the odylic sphere of the other like a thunderbolt, and the mental physician will feel this recoil and want of success, right in the center of the solar plexus. The science of the stars alone contains the real secrets of the healing art divine.

CHAPTER II

THE SOLAR FORCE

"And the Lord set a mark upon Cain
lest anyone finding him should kill him."
Genesis, Chap. IV

At this stage it is necessary to explain several matters of great importance in forming a true conception of astral law. The reader must not suppose that the planets are the primary causes of the fortunes and misfortunes which fall to the lot of mankind generally. This is by no means the case; for the primary cause has its origin within the soul sphere of our parents. The sexual relationship between man and woman has its laws, its harmonies and discords. It is man's duty to investigate, learn these laws, and follow them, especially so when we bear in mind the fact that there is neither morality nor sentiment in the cold inflexible justice of Nature. "Unto every violation of the law there is meted out a penalty." If the attributes of a thief are conceived, a thief will ultimately be born into the world. It matters not what the circumstances or position in life may be, that individual so conceived will be a thief in his heart, and will commit thefts upon some plane or other. Remember, there is no real difference, except in magnitude, between the man who legally by some commercial sharp practice steals a railroad; and the one who, to support his position in life and before the world, lives above his income to the detriment of his creditors; or the poor devil who, under the influence of criminal temptations, robs a bank or steals your watch. All three, when viewed in their true light, are natural born thieves, and each equally deserving, if justice were impartial, of the same term of penance in the house of correction. The false glamor and artificial conventionalities of modern society, however, praise and bow down in adoration to the gifted railroad thief; they pity and condole as unfortunate the man who, by living above his honest income, terminates his career in bankruptcy; but they, with neither pity nor mercy, hurry off to the jail and the treadmill the poor wretch who steals a watch or robs a bank of a few paltry dollars, when, as a rule, it is this one who is most deserving of our sympathy. Ignorance and a neglected childhood may have intensified the evil influences of his conception and birth to an inconceivable extent, and he might, if the world would only let him, become a better and wiser man. It is equally in accordance with the same immutable laws that every species of crime is born into the world. When inflamed passions and cruel thoughts are latent within us, and remain uncontrolled by the higher self during the conjugal union, we must not be surprised if a child with a similar nature is conceived. When such is the case, there is no benevolent God to graciously interfere and prevent a criminal from being launched upon society.

Man has the privilege and possesses the possibilities of choosing the good, and preventing the conception of evil. Therefore if he, either from choice or ignorance, prefers to risk all the natural consequences, Mother Nature, who is no respecter of persons, will write murderer across the brow of the unborn infant in characters as indelible as the mark she inflicted upon Cain.

When the embryonic potentialities of a human soul are launched forth into the matrix they remain there, slowly evolving their organic powers, and are imprisoned within the womb until their magnetic as well as their physical, period of gestation is completed. Nor is it possible for a child to be born and live until the astral influx corresponds exactly to the external polarity of the soul. Only when the heavens are harmonious can that which we term good become manifest upon the earth. Under the opposite condition of the heavens, evil, so called by comparison, becomes externalized.

From the foregoing it will be seen that we are, to a very great extent, what the ignorance or wisdom of our ancestors have made us. As the world progresses, mankind obtains more knowledge. Thus do the rising generations become wiser than their parents. This mental evolution moves forward until the intellectuality of the race becomes exhausted; then, for a time, mankind remains stationary, and at length declines from the summit of its genius to relapse into an ignorant barbarism; when, having regained a supply of latent mental force, the race once more advances, ultimately, to attain unto a still greater perfection than before. Thus do intellectual forces correspond in their apparent motion to the motions of the planets, becoming alternately direct, swift, stationary and retrograde. Men, like planets, have their times of germination, growth, maturity and decay, and races are no exception to this universal law of change. They move in greater cycles only. Their climax of civilization corresponds to the flowering season of the vegetable kingdom; then they run to seed and decay. But in the same racial soil is treasured up the precious seed from the flowers, which, lying dormant, awaits the necessary magnetic and spiritual conditions for its glorious unfoldment.

The stars and planets are the magnetic instruments of the seven creative principles. They influence externally, by their attractive sympathies and repulsive antipathies, the cosmic life forces and physical organisms of precisely the same objects, which, in the realm of spirit, are controlled by their celestial progenitors. By this we mean that the various physical orbs, called planets, stars, etc., act as so many magnetic centers. They are magnetic by solar induction. The sun, itself, is not magnetic, but positively electric. This mighty electric force acts upon the planets precisely the same as an electric current acts upon a piece of soft iron. When a piece of iron is charged with electricity it becomes at once a magnet, its power depending first upon its mass and secondly upon the strength or intensity of the electric current. Shut off the current and the iron ceases to be a magnet. Remove the sun from our system and the planets will immediately lose their peculiar physical influence. Modern science, we know, would contradict this assertion, but Occult science proclaims it to be an absolute fact.

The sum total of those powers which we term "planetary influences," is contained within the potentiality of the Solar Ray. But when so united, as a primal cosmic force, the action of this solar ray upon the human organism and its material destiny is neither harmonious nor discordant, fortunate nor unfortunate. To become potent, in special directions, it is necessary for this solar force to become refracted and resolved into its active attributes. This is precisely what the major planets do. There are six planets, each of which absorbs a single attribute or principle; each one according to its peculiar nature and absorbing affinity. While the solar orb itself retains but one active energy whose potency is embraced within the orange ray of the spectrum. This influence, of course, relates only to the special action of the seven active principles, and does not refer to the solar light reflected by each body, and emitted by the sun itself. Five planets, besides the sun and moon (our earth), absorb the seven rays. The other planets react upon higher planes. That is to say, they radiate one of the same forces upon a higher octave. Each of the planetary bodies, having become magnetically charged with their own special energy, are powerful radiators of the same attribute which they have received from their solar parent. These energies possess a distinctive motion, color and potency, each peculiar to itself, which, when externalized upon man's internal nature, produce a marked contrast in his mental and physical characteristics, briefly, as follows.

THE PLANET SATURN ♄

Saturn absorbs that attribute or energy whose action expresses itself as coldness, and thus produces a nature which is slow and meditative, solitary and reserved, melancholy and repentant. This force corresponds to the blue ray of the spectrum.

THE PLANET JUPITER ♃

Jupiter absorbs a totally different energy than the Saturnine and radiates an influence at once jovial. A happy medium between the fast and the slow, the meditative and the thoughtless, the isolated hermit and the one too easy of access. The influence is cheerful, generous, benevolent, and sheds light and love upon all material surroundings. This force corresponds to the purple or indigo ray of the spectrum.

THE PLANET MARS ♂

Mars absorbs an energy which is the polar opposite of the Saturnine, and therefore radiates an influence which is sharp, energetic, thoughtless, intrepid and fierce. It is destitute of either fear or timidity. An influence which is free with everything and everybody. Briefly stated, the force of the planet Mars is fiery, imperious, combative in the first degree, bloodthirsty and unrelenting. This energy corresponds to the red ray of the spectrum.

THE SUN ☉

The Sun retains and radiates the principle which is at once life-giving and dignified. Just as Jupiter is a compound or happy medium between the energies exerted by Saturn and Mars, so the Sun sends forth an influence which is the happy medium between Jupiter and Mars. It is affable but majestic; proud, but gracious; and blends firmness with kindness, ambition with paternal consideration, combativeness with self-respect, and liberality with discretion. As before stated, this influence corresponds to the orange ray of the spectrum.

THE PLANET VENUS ♀

Venus absorbs an energy which is totally different from any of the preceding, and radiates "the love element" of Nature. This influence is warm and impulsive interiorly, but externally cool and moist, consequently pliable and receptive, clinging and feminine. It is the energy which ever yields to a nature more positive than its own with loving submission; hence the myths of the friendships between Mars and Venus. This energy corresponds to the yellow ray.

THE PLANET MERCURY ☿

Mercury absorbs an energy which, in a general sense, appears to be a compound of all the other planets of the spectrum put together; hence he has been well designated as "the messenger of the gods." The specific action which this orb radiates is purely intellectual and scientific. It is quick and active, intuitional, enterprising, careless, volatile, bright, changeable, and what we call smart. This influence is extremely inventive, and is the originator of all cunning schemes and devices. It is what men term bright and witty. It is that which makes the live man of commerce, and constitutes the leading influence embodied within that sharp, clever and chamelion-like individual who makes a fortune in the real estate business. This energy corresponds to the violet ray of the solar spectrum.

THE MOON ☽

The planet upon which we live, move, and have our being, absorbs an energy which we, as inhabitants, cannot by nature fully understand or appreciate, because we only receive this energy as an astral influx by the reflective action of our Earth's satellite, the Moon. This influence, so far as we, the planet's offspring, are concerned, is neither good nor evil; because it is part and parcel of ourselves. What the influence may be upon the inhabitants of other worlds we cannot say. Therefore, when speaking astrologically, we credit the Moon's reflective power and speak of that body as containing our Earth's attribute of the solar ray. This energy corresponds to the green ray of the solar spectrum.

The foregoing are the seven active principles of Nature, but the ingenious students will notice that two of the major planets have not so far been noticed; we refer of course to Uranus (♅) and Neptune (♆), each of which radiate one of the same forces upon a higher octave. Each of the seven principles enumerated have three planes of action; the spiritual, the astral and the physical. After the seven notes of the magnetic gamut have been sounded, the next note must be upon a higher octave and form a repetition of the first. The first scale being known and its effects understood, it is not necessary for the Occult initiate of these astral powers to wait, for the years of observation necessary to others, in order to tabulate a newly discovered planet. By the laws of correspondences he know at once what that planet's action upon the human organism will be. There is still another planet, more remote from our sun than Neptune, but its action on our organism at present is nil; because the present races have not yet attained to that special state of spiritual and mental development that will admit of its influence becoming manifest. Neither will such a planet become visible to this Earth's inhabitants until there is sufficient mental force of the requisite grade to enable its existence to become apparent.

Such are the sublime facts of Nature's immutable law, that have made the science of astrology true for all time and in all ages. When Uranus and Neptune were shining in their distant heavens undiscovered, mankind was, as a body, impervious to their action. Man's organism did not vibrate in unison with their higher state of action. Thus we see, as man evolves higher powers, more ethereal orbs appear in the celestial hierarchies of the starry heavens for the purpose of controlling and directing him.

The action and inter-action of the planetary influences operate in the following order;—Saturn (♄), Jupiter (♃), Mars (♂), Sun (☉), Earth (⊕), Venus (♀), and Mercury (☿). These are the seven primaries. Then comes Uranus (♅), forming the eighth, or octave expression of the first, or Mercury, and thus do we find, after long years of research and laborious investigation, that this planet rules the higher organs of the brain. Neptune, consequently, represents Venus upon a higher plane. The Earth, whose influence is shown by the Moon, comes next in rotation. When the tenth planet is discovered, its action upon our Earth's inhabitants will be neutral in itself. Its harmonies and discords will depend upon its angular position in respect to the other bodies. Its chief influence will be in the control of our spiritual life forces. Its position, aspect, etc., with respect to the luminaries, will determine our capacity for inhaling the finer ethereal essences of the atmosphere. From this it will be perceived that the influence of the tenth planet will be wholly spiritual; hence, it can only exert its influence upon the spiritual organisms of a more spiritual race.

This chapter contains a brief outline, so to speak, of the interior action of the planets. We shall deal with each orb more fully and in detail from their general standpoint in future lessons, and as a concluding suggestion we would ask the student to think and reason out very closely what we have herein stated by the light of the law of correspondence, the sum and substance of which was formulated for our use by the thrice illumined Hermes Trismegistus, who said:

"As it is above, so it is below,
As on the earth, so in the sky."

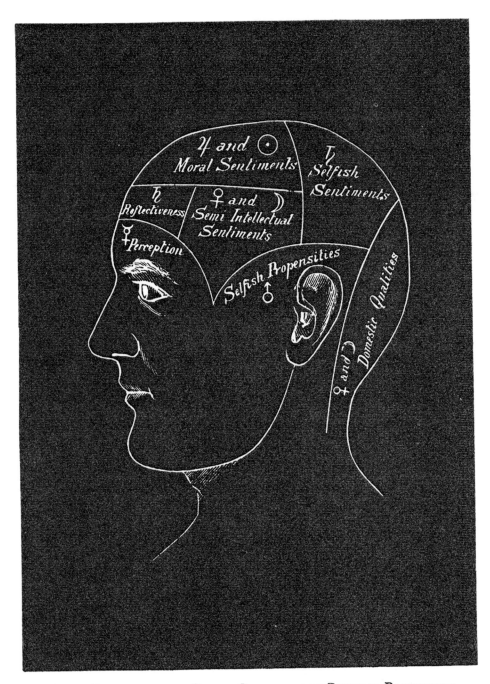

ASTRO-PHRENOLOGICAL CHART, SHOWING THE GENERAL PLANETARY
INFLUENCE UPON THE HUMAN BRAIN.

CHAPTER III

Having briefly explained, in the previous chapter, the origin, nature and power of planetary influence, so far as the planets themselves are concerned, it now becomes our duty to illustrate, somewhat, the principles laid down, and point out the laws or modus operandi by which these influences act and react upon the brain of man, and through the brain, control the whole organism. In order to do this we shall have to digress a little.

Phrenological research has now established beyond dispute certain broad general principles regarding cranial development. But, the great mistake which the devotees of this branch of Anthropology make, is that they allow their enthusiasm to carry them beyond the safe line of demonstrated facts. They are constantly trying to prove that, by the aid of phrenology, they can ascertain the details of man's character; whereas, the very utmost that can be expected as scientifically accurate, is a delineation of the general characteristics.

Phrenology merely points out those relations established by Nature between given developments and conditions of the brain, and corresponding manifestations of mind. Its simple but comprehensive tenet is this: "Every faculty of the mind is manifested by means of a particular portion of the brain, called its organ; the size of which, other things being equal, is proportionate to its power of function." It is the latter portion of this definition that contains the whole mystery of the apparent contradictions with which the phrenologist has to deal. The "other things" are never, in any two cases, equal; hence, the exact action of the brain organs cannot be scientifically demonstrated. As soon as phrenology attempts to define with exactness a person's true character or the powers of the cranial organs, from a simple knowledge of the size of these organs, it becomes a complete failure. The potency, or otherwise, of any organ or group of organs, depends not nearly so much upon their relative size as upon their sensitiveness, or, in other words, upon the state of their etherealization; and this magnetic condition depends solely upon the position and power of that planet which has chief rule over those particular organs. Decisive proof of this assertion, as regards the size of the organs, may be obtained by each student for himself, by carefully noting the heads of individuals. Even among our own personal acquaintances we shall find that it is not an absolute fact that those who possess the largest heads have the most brains, but often the very reverse. In fact, we shall find that the majority of men distinguished in science, politics and literature are those who possess comparatively small but well balanced heads, combined with a fine, highly sensitive organism, while the ordinary citizen or farmer, who is utterly incapable of forming any opinion worth listening to beyond the value of his whiskey, his hogs or his cattle, is possessed of a large head filled, not with intellectual brains, but with coarse animalized "brain stuff" which is utterly incapable of manifesting its powers upon the higher mental planes of our nature.

The old and now much abused Chaldean sages were thoroughly acquainted with these facts, and in order to teach these principles to their youth, they elaborated beautiful imagery in the form of fables and allegories. They gave the nature and power of each group of organs in the human brain to the character of that planet which they knew controlled its activities, and then worked out the facts, so elaborated, into a series of mythical histories of gods and divine personages, who incarnated themselves for the benefit of man. Thus Mars took the character of Vulcan, the god of war; Venus and her innocent companion Cupid were assigned the character of Love and the sympathetic tendencies of the human heart, while the benevolent Jupiter assumed the position of Father, the kindly, generous parent, good alike to all his offspring, and so on with the others.

From this, the student will perceive that when they taught their children that their gods had existed in human bodies, they did not mean to convey the idea of Divine incarnation as we understand the doctrine, but that a portion of the divinity, a refracted ray, had become centered in man, and expressed itself in some special form; thus, a great warrior who brought honor and riches to his tribe or country, through his brilliant victories, was properly considered a son of Mars, because his nature expressed the Martial spirit in what was considered its highest and most potent form. A key to this beautiful Chaldean system will be found in the Astro Phrenological Chart on page 218 of this chapter. The seven principles therein shown are, of course, only general, and indicate those groups of organs over which the planets indicated are most powerful. To descend more into details:

THE PLANET SATURN ♄

Saturn governs the activities of the reflective, meditative and the purely selfish sentiments, such as comparison, causality, covetousness, acquisitiveness and secrecy.

THE PLANET JUPITER ♃

Jupiter governs those activities which, in their expression, show to us the truly noble and generous side of human nature, such as benevolence, veneration, spirituality and hope.

THE PLANET MARS ♂

Mars has chief rule of those activities which generally express themselves as selfishly aggressive. Properly, they are the passions which reveal to us the animal which resides in an active or semi-passive state, within each human soul, upon the material plane of external life. They are known as alimentiveness, destructiveness, combativeness, and the sexual propensities. To these may be added vitativeness and construction.

THE SUN ☉

The Sun has the chief control of those organs whose activities express themselves in man's higher nature as the "Lord" of material creation. They comprise the commanding and dignified elements within us, such as firmness, conscientiousness, pride, approbativeness, and self-esteem.

THE PLANET VENUS ♀

Venus governs those faculties whose activities express themselves as friendship, mirthfulness and conjugality. It also governs the organs of inhabitiveness and those which tend to form agreeable society.

THE PLANET MERCURY ☿

Mercury, in addition to being the general messenger of the gods, rules those faculties whose activities are purely intellectual and mechanical, such as eventuality, individuality, size, form, weight, color, order, calculation and language.

THE MOON)

The Moon governs those organs whose activities are termed the semi-intellectual qualities. They are very desirable expressions of character, viz.: time, tune, ideality and sublimity. She has also influence over the domestic qualities.

Each of the foregoing groups of organs is, to a very great extent controlled by the planet under which it is mentioned, but not wholly so, because every orb has an influence in a minor degree over each and all. But generally speaking, each group will manifest an intense or sluggish action in the brain, according as its controlling orb is powerful or otherwise, in the individual's horoscope at birth, with this difference in its action: if the planet in question be powerful but evilly aspected, then those organs will express the vicious side of the person's nature. For example, the planet Mercury so situated, the intellect will be bright, witty and powerful, but all the energies, under proper conditions, will be devoted to fraud, or at any rate, to very questionable purposes; everything depending upon the plane that the person occupies. As before stated, there is no difference between the criminal who breaks the legal code of laws, and the one who, upon a higher plane, obeys the written letter of the law, but tramples upon the true principles of human justice. The wealthy gambler upon the stock exchange, is no better in reality than the gambling card sharper. But, if the planet is dignified and aspected by benefic rays, then the whole of the above will be reversed, and all that is noble, honorable and manly will be the result.

Having mentioned aspects, it now becomes our duty, briefly, to explain their nature. This we shall do in outline, at present, deferring all details until later.

From what we have already stated, our student will perceive that sympathy and antipathy are the great laws by which the planets affect the human organism. These two forces, or rather let us say the dual action of this one force, constitutes the two modes of motion by which every cosmic principle expresses itself, and the two actions, that is, the action and the reaction, are true polar opposites, of which sufficient has already been stated. Upon the physical plane their effects are correlated as harmony and discord.

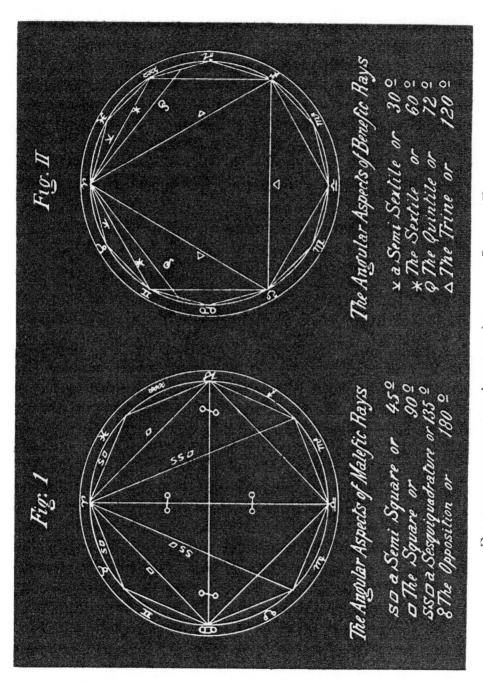

DIAGRAMS SHOWING THE ANGULAR ASPECTS OF STELLAR FORCES.

That nothing, apart from Deity, which has a manifested existence, can exist without form, is a self evident fact, which scarcely requires proof. Therefore, the powers of harmony and discord possess forms which are peculiar to themselves. These forms in Astrological science are angular, and are denominated aspects. The more perfect or complete the angle is, the greater the power its influence exerts upon matter. The symbol of discord is a square, and every inharmonious angular ray constitutes a portion of the square or the angle of 90 degrees. The symbol of harmony is a triangle, and every benefic angular ray constitutes a portion of the trine or angle of 120 degrees; thus we have a geometric expression of evil and good, as shown below.

The student will observe that the discordant rays of magnetic force strike each other crossways from opposing angles, thus +. This conflict produces a violent commotion. There is a fight, as it were, in the current between two powers, while the contrary result is produced in the action of the benfic rays of magnetic force. They impinge upon each other, thus, Y, like the two forks of a river, and then, with their united force flow onward harmoniously. The whole of these angular aspects are illustrated in the diagrams on the adjoining page. Explanation is unnecessary, except that each aspect can be formed from any point of the celestial zodiac, both direct and converse.

We see, therefore, that when the combinations of stellar force flow in straight lines and cut through each other from cross angles, the resultant upon the physical plane is that state which we term discordant and evil. But, when the rays of force flow in straight but convergent angles from or towards each other, then the opposite effects are naturally produced, and harmony, love and prosperity reign.

The student cannot pay too much attention to these Occult facts of Nature's law, because they are true upon every plane of manifested existence.

CHAPTER IV

INTER-ACTION OF THE STARS

The next great subject which requires the student's thoughtful attention is the four Triplicities. These trigons correspond to the four ancient elements, and are therefore, Fiery, Earthy, Airy and Watery. Each triplicity or "Trigon" contains three zodiacal signs, 4 times 3 equals 12, the number of the signs of the sphere. The Fiery trigon embraces the signs of Aries (♈), Leo (♌), and Sagittarius (♐). The Earthy trigon embraces the signs Taurus (♉), Virgo (♍), and Capricorn (♑). The Airy trigon embraces the signs Gemini (♊), Libra (♎), and Aquarius (♒). The Watery trigon embraces the signs Cancer (♋), Scorpio (♏), and Pisces (♓), also see page 399, Wilson's Dictionary of Astrology.

In practical astrology these triplicities are of very great importance, as they shed their potent influence upon the ascendant at the birth of every living being or thing, and impress their peculiar nature upon the temperament of the native. The philosophical principles concealed beneath these so-called ancient elements, are worthy of a far more detailed elucidation than the space of this chapter will admit.

Probably one of the greatest mistakes made by the modern uninitiated astrologer in regard to the actual influence of these triplicities, is that they omit to take into consideration the ascent and descent of the spiritual etherealization of material forces.

Magnetic and electric forces vary in their spirituality like everything else in the universe. That which is superior, by virtue of its higher or more interior emanation, will demonstrate its superiority upon every plane of its manifestation. For example; Aries (♈) is the first and highest representative of the fiery trigon, and those born with this sign rising upon the ascendant of their horoscope will always move upon a higher plane, mentally and spiritually, than those born under Leo or Sagittarius. But, externally, those people born under Aries will show their superiority from a purely intellectual point of view. Their nature will be, chiefly, fiery and mental, consequently quick in action, and prompt in decision.

Leo (♌), the next to Aries, is the second representative of the fiery trigon, and persons born with this sign rising, will always move upon the sensitive and emotional planes. Their nature will be chiefly fiery and sensitive, consequently, hasty and impulsive. They will act without thinking, on the spur of the moment, when under the dominating influence of their susceptible, emotional natures. In this, we see the difference between Aries, which rules the head, and Leo, which represents the heart. Leo persons, when roused to a pitch of passional fury, are absolutely insane in their wild and erratic actions. Like the lion, they are completely blinded by an intense degree of excitement. On the contrary, an Aries person, though susceptible of an equal degree of furious temper, never becomes blind with excitement. Even in his most outrageous conduct, an impartial observer will not fail to see that "there is method in his madness."

Sagittarius is the last and lowest, that is to say, the most external emanation of the fiery triplicity, and illustrates the law of contradictions to perfection. For this reason, those born under this sign live and move, when mentally and spiritually considered, upon the lowest plane of the fiery emanation. Whereas externally and in the eyes of the world, they seem to move in the very highest. Their natures are warm, sympathetic and active, consequently they are generous and benevolent, ambitious and truly jovial. They do as the world does; they progress not of their own internal volition, but by the gentle attraction of the social tide of their surroundings. In everything they are external. They are great admirers of all out-door sports, recreations and pastimes, and as such, they are totally incapable of grasping any form of the higher mental and metaphysical studies. They are, therefore, considered by the masses and the world sound, logical, reasoners, and possessed of sound common sense, and externally they do indeed possess all these desirable qualities.

When viewed from their line of descent, the student will perceive, that in Aries we have the fiery imperial brain, which moulds, guides and acts for itself, independent of the opinions of others. Such extreme natures, when unmodified by other influences, are either despots, cranks or fanatics, according to their bent and station in life. In Leo, we see the emotions and sensitive feelings of the heart, which follow, impulsively, the lead of some mental genius, and form the enthusiastic followers and admirers of those who depart from the beaten path of custom, or proclaim some new truth or system of philosophy, which finds a responsive throb within them. But, they require the thinking brain to direct them; they cannot strike out upon a new path for themselves; they must have some giant mind to support them. In Sagittarius, we see the genial, sympathetic, courteous, neutrality which represents the externally true gentleman. Those who are simply waiting to be led in any direction that the strongest mental force desires to carry them. They love the world and its varied delights, and are, consequently, contented and willing to let others do the thinking for them.

The whole of these remarks are to be considered in a general sense only, and in speaking of any given sign it is, of course, presupposed that the position and aspect of the sun, moon, and planets do not contradict the general tendencies of the sign upon the ascendant. Further, what we have thus far stated in reference to the fiery trigon will also apply to the other triplicities. It is, therefore, quite unnecessary to go over the same ground with each trigon, as the above illustration will suffice to explain the varying powers of each sign, according to the peculiar plane of its manifestation, as Earthy, Airy and Watery. The student has only to bear in mind, when forming his opinion, that his premises and his conclusions must occupy the same plane. Thus, the fiery trigon manifests itself in the combative, aggressive, imperious, commanding and courageous planes of action. The earthy trigon manifests itself in the patient, laborious, plodding, obedient and inert planes of action. The airy trigon manifests itself in the aspiring, philosophical, musical, artistic and volatile planes of action. The watery trigon manifests itself in the dreamy, romantic, changeable, timid and submissive planes of action.

As before stated, the student must understand that these remarks are general and not particular in their application; for instance, we do not mean to assert that because a person is born under a watery sign rising upon the ascendant, that, that person will be dreamy and romantic, or impractical and submissive. This will depend entirely upon the actual position of the planets and their aspects to the sun and moon at the time of birth. But what we do mean to assert is this; that the person then born will possess, deep down and latent, the qualities of the watery trigon, and that under proper conditions and circumstances, it will rise dominantly to the surface and thus manifest the true internal characteristics of the person's nature, while the same conditions and circumstances brought to bear upon one born under the fiery trigon would operate in exactly the reverse direction. Thus we see how and why two different individuals, under the same identical conditions, will differ diametrically in their course of action. Every day adds fresh proof of this.

We must now turn our attention to the purely esoteric aspect of the four triplicities, and view them from their Hermetic and Occult standpoint. The four ancient elements; Azoth, Salt, Sulphur, and Mercury, have been symbolized from time immemorial, as The Man, The Bull, The Lion, and The Eagle. Astrologically these are; Aquarius (♒) "the water bearer," symbolical of The Man; Taurus (♉) the sign of The Bull; Leo (♌) represented by The Lion; and lastly Scorpio (♏) anciently symbolized by The Eagle. In this change of symbols the thoughtful student will find much that is well worthy of his careful consideration, for "hereby hangs a tale." In the esoteric planisphere of the twelve signs, Adam Kadmon, the primordial man, pure, and in perfect accord with the Father, occupied that point of the planisphere now designated by the sign Libra (♎), which signifies the point of equilibrium in the sphere. This esoteric point is where day and night, winter and summer, light and darkness, good and evil are one. Adam Kadmon represents the ideal man, and the very fact that we can form an ideal conception is the absolute proof that we possess the possibilities of attaining unto the ideal and realizing our conception, not perhaps upon this plane, but certainly, when we are translated to the higher. The modern English name for this point of the sphere, "The Balance," which means justice, is a fitting one, as Justice is that which discriminates, upon the external plane, between good and evil, and metes out rewards and punishments. Life, Light and Truth are the same, and consist of spiritual reflection. They are spiritual rays, and when these rays become refracted by passing through the prism of matter, Truth becomes illusion, Life becomes limited by assuming the appearance of death, and Light becomes obscured. This thought is clearly expressed by S. S. Grimke in her book Esoteric Lessons, under the subject "First Lessons in Reality." The spiritually beautiful and eternally true, have no existence in this world where all is change, strife, discord and death, therefore, we see that the divine spiritual ray of good, when it becomes refracted, presents all the forms and colors of evil, the former only, is real and eternal, and the latter is but an appearance, assumed by the fleeting transformations of matter.

This celestial point in Libra is represented by Enoch, in the mysteries of the Jewish Temple, the man who walked with God "and was not." This theological idea was plagiarized by the early fathers of the Christian Church, when they elaborated their Christian mysteries. They make Libra symbolical of their day of judgment, when celestial "justice" will be meted out to all, "both the quick and the dead." This is the point of the planisphere occupied by their divine man. The Cabalistical Adam Kadmon, the Enoch of Judaism, becomes the Emmanuel of the new dispensation. Jesus is the sacrifice required by the divine justice of God's anger (?) for the awful errors of a sinful world of His own creation and management. And Judas, who as a disciple of the son of God, was able to soar heavenward upon the wings of an Eagle (the inward aspirations) falls into temptation, and betrays his master into the hands of his murderers. Thence comes the fall, the divine Eagle of the celestial heavens, becomes the lowly reptile, the treacherous, poisonous scorpion, whose sting is concealed in the most unsuspected part of the body, viz., the tail.

The above will be found useful in the Esoteric translation of signs into principles. The fall, from the Eagle of the heavens to the scorpion of the desert, also applies to the theological fall of man, and scientifically explains the Biblical allegory of Adam and Eve. When the mystic key of the starry heavens is turned with a wise hand, the garden of Eden is no longer an impossible place, but is a divine reality, and the four rivers which, we are told, branch from one head, which rises in the midst of the garden, can all be located and their virtues known.

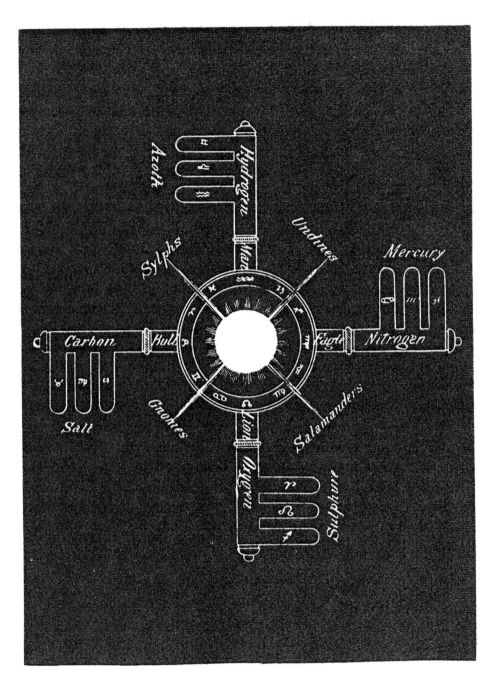

THE GRAND ASTROLOGICAL KEY OF ALCHEMICAL SCIENCE.

CHAPTER V

ALCHEMY, THE STARS AND MAN

By Nature the Zodiac is divided into equal arcs of Light and Darkness, Summer and Winter; which in the technical terms of the science are termed the northern and the southern signs. When the Earth, in her annual orbit round the sun, enters the sign Libra, about the 21st. of March, the sun appears to enter the first degree of Aries, which is called the vernal equinox, and following the opposition point of our earth's journey through space, our sun apparently moves forward through the signs until (about the 21st. of June) the first point of the tropical sign Cancer is reached, and the greatest noonday altitude is attained in the northern hemisphere, and the lowest in the southern hemisphere. On or about the 21st. of September, the sun appears to enter the first degree of Libra, which completes the solar passage through the six northern signs, and the arc of light is over. The following six signs, Libra, Scorpio, Sagittarius, Capricorn, Aquarius and Pisces, constitute the southern arc, termed the arc of darkness. Our chief reason for drawing the student's attention to this preculiar division of the zodiac is, that, it is this division that forms the ground work upon which is based every theological system the world has ever seen. Further, it is the division still observed in all standard works upon Astrological science. But, so far as the real and practical application of the science is concerned, such a division is perfectly unmeaning, and students are advised to pay no attention thereto. The only division the zodiac receives in Chaldean astrology (except the four triplicities) is that which takes into consideration the increase and decrease of the life forces, of the great cosmic life center of all animated nature, viz., the Sun. The zodiac is, therefore, divided into two parts, viz., from Capricorn to Cancer. When the sun crosses the line of the winter solstice, about the 21st. of December, the life forces of the northern hemisphere are at the lowest ebb. It is at this point that God gives the nations the promise of future deliverance. All the crucified saviors the world over were born about the 25th. of December. In those temperate latitudes where snow and ice are unknown, winter is the rainy season, and the people have their bow of promise in the heavens that God will not entirely destroy the world with water.

From the time of the winter solstice the days increase in length, in the northern hemisphere; the sluggish life forces of matter begin to expand; and all things increase in vitality until the 21st. of June; when Sol enters the sign Cancer. This is the highest point of declination north of the equator. It is also the highest point of intensity (in the northern hemisphere) of the cosmic life forces. For a time, these forces remain stationary; then reaction slowly sets in; the trees begin to change their tints, fruits begin to ripen, and the days grow shorter as the Life Wave recedes.

If a complete census of the whole population of the northern hemisphere could be taken, and the actual duration of life, of the people ascertained, we should find a startling contrast between those born from December to June, and those born between July and the end of November. We should find that those who live the longest were born in March, April and May, that is to say, a very great majority would be found to have their natal day in these months. While on the contrary, a majority of the short-lived population would be found to be born during the months of August, September and October. This is only true on general principles, and does not apply to any one individual horoscope; in fact, the remarks in reference to the four triplicities will also apply here. The increase and decrease of the solor light simply governs the vitalizing capacity of the race, and not the individual. Remember this.

Before concluding this general outline of the psychological principles upon which the true astro-masonic science is founded, we must draw the reader's attention to its alchemical aspect, and point out the relation astrology bears to this mystical science of the ancient chemists.

Alchemy is generally supposed to mean the act of transforming the base metal into gold, and as such, it has found more devotees for the prospective wealth which it appeared to offer, than for the spiritual truth it might contain. But like everything else connected with the Occult, "none can obtain the good unless he merits it," and those who obtain the control of any force by evil means must pay a fearful price for it in this world, and a terrible penalty in the next. Therefore, those who do not study the sacred art for its own sake, in search of knowledge, will find nothing but disappointment.

The seven planets represent the seven metals of the ancients. Thus, Saturn is symbolized by lead; Jupiter by tin; Mars by iron; Sol by gold; Venus by copper; Mercury by mercury; and the Moon (Earth) by silver. In this alchemical arrangement we must note the position assignd to the solar orb. It is at least significant.

Saturn, lead		Venus, copper
Jupiter, tin	The Sun,	Mercury, mercury
Mars, iron	Gold	Moon, silver

The precious metal, then, contains the potencies or principles of the other six, consequently, each one of the metals, above enumerated, contains some essential principle that the alchemist requires in the transmuting process; for gold cannot be produced unless the elements of which it is composed are present. Not only must they be present, but they must be mixed in their exact proportion, and then subjected to the purifying resolvent influence of the universal solvent of Nature, "the water of Pythia." This water, we need scarcely add, is the astral light; hence it is, that, each one must make the philosopher's stone for himself; it cannot be bought for dollars and cents; nor monopolized by syndicates, corporations or improvement (?) companies. Some individuals are, from their peculiar organization and temperament, endowed with the power of generating and using the magical forces of the astral light with little or no exertion upon their part, and could, if they only possessed the knowledge, produce phenomenal effects with more ease in three months of training, than others, less magically constituted, could in a lifetime. In fact, there is the same predisposition required to make the successful Occultist as there is in any of the arts and sciences. There is much error in circulation upon this point that requires sweeping away with the brush of truth, especially in regard to Alchemy, which many view in the light of mere chemical formula for gold making. To illustrate this, let us take the art known as music; one person is born who possesses a natural genius for harmony, not only so, but he also has the fine, sensitive touch and mechanical skill to produce harmony; this latter is equally as important as the former. Another is born possessing a natural love for music, but that is all. Now, as long as he lives he will have a great love for music, and be delighted to listen to it, but will never be able to produce the music himself, because he is totally incapable of mastering the details and mechanical fingering, that is so requisite in the skillful musician. Probably the reader is or has been acquainted with many such individuals. It is the same with Occultism. The former represents the natural born magician, the latter the average lover and student of occult science. The former can obtain his knowledge direct from the great storehouse of Nature, the latter only from a long study of the writings of others. But, there is also a third class to be considered in viewing the ranks of the occult, viz., those who occupy a midway plane between the two above noted. It is for this middle class alone that this work was prepared.

The celebrated alchemist, Paracelsus, speaking of the astrological aspects of his science, says in Paragranum I, "If I have manna in my constitution I can attract manna from heaven. Melissa is not only in the garden, but also in the air and in heaven. Saturn is not only in the sky, but also deep in the ocean and earth. What is Venus, but the Artemisia that grows in your garden, and what is iron but the planet Mars;" that is to say, Venus and Artemisia are both products of the same essence, while Mars and iron are manifestations of the same cause. "What is the human body but a constellation (microcosm) of the same powers that formed the stars in the sky? He who knows Mars knows the qualities of iron, and he who knows what iron is, knows the attributes of Mars. What would become of your heart if there were no sun in the universe? What would be the use of your "vasa spermatica" (latent astral germs of subjective life forms) if there were no Venus? To grasp the invisible elements, to attract them by their material correspondences, to control, purify and transmute them by the ever moving powers of the living spirit, this is true alchemy."

The student will not fail to understand the true nature of alchemical science when he compares the above extract from Paracelsus with the previous teachings given in this and other chapters. The man who is dominated by the Martial element and knows it, and then devotes his commercial energies to the realms of Mars, by trading and speculating solely in iron and its products; the Saturnine individual controlled by the earthly trigon, who consciously invests his money, time and abilities in coal mining and trading in lime, clay, bricks and stone: these men, I say, are a long way ahead of those who devote their time and their money to studying and experimenting with the musty old formulas of "Sandivogius," so far as the true alchemy of Nature is concerned, because they have obeyed the commands of true science upon the physical plane. They are using the spiritual and magnetic affinities implanted by Mother Nature within them, to successfully attract to them, their natural correspondences on earth; and then, by the aid of commerce, transforming such base products into the shining yellow gold. Salt, sulphur, mercury and azoth, exist in the human body as well as in the bowels of the earth (the one implies the other), and so does the coveted elixir which resolves all things into their original elements and confers perpetual youth. "He that hath ears to hear, let him hear."

The symbolical diagram at the beginning of this chapter expresses, hieroglyphically, all that the science of alchemy can teach. The twelve signs of the zodiac are divided into their various triplicities, and it will be noticed that each trigon has three planes of manifestation shown by the three wards of the stellar key. These elements are again shown, represented by their chemical equivalents, Carbon, Nitrogen, Oxygen, and Hydrogen; and lastly, the various quadrants represent the realms of elemental life, which live and move and have their being within the four great astral triplicities of the old Chaldean Astrology.

MAN'S ASTRAL ORGANISM.

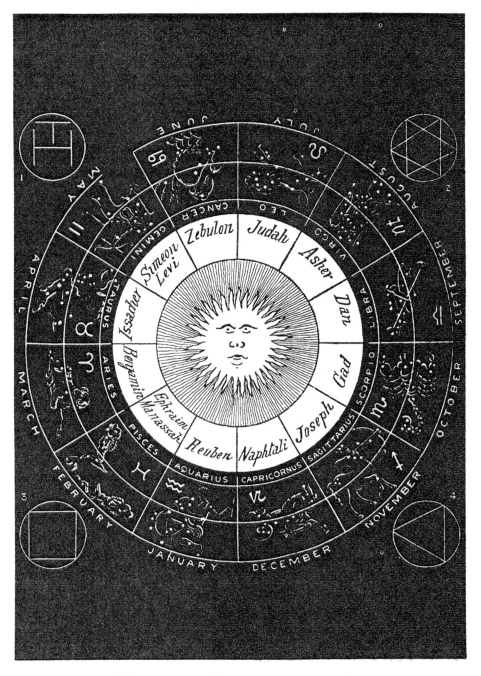

Astro-Kabbalistical Planisphere of the Signs and
Constellations of the Zodiac.

CHAPTER VI

THE NATURE AND INFLUENCE OF THE TWELVE SIGNS

The poet Manilius, so celebrated in the days of Augustus Caesar, in setting forth the astrology of the Romans gives the following beautiful description of the twelve signs and constellations;

> "Now constellations, Muse, and signs rehearse;
> In order let them sparkle in thy verse;
> First Aries, glorious in his golden wool,
> Looks back, and wonders at the mighty Bull,
> Whose hind parts first appear, he bending lies,
> With threatening head, and calls the Twins to rise;
> They clasp for fear, and mutually embrace,
> And next the Twins with an unsteady pace
> Bright Cancer rolls; then Leo shakes his mane
> And following Virgo calms his rage again.
> Then day and night are weighed in Libra's scales,
> Equal awhile, at last the night prevails;
> And longer grown the heavier scale inclines,
> And draws bright Scorpio from the winter signs.
> Him Centaur follows with an aiming eye,
> His bow full drawn and ready to let fly;
> Next narrow horns, the twisted Caper shows,
> And from Aquarius' urn a flood o'er flows.
> Near their lov'd waves cold Pisces takes their seat,
> With Aries join, and make the round complete."

Centaur, the constellation of Jupiter, i.e. Sagittarius.
Narrow-horns, the twisted Caper, refers to Capricorn, the goat.

Everything in Nature, though constituting a trinity in itself, possesses a fourfold application when viewed from the external plane. At least we find this fourfoldness a truth so far as "the things of Earth" are concerned, and therefore, by the laws of correspondences, the same application must hold good in regard to the celestial objects in the heavens. The Hermetic rule is very precise upon this point, viz, "As on the earth, so in the sky." Therefore, we will describe the fourfold aspect of the stars as fully as the limits of the present work will allow. Before attempting this, however, it is perhaps necessary to remind the general reader, that it is well known to students of Occult literature, that behind the external personalities of the twelve sons of Jacob were concealed the various powers of the twelve constellations of the Zodiac. Until quite recently, their correct tabulation has been carefully concealed. In fact, the Kabbalistical and esoteric aspect of the science, what Paracelsus calls the "spiritual astrology," has never yet been committed to writing, except under the dense veil of extremely vague allegorical symbols; because this knowledge formed a portion of "the greater mysteries," and as such, was necessarily confined to the exceptionally favored few. It must in justice be added; that, these favored few thoroughly merited all the knowledge they obtained. Time, however, which regulates all things, very harmoniously, arranges the supply of spiritual truth in exact proportion to the real demand. So that a real, earnest demand having arisen for light upon the spiritual side of Nature, we begin to see the bright rays of truth springing up upon the mental horizon of the western race. The recipients of Occult knowledge, who have been so long waiting in various quarters for the times to become ripe, are now distributing their hoarded treasures, with delighted hands, to the daily increasing number of seekers after truth.

Probably the nearest approach to this spiritual astrology of Paracelsus that has yet been issued from the press, is the remarkable work by H. Melville, entitled "Veritas. A Revelation of the Mysteries", published in London, England.

For the sake of convenience, we shall divide the study of the planets and constellations of the Zodiac into four separate parts, to be designated as Symbolical, Kabbalistical, Intellectual, and Physical. These four planes are entirely separate from each other, and must not be confounded in the student's mind. The Symbolical aspect applies to their purely mystical significance; and the various forms and aspects which they assume in the ingenious imaginations of our early ancestors; who, after viewing the forms and forces of Nature as manifested upon earth, were ever seeking to find their spiritual correspondence "in the sky."

The Kabbalistical aspect applies to their more recondite nature, and to the various occult forces in Nature to which they gave a celestial expression. In this important aspect lies concealed, also, the grand mysteries of the Jewish Temple, the arcane science of the wise King Solomon; and last but not least, the Theosophy of later Judaism, the external form of which is now known as Christianity.

The Intellectual aspect applies solely to the mental plane of humanity, and has reference to the intellectual calibre of the mind. There is often a radical difference between the physical and intellectual natures of the same organism, therefore, the student must be careful not to confound these two aspects of the Man.

The Physical aspect applies only to the gross external plane, the passional and material side of humanity. It shows us the intellectual human animal, as it were, and therefore, is only applicable to those who are living wholly upon that particular plane.

ARIES (♈) THE RAM

The sign Aries, in its Symbolical aspect, represents the Sacrifice. The flocks and herds bring forth their young during the portion of the year that the sun occupies this sign. In addition to the sacrifice, the Ram also symbolizes the spring and the commencement of a New Year, when life, light and love, are to be bestowed upon the sons of earth in consequence of the sun having once more gained the victory over the realms of winter and death. The symbol of the slain Lamb upon the equinoctial cross, is another type of Aries.

Kabbalistically, the sign Aries represents the head and brains of the grand man of the cosmos. It is the acting, thinking principle in Nature called, sometimes, instinct, and again intelligence. Upon the esoteric planisphere, this sign is occupied by Benjamin, of whom Jacob, in his blessing to the twelve sons, says "Benjamin shall rave as a wolf, in the morning he shall devour the prey, and at night divide the spoils." Above all other animals, the wolf is sacred to the planet Mars, and the sign Aries is under the special and peculiar control of this fiery planet. Mars is the most fiery of all the planets, and Aries is the first constellation of the fiery triplicity. The correspondence is significant. The Hebrews concealed this reference to the planetary nature of Mars by combining the wolf and the ram. "The wolf in sheep's clothing" reveals to us the evil action of Mars when malefically posited in his own sign, the Ram. The Kabbalistical gem of this sign is the amethyst, and those born with Aries rising upon the ascendant of their horoscope, possess in this stone a powerful magnetic talisman. Aries is the first and highest emanation of the fiery triplicity, and is the constellation of the planet Mars.

Upon the Intellectual Plane, Aries signifies the martial spirit of destructiveness and aggression. It rules the head; "Out of his mouth went a two edged sword." It is the active will under the guidance of the executive forces of the brain; and those dominated by this influx are imperious, dauntless, and energetic, in the first degree. They will never really submit to the control of others.

Upon the Physical Plane, Aries produces a spare but strong body, of medium height, long face, and bushy eye brows, rather long neck, powerful chest, complexion rather swarthy; disposition courageous, ambitious, intrepid, and despotic; the temper is fiery and passionate. Generally speaking, this sign gives a very quarrelsome, irritable, pugnacious person. His diseases are those of the head, small pox, measles and fevers. Of plants, this sign governs broom, holly, thistle, dock, fern, garlic, hemp, mustard, nettles, onions, poppies, radish, rhubarb and peppers. Of stones, Aries rules firestone, brimstone, ochre and all common red stones.

TAURUS (♉) THE BULL

The sign Taurus, in its Symbolical aspect, represents the powers of fecundity, and also the procreative forces in all departments of Nature. Its genius was symbolized as Aphrodite, who was generally represented as wearing the two horns upon her head in imitiation of the Bull. Many mythologists have been deceived by this symbol, and have taken it to represent a figure of the crescent moon upon the head of Isis, whereas, it was the planet Venus which the ancients intended to symbolize, because she rules the constellation of the Bull by her sympathetic forces. Apis, the sacred Bull of the Egyptians, is another conception of Taurus. And as the sun passed through this sign during their plowing month, we also find this sign used as the symbol of husbandry.

Kabbalistically, this sign Taurus represents the ears, neck and throat of the grand old man of the skies, hence, this sign is the silent, patient, listening principle of humanity; also, it is the governor of the lymphatic system of the organism. Taurus, on the esoteric planisphere, is occupied by Issachar, which means hireling or servant. The patriarch, in his paternal blessing to Issachar, refers to the obedient, laborious nature of this sign, as follows: "Issachar is a strong ass, crouching down between two burdens." This is pre-eminently the earthly Taurine nature, as the ass and the ox are equally remarkable for their endurance as beasts of burden. The Kabbalistical gem of this sign is the agate, and therefore, this stone constitutes a natural talisman for those born with Taurus on their ascendant. Taurus is the highest emanation of the earthly trigon, and is the constellation of the planet Venus.

Upon the Intellectual Plane, Taurus signifies the quickening, germinating powers of silent thought and represents that which is pleasant and good, consequently, those dominated by this influx are able to choose and assimilate that which is good. They are slow to form opinions, are careful, plodding and self-reliant, and patiently await the realization of results. The chief mental characteristics are industry and application.

Upon the Physical Plane, Taurus gives a middle stature with strong, well-knit body, and short, thick, bull-like neck, broad forehead and dark hair, a dull complexion and rather large mouth. In disposition, the natives of the earthly trigon are sullen and reserved. They make firm friends, and unrelenting foes. Slow to anger, they are, like the bull, violent and furious when aroused. Of plants, this sign rules beets, plantain, colts-foot, columbine, daisies, dandelions, gourds, myrtle, flax, larkspur, lilies, moss and spinach. Of stones, Taurus governs white coral, alabaster, and all common white stones that are opaque.

GEMINI (♊) THE TWINS

The sign Gemini, in its Symbolical aspect, symbolizes unity, and the strength of united action, also the truths of matehood. The two bright stars, Castor and Pollux, represent the twin souls. The Greek myth of Castor and Pollux avenging the rape of Helen, is only a repetition of the biblical story of Simeon and Levi slaughtering the men of Shechem for the outrage committed upon their sister Dinah by the son of Hamor.

Kabbalistically, the sign Gemini represents the hands and arms of the grand man of the universe, and therefore, expresses the projecting and executive forces of humanity in all mechanical departments. Upon the esoteric planisphere, the sign is occupied by Simeon and Levi. "They are brethren," says Jacob, "and instruments of cruelty are in their habitations,"—which refers in a very unmistakable manner to the fearfully potent powers of projection that lie concealed within the magnetic constitution of all those who are dominated by this sign. The mystical symbol of the twins conceals the doctrine of soul-mates and other important truths connected therewith. The mystical gem of this sign is the beryl, which means crystal, and consequently forms the talismanic stone for those born under the influence of this potential sign. Gemini is the first and highest emanation of the airy trigon, and is the constellation of the planet Mercury.

Upon the Intellectual Plane, Gemini signifies the union of reason with intuition, and those dominated by its influx express the highest mental state of embodied humanity. They are volatile, free, philosophical and generous. Their magnetic spheres are specially susceptible to the influence of inspirational currents. By nature they are restless and exceedingly energetic. They possess an excess of mental force which impels them headlong into the most gigantic enterprises. Their chief characteristics are intuitional and mental activity, consequently, they are nervous and restless.

Upon the Physical Plane, Gemini gives a tall, straight body, a sanguine complexion, dark hair, hazel or grey eyes, sharp sight and a quick, active walk. They possess a restless but gentlemanly appearance. In disposition, the natives of the airy trigon are volatile and fickle. They are scientific and possess a great passion for all kinds of knowledge; are inconstant, and rarely study one subject very long; are speculative, and possess large imaginations. Of plants, this sign rules privet, dog-grass, meadow-sweet, madder, woodbine, tansy, vervain and yarrow. Of stones, Gemini governs the garnet and all striped stones.

CANCER (♋) THE CRAB

The sign Cancer symbolizes tenacity to life. The crab, in order to move forward, is compelled to walk backwards; which illustrates the sun's apparent motion, when in this sign, where it commences to move backwards toward the equator again. It also represents the fruitful, sustaining essence of the life forces, hence, we see the symbol of the crab occupying a prominent position upon the breast of the statue of ISIS, the universal mother and sustainer of all.

Kabbalistically, the sign Cancer signifies the vital organs of the grand man of the starry heavens, and therefore, represents the breathing and digestive functions of the human family, and also indicates the magnetic control of this constellation over the spiritual, ethereal and vital essences, and the capacity of those specially dominated by this nature to receive and assimilate the inspirational currents. Hence, Cancer governs the powers of inspiration and respiration of the grand man. The sign Cancer, upon the esoteric planisphere, is occupied by Zebulon, of whom his patriarchal father declares, "Zebulon shall dwell at the haven of the sea, and he shall be for an haven of ships," astrologically intimating the home of the crab, which is upon the sea shore. It also expresses the varied powers of cohesion, and the paradoxical truths found in all contradictories. The mystical gem of the sign is the emerald. The stone constitutes a powerful talisman for all natives of Cancer, which is the highest emanation of the watery trigon, and is the constellation of the Moon.

Upon the Intellectual Plane, Cancer signifies the equilibrium of spiritual and material life forces. Those dominated by its influx express the highest form of the reflective powers; they are timid and retiring; are truly passive, and constitute natural mediums. Cancer possesses but little of the intuitional qualities. That which appears to be intuition is direct inspiration. To the external eye, the natives of the watery trigon appear to be slothful; whereas, they are incessant workers upon the higher or mental plane. This sign expresses to us the conservation of forces. Its chief attributes are sensitiveness and reflection.

Upon the Physical Plane, Cancer gives a medium stature, the upper part larger than the lower, a small, round face, pale or delicate complexion, brown hair and small, pensive grey eyes; disposition effeminate, timid and thoughtful; temper mild; conversation agreeable and pleasant. Of plants, this sign rules cucumbers, squashes, melons, and all water vegetation such as rushes, water lilies, etc. Of stones, Cancer governs chalk, selenite, and all soft, white stones.

LEO (♌) THE LION

The sign Leo symbolizes strength, courage and fire. The hottest portion of the year, in the northern hemisphere, is when the sun is passing through this sign. It is the solar Lion of the mysteries that ripens, with its own internal heat, the fruits brought forth from the earth by the moisture of Isis.

Kabbalistically, the sign Leo signifies the heart of the grand man, and represents the life center of the fluidic circulatory system of humanity. It is also the fire vortex of physical life. Hence, those born under this influx are noted for the superior strength of their physical constitution; and also for their wonderful recuperative powers after being exhausted by sickness. The sign Leo upon the esoteric planisphere, is occupied by Judah, of whom his dying parent says, "Judah is a lion's whelp, from the prey my son thou art gone up. He stooped down, he couched as a lion." This sign reveals to us the mysteries of the ancient sacrifice, and the laws of compensation. The mystical gem of Leo is the ruby, and it forms a most potent disease-resisting talisman for all governed by the Leonine influx. Leo is the second emanation of the fiery triplicity, and is the constellation of the sun.

Upon the Intellectual Plane, Leo signifies the sympathies of the heart. Those dominated by its influx are generous even to excess with their friends. By nature they are deeply sympathetic, and possess that peculiar grade of magnetic force which enables them to arouse into action the latent sympathies in others. As orators their earnest, impulsive, pathetic style makes them an irresistible success. An exceedingly fine specimen of Leonine oratory is given in Genesis, 44th. ch. This simple, eloquent appeal of Judah to Joseph, probably, stands unequaled, for its sublime tenderness. The natives of Leo are impulsive and passionate, honest and faithful. Their mental forces are ever striving to attain unto some higher state; hence, their ideas are always in excess of their means to accomplish their large, majestic and grand plans.

Upon the Physical Plane, Leo gives a large, fair, stature, broad shoulders, large, prominent eyes, oval face, ruddy complexion and light hair, generally golden. This is for the first twenty degrees of the sign. The last ten degrees give the same but a much smaller person. Disposition high spirited, resolute, haughty, and ambitious. Of plants, this sign rules anise, camomile, cowslip, daffodil, dill, eglantine, eyebright, fennel, St. John's wort, lavender, yellow lily, poppy, marigold, garden mint, mistletoe, parsley and pimpernel. Of stones, Leo governs the hyacinth and chrysolite, and all soft yellow minerals such as ochre.

VIRGO (♍) THE VIRGIN

The sign Virgo symbolizes chastity, and forms the central idea of a great number of myths. The Sun-God is always born at midnight, on the 25th. of December, at which time the constellation of Virgo is seen shining above the horizon in the east. Hence, originated the primitive idea of the Son of God, being born of a Virgin. When the sun passes through this sign the harvest is ready for the reaper; hence, Virgo is symbolized as the gleaning maid with two ears of wheat in her hand.

Kabbalistically, the sign Virgo signifies the solar plexus of the grand archetypal man, and therefore, represents the assimilating and

distributing functions of the human organism. Consequently, we find
that those born under this influence possess fine discriminating powers
as to the choice of food best adapted to their particular organic requirements. This constellation, as governing the bowels of humanity,
is highly important, since the intestines comprise a very vital section
of the digestive organism and vital fluids. Upon the esoteric planisphere, Virgo is occupied by Asher. "Out of Asher, his bread shall be
fat," says Jacob, "and he shall yield royal dainties." Thus typifying
the riches of the harvest. This sign expresses the fulfillment of the
creative design, hence, the mysteries of maternity are concealed under
this symbol. It also reveals to us the significance of the sacrament of
the Lord's Supper. The mystical gem of Virgo is the jasper, a stone
possessing very important virtues. It should be worn by all natives
born under this sign. Virgo is the second emanation of the earthly
trigon, and is the constellation of Mercury.

Upon the Intellectual Plane, the sign Virgo signifies the realization of hopes. Those dominated by this influx are calm, confident and
contented; they are reflective and studious, and extremely fond of
reading. Consequently, they become the mental repositories of much
external wisdom and learning. Their chief attributes are hope and
contentment. These desirable qualities, combined with the mental
penetration of Mercury, which this sign contains, all conduce to make
the native of Virgo pre-eminently fitted for the close application of
scientific study. They possess large, well balanced brains and very
superior intellectual abilities and make clever statesmen, when thrown
into the vortex of political life.

Upon the Physical Plane, Virgo gives a medium stature, very
neat and compact, dark sanguine complexion, and dark hair; disposition is ingenious, studious and inclined to be witty; rather even temper, but more excitable than Taurine persons. As orators, Virgo persons
are fluent, plain, practical and very interesting. Of plants, this sign
rules endive, millet, privet, succory, wood-bine, skullcap, valerain,
wheat, barley, oats and rye. Of stones, the various kinds of flint.

LIBRA (♎) THE BALANCE

This constellation, in its Symbolical aspect, typifies justice. Most
of our readers doubtless have seen the goddess of justice represented
as a female, blind-folded, holding in her hand a pair of scales. This
conception is purely astrological, and refers to the celestial Libra of

the heavens. The sun enters this sign about the 21st. of September, when, as the poet Manilius says:

> "Day and night are weighed in Libra's scales,
> Equal awhile, at last the night prevails."

Kabbalistically, the sign Libra signifies the reins and loins of the grand celestial man, and therefore, represents the central conservatory or store house of the re-productive fluids. It is also the magnetic vortex of pro-creative strength. This constellation also represents, in its most interior aspect, the equinoctial point of the arc in the ascending and descending cycle of the life atom. Therefore, this sign contains the unification of the cosmic forces as the grand central point of equilibrium of the sphere. Libra upon the esoteric planisphere, is occupied by Dan. The patriarch, in his blessing, thus refers to his celestial nature; "Dan shall judge his people as one of the tribes of Israel." Libra represents the interior equilibrium of Nature's forces, and contains the mystery of the divine at-one-ment of the ancient initiations. Upon the universal chart, this sign becomes Enoch, the perfect man. Its mystical gem is the diamond. As a magnetic talisman, this stone acts as a repulsive force, and combines with the magnetic sphere of those born under its influence, to repel the emanations from foreign bodies, either of persons or things. Libra is the second emanation of the airy triplicity, and is the constellation of Venus.

Upon the Intellectual Plane, Libra signifies external perception, balanced by intuition, the union of which becomes externalized as reason and foresight. Therefore, those dominated by this influence constitute the rationalistic school of the world's body of thinkers. Theoretically, they are strong supporters of such conceptions as universal brotherhood, universal equality and the rights of man. But practically, they seldom (unless it pays) reduce their pet theories to actual practice. The natives of Libra, though possessing a finely balanced mental and magnetic organism, are seldom elevated into very prominent positions. This is because they are too even, both mentally and physically, to become the popular leaders of any radical or sensational party. It is one of the attributes of Libra, to infuse a natural instinct within all born under her influence to accept and adopt the golden mean, or, as it has been termed, "the happy medium." Hence, they generally command respect from both sides on questions of debate.

Upon the Physical Plane, Libra generally produces, when rising at birth, a tall, slender form, of perfect proportions, brown hair, blue sparkling eyes, and a fine clear complexion. The disposition is noble, amiable, high-minded and good. It is perhaps as well to note the fact that this sign often produces dark brown and black hair, and in females, very handsome features. Of plants, this sign rules watercress, white rose, strawberry, primrose, vines, violet, heartsease, balm, lemon-thyme and pansy. Of stones, Libra governs white marble, spar and all white quartz.

SCORPIO (♏) THE SCORPION

The sign Scorpio, in its symbolical aspect, symbolizes death and deceit. It is the allegorical serpent of matter mentioned in Genesis as tempting Eve. Hence, the so-called fall of man from Libra, the point of equilibrium, to degradation and death by the deceit of Scorpio. No wonder the primitive mind, when elaborating this symbol, tried to express a spirit of retaliation; as Mackey says, in speaking of these ancient races,

> "And as an act of vengeance on your part,
> You placed within the sun a scorpion's heart."

thus alluding to the brilliant star Antares.

Kabbalistically, the sign Scorpio typifies the generative organs of the grand man, and consequently, represents the sexual or pro-creative system of humanity. It is the emblem of generation and life; therefore, the natives of Scorpio excel in the fruitfulness of the seminal fluids, and this creates a corresponding increase of desire. A distinct reference to the fruitfulness of this sign will be found in Genesis, chap. xxx, wherein Leah, when she beheld the birth of Zilpah's son, exclaimed, "a troop cometh." (see verses 10 and 11) Scorpio, upon the esoteric planisphere, is occupied by Gad, of whom the dying Jacob says, "Gad, a troop shall overcome him, but, he shall overcome at the last;" intimating the fall of man from a state of innocence and purity, through the multitude of sensual delights, and his final victory over the realms of matter as a spiriual entity. This sign represents the physical plane of the attributes of pro-creation. It contains the mystery of sex, and the secrets of the ancient phallic rites. The mystical gem of Scorpio is the topaz, the natural talisman of those born under this influence. Scorpio is the second emanation of the watery trigon, and is the constellation of Mars.

Upon the Intellectual Plane, the sign Scorpio signifies the generation of ideas; hence, those dominated by this influx possess an inexhaustible resource of ideas and suggestions. Their active evolutionary minds are ever busy with some new conception, and their brains are literally crammed full of inventive imageries. They possess keen perception, fine intuitional powers, and a very positive will. Hence, they excel as medical practitioners, chemists and surgeons. In the various departments of the surgical art, natives of this sign possess no equal. In addition to this mechanical ability, they are endowed with a powerful, fruitful, magnetic life force which they sympathetically transmit to their patients. This is why they become such successful physicians. The sexual desire is naturally very strong, hence, they are liable to excess in this direction.

Upon the Physical Plane, this sign gives a strong and rather corpulent body, medium stature, dark or ruddy complexion, dark hair, features often resembling the eagle; disposition active, resentful, proud, reserved, thoughtful and also selfish. Of plants, this sign rules blackthorn, charlock, heather, horehound, bean, bramble, leek, woad and wormwood. Of stones, lode stone, blood stone and vermillion.

SAGITTARIUS (♐) THE ARCHER

This constellation, in its Symbolical aspect, represents a dual nature, as it symbolizes retribution and also the hunting sports. We find it depicted as a Centaur, with the bow and arrow drawn to its head ready for shooting. Hence, it was frequently used to designate the autumnal sports, the chase, etc. The Centaur was also a symbol of authority and worldly wisdom. Mackey, speaking of this sign, said,

> "The starry Centaur still bends the bow
> To show his sense of what you did below."

Kabbalistically, the sign Sagittarius signifies the thighs of the grand universal man. It, therefore, represents the muscular foundation of the seat of locomotion in humanity. It is the emblem of stability, foundation and physical power. This sign also represents the centers of physical, external, authority and command. Sagittarius, upon the esoteric planisphere, is occupied by Joseph. "His bow abode in strength," says the patriarch, "and the arms of his hands were made strong." It also represents the powers of "Church and State," and the necessity of legalized codes, civil, military and religious. It indicates to us the organizing powers of humanity, and the absolute necessity of "the powers that be" in certain states of development. We see in Joseph, the Egyptian ruler and law-giver, a true type of real authority. The mystical gem of this influx is the carbuncle, which is a talisman of great virtue to its proper natives. Sagittarius is the lowest emanation of the fiery trigon and is the constellation of Jove, the planet Jupiter.

Upon the Intellectual Plane, Sagittarius represents the organizing power of the mind; hence, this influence indicates the external powers of command, discipline and obedience, to the ruling authority of material institutions. Persons of this nature are loyal, patriotic, and law abiding. Such natives are generous and free; energetic and combative; hasty in temperament; ambitious of position and power; also charitable to the afflicted and oppressed. They possess strong conservative qualities; and their chief mental characteristics are prompt decision, self control, and the ability to command others.

Upon the Physical Plane, this sign usually produces a well formed person, rather above medium height, sanguine complexion, oval face, high forehead, bright brown hair, fine clear eyes; in short, handsome. In disposition, the native is quick, energetic, fond of out door sports and recreations; hasty tempered, jovial, free and benevolent. Of plants, this sign rules agrimony, wood betony, feather-few and mallows. Of stones, Sagittarius governs the turquois, and all the stones mixed with red and green.

CAPRICORN (♑) THE GOAT

This sign, in its Symbolical aspect, typifies sin. The scapegoat of the Israelites; and the universal offering of a kid or young goat as an atoning sacrifice for sin, are significant. The different qualities of the sheep and the goat, from a symbolical standpoint, are used by St. John in his mystical Apocalypse. The Redeemer of mankind, or Sun God, is always born at midnight directly Sol enters this sign, which is the winter solstice, "The young child" is born in the stable and laid in the manger of the goat, in order that he may conquer the remaining signs of winter or death, and thus save mankind from destruction.

Kabbalistically, the sign Capricorn signifies the knees of the grand macrocosm and represents the first principle in the trinity of locomotion, viz., the joints; bending, pliable and movable. It is the emblem of material servitude and as such is worthy of notice. Capricorn, upon the esoteric planisphere, is occupied by Naphtali, whom Jacob says, "is a hind let loose, he giveth goodly words." Here we have two very distinct references; the first, to the symbol, a hind or young deer, i.e., a goat with horns, (goats and deer are equally significant of the earthly, mountainous nature, and are fond of high hills); the second, is the Christmas proclamation, he giveth goodly words, "Peace on earth, good will toward man." This sign represents "regeneration," or re-birth, and reveals the necessity of "new dispensations." The mystical gem of this constellation is the onyx, sometimes called "chalcedony." Capricorn is the lowest emanation of the earthly trigon, and is the constellation of the planet Saturn.

Upon the Intellectual Plane, Capricorn signifies external form, and those dominated by its influx are among the very lowest in the scale of true spirituality. The brain of this influence is ever on the alert to seize and take advantage of circumstances. The sign gives a purely scheming mentality; the intellectual nature is directed purely to the attainment of selfish ends; the penetrating power of the mind is great. The natives are quick as lightning to see in others the weak points that they may work to their own advantage. They are indisposed to do any real hard work unless they see some great benefit therefrom in the immediate future. It is a very undesirable influence.

Upon the Physical Plane, Capricorn generally gives a medium stature, slender, often ill proportioned; plain looking, energetic in their own interests, and indolent in the employ of others. Frequently these natives have a long sharp chin and slender nose, with small piercing eyes. They are almost always narrow chested. In disposition, they are crafty, subtle, reserved and often melancholy. At the same time, natives of Saturn are often miserly. Of plants, this sign rules hemlock, henbane, deadly nightshade and black poppy. Of stones, Capricorn governs coal and all black or ash colored minerals.

AQUARIUS (♒) THE WATER-BEARER

This sign symbolizes judgment. This constellation forms the starry original of the urn of Minos, from which flow wrath and condemnation or blessings and reward, according to the works done in the body, irrespective of theological faith. The earlier baptismal urns of the primitive Christians, and the elaborate stone fonts of the later churches, are relics of this great astral religion.

Kabbalistically, the sign Aquarius signifies the legs of the grand archetypal man, and therefore, represents the locomotive functions of the human organism. It is the natural emblem of the changeable, movable and migratory forces of the body. The Water-bearer, upon the esoteric planisphere, is occupied by Reuben. "The excellency of dignity and the excellency of power," says Jacob, "unstable as water thou shalt not excel." A simple but magnificent astrological description of this sign, which, from time immemorial, has been symbolized by two wavy lines ($\approx$), like the ripples of running water. This sign signifies consecration, and not only contains the rites and mysteries of consecration, but will reveal to the student the potency of all sacred and dedicated works. The mystical gem of this sign is the sky blue sapphire (not the dark or opaque sapphire). Aquarius is the lowest emanation of the airy trigon, and the constellation of Uranus.

Upon the Intellectual Plane, Aquarius represents popular science, and consequently, the truth of material phenomena. Those dominated by its influx constitute the school of inductive philosophy; the grand basis of all exoteric science. They represent the intellectual and scientific spirit of their age and generation; and cannot advance one step beyond those classes of facts which are demonstrable to the senses. Elegant in form, they are brilliant in intellect.

Upon the Physical Plane, Aquarius gives a medium stature, plump, well-set and robust; good, clear, sanguine complexion; sandy or dark flaxen hair; very prepossessing appearance; disposition elegant, amiable, good natured, witty and very artistic; fond of refined society. Of plants, this sign rules spikenard, frankincense and myrrh. Of stones, Aquarius governs black pearl and obsidian.

Pisces ($\times$) the Fishes

This sign symbolizes the flood; chiefly because, when Sol passes through this sign the rainy season commences; clearing away the snows of winter, the melting torrents of which flood the valleys and lowlands. This sign is also the terminus of Apollo's journey through the twelve signs.

"Near their loved waves cold Pisces keep their seat,
With Aries join, and make the round complete."

Kabbalistically, the sign Pisces signifies the feet of the grand cosmic man; and therefore, represents the basis or foundation of all external things as well as the mechanical forces of humanity. It is the natural emblem of patient servitude and obedience. This sign, upon the esoteric planisphere is occupied by Ephraim and Manasseh, the two sons of Joseph, who received their portion in Israel as the two feet of the grand, archetypal man. It signifies confirmation, also baptism by water. It also indicates to us the divine purpose of the great cycle of necessity; commencing with the disruptive, flashing, dominating fire of Aries, and terminating with its polar opposite, water, the symbol of universal equilibrium. The mystical gem of Pisces is the chrysolite (white and glittering). Pisces is the last emanation of the watery trigon, and is the constellation of Neptune.

Upon the Intellectual Plane, Pisces represents mental indifference. It is the polar opposite of the head. Those dominated by its influx express a peculiar indifference to those things which generally interest others. They take all things as they come, and pay no serious attention to any. They live and die in accordance with St. Paul's advice, being "all things to all men."

Upon the Physical Plane, this sign gives a short, fleshy body, brown hair, pale complexion, moist, watery eyes (fishy looking); disposition negative, timid, listless and harmless. Their nature is peaceable, but their actions are influenced by their surroundings and friends. Of plants, this sign rules all sea weeds, also ferns and mosses that grow in water. Of stones, it governs coral, rock, pumice and gravel or sand.

THE OCCULT APPLICATION OF THE TWELVE SIGNS

The four triplicities symbolize the four cardinal points of the universe. To us, on our present external and physical plane, they signify the four opposite points of space as represented in the compass and cross (hence the sacredness of the cross as a symbol in all times and ages) and the four Occult elements, Fire, Earth, Air and Water. They each correspond to a particular quarter of the heavens. Thus, the Fiery Trigon corresponds to the positive-azoth; and is expressed in the glowing, flaming, eastern horizon at sunrise; the beginning of the day. Similarly, primary molten fire was the beginning, or first condition, of the present order of things on our globe; and stands for that principle of heat termed caloric, which sustains the animal, vital life force of all animate beings upon the face of the planets.

Upon the Intellectual Plane, Fire represents zeal, animal courage, daring; and in fact, all that pertains to action and activity. While on the higher (esoteric) plane, Fire implies the interior apprehension of the meaning and significance of action as displayed in the trinity, and expressed by fire of three terms as Aries, Leo, and Sagittarius; Aries (♈) the intellect; Leo (♌) the emotions; Sagittarius (♐) the offspring of the intellect and emotions; the external result or consummation of the two; that point which is neither the one nor the other; but where the two are one.

The Earthly Triplicity stands for the frozen, inert north, as a symbol of frigidness, hardening, crystallization, death. It is concerned with all phenomena that is most external and palpable to the external senses; the solids, metals, fabrics.

Upon the Intellectual Plane, it is concerned with the relations of solids to each other, from which is especially evolved form, proportion, sound, etc. The same may be said of the metals dug up from the bowels of the earth, of the commerce, arts and industries resulting therefrom. Esoterically, the earthy trigon denotes the comprehension of the spiritual qualities evolved from the earthy activities; or, rather, that one spiritual quality of three-fold formation expressed in three mystical terms; Taurus (♉), servitude or spirit of patient work; Virgo (♍), formation and re-formation; Capricorn (♑), the result of the union of Taurus and Virgo, which leads either to the higher plane in the spiral of existence; or to the lower plane on the downward course to darker realms of being; more earthy, hardened and dead.

The Airy Triplicity represents the west; the scene of the setting sun; which signifies the dying of the day, of sense and of matter; which is only the promise of another day; an advance to a higher plane. This brighter day is denoted by the airy trigon; and is concerned, upon the external plane, with the priestly, political and social relations of human life. That is to say, it represents the higher qualities of these relations. It is, therefore, symbolized by the invisible element, air; the great medium of motion. Its esoteric significance is comprised in the arcana of the one true science. After first having a knowledge of the twins (♊ Gemini) external, the internal science attains unto the adjustment and equilibrium or balance (♎ Libra) of the two; so that they exactly blend in the divine equipoise of harmony and wisdom; thus realizing only the rippling waves (♒ Aquarius) of peaceful results; instead of the downpouring floods and cataclysms; both social and physical; which otherwise result from the unbalanced scales (♎ Libra); when external and internal antagonize, as two hostile and absolutely separate and dual forces; instead of balancing as two modes of one and the same eternal motion, the one life of the universe.

The Watery Triplicity, symbolical of the south, is the exact opposite of the earthy north. It is the frozen, melted; the hardened, liquefied; the renewal of the crystal into other forms; and the resurrection of death into life. The watery trigon signifies the constant effort in Nature to adjust opposites and contradictories; to bring about chemical changes and affinities as especially seen in fluids; and as so perfectly symbolized in that great distinguishing feature of water, viz., to seek its own level. On the external plane of human life, the watery trigon denotes love (∞); sex (♏ Scorpio and ♂ Mars); and offspring (♓); the external results of the union of the two (love and sex). On the more esoteric planes, Cancer (♋) symbolizes tenacity to life, hence, the desire for immortality; which, combined with a knowledge of the mysteries of sex (♏ Scorpio and ♂ Mars) or generation and regeneration, leads the immortal soul to the termination of its earthly pilgrimage and material incarnations, in the union with its missing half or Pisces (♓), which is symbolized, upon the celestial equator (equilibrium), as the two fishes bound together by the cord (of love). Having regained this equator and passed from the lower arc of matter, the soul enters once more upon the spiritual path of eternal conscious life.

The reader will now perceive that the four great trigons are but the different series of attributes within the human soul or microcosm; and further, that the twelve constellations of the zodiac reveal the mystical signification of Adam Kadmon, the archetypal man of the starry planisphere. Thus; Aries (♈) rules the head, brain and the fiery will; Taurus (♉) the neck and throat, the ears, the listening requisites of obedient servitude; Gemini (♊) the hands and arms, or projective and executive powers; Cancer (♋) the breast, bosom and lungs, which signify life and love; Leo (♌) the heart and its varied emotions; Virgo (♍) the bowels, the navel or maternal, the compassionate and formulative qualities; Libra (♎) the loins or physical strength, the power of balancing the mental faculties; Scorpio (♏) the generative organs and the procreative attributes; Sagittarius (♐) the hips and thighs, the seat or foundation of volitional force, the migratory instincts; Capricorn (♑) the knees, tokens of humble submission to the higher powers; Aquarius (♒) the legs and ankles or active powers of movement and locomotion; and lastly, Pisces (♓) the feet, the foundation of the whole frame, which should ever be capable of finding and sustaining its own level unaided, lest the grand human temple fall to the ground. Thus we begin with fire and terminate with water. These constitute the two poles of the human magnet.

NOTE: To obtain the celestial application of the above, the points must be reversed; north becomes south; east becomes west, and so on.

MAN'S PLANETARY ORGANISM

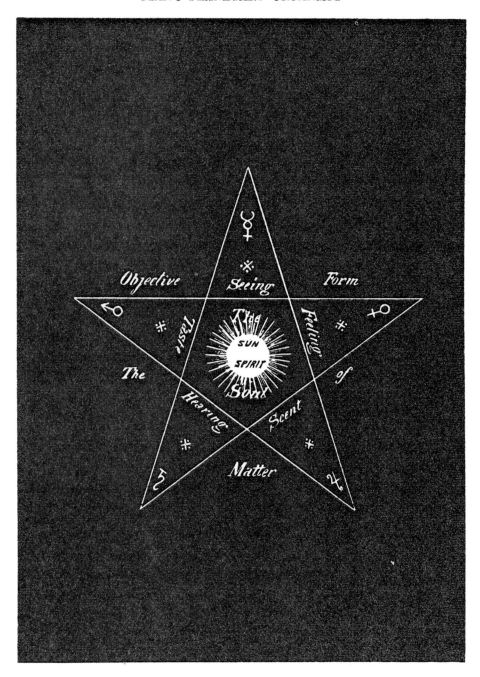

THE UNION OF THE SOUL AND STARS.

CHAPTER VII

THE NATURE AND INFLUENCE OF THE PLANETS

Before describing the nature and influence of the planets as known to the initiates of Hermetic Philosophy, it is necessary to point out to the reader the difference between the nature of a planet and a constellation. The twelve signs constitute the innate, latent possibilities of the organism, and as such represent the constitution as a whole. In this light we have considered them in the previous chapter. While on the other hand, the planets constitute the active forces which arouse these latent possibilities. In this duplex action of sign and planet, both natures come into play and produce the various results of external life. Man, the microcosm, is merely the sounding board, so to say, the re-acting point for their ethereal and magnetic vibrations. Further, while the twelve signs represent the human organism as a form containing latent possibilities; the sun, moon, and planets, represent the spirit, soul, and senses, of that organism. Man consists of body, soul, and spirit, as described in Section II, Chap. II. As at present manifested, he has five physical senses as stated in Section III, Chap. IV. The constellations are the body; the Moon is the soul; the Sun is the spirit; and the five planets; Saturn, Jupiter, Mars, Venus, and Mercury, represent and express the five physical senses. It is in this light that the reader must consider the various natures of the planetary influx, described in this and the succeeding chapters. A great many students of the mystical science fall into serious error through failing to grasp this relation of the stars and the planets.

It must also be borne in mind, that; when considering the actual influences at work in a given horoscope; those signs only which contain one or more planets will be the dominant forces within the constitution; mental, physical, or both; according to the plane occupied by the person. To ascertain the particular plane a person occupies, is a very difficult matter with most students. It can only be gauged and understood by those who possess the interior senses of the soul in such an advanced state as to be capable of spiritual perception, either of sight or feeling. Therefore, the perfect astrologer is the perfect man. There are, however, many degrees of perfection; and the reader, as well as the writer, must feel thankful for the degree which he may already possess; and set to work in real earnest to attain a still greater degree of spiritual perfection.

THE SUN ☉

The symbolical aspect of the glorious orb of day, undoubtedly, first occupied the attention, veneration, and worship, of the primitive races of mankind. Every thing in Nature depends absolutely upon the presence, and kindly support of the shining sun, for its existence and life. The literal interpretation of the Hebrew name for the sun, Ashahed, is "the all bountiful fire;" which is perfectly in harmony with the solar orb.

It is utterly impossible, in the brief space at our command, to give even the remotest conception of the innumerable ramifications connected with the various mythologies which typify the sun. We will, therefore, only add that Osiris of Egypt, Chrishna of India, Belus of Chaldea, and Ormazd of Persia, are merely different personifications of the sun.

Kabbalistically, the Sun represents the central spiritual source of all. It is the divine Ego of the grand man, and therefore, signifies the spiritual potentialities of creative power. It is the great I AM of all things; both spiritual and temporal; and is, in itself, the grand conservatory of Life, Light and Love. Upon the esoteric planisphere, the Sun becomes the great archangel Michael, who defeats Satan and tramples upon the head of the serpent of matter; and thenceforward, guards the way of life and immortality, with the flaming swords of solar power. In this sense the sun represents the positive, aggressive, controlling forces of the cosmos, as the forces of the sun are electric.

Astrologically considered, the Sun constitutes the central life principle of all physical things. His influx determines the absolute measure of physical vitality within each human organism. When the solar ray is not vitiated by the discordant configurations of malefic stars, the individual then born, will enjoy a sound constitution; more especially so, if the sun at the moment of birth is between the ascendant and meridian; or, in other words, during the increase of the diurnal sunshine, which is from sunrise to noon.

Upon the Intellectual Plane, the Sun governs the higher group of the selfish sentiments and lower group of the moral qualities; the former, represented by firmness and self esteem; and the latter, by hope and conscientiousness. Those dominated by this influx are the natural born leaders of mankind. By their high-minded presence, they proclaim their "right divine to govern." They are proud and ambitious, yet magnanimous and noble. Hating all mean, petty and sordid actions, they express the very highest form of true dignified manhood.

Upon the Physical Plane, the position of the sun in the horoscope is one of vital importance; for on this, in a male natus, hangs the vital thread of life. If evil rays concentrate thereon; the life will be of short duration; unless counteracting aspects intervene.

When the sun is afflicted at birth, his influence upon the native through life, will be malefic. When this is so; even minor evil directions to the sun and moon combined, will bring about destruction of life; the nature of which will be similar to that of the afflicting planets. And note this: for prosperity and success in life; it is essential that the luminaries be well aspected and favorably situated in the celestial figure. When the sun and moon are afflicted at birth, depend upon it, that person will have a very hard struggle against an adverse fate all the days of his life; and it will not require the powers of an inspired prophet to foretell his general destiny. "From evil, discord and suffering are born."

The Sun, rising at birth, confers courage, pride, ambition, and to a certain extent, good fortune. But, if afflicted by Saturn, the native will suffer much in health, and be correspondingly unfortunate. If afflicted by Mars, the native will be cruel, rash and quarrelsome. Such a one will have little respect for the feelings of others; unless Jupiter or Venus cast beneficent rays. Generally speaking, the Sun when rising at birth gives a person of strong frame, good forehead, large eyes, sharp sight, tawny or brown hair. If well aspected and dignified, the disposition is noble, generous, and proud, yet humane, and courteous; a truly faithful friend and generous foe. He is profuse in his manner, and loves magnificence. If evilly aspected and ill dignified; then the native is mean, proud and tyrannical to those under his authority, but a submissive sycophant to his superiors; shallow minded and thoroughly unfeeling.

THE MOON ☽

The symbolical aspect of Luna, like that of the Sun, cannot be detailed. From time immemorial the fair goddess of night has been venerated and worshiped as the universal mother; the feminine fructifying principle of all things. In the poetical conception of the Hebrews, the moon was called Ash-nem or Shenim, the state of slumber and change. Without a complete knowledge of astrological science, the weird truths concealed beneath the veil of Isis, can never be properly understood. Astrology alone, is the true key to the fundamental principles of Occultism. The secret of the tides; the mysteries of gestation; and the alternate periods of sterility and fruitfulness, caused by the ebb and flow of the magnetic life currents throughout every department of Nature; are discoverable only by a comprehension of the divine goddess of our midnight skies. This knowledge was the sublime attainment of the sages, "who," says Bulwer Lytton, "first discovered the starry truths that shone upon the great shemaia of the Chaldean lore." Chandra of the Hindoos; Isis of the Egyptians; Diana of the Greeks; and others, are all, the moon.

Kabbalistically, the Moon represents the soul of the grand man. It is, therefore, the celestial virgin of the world, in its mystical application; the emblem of the Anima Mundi. Upon the esoteric planisphere, Luna becomes transformed into the Angel Gabriel. Upon the universal chart, we see her expressed as the divine Isis, the woman clothed with the sun. As Isis, she represents the grand initiatrix of the soul into the sublime mysteries of the spirit. The Moon, also, represents the moulding, formative attributes of the astral light. She, also, stands as the representative of matter. Hence, in her dual character, she reveals to us her forces which are purely magnetic; and as such, they stand as the polar opposite of those of the Sun, which are electric. In their relation to each other, they are woman and man.

Astrologically considered, volumes might be written regarding this orb. When we consider her proximity to our earth, and her affinity with it, as well as the rapidity of her motion, we cannot help granting to her the highest position, as an active agent in every branch of judicial astrology. Her influence is purely negative, however; and in herself alone, or when void of the configurations of the Sun and planets; she is neither fortunate nor unfortunate. But, when configurated with other orbs; her influx becomes exceedingly potent as she receives and transmits to us the intensified influence of those stars aspecting her. The Moon, therefore, may be called the great astrological medium of the skies.

Upon the Intellectual Plane, Luna governs the physical senses, and to a great extent the animal passions also. She controls the lower forms of the domestic qualities, and the lower group of intellectual faculties. Those dominated by her influx are changeable in their nature, submissive and very inoffensive. Magnetically, their odylic sphere is purely mediumistic; hence, they become inactive and dreamy. Generally, Luna natives may be said to be rather indifferent characters, lacking anything and everything that may be called strong and decisive. They are given to roaming about, or constantly moving their residence from one place to another.

Upon the Physical Plane, the influence of the Moon is convertible in its nature, being harmonious or discordant according to her relative position to the sun and major planets. If the moon be dignified at birth; she renders the native more refined, engaging, and courteous, than he otherwise would be. Should she also be well aspected; such a position will confer refined, artistic tastes, easy disposition, and good abilities. On the contrary, should the moon be ill dignified or evilly aspected, the native then born will be a shallow-minded, evil character, prone to dissipation, slothful, and void of proper business foresight, consequently, improvident. If the horoscope be a strong one in other respects, and points out sterling ability; then these aspects will tend rather towards making the person diplomatic. These aspects are also a strong indication, when unassisted by benevolent rays, of ultimate insanity. Very great consideration is necessary upon these conflicting points. In addition to the indifferent disposition above mentioned; the Moon, when rising, usually produces a medium-sized body, fair or pale complexion, round face and grey eyes; the forehead wide but not high; temperament phlegmatic.

THE PLANET MERCURY ☿

In its symbolical aspect, the planet Mercury was most prominent as "the messenger of the gods." A thousand myths have been elaborated regarding "the fleet-footed Mercury." In the fertile imaginations of the early Greeks, the spirit of Mercury was ever on the alert to manifest its powers. His actions though sometimes mischievous, were often beneficial. It seems that the central idea of these ancients was to typify or express in external form the restless activities of the mercurial mind; hence, wings were placed upon his head and feet.

Kabbalistically, the planet Mercury signifies perception, and therefore, represents the power of sight within the grand body of the celestial man. It is the active power of self-consciousness within humanity, and the ability to see, perceive and reason. Upon the esoteric planisphere, Mercury becomes transformed into the angelic Raphael, the genius of wisdom and art. We see, therefore, that the esoteric forces of this orb are those which tend to elevate mankind from the animal planes to those of the human.

Astrologically considered, the influx of Mercury is mental and restless. No system of mere human invention would have dedicated to an almost invisible star; the least and most insignificant of all primary planets; the government of man's intellectual nature. Any fanciful system would have attributed such an important group of mental qualities to the Sun, or to the lordly Jupiter. The experience of the ancients, however, showed them that, neither the Sun nor Jupiter possessed any such influence; and it is upon the experience of ages, that the truths of astrology are founded; and the rules made for their application.

The qualities of Mercury may be well expressed by the American phrase, "get up and get;" for energy, intellect, and impudence, constitute the chief characteristics of the purely Mercurial native. There is nothing too hot or too heavy for his ingenuity; nor is there anything too great for his fertile brain to accomplish. The United States, as a whole, are ruled by Gemini, the constellation of Mercury, and the restless energy, commercial enterprise, and scheming abilities, of the typical American are well expressed by the singular influence of his patron star.

Upon the Intellectual Plane, however, the planet Mercury is truly the genius of wisdom, and governs the whole of those mental qualities denominated perceptive. The oratorical powers are likewise ruled by this planet. Those dominated by its influx are ingenious, inventive, witty, sarcastic, scientific, and possess remarkable penetrative power. They are profound investigators of all those sciences that aid in the promotion of commerce.

Upon the Physical Plane, Mercury rules the brain and tongue. When strongly placed at birth, the person will possess a vivid imagination and retentive memory; and also be noted for mental capacity and power of persuasion. Such a position, if configured with the Moon,

will give an unwearying fancy and strongly incline the mind towards
the curious and Occult side of Nature. Should Mercury be ill dignified
and void of the good aspects of other orbs, and at the same time be
afflicted by Mars; he will produce a liar and an unprincipled, shuffling
nature, incapable of attaining or appreciating the higher mental and
moral standards. If strong or well aspected, and below the horizon,
he inclines the native to mystical and Occult studies; but if above the
horizon and dignified, he confers a more external influence and produces orators, statesmen and teachers. One of the chief attributes of
this planet, when well placed above the horizon, is that of literary
ability. All such natives possess genuine talent in this direction. It
may, therefore, be safely said that Mercury confers the ideal when
below, and the practical when above, the ascendant at birth. Physically,
Mercury gives a medium stature, strong but slender frame, exceedingly active, sharp piercing eyes, thin lips, well cut features and confident look. The complexion depends upon the Race.

THE PLANET VENUS ♀

In her mythological and symbolical aspect, the planet Venus
has been venerated, the wide world over, in her dual character of
Love and Wisdom. The bright star of the morning, proud Lucifer,
was the harbinger and genius of wisdom; and truly, none of the stars
of heaven can compare with the brilliance and glory of Venus when
she shines as the herald of day. As the goddess of Love she is equally
prominent. The ancient Greeks also represented her as Aphrodite,
wearing the horns of her sacred Bull, Taurus.

Kabbalistically, the planet Venus signifies the Love element within
the soul, of the grand archetypal man; and therefore, represents the
sense of feeling within embodied humanity. It consequently expresses
the clinging, yielding, feminine portion of the human constitution.
Upon the esoteric planisphere, Venus becomes the celestial Anael,
prince of the astral light. In this character we behold her powers of
transformation, and the "conservation of forces." As Isis represents
the astral fluid in a state of rest, pregnant (by the Holy Ghost) with the
things TO BE, Anael represents the same fluid in action. Therefore,
the Moon and Venus form the kabbalistic symbols for the two modes
of motion within the soul of the universe.

Astrologically considered, the planet Venus may be said to represent mirth, joy, and conviviality, as the influx inclines those under her rule to pleasure-seeking, and grand display. The pleasures of society are especially governed by Venus. Balls, parties, concerts, and receptions, possess almost irresistible attraction to those born under her influence. If afflicted in a feminine horoscope, without strong counteracting rays, the native becomes "unfortunate" and suffers from the loss of virtue, hence the position of Venus is very important.

Upon the Intellectual Plane, Venus controls the higher group of the domestic qualities, and also the ideal, artistic, and musical, sentiments. Those dominated by her influx excel in music, art, and poetry, and become noted for their refined accomplishments. But, at the same time, they lack true moral power. They are guided impulsively by their sentiments, passions, and desires. Reason is conspicuous by its absence when their desires are aroused. Hence, the danger of being misled by flattery and sentimental nonsense is very great, when Venus is not protected by harmonious rays.

Upon the Physical Plane, when Venus has chief dominion over the mind of the native; she induces a strong predilection for society, and inclines to dancing, music, drawing, etc. She also confers a good humored, witty, kind and charitable disposition. Men dominated by this influx are always great favorites with the fair sex; but they are thoroughly deficient in firmness and self-control; and, if ill dignified, the male native will often find himself in awkward affairs; and is liable to fall into intemperance. A friendly aspect of Saturn in such cases would do much towards cooling and steadying the native's character and inducing reflection. Women born with Venus in the ascendant generally display the most amiable, engaging and fascinating qualities. If well aspected, they are neat and artistic in their dress and personal appearance; elegant in their homes and generally as virtuous as they are beautiful. It has been truly said, "The general disposition derived from Venus is that of mildness and genuine good nature; and whatever defects may fall to the lot of the native, they are seldom great ones; and are more the results of weakness and a strong animal nature, than constitutional wickedness or a desire to do wrong." In this we fully concur, and will only add that the chances to do wrong are multiplied by a prepossessing externalism. They are of medium stature, of fair clear complexion, bright sparkling wicked eyes, handsome features and beautiful form.

THE PLANET MARS ♂

This planet, of all others, in its symbolical aspect, was the object of divine honors in the eyes of the ancient world. Mars seems to have been the most sincerely worshiped, of all the gods, by our northern ancestors. The greatest glory, in their rude times, was enjoyed by the greatest warrior. Hence Mars, in his universal character, represented the god of war. He was also symbolized as Vulcan, the celestial blacksmith, who forged the thunderbolts of Jove. This indicates the rule of Mars over iron, steel, fire, and edged tools.

Kabbalistically, the planet Mars signifies alimentiveness within the grand man, and therefore, represents the sense of taste in the human constitution. We have a direct reference to the expression of these martial forces in reference to the physical sensations in the New Testament, viz.: "eat, drink and be merry, for to-morrow we die." Upon the esoteric planisphere, Mars becomes transformed into the angel Samael (Zamael), wherein are shown the highest attributes of this spirit. As such, it represents the power and ability to appreciate the higher, finer, and more ethereal essences of the life wave, and therefore, to have dominion over the powers of absorption and assimilation.

Astrologically considered, Mars typifies and embodies, in his astral expression, the spirit of cruelty, bloodshed, and of indiscriminate destruction. The true son of Mars is a genuine pugilist of the first water, and is never so happy as when thoroughly engaged in vanquishing his opponent. A type of this questionable spirit of enterprise may be found in the history of Great Britain. England is ruled by the sign Aries, the chief sign of Mars, and the typical Englishman is a Mars man. No better subject for study can be found to illustrate Mars, than John Bull. He is always fighting some one, and his past history for a thousand years upon land and sea, is the record of brilliant victories with very, very few reverses.

Upon the Intellectual Plane, Mars represents the spirit of enterprise, energy, and courage. Without a spice of this orb all men would be shiftless, effeminate cowards. Those dominated by the Martial influx are mechanical in the highest degree; and possess an unconquerable, untiring, energy, and potent will.

Upon the Physical Plane, Mars signifies all those who are in any way engaged in the production of iron and steel. All Martial men prefer some business where sharp instruments, iron or fire are used, as in the case of butchers, barbers, blacksmiths, etc. When the planet is rising at birth, it always imparts a certain kind of ruddiness, either upon the face or hair, a fiery look, and gives to the native a dauntless, manly, appearance. If located in the second angle, it causes the native to become improvident and to spend money thoughtlessly. Such a person never becomes wealthy, but always lives up his means. Located in the 10th. house or mid-heaven, it never fails to cause the native much suffering from slander and consequent detriment of character. When we compare the native of Mars with that of Saturn, we find them as polar opposites. The latter is like a slow, lingering consumptive disease, and the former like a raging fever. No matter who or what they may be, depend upon it, you will always find the native of Mars fiery, headstrong, furious in temper, and in respects cruel and destructive; and yet withal, they are generous to excess with their friends, and fond of good company. The general description of a true Mars man is somewhat as follows; medium height, strong, well made body, ruddy complexion, piercing eyes, square set jaw, bold determined look, and quick, quarrelsome temper. The color of the hair is variable, but it has generally a fiery tinge.

THE PLANET JUPITER ♃

Under its symbolical aspect, we find Jupiter universally recognized among the ancient Greeks as Jove, the celestial father of all. Under the remoter Aryan symbolism, we find it represented as the "All father of Heaven." Both conceptions, Greek and Aryan, are identical. In the rude conceptions of the hardy sons of the north, we see the planet Jupiter depicted as Thor, from which comes the saxon Thors-day and the modern English Thursday, the day over which the planet was supposed to rule.

Kabbalistically, the planet Jupiter signifies ethereal absorption within the grand man. It therefore, represents the power of scent or smell within the body of humanity. It is the sense by means of which the developed soul perceives and partakes the finer aromatic essences of Nature. Upon the esoteric planisphere, Jupiter becomes transformed into the celestial Zachariel or Zadkiel, and thus represents the impartial spirit of disinterestedness. In this capacity, it signifies the principles and philosophy of arbitration; the perfect adjustment of equilibrium by the withdrawal of disturbing forces. As symbolical of the attributes of ethereal absorption, we are frequently reminded of this planet by the Kabbalistical writers, of the books of Moses, who intimate that "a sweet smelling savor" was acceptable to the Lord during the sacred rites of the temple service.

Astrologically considered, the planet Jupiter is the largest, and next to Saturn the most potent planet in our solar system. He signifies all that is truly good and charitable in human life. His action is truly noble, far removed from the sheepish timidity of Saturn, or the impudent forwardness of Mars. The genuine son of Jupiter fills the atmosphere around him with genial warmth. His soul is brimming full of honest good nature. Utterly incapable of practicing fraud himself, he never suspects it in others; hence, often becomes the victim of others' schemes and duplicity. This planet's nature suggests itself, when we say that, he takes every man to be honest until he is proven to be a rogue; and when this is proved, will forgive him once or twice before punishing him.

Upon the Intellectual Plane, Jupiter signifies the higher moral nature, the humanitarian qualities, and is the author of all noble and charitable institutions and enterprises. Those dominated by his influx express the highest form of human nature. There is something truly royal in this planet's influence, a mixture of the father, patriarch, and king. Such natives do much to redeem mankind from their general depravity. There will always be found in the natives of Jupiter, upon the intellectual plane, a fine sense of discrimination; hence, they possess rare qualities of justice, which entitle them to be judges of the people. When they err, it is always on the side of mercy.

Upon the Physical Plane, Jupiter may be called the greater fortune, when he rules over a nativity. He gives a sober, manly, commanding presence. The native is sober and grave in his speech, but, at the same time kind and sympathetic. If well dignified, he makes the native sincere, honest, and faithful; generous, liberal, prudent, and aspiring; strongly given to religion and moral sentiments; and generally speaking, all that can be desired, where morality, integrity, and faithful service is required. Located in the 2nd. house, and well aspected, he brings great wealth to the native. Dignified in the 10th. house, he confers the highest honor upon the native. Such persons always attain unto very important and responsible positions, which they fill with dignity to themselves, and honor to those who promote them. This planet's position, unafflicted in the 7th. house, confers great matrimonial felicity; in the 11th. house, faithful and powerful friends; in the 5th. house, great gain and benefit through his offspring. But, when Jupiter is afflicted and ill dignified, then his nature is greatly altered. The native is generally a pretender to all these noble qualities. He externally simulates them, but at heart, he is a shallow, scheming hypocrite, a wolf in sheep's clothing. He is the judge who renders his opinion according to the price. He is hollow, a fraud and a sham. The Jupiter man is generally a tall, well made, rather fleshy, generous looking, dignified person, sanguine complexion and brown hair.

THE PLANET SATURN ♄

Old Father Time, with his skeleton-like form and deathly scythe, is doubtless, well known to most of our readers. This is one of the many forms assumed by Saturn in his symbolical aspect. With the ancient Greeks he was known as Kronos, holding the cycle of necessity and eternity in one hand, and the symbol of death in the other; thus typifying eternal change of form, sphere, and function. Among the ancient Hebrews, Saturn was called Shebo, a name that literally means seven. It is composed of Ash-sheb, which means the star of old age; thus expressing the symbol of this planet.

Kabbalistically, the planet Saturn signifies silent meditation, and thus corresponds to the auricular attributes of the grand man; and therefore, represents the senses and powers of hearing, listening, etc., within the constitution of humanity. We see, therefore, the mystical significance of the Kabbalistical conception of this orb, as silent meditation. In order to meditate, there must be silence; hence listening, hearing. Meditation is but the listening of the mind to the inspirations of the soul. Upon the esoteric planisphere, Saturn becomes the angel Cassiel, the genius of reflection in the astral light. It also presents to us the occult side of all theological mysteries; hence, the medieval conception of this planet as the isolated hermit. It is in this sense, that, we find it symbolized in the Tarot; a system worthy of greater attention than seems to be paid to it by modern students of occult science.

Astrologically considered, the planet Saturn may be truthfully said to be the most potent and malignant of all the planets. This is not so much on account of the marked character of his influence, as the imperceptible, subtle manner, in which his influx undermines the vitality of the physical organism of those it afflicts. Mars comes like a thunderclap, and gives every one to understand that there is something decidedly wrong. But Saturn is exactly the reverse. His nature is slow and patient, cunning and stealthy. At least, a good half of our world's suffering is due to the action of this planet; and in fact, nine-tenths of the ills of human life are due to the malignant rays of Mars and Saturn combined. Mars commits crime in a passionate and unthinking manner, and very seldom indeed is guilty of premeditated wrong. Saturn is the reverse. He thinks over all his plans very carefully before he attempts to put them into execution, and seldom makes a mistake.

Upon the Intellectual Plane, Saturn governs the higher group of the selfish sentiments, and the whole of the reflective qualities. Those dominated by his influx are retired, reserved, slow in speech and action. They express the highest form of reflection; consequently, they are studious, scientific and close reasoners. They generally tend to exclusiveness; hence, the hermit is a true type of this planet's action. They excel in all Occult studies.

Upon the Physical Plane, the only good that Saturn can do, is to strengthen the mentality, cool the passions, and make the native selfish and careful of his especial interests. When a person can claim these favors, he is exceedingly fortunate; because almost every aspect and position of this planet is rather more of a misfortune than a blessing. In nature it is cold and selfish, and is very apt to create a miserly disposition. If located in the mid-heaven, it brings ultimate ruin and disgrace. The horoscopes of Napoleon I and Napoleon III are splendid examples of this position. Both were born with Saturn in the M. C. (mid cusp) and both attained to heights of fame, and then suffered from disgrace, and died in exile. When Saturn is exactly upon the zenith and afflicting the sun and moon, the child then born will not live twelve months. If in the ascendant, it makes the person timid and miserly, and generally produces a weak circulation. If in the 7th. house, the native may expect a miserable life when he marries. When in the 5th. house, the children of the native seldom live, unless one of the horoscopes, especially the wife's, counteracts this. The chief thing to note is whether the planet is well aspected or dignified. If such is the case, the native is much superior, and the influence is chiefly upon the mental plane. The native of Saturn is a thin, spare, lanky person; small, sharp eyes and black hair; and inclined to melancholy.

We have now completed our descriptions of the seven planetary principles of Occult philosophy, and will now add an outline view of the two remaining orbs, Uranus and Neptune; both belong to a higher octave.

THE PLANET URANUS ♅

Uranus, the mythological parent of Saturn, commences the first series of a higher round or cycle of celestial influence. His nature is that of Mercury upon a more interior plane, and that of Mars and Saturn combined upon the lower or physical plane. As Mercury is the first of the planets, Uranus is the eighth or octave expression of the first; consequently, we can only properly observe the real influx of this planet upon the higher or mental plane. This fact must be carefully noted. When Uranus is dignified and well aspected at birth, he will act as a benefic, and vice versa. A great number of otherwise tolerably good artists of astral science, make a very serious mistake in taking this planet solely as a malefic.

Astrologically considered, the planet Uranus has not so far been able to exert his full power upon the human brain, except in rare instances. The age is not yet ripe for his influence. Comparatively few possess the necessary etherealization of "brain stuff" for this planet to fully express his action. These few are, almost without exception, to be found in the ranks of Occult science and spiritualism. The natives of Uranus are always ahead of their time. They are veritable reformers upon the plane they occupy in humanity. Their contempt for the conventionalities by which they find themselves surrounded, always creates the active hostility of those who admire the forms, customs, and opinions of "society." Consequently, they have many bitter enemies. They are always persecuted by popular opinion and the leaders thereof. But, the Uranian soul does not care for consequences. His dauntless, intrepid spirit acts with perfect independence. Under these circumstances, Uranus always becomes a disturbing force, amid shallow, false or purely artificial conditions of life. This only adds further proof, if that were necessary, that the age is not yet ripe for the full action of this weird and eccentric orb.

Upon the Intellectual Plane, Uranus rules the ideal sentiments and the imagination to a very great extent. Those dominated by his influx possess the most extraordinary abilities in special directions. They are real geniuses, whose talents are so strange and erratic that they seldom, if ever, become appreciated. They are inventive, original, acute observers, possessing large perceptive and executive powers, but much given to roaming over the face of the earth; in other words, are Bohemians.

Upon the Physical Plane, Uranus tends to make the native an object of comment, and those under his influence are odd in their ways, very eccentric, and stubborn to the last degree. They are strongly argumentative and opinionated. What they say is to the point, and asserted with a startling amount of confidence. If well aspected and dignified, Uranus produces sudden wealth. Cases of un- expected wealth, from the poorhouse to the millionaire, are exactly the style of Uranus. When evilly aspected, etc., then he becomes malefic in the highest degree, and brings sudden reverses, quite as unexpected as his gains. Sudden failure, collapse of banks and other commercial squalls, which bring down the rich to the condition of poverty, are generally due to Uranian influence. When Uranus afflicts the significator of marriage in the natus, or is located in the 7th. house, illicit connections are brought about, both before and after the legal unions. This planet is the great significator of the Occult, and his influence never fails to produce mystics.

THE PLANET NEPTUNE ♆

This planet is the most recently discovered of the primary planets, and constitutes the present "scientific frontier," so to say, of modern astronomy. But, it is not the last, as there are others still more re- mote, whose action upon the mental and nervous constitution of man- kind, at present, is nil. Each orb becomes visible to our earth only when the planetary life which it evolves is susceptible to the action and re-action of its influx. But at present the influence of Neptune is very small, except upon certain organisms; therefore, we are not prepared for the revolutions of still more ethereal forces. As the race evolves higher susceptibilities, the influence of Uranus and Neptune will increase, and that of Mercury and Venus will wane. Neptune ex- presses all the higher qualities at present known to us.

Astrologically considered, Neptune is the octave expression of the planet Venus; consequently, its influx relates to the affectional and emotional qualities. This love, however, is purely platonic, and at present, ideal. The influence is mild and genial, but it possesses no power of the lower orb upon vitality; consequently, is utterly power-less to sustain physical life when the Hyleg is afflicted, either by posi-tion or direction. This must be borne in mind or serious error will occur in astro-delineations.

From what has been stated, it will be apparent to the reader that the present generation has very little affinity with such ethereal in-fluence; therefore, the chief points to watch are those wherein Nep-tune is located in the ascendant, mid-heaven, seventh house and lower meridian. At these points, only, will the influx be strongly man-ifested, or, in other words, when the planet is "angular."

Upon the Intellectual Plane, Neptune controls the platonic spirit of Universal Brotherhood which, strangely enough, since the planet's visible manifestation has been so loudly preached and theoretically accepted, but practically, entirely ignored by those who are most clamorous for its general recognition. Those dominated by its influx are pleasant, agreeable, pure, simple and also romantic. They desire the simple arcadian life of the golden age. They sigh for all things in common; consequently, they are considered by modern thinkers as impractical visionaries. The world of Neptune's influx is decidedly Utopian.

Upon the Physical Plane, this planet has but little influence in the present age. His aspects (when powerful) with the Sun and Moon, tend greatly towards the production of clairvoyance. If located in the ascendant, Neptune always produces large, blue, dreamy-looking eyes. In fact, the eyes of such natives are the most conspicuous fea-ture they possess. This position also confers a strong predilection for books of romance and an aversion to hard, dry, matter-of-fact science; also, strangely enough, such natives manifest an aversion to water. When located in the 10th. house, the native generally obtains some pleasant, easy position, such as private secretary to some nobleman or philosophical institution; where the duties are light and the salary more or less heavy in proportion to the absence of actual work. When in the 7th. house, such a position indicates a pleasant married life, and if, in aspect with the Moon, with a rather impractical partner. In the 4th. house, it is a testimony of a natural death.

THE LOST ORB ★ ☽

Strange as it may seem, it is, nevertheless, a fact, that there is a missing planet. It has been allegorically expressed by Jesus as the prodigal son; by Moses as Abel; and by the prophets of the Scandinavian Edda as "Ragnarok." To our esoteric system there are ten celestial bodies somewhere, viz. the Sun and nine planets. At present we have only nine in all. Where, then, is the lost one? The exalted adept alone, can solve this problem. Suffice it to say, that it symbolizes the missing soul within the human constitution. Pushed out of the line of march by disturbing forces; this orb became, for a time, the prey of disruptive action and ultimately lost form; and is now a mass of fragments. The ring of planetoids, between the orbits of Mars and Jupiter, indicate to us the empty throne of Abel, whom Cain (Mars) slew in his anger. The time will ultimately come when this orb will be re-constituted, and Abel will rise up from the dead. Until that time, the missing soul will seek its physical mate in vain, except in rare cases. When this day shall arrive, the Utopia of Neptune and the Millennium of St. John will begin upon earth. May that time speedily arrive.

Each planetary chain consists of seven active orbs and three latent ones. When one becomes latent, another becomes active. Remember this occult fact. THEY CORRESPOND TO THE TEN SEPHIROTH OF THE KABBALAH.

Zenith
Noon

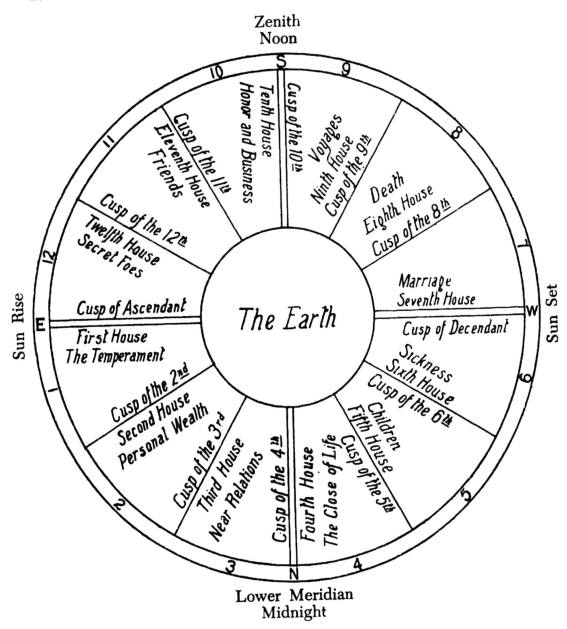

Sun Rise

Sun Set

Lower Meridian
Midnight

DIAGRAM SHOWING THE TWELVE HOUSES OF THE HEAVENS
AND THE INFLUENCE OF THE STELLAR INFLUX
REFLECTED FROM EACH HOUSE.

CHAPTER VIII

THE PRACTICAL APPLICATION OF THE SCIENCE OF THE STARS

The next branch of this celestial science which requires our notice, is the practical application of the various laws, principles and influences, in their direct relation to man and his material destiny. Therefore, we will first present a brief outline of the scientific basis, so to say, upon which the action and inter-action of stellar influences repose, and then offer a few concluding words of general advice.

The magnetic polarity of any given geographical point on our earth's surface is changing every moment. This continual changing in the earth is accompanied by a corresponding change in the electric and more ethereal vital currents of the atmosphere. Both of these varying conditions are caused, primarily, by the diurnal motion of the earth upon its axis from west to east, which causes the whole heavens to transit the visible horizon from east to west during the space of one natural day, of 24 hours. The secondary causes are the various motions and aspects of the Sun, Moon and planets, as they relate to the positions of the earth in her annual orbit about the Sun. The primary basis, the diurnal motion of the planet, claims our attention first. We will, therefore, briefly examine its nature and philosophy.

The real motions of the earth are the only motions that have any real influence upon the physical organism of the earth's inhabitants. These motions determine the length of the day, measure out to us the proportion of light and darkness, regulate the seasons, and fix with the hand of fate, the exact duration of the year. All these have a manifest influence upon the organism of man.

As our mother earth revolves upon her axis, the whole of the celestial heavens seem to rise, culminate and set upon every portion of her surface. Though this rising and setting is only an appearance, so far as the heavens are concerned, it is absolutely real to the earth's inhabitants, because the influences, as they transit the earth from east to west, are exactly the same as if the earth was the stationary center of our solar system, and the heavens were revolving around it.

The varying conditions of the astral and magnetic forces are caused by the various angles, at which, in their apparent motions, the stellar influx is reflected to any given point of the earth. For instance, the conditions at sunrise are practically different from the conditions prevailing at noon, when the Sun is shining upon the meridian. At sunset we see another wonderful difference manifested, possessing nothing in common with either noon or sunrise. Then, again, we have the midnight state of the earth and the atmosphere, in which the conditions are the polar opposite of those in force at noon. These cardinal points of the day indicate the greatest changes, but, as a matter of course, these changes, from one to the other, are gradual. To measure this gradual angular change, the ancient astrologers divided that space of the heavens visible at any moment into six houses or mansions, as they termed them, and the opposite or invisible arc into the same number, making twelve in all, designated as the diurnal and nocturnal houses of the heavens. Modern astrologers follow out the same principles, because, being founded upon the rock of absolute truth, their influence can be verified in every correctly calculated horoscope, when the plane occupied by the native is taken into consideration.

These twelve houses contain, like the signs of the Zodiac, 30 degrees of space each, but unlike them, the house distance is measured by degrees of right ascension, or time, instead of celestial longitude. This is the only real relation existing between the twelve houses and the twelve signs. The various symbolical relations between the two, such as Aries being the regent of the first mansion and so on, possess no influence or importance in the practical application of the science, but pertain to the realm of Kabbalistical mythology.

If the reader will draw a circle three inches in diameter, and then, in the center of this, a smaller circle about one inch in diameter, he will possess two mathematical ideas in objective form. The smaller circle will represent the earth, the larger one the heaven around it. If we now divide the larger circle into quadrants, we shall see the angles which represent the four cardinal points of the day, and, upon a more extensive scale, the seasons of the year. These are no mere fanciful ideas, but they are external symbols of living realities upon the external plane of phenomena. If the reader will now divide the larger circle into twelve equal parts, he will possess another outline chart representing the twelve houses of the heavens, with the earth in the center. The horizontal line upon the left represents the eastern horizon or the point, in reference to the earth, which is occupied by the sun at sunrise. The perpendicular line above the horizon, marking off one quadrant of the circle, represents the zenith or meridian occupied, at noon, by the sun in its daily transit. Now between these two points, the horizon and the meridian, we have two angular lines which divide the quadrant of 90 degrees into three parts containing 30 degrees each. These are the three south-eastern houses which mark off the angular changes of solar and astral influx between sunrise and noon. The horizontal line opposite to and parallel with the line of the horizon, shows that point of the heavens which is occupied by the sun, in reference to the earth, at sunset, and the two angular lines between it and the meridian indicate the changes of terrestrial and celestial conditions between noon and sunset. Thus, in the space of the daytime, the sun, stars and planets (if there should be any situated in that part of the heavens) have made the transit of the diurnal arc of six houses. During this time every conceivable change of polarity that is possible under solar influx has been manifested upon the earth, and thousands of human beings have been ushered into physical existence, each and all differing more or less widely from each other, according to the influence dominant at the exact moment of mortal birth. It is needless to repeat this description of the six nocturnal houses; it is similar; the perpendicular line opposite the zenith is the lower meridian where the sun is situated at midnight; then, still moving forward in its ceaseless round, the sun arrives upon the horizon again, at sunrise, to commence another day. In order to give a clearer idea of this thought than words can possibly convey, we insert a diagram which explains itself. We have only to add in this connection, that the earth is divided into positive and negative halves, which are continually changing from one to the other; the half under the sun's rays is always positive; that portion under the shades of evening is negative. Day and night then, like the sun and moon, are the polar opposites of each other, and so are the individuals born under the two conditions.

From the foregoing, it will be seen that any number of individuals, born during the course of a single day, at different times, will differ widely in their physical temperament and mental bias. Not only so, but, they will differ just as widely in their fortunes and destiny. Herein, then, we see the grand basic principles of this science; which accounts, in a most philosophical manner, for the wonderful diversity in human beings; so that, scarcely any two are alike in mind, form, or feature; because no two are born exactly at the same moment of time, under exactly the same position of the heavens. For instance; suppose one hundred children in different parts of the world were born at the same precise moment of time, the difference in the latitude and longitude of their respective birthplaces would render it probable that no two would be alike; because of the different aspects presented by the heavens to different portions of the globe at exactly the same moment. The reader has only to bear in mind that, it is sunrise, noon, sunset, and midnight, every moment; at some point on the earth; in order to realize the great natural difference that exists between those who are born at the same moment of time in different parts of the world.

The secondary causes which regulate and modify the astral and planetary influx are the apparent motions of the sun, moon, and planets, in their orbits; as they either approach each other or recede. As before stated, it is the real motion of a planet which affects its inhabitants; therefore, we need not repeat the reasons we have already given. When our earth is so situated as to appear to an observer in the sun to be moving through Cancer; the sun appears, to the inhabitants on earth, to be passing through the opposite sign, Capricorn; and so far as the earth is concerned it really is; because the solar center stands between the earth and the sign; and the solar influx is, consequently, impregnated with the magnetic qualities of Capricorn; with which it permeates the earth. Hence, when we speak of the influence of the sun in Capricorn or any other sign, though only an astronomical appearance, we mean exactly what we say. Further, when the earth, by its progressive motion, moves faster or slower in a different direction from other planets and causes them to become alternately stationary, direct in motion, or retrograde; we know that these are purely appearances, so far as the planets, themselves, are concerned; but their influx is just the same on earth, as if it were a reality; because the real movements of our earth place them in those positions, in reference to the apparent position of the sun. The various angular distances so formed, termed aspects, are so potent in their magnetic effects; that some times, the whole good or evil influx of a given planet is completely polarized by them; and, almost always, these aspects are found to constitute very important factors in the native's horoscope.

The reader will perceive from the foregoing statement of astral principles, that in order to properly gauge and apply the actual influences in operation at a person's nativity; two primary considerations are necessary, viz.: the time and place of a person's physical birth. Without these, nothing reliable can be scientifically determined. And any system of astral, planetary, or solar influences; that pretends to determine the celestial influences upon man; which ignores these essential elements, is thoroughly inaccurate; if not utterly misleading.

Before concluding these brief remarks upon the basis of this science, we would point out the fact, for the benefit of some of our readers; that ancient astrology is not, as so many seem to think, "an exploded science;" and further, we wish to point out another very important fact, viz.: that, not a single individual can be found, who talks or writes of this astrological explosion; who himself, understands the fundamental principles of the science he is defaming. Many superficially learned individuals think that the old geocentric system of Claudius Ptolemy was the only foundation upon which the ancient astrology rested; and that, when the present Newtonian system overturned the Ptolemaic theory of a "primum mobile," the astrology of the ancients was buried amid the ruins. We need scarcely add that, such superficial minds are in sad need of a little true light. The observed effects of certain positions of the heavens; be they apparent or real; is the only foundation of judicial astrology; and it was upon the continuous observations of ages, that the old Chaldean sages formulated their wonderful science of the stars. The eclipses of the Sun and Moon, the conjunctions of the planets, and the exact length of the solar year, were all correctly computed, ages before the days of Abraham. In reality, it makes little difference to astrology; whether the earth moves about the Sun or the Sun moves about the earth; for it rests upon the absolute fact that, one of them does indeed move.

So far as the physical organism of man is concerned; the planet which gave it birth is its center and the focus of all celestial influences; hence, the earth and its motions are the only ones of vital importance upon the material plane. We would point out to all would-be heio-

centric astrologers who desire to formulate special "solar" systems
of planetary influence for themselves; that, the whole basis of their
system rests upon a mere question of terms; and is as much an appearance as the geocentric conception. The orbits of the planets, of our
solar system, are so small and insignificant compared with the inconceivable distances of the constellations; that to say that a planet
is in any particular sign or constellation; is nothing but asserting, that
which is only an appearance. It is only removing the point of observation from the earth to the Sun. Both are optical illusions; but, in this
removal, the illusion is intensified. What are the signs of the Zodiac
but apparent lines and apparent spaces? They certainly have nothing
to do with the real constellations of the heavens at the present day.
Nevertheless, their influence is a demonstrated fact. These signs are
nothing more nor less than angular distances in the heavens, which
mark off the increase and decrease of the solar influx, upon the northern
and southern hemisphere of the earth. Surely then, the system which
adopts one series of appearances is very incomplete; that does not
include the whole, embracing a map of the heavens. Away then
forever, with this pseudo-scientific sentimentalism which speaks so
much of realities; when in very truth, it is embracing nothing, but
an aggregation of shadows and appearances.

The various mathematical details, which constitute the external
and purely practical department of the science of exoteric astrology,
can be thoroughly studied out by each interested reader for himself;
from the numerous books published upon the subject. To guide the
student of this science, we will say that "The Dictionary of Astrology,"
by James Wilson, and "The Text Book of Astrology," vol. I, by A. J.
Pearce, are among the very finest works.

Our advice to any one commencing the serious study of The
Science of the Stars, is to carefully read and reread the works just
referred to; then master the mathematical and mechanical details;
thirdly, make yourself familiar with the various aspects, characters,
etc., of the planets; and lastly, study closely the occult laws and
esoteric principles relating thereto as given in this work. When this
course of study is completed, you may commence experiments by
erecting the horoscopes of yourself and friends; and note how far
the observed results agree with your astrological deductions. If this
advice is followed out, you cannot go very far wrong; for it is upon

the full realization of the occult and philosophical principles underlying this external formula, that a real knowledge of astrology consists. It is this absolute knowledge of the stars, that always distinguishes the true artist from the astrological pretender, and "fortune telling" imposter. It is these latter charlatans who, by their unprincipled methods and villainy, have caused the very name of astrology to become the synonym of superstition and fraud in the eyes of nineteenth century intelligence. So different are the people and the conditions which surround us; from those who lived in the days of old, when the wise men of Chaldea communed with the beautiful constellations of heaven; and learned therefrom, the mighty secrets of the soul's origin and destiny; as well as the material details of their physical lives. The same book of Nature is open now, as then; but, only the pure in heart can read its pages and trace the mystical chain of life, as depicted by Nature through the stars, to Nature's God.

THE SOUL AND THE STARS

The beautiful, twinkling, glittering stars,
The rivals in splendor of Venus and Mars,
They come and they go,
Moulding the powers of our weal or our woe.

Shining serene in the heavens above,
Nightly teaching us lessons of love,
No discords nor jars
Appear to disturb these beautiful stars.

The soul seems to claim these jewels on high,
And struggles to soar to its source in the sky.
But sorrow and pain
Are the pathways that carry it homeward again.

How oft have we dreamed, when gazing above,
That the purified soul — the offspring of love,
When freed from earth's load,
Would find in the stars its peaceful abode.

So fondly we think of our homes in the sky,
Joined with the soul for whose presence we sigh;
Where Saturn nor Mars
Can embitter our joys mid the beautiful stars.

CONCLUSION

THE MYSTICAL CHAIN; OR, THE UNION OF THE SOUL AND THE STARS

As the soul unfolds in true spiritual light, the manifest unity between man and his divine source; also between man and the myriad creations of the infinite universe; become a self evident and absolute fact. But, unfortunately, the undeveloped soul sees none of these great facts of unity and identity; nor perceives the vital relations existing between the soul and the stars. The facts of the one seem to him totally irrelevant to the facts of the other; while, on the other hand, to the initiated seer, a true knowledge of the soul is impossible without a perfect understanding of the stars. Equally, are the stars incomprehensible, apart from the soul. Man, the microcosm, is, in himself, a miniature universe; composed of infinite atoms; which are in a constant state of action and re-action; not only among themselves; but also, with the infinite atoms of the larger universe, the macrocosm. Hence, a true science of the soul cannot be founded which does not also include a true science of the stars. It also follows; that deductions based upon a comprehension of these higher relations, which are self evident to the seer; will appear to the ordinary undeveloped human being as quite irrational and illogical; since the premises are, to him, incongruous and unrelated. With such, all efforts at enlightenment are quite futile in the present state of evolution; but for those souls struggling to awake to the higher truths of their existence and destiny; this conclusion is added, to help them, to grasp, this grand union of the soul and the stars; this mystical chain, which binds the infinite multiplicity into unity, as well as diversity into identity.

We have, therefore, to regard man in a somewhat different light from that in which we have hitherto considered him, viz.: we have now to behold him as a grand, intelligent, spirito-material center, for the expression of astro-celestial forces, upon the internal and external planes of God's universe. Man, broadly speaking, is a duplex mirror, reflecting the stellar forces in two directions; 1st., the astral influx from his body to the planes below humanity; 2nd., the finer ethereal essences of the stars from his soul to the aerial races in the spheres above. The first comprises seven degrees of sub-mundane life, from man to the mineral, forming as it were a lower octave of existence;

the second is the ascending scale, or the higher octave of existence, containing seven degrees of super-mundane life between man and the angel. These seven degrees of super-mundane existence are the aerial races of bright, immortal souls; the spiritual superiors of humanity; in so far as concerns the realms they inhabit; and the more etherealized conditions which surround them. These are the planetary angels mentioned in the Ritual of divine magic. Planetary angels do not exist upon the various objective planets, as so many occultists imagine; but in the series of seven spheres between the planets and the sun. But, on the other hand, these aerial races are very much inferior to man; both in spiritual quality, soul power, and penetrative force; and are utterly incapable of entering upon the physical struggles of external life; hence, they are a purely subjective race; and are never incarnated in matter (as we understand the term). They depend upon the more positive spirit of humanity (which alone is capable of entering and subjecting material forces) for all their knowledge of external conditions.

The first degree in the higher octave consists of those souls who have the most penetrative force, next to man; and are, consequently, nearest to our physical conditions. Each degree in the ascending scale becomes less potent (materially); more ethereal and refined; until it blends, in the seventh, with the purely spiritual or angelic world.

In the lower octave of existence, viz.: the seven degrees of sub-mundane life; countless beautiful worlds are open to the inspection of the spiritual sight. We will briefly recount what we ourselves have witnessed therein, as we speak of each degree.

The first degree in the lower octave is that of the crystallized mineral, in which the life atoms are latent, so to say. The rocks and stones are of both sexes, and impregnate each other with their magnetic forces. Their sympathies and antipathies constitute their laws of natural selection; which we see manifested externally by the vegetation they produce from their soil. The second degree pertains to the subjective spaces of the mineral world. The busy races within the higher rounds of the mineral zone (the anima mineralis), are beautiful in every detail; each life atom busy at its appointed task; happy beyond conception in its lowly spiritual state. As yet the scintillating monad knows nothing of the greater worlds above. To it the mineral waves are the alpha and omega of its ideas. The third degree of life passes in review as the vegetable kingdom, of which sufficient is already known to the reader. The higher we go the brighter the little creatures become. When we ascend to the fourth degree of life, we behold the loveliest scenes that fairyland can present to the eyes of the seer. The exquisite form and variety of these dazzling elemental sprites are beyond language to describe. Each vortex or space of the anima floralis constitutes a veritable paradise of beauty; a wondrous world of delights; in which, the nymphs of the flowers and the bright fairies of the floral world, sport like butterflies, in the luminous ether of their round. The fifth degree passes before us as the animal kingdom. The sixth degree of life expresses itself as the semi-human round, the external correspondence of which may be seen in the ape family. This realm of sub-mundane life contains the astral world of the apes. It is these astral forms that are used by certain magicians (after the human principle has vacated them) for occult purposes. They become the trained elementals of magical science. Their chief quality is imitation; and under the influence of their master's mind they will personate anything; from an angel of light to a goblin damned. The sixth degree is a world in which the soul begins to put forth its attributes of self-consciousness; a realm wherein the struggling monad gathers together the results of past sub-mundane victories; and prepares to graduate to that higher life round; wherein, it may commence to assume the human form. The seventh degree of life is the embryonic human round; a spiritual zone or soul world, wherein exists the multitudes of prepared souls awaiting the conditions of their final incarnation. It is the realm of anxious expectations and glowing ideals of what external human life may be. It is from this state, or degree of life, that the human soul takes its last plunge into objective material conditions; from which, it emerges to the surface as the self acting, self conscious, individual man.

Let us now briefly turn our attention from man to the planet, which he inhabits; and trace the correspondence. The planet, like the man, may be designated as a duplex mirror; reflecting stellar and planetary influx in two directions; 1st., to the various realms of elemental existence (corresponding to sub-mundane life); termed cosmic elementals; belonging to the four occult elements of Fire, Earth, Air, and Water; 2nd., to the astro-magnetic zones of the planet (corresponding to the super-mundane realms), termed magnetic elementals. The magnetic elementals are intelligent spirits known by various names; such as fairies, fauns, elves, nymphs, etc. One very important distinction must be noticed here; between sub-mundane and super-mundane realms on the one hand; and cosmic elementals and magnetic elementals on the other hand; viz., that the two former are various degrees of human soul life; hence possess the germs of immortality, when the human state is attained; while the two latter are not souls; and although they depend upon the soul of man for their differentiated existence, yet they do not derive their supply of sustenance from him; but from the latent forces within the planet, of each orb, of the planetary chain; hence, they live only so long as the planet is able to sustain them. Therefore, they are not immortal. When the planet has fulfilled its material purpose, they, along with the orb which gave them life, become a thing of the past.

We have now reached a most important link in our mystical chain, viz.: since embodied man is the highest form of manifested existence upon the planet, he is the grand polarizing point for all four of the forms of existence, we have been describing. The human organism is, therefore, the grand radiating center upon which the two vast realms, stellar and psychic, impinge; and is the material link, uniting the soul and the stars. Thus, in very truth, is man the microcosm; and the sacred adytum of the mysteries.

In order to render this more manifest, let us now endeavor to form as clear an idea as possible of the nature and modus operandi of stellar influx, as transmitted to man from our solar system; for, when we comprehend that portion of the mystical chain, then we can form some faint conception of the continued and unbroken chain, which binds our solar system to other systems and constellations; on and on, to the very interior of the soul, of the universe. First, then, stands our Sun; and around it, like a group of obedient children, are the seven planets of the mystical chain; (there are more than seven planets in the solar system, but only seven in each octave of life); each orb giving birth to an entirely different degree of life; so that the seven mystical degrees are completed. Each orb produces innumerable types of fauna and flora, corresponding to the action of its own peculiar grade of spiritual force. Each, therefore, comprises a miniature universe of its own; and yet, at the same time; each planet contains all the forces

of the other six; only that, these six forces are latent; in so far as to
lend all their force, for the more complete manifestation of the dominating one. Hence it follows, that our earth contains, in addition to
its own dominating degree of life, the latent forces of the various
grades of life active upon the other planets; so that Mars, Venus,
Mercury, etc., are here with us; just as much as they are in the far
off spaces. Herein is contained the great mystery of planetary influence upon man; for man, as before stated, is the highest type of
life upon the globe; and becomes the great radiator of the different
grades of life of the seven planets, comprised within the one he inhabits. His sensitive sphere becomes the means of arousing countless races of astro-magnetic elementals into life and motion; and also,
into obedient servitude; if he only possesses the knowledge to direct
them; for each grade of planetary influx renders service and protection
to the corresponding grade of men. Thus; Mars to the martial natures,
Saturn to the saturnine, and Jupiter to the jovial, and so forth. The
interior secrets of the talisman and the mysteries of magic are concealed here; and the portals are open, for the soul's exploration. This
also, is the philosophic basis for the various statements that; certain
planets rule certain soul attributes, mental qualities, physical instincts,
classes of animals, plants, herbs, trees, minerals, precious stones, etc.

The reader who has followed us thus far, is now invited to join
us in a short trip to the astral world and there behold man as he presents himself to the vision of the seer. A most wonderous and dazzling
picture is before us, undreamed of mysteries connected with the
human form divine. Let us examine more closely. First, we observe,
that from the spinal column of the stately form of man; and from the
base of his luminous brain; issue living streams of vitalizing force;
which, as they flow from the various points of his odylic sphere; become refracted into the seven rays of the spectrum. These rays of
living force from different individuals, become mutually attracted
toward each other; each color blends with its kindred color from other
organisms, and gravitates to its own particular level in the prismatic
ocean of life; until the whole of this mighty planet, with its millions
of human beings scattered over its throbbing surface; presents to the
eye of the initiated seer a perfect network of luminous springs, creeks,
rivers, and oceans of force; flowing from the radiating organism of
man. We also observe; that these luminous oceans gradually assume

the form of a spiral belt, which encircles the planet—penetrating to its very center; and then expands itself, mist-like, within the planet's atmosphere; where a prismatic reflection is cast around the earth; constituting a sort of astral rainbow (if we may use such a term); which is strictly confined within the limits of the planet's gaseous envelope. This prismatic reflection is the astro-magnetic sphere, wherein are formed the astral zones of the magnetic elementals, of planetary influx, to which we have previously referred, as forming the grand mystic links in the chain of life; which binds the organism of man to the soul of the stars.

So far, we have only beheld our human duplex mirror from the spinal column and the base of the brain; as he reflects the astral influx from his body to the lower octave of life, termed sub-mundane; we will now, therefore, regard the other half; or polar opposite surface of our duplex mirror; wherein, the stellar forces are reflected from the soul to the higher octave of life; the realms of super-mundane beings.

We first observe, that, the odylic sphere of man; which forms the oval surface of our living mirror; is constantly polished by the vivid lightnings of the immortal soul within; next, we see that the forces reflected from it are received directly from above, in an angle to the left of the sphere; and that, after passing through and leaving one portion to sustain the form and its functions; and also another portion to be radiated to the sub-mundane planes; then, the higher and more ethereal principles undergo a change of polarity; and are reflected upward again, in an angle to the right of the sphere; to the aerial races of super-mundane life. Let us now, therefore, enter within the occult spaces of humanity, upon this spiritual plane; and describe the phenomena as it passes in review before our spiritual sight.

We perceive that, from the millions of earth's inhabitants there issues continual rays of reflected light; each ray partaking of the peculiar color represented by the soul from which it is reflected. As these rays ascend, they converge into streams and oceans, within the astral light above the planet's atmosphere; (whereas, the former astral belt, just described, was confined within the limits of the planet's atmosphere). All of these luminous oceans of etherealized light seek their own plane, and maintain a strict relation to each other, with the mathematical exactitude of the solar spectrum. We also notice that, these oceans flow in one continual direction, viz.: in the opposite direction to the orbital motion of the earth. They flow backward in the orbit. The writer cannot be positive upon this point, as these are his own actual experiences, and are related here as they actually appeared to him in the realms of spirit. It may be that, this backward motion is only an appearance, caused by the earth moving forward; just as the landscape from the window of a car in motion, appears to the occupant to be moving. But, in flowing backward, these oceans graduallly ascend, assuming the spiral form; the first round being about the same circumference as the earth's annual orbit about the Sun; but, increasing in size with each spiral, in the ratio of 1-2, 4-8, 16-32-64. These spirals assume their own special color; commencing, first with that which is nearest to the earth, which is Red; the 2nd. Orange, the 3rd. Yellow, the 4th. Green, the 5th. Blue, the 6th. Indigo, and the 7th. or last Violet. What there may be beyond this, we cannot tell. All that we do know is, that it is the realm of the angels. These spirals, which we have just described, constitute mighty zones; which encircle an ethereal sphere or world of the same identical color; similar to the bright rings round the body of Saturn. The clairvoyant medium, Andrew Jackson Davis, undoubtedly saw these beautiful etherealized zones, when he described "the summer land" in his "Stellar Key." But he was quite mistaken in supposing them to be the homes of disembodied humanity. As the reader has seen, they are inhabited by aerial races, who cannot penetrate the outer envelope of crystallized force; called objective matter. We need scarcely add that, these are the seven graduated spirit worlds, between the earth and the Sun; constituting the chain previously mentioned. These spheres are the seven etherealized worlds, which form the subjective arc, between the planet and its parent center—man and the angel.

Still gazing at this sublime panorama of Nature's wonderful formations, within the spiritual spaces of the astral light; we perceive that these astro-spiritual zones or belts contain the etherealized materials and essences of earth; which sustain the external life forces of the aerial races, who inhabit these glorious worlds. The first world, as we have previously shown, is nearest to our physical conditions and absorbs the coarsest portions. The next, being more ethereal, absorbs the next in spiritual quality. The finer the essence, the higher it ascends; so that the most ethereal of all reaches the confines of the angelic world; and diffuses its violet aromas within the spaces that are divine. As we perceive this fact; we instantly comprehend the grand connection of the whole universe. MAN stands upon the central rung of the cyclic ladder, as the meeting point of the equilibrium, between the upper and the lower manifestations, of the great ONE LIFE. In MAN lies concealed the sacred mystery of the lost word. He is the wonderful microcosm. By his duplex action of body and soul, he becomes the grand conservator; the generator; and the radiator; of spiritual and material life forces; first, absorbing the currents of the life wave, then separating it into its triune qualities; retaining one, then re-polarizing and transmitting the grosser portions, in the form of an astro-magnetic fluid, to the planes of life below; and reflecting, from the mirror of his soul, in the form of an astro-spiritual essence, the finer and more ethereal portions, to the realms above. What awful and unsuspected mysteries lie concealed within our being! Verily, no mind can grasp all the mysteries of man.

Reader, the oceans of purified life essence; forming these spiral zones of the interior heavens; which extend from the celestial worlds to the earth; from the angels to man; and then, in a grosser form, extend to our planet's very center; is the mystical chain of the great one life; that unites man to all below him and binds him to the immortal realms of life above. It is the spiral cycle of necessity traversed by the life atoms; in their descent into matter, and in their ascent into the realms of conscious spiritual existence. It is the spiral cord of Nature whose vibrations, throughout the wide universe of manifested being, proclaim the unbroken union between the soul and the stars. The same yesterday, to-day and for evermore.

The mysteries of man are the mysteries of God, and who can solve them here on earth? The soul answereth, "none." So be it.

In conclusion, we will only add that as a child of God, or the crystallization of force; as a spiritual entity, or a thing of dust; man's birth-right is ever the same; a progressive conscious immortality. He is the sustainer of the universes below, of which even occultists have scarcely dreamed, and he is the generator of the essences which sustain the life of myriads in brighter worlds than ours.

FINIS

The

Light of Egypt

or

The Science of the Soul and the Stars

VOLUME II

BY

THOMAS H. BURGOYNE

Zanoni, ⅂

"Write the things which thou hast seen, and the things which are, and the things which shall be hereafter; THE MYSTERY OF THE SEVEN STARS, which thou sawest in my right hand."

Revelations, Chap. I, 19 and 20.

H. O. Wagner
P. O. Box 20333 Montclair Station
Denver 20, Colorado.

REPRINT EDITION 1963

The first edition of *The Light of Egypt,* Volume II, was copyrighted in 1900 by Henry Wagner M.D. and published by the Astro
Philosophical Publishing Company of Denver, Colorado. This book
is a reprint of the first edition which has been out of print for many
years.

H. O. Wagner.

Dedication

To the Budding Spirituality of the Occident and
The Rising Genius of the Western Race,
This work is respectfully dedicated,
By the Author

CONTENTS

The Science of the Soul and the Stars

VOLUME II

PUBLISHER'S PREFACE

No explanation is thought necessary, further than to corroborate the author in all he has said in his somewhat unusual preface.

We have enjoyed, immensely, our work of giving to the world this remarkable series of books on Occultism, and appreciate the large patronage they have received from the reading public, for which we return our sincere thanks. We hope the near future will give us the work referred to by the author in his preface, as doubtless it will be a great revelation of Occult laws that govern our little Earth in its relation to our Sun and solar system, of which it forms a part, and give much light on those subjects that have been shrouded in mystery.

"The Light of Egypt" will be found to be an Occult library in itself, a textbook of esoteric knowledge, setting forth the "Wisdom Religion" of life, as taught by the Adepts of Hermetic Philosophy. It will richly repay all who are seeking the higher life to carefully study this book, as it contains in a nutshell the wisdom of the ages regarding man and his destiny, here and hereafter. The London and American first edition, also the French edition, Vol. I, met with lively criticism from Blavatsky Theosophists, because it annihilates that agreeable delusion of "Karma" and "Reincarnation" from the minds of all lovers of truth for truth's sake.

"The Tablets of Æth" is a great and mighty work, as it contains the very quintessence of Occult and Hermetic philosophy, as revealed by spiritual law. "Penetralia" is a new revelation, and invaluable to Occult students, as it is the personal experience of a developed soul.

To all lovers of Truth we respectfully recommend this Book of Books, as it has justly been called by many who are competent to criticise its teachings. It was the author's wish that his name be withheld from the public, knowing full well that the teachings contained in his works will prove his motto: *"Omnia Vincit Veritas."*

Now that our author has passed beyond the power of the world to flatter or condemn, and has given his thought for the uplifting of the human family, it is but simple justice that he be made known to the world as its teacher of a higher thought than has preceded him. He shrank from public notoriety, and modestly refused to be publicly known to the world as one of its spiritual leaders for the cycle upon which the Earth and its inhabitants have entered, but the time has come to announce publicly the authorship of the works published anonymously under the symbol of , , and his writings are to be judged by their merits, and not by prejudice nor personal bias as viewed from the human plane of life.

He moved in the world, comparatively unknown to the world at large, and his greatest friends, though mystified, did not understand his true worth in spiritual greatness. The mask, or person, often hides from view the angel in disguise. Therefore our author must be judged by what he has written, and not by his personators and calumniators. The true student of Occultism always judges the tree by its fruits. If the writings of our author are judged by this standard, they will stand as a beacon light to higher rounds than ours.

PREFACE

These lessons were issued to a few of my pupils as "Private Studies in Occultism," several years ago. The time has now come to give them to the world as a companion to the first volume of "The Light of Egypt."

It is the duty of Occult students to familiarize themselves with the subjects herein discussed. They should know the ideas of our ancestors regarding them and be familiar with their thought, in order to appreciate the sublime wisdom and knowledge of Nature as taught by them, otherwise we are sure to do them, as well as ourselves, great injustice. The history of Occultism bears out the fact that there is very little that is new to the present time.

The arrangement and classification of thought differs during each cycle of time on the different spirals, and, like the fruitage on lower rounds of Nature's progressive wheel of destiny, variety and quality are diverse, so, likewise, do we find the mental manifestations. This age, however, is blessed with a great variety and abundance of thought, in clear-cut language, that should enlighten the races of the Earth with Mother Nature's modus operandi in every department of human thought.

We hope these chapters will aid to this end, and doubtless many students will find in them the key to unlock the mysteries veiled in symbol and hieroglyphic by ancient writers. The author's object has been to make plain and easy of understanding these subjects. Much, however, has been left for private study and research, for many large volumes might be filled if a detailed description of each subject were entered upon, which task is left for those who feel so inclined. A rich reward is in store for those spiritual investigators who will follow out the paths and lines herein mapped out on Spiritual Astrology, Alchemy, and other subjects. Meditation and aspiration will open up hidden treasures that will prove a boon to Occult students, for Astrology and Alchemy are the two grand sciences that explain the why and reasons for what we see and experience on every plane of life. In this age there should be no concealing of these Divine truths. We cannot hide anything in the air, and for this reason the Sun in Aquarius will unearth and reveal to man all that the present cycle has to give during the Sun's passage through this airy sign.

The watery sign, Pisces, through which the Sun manifested during the past 2,160 years, gave up to man their secret powers and hidden attributes in steam as a motive power, which man has completely mastered. He will likewise master the airy forces during the present sub-cycle of the Sun in Aquarius. Already we see him using liquid air and compressed air as a motive power, which will gradually take the place of steam as the Sun gets farther into the sign, or constellation, of Aquarius. Men will become immensely wiser than they have been, and it is to be hoped they will leave the written record of their achievements in science and art to show to future races their status of mind on every subject for the edification and enlightenment of coming races.

Our ancestors were denied this great privilege. Consequently their wisdom is only symbolized to us in a way that it is difficult to read and interpret correctly, yet we who have the key to their symbols can read accurately the truth they wish to convey, which stands out clearly to all capable of understanding and interpreting symbolism and correspondence correctly. History and Nature repeat themselves in every cycle of time; therefore these forces and potentialities are natural to the sign through which the Sun manifests. We can go backward or forward through the Sun's Zodiac and read correctly the history of the hoary past, as well as the present and future, by bearing in mind the sign and cycle in manifestation at any given period. When the proper time arrives, a work will be given to the world to prove to mankind the law of cycles.

God is present in all ages and races, manifesting His love and wisdom throughout infinite creations, and that He records, in His own way, the most detailed record of any event which takes place, thus giving to man a complete history of His works and will, for man's enlightenment, so that he, too, may cooperate intelligently with his God in every way that intelligence wills to manifest. Prehistoric history is not blotted out from Nature's laboratory. The Astral Book of Karmic evolution will one day reveal its hidden treasures to a waiting world in such a manner as to surprise and enlighten mankind as the recording angels give up those gems of truth they have so jealously guarded for untold cycles of time, simply because the time was not ripe for its divulgence.

There is a time for everything, and when that time arrives all past history of our planet's evolution will be written in an intelligent manner for the illumination and education of man as the masterpiece of the Living God. In this way man will worship Deity and perfect his God-nature, even to Angel-hood.

If this volume of "The Light of Egypt" meets with the same appreciation that was accorded the first volume, which has passed through four editions, and is still growing in favor every day (besides being translated into the French), the author will feel that his efforts have not been wasted, and he trusts the race will have been made better for having read his writings.

As this is his posthumous contribution to the world, the author wishes, in this connection, to pay a debt of gratitude and grateful recognition to his esteemed pupil and friend, Dr. Henry Wagner, who has so generously published nearly all of his writings. Without his aid and assistance we would not have been able, of ourselves, to have given these works to the world. Therefore, honor to whom honor is due.

Mrs. Belle M. Wagner has been chosen by the Masters as my spiritual successor and representative of the Hermetic Brotherhood of Luxor, and thus perpetuate the chain of outward connection between those in the realm of the higher life with those upon the outward plane.

She is our choice, and a most worthy one to take my place.

I make this statement in this connection for the benefit of my pupils and Hermetic students generally, as I am being personated by frauds and imposters, claiming to be Zanoni. *Verbam sap.*

It is my request that a fac-simile of my signature and symbol accompany this preface.

Dictated by the author from the subjective plane of life (to which he ascended several years ago) through the law of mental transfer, well known to all Occultists, he is enabled again to speak with those who are still upon the objective plane of life.

The additions found in this volume, not in the original manuscripts, have been supplied in this manner. The two planes of life, the objective and subjective, are scientific facts, no longer disputed by well-informed minds, and the exchange of thought will become almost universal among educated minds during the present cycle. Hence great progress will come to the Earth during the next 2,160 years, while the Sun manifests his glorious influence through the symbol of the Man.

Thanking each and all who have aided in any way to give my writings to the world, I am, in love and fraternal greetings, ever yours.

Omnia Vincit Veritas.

Very Truly
T. H. Burgoyne.

INTRODUCTION TO VOL. II

What study is more sublime, inspiring and profitable, in the highest sense, than the "language of the stars"—those silent monitors of the midnight sky, who reveal *His Will* as secondary causes in the administration of universal law? The science of the stars is the Divine parent of all science.

The more earnest our study, the more recondite our research and thorough our investigation of the "Science of the Stars," the more fully shall we realize the truth of the teacher's words: "Astrology is the key that opens the door to all occult knowledge." It is the key that unlocks the mysteries of man's being; his why, whence, whither. Within the temple of Urania lies concealed the mystery of life. The indices are there, written by the finger of the Infinite in the heavens above.

It is our privilege to make this language our own, and it should be the earnest work of every true student of Nature to acquire a right understanding and correct interpretation of these Divine symbols. And, as thorough students of any language seek out the derivation of words and expressions, search for the root, or stem word, and its origin, so should the student of astrology, by sincere desire and earnest study, seek to know the origin and root of these starry words and complex expressions of the "language of the stars."

The Sun, Moon and five planets* of our solar system are to us symbols of the reflected and refracted rays of the triune attributes of the great Central, Spiritual Sun: Life, Light and Love, analogous to the three primary colors in Nature, which become still further refracted into four secondary or complementary colors, rays or attributes, the seven constituting the active principles of Nature, the seven rays of the solar spectrum, the seven notes of a perfect musical scale, there being throughout a perfect correspondence, and all are but different modes of vibration or activities of the Supreme Intelligence.

And, as we know, the seven rays of color reflect an almost infinite variety of tints, that, octave upon octave, are built upon the seven natural tones in music, so, also, are these seven active principles divided and subdivided into innumerable forms, qualities and mani-

---

* Uranus and Neptune belonging to a higher octave.

festations of the first trinity—Life, Light, Love, life being the manifestation of the second two, love and wisdom, which in turn are the
dual expressions of the "One."

Upon the knowledge of these Divine truths Pythagoras built the
theory of the "music of the spheres." Let us pause and listen to this
celestial music.

Suns and their systems of planets sound forth the deep bass tones
and rich tenor, while angelic races take the silvery treble of the Divine
melody, octave upon octave, by more and ever more ethereal system
upon system, to the very throne of Deity—the Infinite, Eternal source
of Light, Life and Love. Let us learn, through the knowledge of the
stars, to attune our souls to vibrate to the Divine harmony, so that
we may take our places in the celestial choir and blend our voices with
those of the celestial singers, chanting the Divine anthem: "We Praise
Thee, O God!"

To resume. If we would gain a correct knowledge of astral
science we should study astrology in its universal application, side by
side with its more intricate phase and the details, as manifested upon
the individual man and his material destiny.

Let us digress for a moment. The intellectual minds, the material
scientists, who cavil at the "science of the stars," declaring it to be
mere fortune-telling, consequently false, do but air their ignorance of
this most profound subject, not knowing that it embraces and contains
all sciences, all religions, that have ever been or ever will be, comprises
all history of every age, of races, empires and nations; that it is the
only true chronology, and marks the destiny, not only of personal man
on every plane, but of the human family as a whole. All mythologies
find their explanation in this starry language, and every religion is
founded upon the movements of our solar system. The rise and fall
of empires and races of men are written in its pages.

To master as far as we are capable, and our limited space of life
here will permit, we must pursue the study in its broad sense, as already stated, in the external application of the starry influx and upon
the interior planes of action from God to the mineral, the mineral to
man; aye, and man to the angel, finding in every section a complete
and perfect correspondence.

To master the alphabet should be the first step, whose vowels,
diphthongs and consonants are the planets and shining Zodiac. It is

very essential to clearly comprehend the action and reaction of the planets upon the human organism, as an integral part of the universal organism; ever remembering that the starry vowels, in combination with the consonants, or Zodiac, form the infinite expressions comprising the language of the starry heavens in their threefold manifestation upon the external planes of life; while the radiant constellations are the ideas which find expression through this language, which is likewise a science, accurate in its mathematical construction and perfect in geometric proportion.

The student should ever bear in mind that astrology, like every other science, is progressive. The underlying principles are always the same. These are like the "laws of the Medes and Persians," but the plane of action is constantly changing.

It is a well-established and indisputable truth that from the Sun, the solar center of our system, is derived all force, every power and variety of phenomena that manifests itself upon Mother Earth. Therefore, when we remember that the solar parent passes through one sign of his celestial Zodiac in 2,160 years, a twelfth part of his orbit of 25,920 years, we see that from each sign in turn he (the Sun) rays forth an influx peculiar to that special sign; and, as there are no two signs alike in nature or quality, hence the passage of the Sun from one sign into another causes a change of polarity in planetary action, which can be fully demonstrated and conclusively proven. It follows, as a natural sequence, that the rules formulated and taught by astrologers in reference to the plane of planetary influence in one sub-cycle will not hold good in the next. To illustrate: In the year 1881 the Sun passed from the sign Pisces into Aquarius, thus beginning a new cycle of solar force. The human race has entered upon a cycle in every respect differing in nature and action from the past cycle of 2,160 years. The sign Aquarius is masculine, electric, positive. It is intellectual in character, scientific, philosophic, artistic, intuitive and metaphysical. It is the sign of the Man. The truths of the past are becoming etherealized. Our solar parent has scarcely crossed the threshold of the sign Aquarius, and already we observe in many directions the activities of the peculiar influx. True, it is but the first flush of the dawn of a new era, the harbinger of a glorious day to our race. In the light of this truth, ponder well on the nature of the influx radiating from the solar center, each orb of his shining family absorbing a different ray, or attribute, of solar energy, corresponding to its own peculiar nature. The Earth, in her annual passage about her solar parent, receives the harmonious or discordant vibrations of this astral influx according to the many angles she forms to the various planets.

We see, then, that the Earth is enveloped in an atmosphere, or zone, of occult force we recognize as humane, mental, positive, etc., acting and reacting upon the human family through the laws of vibration in strict and exact ratio to its interior capacity to receive and ability to externalize upon the material plane of being. The results, as far as this stage of existence goes, will be manifest as man vibrates harmoniously or otherwise to the stellar cause.

The present sub-cycle producing an entirely different influence to that of the past cycle, whose force was watery, magnetic and feminine, causes a warring of elements, confusion and uncertainty, until the old are displaced by the new conditions. We should learn from these facts that it is folly to brand as false and condemn as worthless the rules and formulas, and even religious thought, of the past when we find upon careful investigation and crucial tests their inadequacy to account for present conditions. They were true in their cycle, and applied to past conditions and states of mental development. But in this new era, upon whose threshold we now stand, the vibrations become more intense. Man's whole nature is being tuned to a higher key. We must not forget that these cycles apply to the race in their effect, and to the individual only as an integral part of the whole. To illustrate. The sign Aquarius is an electrical, positive, masculine influence, and will consequently manifest its chief activities upon the masculine qualities of the human soul; and to-day we have evidence of this in the gradual enfranchisement of woman, arousing the positive attributes of her nature in demanding equal rights with her brother, man, in the political arena, as she has already done in the educational field. The masculine portion of the race is becoming more aggressive, mentally, asserting greater individuality, independent thought and action. The intellect of the race is being directed, however slowly, into scientific channels, while the human soul is slowly awakening to a sense of a deathless immortality and a desire for spiritual truth. It is slowly but surely shaking off the yoke of an effete priesthood and the fetters of superstition and tyranny.

Intelligent man talks of the new scientific and intellectual era that has dawned upon the world; of the necessity for a new religious system, based upon scientific truths, which can be demonstrated, combined with the pure spiritual essence found in all systems of religion; a religion with more spirituality and less theology; a broader charity and less dogma, and deeper love for God and man, its only creed.

We must now consider the astral influence of the cycle upon the physical organism of mankind, and particularly of the Western races, who are moving upon the upward arc of the cycle. It is quite evident that a radical change must take place in the physical form and constitution with the influx of more intellectual, ethereal and spiritual vibrations. The organism must become more refined and compact, a greater degree of sensitiveness be attained, with a highly nervous system. The forerunner of this superior organism is now apparent in the numerous schools of physical culture and gymnasiums throughout the land, the many articles and pamphlets on deep, rythmic breathing disseminated among the people, and last, but not least, the various schools of mental healing, etc. The masses look on and wonder, while they exclaim: "What marvelous changes are coming to the world!" but are utterly ignorant of the cause of the mysterious change. To the student of Hermetic Philosophy there is no mystery involved. He knows the cause, and confidently watches for the effect.

Each one must seek to comprehend for himself, according to the light he may receive, basing his premises upon the *true principles* of astrology, carefully noting the triune aspect of planetary influence upon humanity, ever remembering that the Sun and Moon are the great factors in human destiny, and that his premises and conclusions must occupy the same plane. Having acquired a knowledge of the science in its application to the individual, take the broader field, or universal aspect, as it applies to human races, and you will find the rise and fall of nations, empires and families marked upon the celestial dial, and in perfect accord with the influence of the Sun and planets upon Mother Earth, in her various movements. And last, but most important, seek with an earnest desire for truth to learn the relation of those glittering constellations of the shining Zodiac to the human soul and their influence in shaping its eternal destiny. This will reveal the whole of involution and evolution in a general sense.

A faithful, earnest and devout study of the "Science of the Starry Heavens" will lead us on to other planes of thought, relating to still more interior realms of knowledge than we perhaps now dream of, and, in the words of the master: "A true knowledge of the stars will include a true knowledge of the soul," and we shall realize "the mystical link that binds the soul to the stars."

MINNIE HIGGIN.

CHAPTER I

THE ZODIAC

To the ordinary astrologer the Zodiac is simply a band of space, eighteen degrees wide, in the heavens, the center of which marks out the pathway of the Sun during the space of one year of 365 days, etc.

The twelve signs are to him simply thirty degrees of the space (12 times 30 equal 360), bearing the names of the constellations which once occupied them. Nay, he, as a rule, still imagines in some sense that the signs (constellations) are still there, and that the power and potency of the twelve signs is derived from the stars which occupy the Zodiacal band of the skies.

But this is not so, as any ordinary astronomer well knows. This single fact, i.e., the gradual shifting of the constellations, the *displacement*, let us say, of the starry influx from one sign to another without any *allowance* being made in the astrologer's rules for any such change, has been one of the greatest obstructions to the popular spread of the art among *educated minds*. Argues the scientist: The "fiery influence of Aries," if depending upon the stars of that constellation, ought now to be shedding forth their caloric from the sign Pisces, and Aries ought to be lumbering along with the earthy Taurine nature. So, also, the lords of these signs ought to be changed, but that they are not can be proved by the fact that our earliest records of that dim, historic past show, equally as well as your latest "text-book," that Mars is the lord of Aries—a fiery planet in a fiery sign; but astrologers still say that Pisces is watery and Aries fiery, *which is not the case, if the stars have any influence at all*. "It is not necessary," say these logical thinkers, "to learn your abstruse science if we can demonstrate that the very basis upon which your conclusions rest is in every sense fundamentally false." The scientific facts of the case are as follows: The influence of the twelve signs, as described by astrologers, is a delusion, because in all ages they are reported the same; whereas *we know* that every 2,160 years each sign retrogrades to the extent of thirty degrees, and, as your art does not make allowance for this, it is false. For, if the influence of the twelve signs does not emanate from the stars occupying the space of those signs, it must emanate from nothing—a doctrine well suited, no doubt, to musty old sages of your superstitious

Chaldea, but quite out of court in our progressive age—the last decade of our cultured and scientific nineteenth century.

So far, so good. And so the world rolls along its bright pathway in the heavens, little heeding the logical conclusions of an exact science. But to an initiate of those inner principles of our planet's constitution all these mental conflicts have a meaning and a purpose within Nature's divine economy; for it is neither wise nor expedient that the masses, with popular science in the lead, should grasp the truths which Mother Nature reserves *alone* for her own devoted priests.

The shining Zodiac, with its myriad constellations and its perfect galaxy of starry systems, derives its subtle influence, as impressed astrologically upon the human constitution, from the solar center of our solar system, NOT FROM THE STARS which occupy the twelve mansions of space. *Aries*, the fiery, and *Pisces*, the watery, *are always there*, and, instead of its being an argument against astrology, it is one of its grandest truths that, in all ages and in all times, Aries, the first sign of the Zodiac has been found *ever the same*, equally as well as Pisces the last.

In order to convey our meaning, let us digress for a moment and bring forth a fitting illustration. The condition of our atmosphere and the surrounding objects—vegetation, etc.—have a peculiar condition and a magnetism wholly their own when surveyed exactly at sunrise. There is a freshness and peculiar sense of buoyancy not visible at any other time. If this state could be registered by any instrument and compared with any other set periods during the day, it would offer a remarkable contrast. Two hours later there is a very different influence, and at noon there is a wonderful contrast. The same may be said of sunset, and again at midnight; and, lastly, note the difference two hours before dawn. This is the coolest period of the whole twenty-four hours. These are facts, and yet our hearts are all beating to the same life-flow, and the Earth is no farther away from the parent Sun; and yet it is the angle at which we, THE INHABITANTS, receive this Sun's light that makes all the difference between dawn and sunset, noon and midnight.

When to these facts it is further added that it is sunrise, noon, sunset and midnight at the same instant, all the time, to some of the various, different portions of the globe, it demonstrates most conclusively that the Earth itself is enveloped, so to say, in a complete circle of conditions very similar to the twelve signs of the celestial Zodiac.

If we apply the foregoing illustration to the twelve signs of the Zodiac, we shall see a perfect analogy. We shall find that when the Sun reaches the celestial equator, so that it is equal day and equal night on the Earth, that he is on the line of the celestial horizon; it is cosmic sunrise. Hence Aries, the fiery Azoth, begins his active influx, and extends for thirty degrees, equal to two hours of the natural day.

It is the fiery red streams of awakening life that we all manifest at sunrise; then comes a change of magnetic polarity after the first fiery flush of cosmic life; the gleeful chattering of the birds and the cackling of the poultry. A reaction is noted; all things before active become restful and quiet.

So it is with vegetation, so it is with infant life, and so it is with cosmic conditions.

This corresponds with the sign Taurus. It is the solar influx, thirty degrees removed from his point of equilibrium toward the North. As this sign represents the powers of absorption, we see that at this period vegetable and animal life is quietly absorbing, for its own use, the fiery streams of solar life.

Again we view the activity of solar influx from a different angle and change of polarity, and all things become active. It is executive force. This corresponds to the sign Gemini. It is the solar influx, sixty degrees removed from his point of equilibrium. Then comes another change of magnetic polarity. It is rest from labor; it is noon.

This corresponds to Cancer. The analogy is perfect. It is the solar influx, ninety degrees removed from his point of equilibrium toward the North, and the highest point in the arc of his apparent journey and of cosmic life. It is the equilibrium of life forces.

Again the fiery influx begins its activity, and, as the hottest part of the day is about two hours after noon, or middle of the day, so is solar influx most potent at this point in the Zodiac.

This corresponds to the sign Leo. It is the solar influx, removed 120 degrees from his point of equilibrium and thirty degrees toward the South. And so on month after month, until the last one, Pisces, which well corresponds to the watery skies of February and the lifeless period two hours before dawn of a new day upon the Earth, a new year to man and a new cycle in the starry heavens. The Zodiac, then, as it applies to the human constitution and the science of astrology, has its foundation in the Sun, the center and source of life to the planet; and the twelve signs are the twelve great spaces of our Earth's annual orbit about her solar parent, each one typical of its month, and each month typical of its corresponding action upon our Earthy conditions.

As each sunrise is different in its aspects, so are no two signs of the Zodiac alike. The sunrise on the first of March is wholly different from the sunrise upon the first of May. So is the beginning and ending of each sign, and the beginning and ending of each natural day, peculiar unto itself.

When we reflect upon the inner laws of this action and inter-action, we come nearer and nearer to the one great occult fact, viz.: *The Divine Oneness of life.*

We find a perfect analogy between the destiny, the life, and ex-pression of life on the Earth, and the life and material destiny of embodied man. He, too, has his sunrise, the beginning of a new day of life, the seedtime, the flowering season, when life wears a roseate hue; the ripening fruits of experience, his harvest-time—it may be tares or golden grain; his gradual decay, the ebbing of the life forces and the icy winter of death; his gentle zephyrs and destructive hurricanes, floods and tempests, periods of drought and plenty. Within his triune constitution there are spring tides and low tides of physical, intellectual and spiritual forces. Man also makes the annual journey about the solar center, when, at the beginning of each new year to him, the life forces of his soul are renewed, regalvanized, so to say, according to the magnetic polarity of his constitution.

And so, every form of life has its Zodiac, its orbit of life and destiny. It may be infinitesimal, or vast beyond conception, each in its own peculiar plane. So we see that, the whole visible universe is one vast organism, the medium of expression for the invisible, real universe— the soul and God, the great central Sun, the eternal center of all life, binding the whole into unity—*one life.*

The celestial signs of the shining Zodiac have no existence to us apart from the graceful and unwearying motion of our Mother Earth. She alone makes our seasons, years and destiny; and she alone, by her motion about the Sun, determines the thrones and mansions of the planetary powers.

The astrological Zodiac of a Saturn or a Mars cannot be like ours. Their years and seasons are peculiar to themselves and their material conditions; hence the twelve constellations have no existence as objective facts of concrete formation or cosmic potentiality. No! But as unalterable symbols of occult truth, the starry pictures of the shining constellations have an eternal verity. They pertain to the living realities of the human soul and its varied experience.

What the mysteries are, and what connection they have with the twelve constellations, will form the subject of our next chapter.

CHAPTER II

The twelve great constellations of the zodiacal belt which forms the Earth's orbit and the Sun's shining pathway around the celestial universe have been considered as mere imaginary figures, or emblems, invented by an early, primitive people to distinguish the monthly progress of the Sun and mark out, in a convenient manner, the twelve great divisions, or spaces, of the solar year. To this end, *it is thought*, the various star groups, termed constellations, were fancifully imagined to represent the various physical aspects of the month, under, or into, which they were consecrated by the Sun's passage during the annual journey, so that, in some sense, the twelve signs, or constellations, were symbolical, not only of the seasons, but also of the labors of the year.

That such a system seems perfectly natural to the learned mythologist, and that granting the ancients so much is a very great concession toward this *childish knowledge* is, of course, quite excusable when we are constantly told, or reminded, that actual science—that is to say, *"exact science,"* does not date backward more than a couple of centuries at most.

Even the modern astrologer, much as he descants upon the influence of the twelve signs, has but little, if any, real knowledge of this matter above and beyond the purely physical symbolism above mentioned. And perhaps it is as well that such a benighted condition prevails, and that the Divine, heavenly goddess is unsought and comparatively unknown. The celestial Urania, at least, in such isolation remains pure and undefiled. She is free from the desecrating influence of polluted minds.

Such, in brief outline, is the general conception of mankind regarding the shining constellations that bedeck, like fiery jewels, their Maker's crown, and illumine with their celestial splendor the wondrous canopy of our midnight skies. Is there no more than a symbol of rural work in the bright radiance of the starry Andromeda, the harbinger of gentle spring? Nothing, think you, but the fruit harvest and the vintage is in the fiery, flushing luster of Antares and the ominous Scorpion? Are men so spiritually blind that they can perceive nothing but the symbol of maturing vegetation and the long summer's day in the glorious splendor of Castor and his starry mate and brother, Pollux?

It would, indeed, seem so, so dead is the heart and callous the spiritual understanding of our own benighted day. To the initiate of Urania's mysteries, however, these dead, symbolic pictures become endowed with life; these emblems of rural labor or rustic art transform themselves from the hard, chrysolitic shell and expand into the fully developed spiritual flowers of spiritual entities, revealing in their bright, radiating lines the awful mystery of the soul's genesis, its evolution and eternal progressive destiny amid the mighty, inconceivable creations yet to come; pointing out each step and cycle in the soul's involution from its differentiation as a pure spiritual entity, a ray of Divine intelligence, to the crystallization of its spiritual forces in the realms of matter and its evolution of progressive life; the same eternal symbols of the springtime, the glorious summer, the autumn and winter of its eternal being.

In making this attempt, probably the very first within the era, to convey in plain and undisguised terms the interior mysteries of the twelve constellations, the reader and student is advised to ponder deeply upon the outlines presented. The subject is too vast to present in one or two chapters. Therefore we hope that this revelation may incite the student to further research. The real significance, the true, spiritual importance of such mysteries, can only be realized and fully appreciated after prolonged meditation and careful study.

With this brief digression, which we consider needed advice, we will resume our task, and attempt to usher our student into the weird labyrinth of Solomon's starry temple—"the house not made with hands, eternal in the heavens."

I. Aries ♈

"First Aries, in his golden wool."

This constellation represents the first Divine idea, the "word" of the Kabbalist, and the first active manifestation of the glorious En Soph. In other words, it is *mind in action*, the first pulsation of Deity in the dual aspects of "Lord and Creator." To the human soul it is, and always typifies, the unknown, invisible power which we term *intelligence; that which knows*, and gives unto each Deific atom of life that distinguishing, universal, yet deathless force which not only constitutes its spiritual identity and physical individuality, but enables it to pronounce, in the presence of its Creator, those mystic words: "I am that I am." In other words, this beautiful constellation symbolizes the first pulsation of that ray of pure intelligence which constitutes the Divine Ego of the human soul. It is the force that impels ever onward the life atom in its evolutionary progress, and reveals to us the beginning, or first manifestation, of the Divine Ego as an active, self-existing atom of Infinite spirit, within angelic spheres.

Seeing the actual, spiritual reality symbolized in Aries, how easy it is to note its full significance upon the external plane when refracted and reflected into the planes below through the complex action of the human organism, conveying the same radical influx in the first astrological month and the first sign of the Zodiac. We can read a perfect parallel in the astral influx upon the human body, as set forth in the "Light of Egypt," vol. 1, which says Aries symbolizes the sacrifice and represents the springtime, the beginning of a new year. The first action of pure intelligence brought forth the first expression of form, and led to the sacrifice of its angelic state, and, having gained the victory over the lower realms of matter, once more the springtime of a new life, with the promise of life, light and love.

The sign Aries represents the thinking powers of humanity; in short, the active, intellectual being, the lord of material creation—Man; and in its cosmic relations, as shown under "The Occult Application of the Twelve Signs" (vol. 1), we find the same perfect analogy.

II.   Taurus ♉

"He (Aries) turns and wonders at the mighty Bull (Taurus)."

The second constellation of the shining twelve represents the first reaction of spiritual conception. In other words, it is the mind's attention to its own ideas. In the Kabbalah it represents that peculiar state of executive force whereof it is symbolically said: "And the Lord saw that it was good," after each act of creation.

When intelligence first manifests itself form is a matter of necessity, and, as no form can possibly exist without matter, so Taurus is the first emanation of matter in its most etherealized state. Hence it is feminine, Venus the ruler thereof, and it represents the first pure form of the human soul, as it existed in its bright paradise within the angelic spheres of its parents, and reveals to us the first surprise of intelligence in embryo, the first sensation of consciousness, so to say—conscious of its Divine selfhood. Hence "He (the male spirit of pure fire, Aries), glorious in his golden (solar) wool, turns (expressing reaction) and wonders at the mighty bull (or material form)." Thus the first idea of pure intelligence in embryo, the result of action in Aries, becomes objective to its consciousness and is surprised at its own conception. It is the first sensation of pure, Divine love within angelic realms, and it (the male spirit of pure fire) sees that it is good.

Bringing this spiritual reality within our conception, and comparing it with its reflected astrological influx, what a beautiful harmony we find, and yet so simple that verily we cannot refrain from once more quoting our old-time, worn, yet, nevertheless, golden law: "*As it is above, so it is below; as on the Earth, so in the sky.*" Reflecting that Taurus is an Earthy sign, and a symbol of servitude, we see that matter is ever the servant of spirit, a necessary means for the manifestation of intelligence, again recognized in the fecundating forces of this astrological sign on every plane of its action. And it is ruled by Venus, the love element in Nature, her sympathies ever finding expression in this beautiful sign. What can be clearer, more understandable, than, that the involved principles and Deific attributes, as represented by the shining constellations, when refracted through the human organism, so complex in its constitution, reflects qualities which are the external and parallel expression of the subjective principles, and, further, that form is absolutely necessary for the manifestation of intelligence?

III.   Gemini ♊

"He (Taurus) bending lies with threatening head, and calls the Twins (Gemini) to rise. They clasp for fear and mutually embrace."

This bright constellation (Castor and Pollux), Gemini, is spiritually representative of the second spiritual action. Hence it is, of course, a masculine sign and positive. We have witnessed act I of the soul's drama, and, as some have said, tragedy, and in this, the third of the shining twelve, we find the opening scene of act II, viz: The evolution of the twin souls, or, more correctly, the differentiation of the Divine soul into its two natural component parts—male and female.

Here we approach one of the most arcane secrets within the wide scope of Occult philosophy, hence must be exact, and at the same time clear, in our statements. Note, then, that after the male spirit of pure, ethereal, divine fire (Aries) had conceived the first idea, and Taurus, the material envelope, had given that idea objective existence to its (the Ego's) consciousness, we find *sensation as the result.* No sooner sensation than aspiration; i.e., longing. This closes the action and the reaction.

Ever, in obedience to the unsatisfied wants of an immortal soul Nature immediately responds. Hence "He bending lies with threatening head, (that is demanding)," and calls the twins (the twin souls) to rise (to appear or evolve forth)," and as a first rude shock caused by their separation, or, rather, by their separate existence as two distinct, yet mutually dependent, forces, we have the context.

"They clasp for fear and mutually embrace."

This most impressive scene in the soul's drama is one of profound interest and sublime beauty.

In the Kabbalah we find the same parallel, wherein it is stated: "And so God created man in His own image (the action of Aries and Taurus); in His own image (mind) created He him, male and female created He them." In other words, Aries, Taurus and Gemini are thus spoken of in pure allegory.

The mundane Bible of the Jews, like everything else esteemed sacred, finds its original and perfect expression in the great Astral Bible of the skies.

To the average student the evolution of the Twin Souls is a profound mystery, embracing, as it does, the whole of involution and evolution, seeing that this beautiful constellation represents to us the first recognition, or consciousness, of the Divine Ego of its dual forces, sensation and aspiration, called forth by the action of Aries and Taurus. How beautifully has the poet expressed this first pulsation of Divine love: "They clasp for fear," etc. Evolved by the Divine will of pure intelligence, they must ever remain as separate, yet mutually dependent, forces, positive and negative, male and female, upon whose action and reaction rest the perfect evolvement of the powers and possibilities of the One.

In order to clearly grasp the whole of these ramifications, we again invite our student's careful attention to the same sign, Gemini, in its astrological aspect, as it is representatively expressed by refraction upon the human organism. We find that this sign (the representative of the constellation always) signifies the union of reason with intuition, and that it governs the arms, hands and executive forces of man.

Surely, as we reflect upon the almost marvelous inter-relationship between things spiritual and things temporal, we must conclude, with the man Jesus, that "They have eyes but they see not, and ears, but alas they hear not."

If it were not so man would, indeed, by virtue of the latent forces within him, take the kingdom of Heaven by storm and reign supreme as enthroned king of all material forms. Man, in his blindness, has relegated intuition to obscurity; has neglected the cunning of the left hand and debauched the pure love of the divine state. Consequently, the executive forces within him are unbalanced, thus rendering him the slave of material forms, instead of being their lawful sovereign. Therefore, not until, with clean hands and pure heart, he restores intuition to her throne, united with reason, can he hope to *comprehend* the reality of this arcane mystery of the twin souls, Gemini.

IV.   Cancer ♋

"And next the Twins with an unsteady pace Bright Cancer rolls."

In this beautiful constellation we witness the reaction of Gemini, the closing scene in act II. Hence it is, of course, a feminine force we are observing. In other words, it is that period (or rather one of them) wherein the Kabbalah expresses the reaction of the En Soph, via his Creators, as "And behold the Lord saw everything that He had made, and behold it was very good."

Just so Cancer, spiritually interpreted, means equalizing, hence *harmony*, which is indeed very good as contradistinguished from chaos.

To the human soul Cancer is the period of exalted rest. It is the highest point in the arc of the Divine Soul's Angelic Cycle. From this glorious, but subjective, summit or altitude in the realm of spirit it must descend.

Restless energy and the still unsatisfied longings of its own immortal nature are the forces that bring such evolution about. Having evolved the dual forces of its divine nature, the Ego sees that it is good and rests from its labor. But as this exalted state is purely subjective, and ideal, it must of necessity, to satisfy the longing for further unfoldment and desire to know, descend into material realms and conditions. From this point begins the soul's involution downward, until the lowest point in the arc is reached, viz., Capricorn.

Refer now to the sign Cancer, and carefully study out the parallel upon its astrological planes and also under its Occult aspects, as given forth in the "Light of Egypt," Vol. I, where we read: "Cancer rules the respiratory and digestive functions of humanity, and governs the reflective organs of the brain." Note the parallel. Within subjective realms the Divine soul has inspired and assimilated all that is possible to that angelic state, and knows a period of blissful rest. But the longings of its immortal nature urge on the soul. So we see that the sign Cancer symbolizes tenacity to life; to live we must breathe and eat and assimilate upon every plane of our being. It necessarily follows that, the mentality expressed by Cancer must be susceptible to inspirational currents; to inspire is to indraw. In its application, we find that this sign symbolizes love. How beautiful the harmony and contrast of the constellation and its astrological representative.

V.   Leo ♌

"Then Leo shakes his mane."

Herein is typified the third grand spiritual action which, as we find throughout Nature, travel in pairs; hence Leo is a positive, masculine constellation.

Having attained the highest point in the super-celestial states of subjective, embryonic existence; having evolved sensation and aspiration; now, inspired by a desire for immortality, the *dual soul* of the Divine Ego is once more impelled forward; but, as all evolution works in spirals, it cannot ascend higher without first apparently descending lower; so ever onward in its eternal march. This beautiful constellation symbolizes the first action on the downward portion of the arc. It is the affinities of the heart, so to say, working from within to without.

Matter, in its more etherealized form, begins to assert its sway. The allegorical serpent of Eden is working upon the feminine portion, symbolized by the heart, and, like a magnetic tractor, the soul's affinities are drawn downward, and, as if in defiance of all responsibilities, consequences, and Karma, the soul, lion-like, "shakes his mane in the imperiousness of deathless courage."

As we read these weird allegories, written by Deity in the starry vaults of heaven, the interested soul bows in reverence and awe before that almighty power we term Providence, and the profane call God.

No man has altered these pure records of divinity; no finger has interpolated one single line. They are as beautifully clear to the soul now as they were in the very dawn of Nature's awful creation.

To the Initiate into Urania's mysteries it is unnecessary to draw a parallel between the constellation and its astrological sign. They are too clear, magnificent and impressive to escape notice. To the majority of students the resembance may not be so apparent, hence, for their benefit, we will point out a few aspects of this interesting parallel.

We read that the sign Leo is the "solar Lion of the mysteries, that, ripens with his own internal heat the fruits brought forth from the Earth by the moisture of Isis (the soul)." Just so, the Divine Ego, by its eternal energy and strength, the pure fire of intelligence, externalizes through material forms the principles involved in the downward portion of the arc, as qualities and attributes of the soul (reflected in the physical man as traits and qualities). Again we are told, "this sign reveals to us the ancient sacrifice and the laws of its compensation." In the imperiousness of a deathless courage, the soul defies all consequences and responsibilities. Surely, this is the supreme sacrifice, to leave its pure, Edenic state to gain knowledge, to evolve its latent forces. And from this lion of the Tribe of Judah, is born that Divine love and sympathy which ultimately redeems and purifies the soul and saves it from death in matter. The laws of its compensation are fulfilled in the prefected man.

In its intellectual aspect, we learn that the mental forces of those dominated by this sign are ever striving to attain unto some higher state. Their ideas are grand, compared with the nature of the constellation, and all that it implies. The reflection is clear, natural and beautiful. When we reflect upon this awful period in the involution of the dual souls of the Divine Ego, as symbolized by the constellation, and the grand truths represented by the astrological sign when refracted through the human organism, the reason for Leo being named the Royal Sign becomes quite plain.

VI.   Virgo ♍

"And following Virgo calms his rage again."

Beautifully expressive are these lines to those who read their mystic import aright. Virgo is the reaction of the leonine force, and is, consequently, a feminine symbol.

Action and reaction are the eternal laws upon which the cosmos is founded. They constitute the inseparable affinities, attraction and repulsion, of everything within the realm of manifested being. In this mystic constellation, we see the first ideas of maternal instinct arise. This is a necessary result of the impulsive action of the heart in Leo—the reaction from a state of imperious, defiance. The heat of rage or energy and deathless courage results in the *ideas* of something to be encountered, overcome, and of self-preservation. The dual soul descends still another volve in the spiral of its celestial journey toward crystallized forms.

Virgo, the Virgin of the skies, and eternal symbol of that Divine, immaculate conception, shows wherein these forces lie. Here is conceived, in a pure, holy sense, the first instinct of love within the dual soul. It represents that awful period in the Biblical Garden of Eden, wherein the *virgin wife* stands before the tree of knowledge, of good and evil, where she is fascinated by the allurements of matter and is unconsciously becoming enveloped in the coils of the serpent. In other words, after the cosmic force had *shaken its mane* in defiance of material forces, it is the reaction of his subjective half which sees *how good* material things are; or, in other words, "and following Virgo calms his rage again." The masculine half, or positive force of the soul, yields to temptation and is soothed by the alluring prospects.

It will be noticed in this connection that pity, reflection, and compassion, are the peculiar actions of the sign Virgo in the Zodiac (not the constellation), and that astrologically it governs the bowels. This symbolism is really very beautiful when closely compared and studied. That immaculate conception of pure love of the soul for its other half, upon the astrological plane, becomes refracted and reacts as compassion and pity. Again, the soul, within subjective realms, sees how good material things are, and its refraction represents the assimilating functions of the human organism. It also reveals to us the significance of the Lord's Supper. At this stage of its journey, the Divine Ego knows for the last time that close communion with the twin soul before the crucifixion, the wine typical of the sacrifice, the bread, and the sustaining forces, of its own immortal being.

The intellectual aspect of the sign Virgo forms a perfect analogy to the constellation, and is too evident for further remarks.

VII.   Libra ♎

"Then day and night are weighed in Libra's scales;
Equal awhile, at last the night prevails."

Another volve in the spiral, and we reach the grand climax of
the soul's journey, within the spiritual world.

The nature of this constellation was, for ages, concealed from all
but Initiates; for the reason that, it contains the most important
mysteries connected with the human soul. It is the grand transition
arc between the spiritual world and the astral world; in other words,
between ideal conceptions and elemental forms, between the world of
design and the realms of force.

One of the chief mysteries of Libra is, that, it is androgyne, or bi-
sexual, in nature. So far the dual soul has evolved within the realms
of spirituality; here it stands, in the celestial balance, between the two,
giving way to temptation, takes the forbidden fruit and instantly
awakes from its purely spiritual state to become surrounded by the
illusions of matter. The struggle of the soul with the attracting forces
of matter is very clearly expressed in the line:—

"Equal awhile, at last the night prevails."

In other words, astral and physical darkness bedim the soul's
spiritual sight, and, leaving the realms of innocence and bliss, they
sink into the vortex of the great astral world.

The celestial state is now forever lost as a realm of angelic innocence. It can only be regained amid trial, sorrow, suffering, and
experience, and, when regained, it is as Lord and Master, not as the
innocent cherub. But when, having gained or reached the equator of
the upward arc of its progress, and, united once more to its missing
half, gives expression to that deathless force with which it started
from the opposite point, Aries: *"I am that I am;"* no longer an embryo, but being within the *universal soul* of being. Before closing this
symbolic constellation, we must reveal the mystery of its *bi-sexual
nature.* In the higher or first portion of the sign it is ⌒, positive to
some extent, and masculine. The soul is still within the Garden of
Eden and pure, clad in the raiment of God, and is represented by the
Chaldean statues of "The Bearded Venus," or Venus, the Angel of
Libra, as a morning star, bright Lucifer. But in the latter half, after
the fruit of the tree of knowledge of good and evil (positive and neg-

ative, you see) has been partaken of, bright Lucifer falls. The Sun of the Morning, shorn of his glory, becomes the symbol of night, or Vesper, the evening star, and the symbol is thus ⚍, and the soul loses its heavenly raiment, or spiritual consciousness, and becomes clothed with matter, the symbol of night.

The sign Libra in the Zodiac, in its astrological aspect, is a very external correspondence of all the foregoing.

VIII. Scorpio ♏

"And, longer grown, the heavier scale inclines,
And draws bright Scorpio from the winter signs."

We now behold the gates of Paradise guarded by the *flaming sword* which points to the four quarters of the world. This sword is, according to Genesis, "to guard the way of the tree of life," and such, esoterically, it really is.

The soul is no longer dual, but separated into male and female personalities; "and behold they see that they are naked." Stripped of their spiritual raiment, they feel the chill of matter and the lusts of an animal nature. They need clothing, "so God made them coats of skin." Sex is the symbolism herein typified, and the evolution of the animal passions of procreation, of multiplication and evolution. It is the complete entry of the soul into elemental conditions, and the flaming sword guarding the four quarters of the Earth to the way of life are the four great realms of the astral world; the way to physical life in concrete forms; and the way to life eternal through the realms of the Sylphs, Gnomes, Undines and Salamanders. They are the basis of all matter, known as Air, Earth, Water and Fire. Here we see that, through the evolution of sex and its accompanying desire for pro-creation, these blind forces of Nature find their avenue of expression. Spiritual consciousness almost lost, and without reason, the soul be-comes the prey, so to say, of these forces of the astral world, which is the realm of design. The soul's creations must be met and van-quished upon the upward arc of the Cycle of Progress. They guard or oppose the way to eternal life. Here the soul, having gained the victory, stripped forever of its earthy raiment and the lusts of the flesh, arrayed once more in its spiritual raiment, purified and sanctified, it will stand once more at the gates of Paradise, where, reunited with its missing half, it will partake of the fruit of the Tree of Life and become as Gods. Astrologically the correspondence is perfect, and so thinly disguised as to need no explanation.

IX.   Sagittarius ♐

"Him Centaur follows with an aiming eye,
His bow full-drawn, and ready to let fly."

Deeper and deeper sinks the soul into material forms. The evolution of sex has produced the necessary avenues for the entrance of countless forces, and the soul is now rapidly losing the last vestiges of its spiritual conscience. In other words, Sagittarius symbolizes that state of the soul wherein it is descending to its polarizing point, and is, therefore, the vortex of innumerable opposing forces, seeking expression in different forms.

"It is the bow (strength or force of the soul), FULL-drawn and ready to let fly" its arrows (of energy) in any direction that may afford proper opportunity. Here we see the expression of that deathless, fiery force, and imperious daring and courage, within more material states; the primal fire reflected from another angle.

But everything is unsettled. It is a masculine force, and restless, and is represented under the allegory of the "Tower of Babel" and the utter dispersion of the people (entities) to the four corners of the Earth, and finally becomes involved in dense matter, and its migrations are at an end on this side of the Cycle of Necessity.

Upon the astrological plane, the zodiacal sign Sagittarius rules the motive forces and the pedestrian instinct, the thighs, or basis of locomotion; hence, we see, even here, a most perfect analogy. This sign symbolizes, also, the governing forces of humanity, which see the necessity of law and order; hence government. In this expression, we find the bow (strength or force) ready to let fly its arrows of energy in any direction the opportunity may afford; when refracted upon the human organism and reflected upon the external plane, these forces manifest as the restless spirit, that ever impels onward, seeking new fields of expression, out of which develops a sense of order, restraining and training, or the governing of self and control of others. When we reflect upon these symbols of starry truths the mind bows in reverence before the wisdom that created them.

X. Capricorn ♑

"Next narrow horns the twisted Caper shows."

The Goat, and in the realms of spirit, the crystallized mineral is the reaction of the former, and shows to us death, inertia and rest; hence Kronos, or Saturn, the symbol of death, is lord of this state and condition. It is the polarizing point of the soul's evolution in matter, and therefore, forms the lowest arc in the Cycle of Necessity.

Herein we behold the soul, imprisoned within the mineral state. The fire of the flint, and the spark in the crystal, are the only avenues of its lonesome expressions. But, as the lowest point, it is also the promise of a higher, and the symbol of a higher state, and the symbol of another spiral in its endless life.

This constellation, as the symbol of inertia and death, is also the symbol of awakening life, and prepares the soul for the more perfect expression of its powers in its forthcoming upward journey. If we pause for a moment and consider the force and power necessary to evolve out of this dark, dense, mineral realm, the foregoing sentence will become clear and forcible. Hitherto, the soul has been slowly drawn down into coils of matter, imprisoned by material forces. It has penetrated the lowest depths, and can go no farther. Rest here, is to gather strength, force. Mark well the difference and parallel between Cancer and Capricorn, opposite points in the arc. Cancer is the symbol of exalted rest within angelic realms; Capricorn the symbol of rest in dense matter. From the former state the soul is impelled forward on its downward journey; from the latter state the soul awakens to the struggle for life on the upward arc; and must now give expression to the positive powers of its immortal being, which have become involved in material form; that shall make it the master, and give it the victory over death and material forces. Surely, this is truly the promise of a new day, and higher state of existence.

It will be instructive to study this by a comparison of the zodiacal sign, Capricorn, as set forth in the "Light of Egypt," Vol. I, wherein we read: "This sign signifies the knees, and represents the first principle in the trinity of locomotion, viz., the joints, bending, pliable, movable." The analogy is perfect. The soul, which has been pliant, bending to material forces, now reverses this action, and bows the knee in awe and reverence to the higher powers of its being. When refracted upon the human organism, we find that the cold, lonesome state, and weary struggle within the mineral realm, becomes love of *self*, directing its energies to the attainment of selfish ends. What could be more natural?

XI.   Aquarius ♒

"And from Aquarius' urn a flood o'erflows."

The soul, released from its crystallized cycle of matter, now rapidly evolves into states, though material, yet entirely different. Its previous arc, from Libra to Capricorn, has been amid inorganic matter. It is now rushing with lightning speed upon its weird, toilsome, upward, journey through purely organic forms, from vegetable to animal; and, as all organic forms have their primary origin in water, so does this celestial urn express the primary conception of this physical state. Further, to more fully express this, Aquarius is typical of man, as prototype of the last grand goal of the soul's future material state—in other words, the last quadrant of the four elements, viz.: Bull, Lion, Eagle, Man.

There is something exceedingly significant in all this, and the more we ponder on this spiritual allegory of the shining constellation, the more we are impressed with the divine wisdom of those early instructors of our race, who thus preserved truth in an incorruptible form.

From this weird, but beautiful constellation, we learn how the soul has progressed, finding innumerable avenues of expression of its latent forces; the manifestation of its powers in the various chemical changes, and development of functions expressed through countless forms, on the lower planes of existence. The sacrifice of its angelic innocence, the imperious defiance and deathless courage, symbolized by Leo, have obtained the victory over the lower kingdoms; which will be incorporated into his vast empire. Yet, unstable as water, it cannot excel; or, in other words, cannot rise to a higher state within this arc, of its progressive life.

We find that the astrological expression of this constellation, the sign Aquarius, governs the legs, and is the natural emblem of the changeable, moveable, migratory forces, of the body, forming a perfect parallel with its interior symbol. There is a great deal contained in this zodiacal sign worthy of deep study and reflection.

XII.   Pisces ♓

"Near their loved waves cold Pisces take their seat,
With Aries join, and make the round complete."

Once more a reaction—the last scene of the soul's impersonal drama. The constellation of Pisces is the symbol of rest and expectation. The soul has now completed the first round, or rung, in the Cycle of Necessity; and its next state is that of incarnated man. It has triumphed over every sphere below, and defied, in turn, every power above, and is now within that sixth state of the embryonic soul-world that transforms all its past knowledge, sorrow, and suffering, into experience; and produces the impersonal man.

It has traveled through constellated states within matter and spirit, and, as a human soul, with reason, intuition, and responsibility, it will, in its next state, become subject to those same powers when reflected from a different plane. The twelve constellations of its soul will manifest a complete rapport with the twelve signs of solar light and power.

With this we close. The mystic sign of this constellation is ⚎, or completion, a seal and a sign of its past labors.

And, as we have seen, the shining constellations are the soul's progressive history from its genesis, to its appearance within embodied conditions as man; and so, by correspondence, are the twelve solar signs symbols of man and his material destiny. The foundation has been laid, the material and resources are at hand, for his kingdom is exclusive. With his own hands he must build his temple (the symbol of the perfected man), each stone accurately measured, cut, polished, and in its proper place, the proportions symmetrical, hence, harmonious; the keystone of whose arch is *Will*, its foundation love. This accomplished, he will have completed the second round of the great Cycle of Necessity.

And who, after contemplating the wondrous harmony of this beautiful system, and the complete accord of each part, can refuse to agree with the truly inspired Addison that—

"Ever moving as they shine,
The hand that made us is divine."

CHAPTER III

THE SPIRITUAL INTERPRETATION OF THE TWELVE
HOUSES OF THE HOROSCOPE

As a sequel to the foregoing subjects, viz., the Zodiac and constellations, we will add the spiritual interpretation of the twelve houses
of an horoscope, which completes the triune expression of these celestial symbols of eternal truths.

In revealing this mystery, we would impress upon the mind of the
student that the order of the Zodiac is the reverse of the external, in
its spiritual application, to the twelve houses of the horoscope.

As the four cardinal signs, viz., Aries, Cancer, Libra and Capricorn, correspond to the four angles of a natal figure, it is our purpose
to explain, first, the symbology of the four angles, or cardinal points;
believing the whole revelation will thus become clear and forcible.

The four angles of the horoscope correspond to the four elements,
the four triplicities, and the four cardinal points, or epochs, in the
soul's involution from pure spirit to the crystallizing, inert, mineral
state.

The first angle is the ascendant, or House of Life. It is the eastern
horizon, and symbolized by Aries. Upon the interior, this first angle
stands for the birth, or differentiation, of the Divine Ego, as the result of the creative action, or impulse, of the Deific mind.

The Ego rises upon the eastern horizon of celestial states, a glowing, scintillating atom of pure intelligence, an absolute, eternal Ego,
rising out of the ocean of Infinite Love.

The South angle, meridian, or Tenth House, pertaining to honor,
etc., is symbolized by Cancer; the highest point in the arc of the soul's
involution, as a differentiated atom of Deity within angelic spheres.

Having evolved the first dual expression of its (the Ego's) self, the
twin souls—Sensation and Aspiration, or Love and Wisdom, the Ego
rests awhile, radiant with celestial love and wisdom, and inspiring
the Divine breath of life.

Again the restless impulse of the creative purpose arouses the Ego
to further action. The culminating point has been reached, and now
must begin an apparent downward course toward the western horizon.

The seventh angle, or House of Marriage, etc., is represented by

Libra (the Balance), or point of equilibrium; where the two souls are still one, balanced upon the western horizon. The alluring temptations of material illusions draw the souls downward, and, divorced from their celestial state, the radiance of Divine love becomes obscured, until the twilight of consciousness of that former state is lost in the night of material conditions.

This house signifies, also, law, and open enemies, and (Libra) justice. Sex is the law. The antagonism is surely too apparent to require explanation.

The fourth angle, or Nadir, the point opposite the M. C., signifies the frozen North, and is symbolized by Capricorn, the crystallizing point in the soul's involution. It is death, inertia; that is, crystallization of the soul's spiritual forces. It is the lowest point of the arc in the monad's downward journey. It is the night, before the awakening of a new day upon a higher plane of existence.

The remaining houses are the lights and shadows that, fill out and complete the picture, upon this, the first round of the Cyclic Ladder.

The Twelfth House, symbolized by Taurus, represents the first expression of form of the human soul. It is matter in the most etherealized state. It is the trail of the serpent; the silent, secret, tenacious, negative principle; that ultimately draws the soul down into the vortices of gross matter and death.

The Eleventh, or House of Friends, whose symbol is Gemini, the Twins, expressive of the first emanation of this sublime relationship, the dual attributes, love and wisdom, closest friends. It is sensation and aspiration, which enable the spirit to attain to the exalted state indicated by the Tenth Mansion.

The Ninth Mansion of the celestial map is the House of Science, Art, Religion, Philosophy, etc., and its symbol is Leo, the Heart, with its emotions, love, and longings, and sympathies. Having evolved the twins, and inspiring the Divine breath of wisdom; glowing with Deific love, the Ego aspires to know; and all the sympathies of the soul are aroused. Dauntless and fearless, defying all opposition and consequences, It (the Ego) is ready to sacrifice this angelic state and explore the boundless Universe in pursuit of knowledge, and goes forth on its long voyage upon the ocean of Infinite, fathomless love and wisdom.

The Eighth, or House of Death and Legacies, is symbolized by Virgo, the virgin wife, standing before the "Tree of Knowledge of Good and Evil," fascinated by the flattering prospects of greater power and wisdom. Desire and sympathy draw the soul down into realms which lead to death, and the beginning of a heritage of sorrow.

The Sixth, or House of Sickness, Menials, and Sorrow, is symbolized by Scorpio. The fall, from Libra through Scorpio (sex), created the first condition of what we recognize as sickness and affliction. It is evident that this house is related to the elementals of the astral plane, which become the servitors of man.

The Fifth, or House of Children, etc., symbolized by Sagittarius, signifies the offspring of sex (Scorpio), entities sent forth to people the Earth, to take their chances of life, speculating on its future course, fearlessly eager for the struggle, gaining pleasure in its migrations and activities.

The Third House is symbolized by Aquarius. This is the first step of the upward journey, or evolution, from the inert mineral state. The changes are now rapid; the journeys innumerable; through mineral, vegetable, and animal planes, of existence. Here, the Soul Monad brings into actual practice the knowledge gained on its long voyage. The magical powers of the soul are brought into action to effect these changes in form and function, conquering material forces and planes of life, transmuting Nature's elements to its uses and purposes, and writing its history, as it journeys ever onward, step by step.

And further, this house stands in opposition to the Ninth House, symbolized by Leo; longing to expand its (the Ego's) possibilities through trial and suffering; gaining knowledge through bitter experience; yet fearlessly braving all things; guided and sustained by the imperial will of spirit. The recompense promised by that supreme sacrfice has been won in Aquarius—the Man—consecrated now to a higher existence, baptized in the waters of affliction (experience), ready to be transmuted into actual knowledge. This is Aquarius, and the Third House.

The Second House, signified as Pisces, the House of Wealth, that which has been accumulated on the long and toilsome journey— the wealth of experience, acquired through trials and struggles. And now, with higher, greater possibilities, the soul eagerly awaits the hour when it shall be born again, a conscious, responsible human being, to begin the second round of the Cyclic Ladder; on this second round, to externalize the knowledge gained, to evolve the involved attributes and forces of being,—a creature of will and intellect, to work out its destiny, as the lord of material creation.

Observe, the order of the Zodiac is reversed upon the external human plane. But, Aries is always symbolical of the first angle, and Libra of the seventh, being the point of equilibrium, while the tenth, or South, angle becomes Capricorn and the fourth Cancer. The mission of the soul now is to evolve the positive, spiritual attributes.

Aries rules the brain and the fiery, imperial will. It signifies courage, daring, etc., the first qualities necessary for the battle of life. Ruling the head, the sign and house show us the ability of man to view the field of action, to mark his chart, and arm for the war (which will be incessant); responsible for his acts, a creature of unfolding consciousness, an individual, whose measure of free will enables him to wander so far North or South of his celestial equator, within his orbit, or Zodiac.

The South angle, or Tenth House, now ruled by Capricorn, tells of the honor, position, fame, etc. (or the reverse) acquired by patient labor. The crystallized material gains, the concrete result of ambition, skill, and talent, which will, at the close of his earthly career, become liquefied by the universal resolvent; symbolized by Cancer upon the opposite angle, symbolical of the grave, the end of mundane affairs; when they will be mirrored forth in new forms in that great white sea, according to the manner in which he gained his worldly accumulations and prestige.

The seventh angle is Libra, House of Marriage; that all-important relation which may make or mar a life, the Balance is so easily disturbed in its equilibrium. To preserve its harmony, equality must reign, blending love and wisdom. It is the perfect poise of body, mind, and soul, achieved by loving obedience to the higher laws of our being and the true union of intuition and reason.

The Second House, now represented by Taurus, shows us that personal wealth and possessions must come through patient servitude, steady application, and diligence, in being able to choose and assimilate the knowledge, that will enable man to battle with material conditions, and wrest from the abundant sources of Mother Nature his share of treasure and experience. It is the battle-ground to which humanity, armed with brain and will, life and energy, goes forth to battle with material forces for the bread he must earn by the sweat of his brow, and through the silent, subtle forces of mind and soul conquer matter, thus storing up a wealth of knowledge and experience.

The Third House is ruled by Gemini, the Twins, Reason and Intuition, the brethren who aid and guide us on our many journeys in the pursuit of knowledge. As this sign governs the hands and arms and the executive forces of humanity, we see, that, the hands become the magical agents of mind, moulding into outward form the ideas conceived in the mind, projecting these into the field of active life, that he may write a bright record in the Book of Life. The hands should be kept clean, the images pure; and the perfect poise gained by the equal exercise of love and wisdom, intuition and reason, making the basis of education; the evolution of the interior or real self. This is the true meaning of this house upon the external plane. It is Occult, because it means projecting the powers of the soul into conscious life, externalizing the qualities and magical forces of spirit, as shown in the first instance by Aquarius. This can be accomplished only through pure desire and aspiration. Otherwise, the unbalanced scales, with floods and cataclysms, will be the results.

The Fifth House, ruling children, etc., is symbolized by Leo (the Heart). The joys and sorrows that offspring of every kind bring, all belong to this House of the Heart. The sacrifice indicated is too obvious for comment.

The Sixth House governs sickness, disease, etc., and its symbol is Virgo, an Earthy sign, clearly showing us that the material form is the matrix, out of which are born disease and suffering. But, the perfect assimilation of the fruit of the "Tree of Knowledge of Good and Evil;" transmuting the trials, experiences, sorrows, and suffering of the physical and external life into true wisdom; makes man master of his material universe; and the blind forces of Nature become his servants. Having accomplished the task, and attained the harmonious poise, or balance, in Libra, the individualized soul arrives at the eighth step in the journey.

The Eighth House, or House of Death and Legacies (Scorpio). The old Adam dies. The sensuous has no place in the balanced, harmonious being, but recognizes sex as the law, the door to regeneration now, and that a new legacy is awaiting him.

The Ninth House, Sagittarius, where, with the knowledge acquired, self sits in judgment upon the works of the hands and mind, whether or no they have been well done; the sacrifice of the lower nature properly made, control of the triune being established, the transmutations correct and accurate, assimilation perfect and free from dross, harmony gained by loving obedience to the higher law of being, and thus becomes ruler of his kingdom; the long journey almost accomplished, so far as Earth is concerned, perceiving and understanding that all sciences, philosophies, and religions, have their origin from one primal source. Having penetrated the depths in reverent obedience to the Divine law of creation, and evolved the attributes of the dual constitution, the forces of his being become crystallized. He has reached the culmination of his earthly pilgrimage, and stands forth the perfected human reflection of the higher self.

The Eleventh House is represented by Aquarius on the human plane. Friends surround and welcome him. These friends are the pure thoughts, noble impulses, lofty ideals, and generous deeds. The bread cast upon the Waters of Life returns to nourish and sustain him in his encounter with the secret foes, symbolized by the Twelfth House and Pisces. The idols, false ideas, and vampires of his own creation, are to be cleansed and washed away by the Waters of Love, the universal solvent that is ever seeking to bring about change and new forms; born again of water to make the round of the astral Zodiac, until, having again reached the equator of the ascending arc, where he is reunited to the missing half of his soul, the true friend of the Edenic state; the highest point in the arc of human progress won; the honor and glory of a perfected soul; the Lord and Master, the "I am that I am," to rest in peace in the heart of Infinite Love and Wisdom.

CHAPTER IV

There is one species of Divine revelation which has not, and cannot, be tampered with, one great Bible, which forms the starry original of all Bibles.

This sacred Bible is the great Astral Bible of the skies; its chapters are the twelve great signs, its pages are the innumerable glittering constellations of the heavenly vault, and its characters are the personified ideals of the radiant Sun, the silvery moon, and the shining planets, of our solar sphere.

There are three different aspects of this sacred book, and in each aspect the same characters appear, but in different roles, their dress and natural surroundings being suited to the natural play of their symbolical parts. In fact, the whole imagery may be likened unto a play, or, rather, a series of plays, performed by the same company of artists. It may be a comedy, or it may be melodrama, or it may be a tragedy; but the principles behind the scenes are ever the same, and show forth the same Divine Oneness of Nature; demonstrating the eternal axiom: *One truth, one life, one principle, and one word,* and in their fourfold expression, is the four great chapters of the celestial book of the starry heavens.

In this aspect the visible cosmos may be represented as a kaleidoscope. The visible constellations, planets, and other heavenly bodies, are the bits of colored glass; and Deity the invisible force, which keeps the instrument in motion. Each revolution produces a different pictorial figure, which, complete in its harmony of parts, is perfect in its mathematical proportions, and beautiful in its geometrical designs. And yet each creation, each form, and each combination of forms, are produced by the same little pieces of glass; and all of them, in reality, are optical illusions; i.e., natural phenomena, which deceive the physical senses. So it is with Cosmic Nature.

It must not, however, be supposed, because of this perfect and continual illusion of Nature's playful phenomena, that all visible creation is purely an illusion of the senses, as some cranky metaphysicians would have it, because this is not so.

Going back again to our kaleidoscope, we can clearly see that without it, and its tinted beads, no such optical illusion is possible. There is, then, a basis of spiritual reality to all visible physical phenomena; but this basis lies concealed, because of the perfect illusion which the reflected image produces upon the material plane of the physical senses. The beads themselves are real. These are the basis, and the different pictures are the result, not of the beads, but of the angle from which they are reflected to our earthly vision. In other words, *the plane from which we behold the phenomena.*

Hence, the nearer we approach the Divine center of our being, the less complicated Nature's original designs become, and the farther we are removed from that central source, the more weird, mysterious, complicated, and incomprehensible, does Mother Nature appear, to the finite human mind. And this is especially so, to man's theological instinct, his religiosity, that constitutes one of the fundamental factors of his being.

Nature is ever *one* in her original truths and their duplicate reflections; but ever conflicting and contradictory in her multiplied refractions through the minds of men. Therefore, we will present the primary concept of that grand Astro-Theology formulated by man's great progenitors; and view the simple machinery, by which they typified to the primitive mind a general outline of Nature's Divine providence.

All sacred books begin with an account of physical creation, the culmination of which, is the appearance of man and woman, as the parents of the race; and, while they will differ considerably in detail and make-up, the basic ideas embodied are essentially the same in all cosmo-genesis; so that in the Jewish Bible, accessible to all, one can read the primitive story of creation from a Jewish point of view, and, when read, rest satisfied that he has read the revelation vouchsafed to man in every age and in every clime. The only difference is one of mental peculiarity and national custom, along with climatic conditions. Hindoo, Chaldean, Chinese, Persian, Egyptian, Scandinavian, Druidic and ancient Mexican are all the same—different names and drapery, to suit the people only, but essentially the same in the fundamental ideas conveyed.

THE CREATION OF THE WORLD

The simple story of creation begins at midnight, when the Sun has reached the lowest point in the arc—Capricorn. All Nature then is in a state of coma in the Northern Hemisphere, it is winter time, solar light and heat are at their lowest ebb; and the various appearances of motion, etc., are the Sun's passage from Capricorn to Pisces, 60°, and from Pisces to Aries, 30°, making 90°, or one quadrant of the circle. Then begin in real earnest the creative powers, it is spring time. The six days are the six signs of the northern arc, beginning with the disruptive fires of Aries. Then, in their order, Taurus, Gemini, Cancer, Leo, Virgo; then Libra, the seventh day and the seventh sign, whose first point is opposite Aries and is the opposite point of the sphere, the point of equilibrium, equal day and equal night, it is autumn. It is the sixth sign from Aries, the first creative action, and so the sixth day following the fiery force, wherein God created the bi-sexual man. See Genesis, 1:5-27: "So God created man in His own image; in the image of God created He him, male and female created He them."

It is the seventh, or day of the Lord (man), the climax of material creation and Lord of all living things, and he rests in the blissful Garden of Eden. This seventh day and seventh sign is the concealed sacred Libra (♎), the perfect union of the sexes. Then comes the fall from Libra, through Scorpio, and banishment from the Garden of Eden. That is the victory of Satan, or Winter, over Summer, etc. It is useless to repeat the same old, old story. The yearly journey of the Sun around the constellated dial of Deity is the Astro basis of all primitive cosmology.

THE SCHEME OF REDEMPTION

In addition to the creation of the world and the fall of man through sin, we find all people in possession of a grand scheme of redemption, and, like the former, we shall find them all essentially the same. They all require a mediator between the angry God and disobedient man, and they all require that this mediator shall be Divine, or semi-Divine. Nothing less can satisfy Deity's demands; or, rather, let us say man's own carnal imagination. It is simply another turn of our cosmic kaleidoscope, and behold! the actors have changed. Capricorn becomes the stable of the Goat, in the manger of which the young Savior of the world is born. As a type of all, we will take the Gospel Savior. It is again midnight. The Sun enters the sign Capricorn on the twenty-first of December. This is the lowest point of the arc, South, and for three days he is stationary, or in darkness. And now it is Christmas Eve. He (the Sun or Savior) begins to move, and at midnight is born as the celestial Virgo is rising upon the Eastern quadrant of the skies; hence the Sun-God is born of a Virgin. Then comes the flight to escape Kronos, or Saturn (ruling Capricorn), who kills the young babes. There is a period of silence in the God's history while the Sun is in transit through the signs Capricorn and part of Aquarius. That is, he is hidden or obscured by the clouded skies of this period. We hear of him but once again until he, the Sun-God, or Savior, is thirty years old, or has transited thirty degrees of space. He has entered the sign Aquarius (symbolical of the Man.) Now begins the period of miracles.

Let us digress for a space, and refer to our chapter on the constellations. We shall find a perfect analogy between this miracle-working period and the constellations Aquarius and Pisces, as therein given. The first miracle we read of is turning water into wine. This may be seen in a threefold aspect. The Sun-God changes by his life-forces the waters of winter into the rich vintage of the harvest, where the Virgin (Virgo) Mother again appears. Again, the wine becomes the blood—the life offered up on the vernal cross to strengthen, renew and make merry with new life our Earth and its people. The devil (or winter), with his powers of darkness, is defeated and man saved. The final triumph is the crucifixion in Aries, the vernal equinox, about the twenty-first of March, quickly followed by the resurrection, or renewal of life. Then the God rises into heaven, to sit upon the throne at the summer solstice, to bless his people. We read, that, the Savior of mankind was crucified between two thieves. Very good. The equinoctial point is the dividing line between light and darkness, winter and summer. In other words, the Sun is resuming his northern arc, to replenish the Earth with his solar force and preserve his people from death in the coming winter. The life of a Buddha, a Krishna or a Christ, are all found in their completeness in the life of *Horus*; while the Father, Son and Holy Ghost are *Isis, Horus* and *Osirus*. The same trinity, under different names, are found in all nations. It is the *Sun, Moon* and *Human Soul*, which is the only true mediator of Man.

There is another version of this celestial crucifixion, wherein the Sun-God-Savior, after the supper of the harvest in Virgo, is crucified at the autumnal equinox upon the equator. We read that he was dying from the sixth to the ninth hours—three hours, three signs, or from the 21st of September to the 21st of December, when he is laid in the tomb. This is the lowest point of the Sun's journey in the southern hemisphere, and darkness holds the balance in our northern hemisphere. The three days in the tomb are the three months, or three signs, before the vernal equinox, or the resurrection, the rising out of the South to bring salvation to the northern portion of our Earth.

We have now only to glance over various diverging lines of the same cosmology and the same redemption. All these allegories typified *truths*. They all teach the Initiate the mysteries of creation, of man's destiny and his necessary Cycle of Material Probation. Some of the most beautiful parables may be read in this light. Abraham, and the story of his wanderings in the deserts of Asia Minor; of Lot and his unfaithful wife, are to be seen still written in the heavens. Hagar and Ishmael are still there; so also are Esau and his brother Jacob; the story of Joseph and his brethren; of Sampson and his twelve labors. This is the same beautiful story. The Sun, shorn of his glory, or solar force, at the autumnal equinox, stands upon the equator between the two pillars of the temple (or light and darkness), and pulls down the temple (or signs) into the southern hemisphere. And behind this we have the eternal truth of the soul, when, giving way to the allurements of matter (Delilah), the soul is shorn of its spiritual covering, or conscience, and sinks into matter and death. And the story of David and Goliath can be read to-day as clearly as of yore.

They are eternal, spiritual verities of human nature, and record, not only the history of the human race, its mutations and transmutations, but of the individual man and the suffering and delusive joys of his material life. Aye, more! It is the record of all his past existence and a type of his eternal destiny in the future.

Another turn of our cosmic kaleidoscope, and lo! the scene changes —the play extended, the angles greater, caused by the revolution of our solar parent through his celestial Zodiac. As the Sun passes out of one sign into another, or, in other words, forms a different angle to his own center of force, a new dispensation is born to the world;

or, rather, re-born under a new guise. The great Sun-God appears
to change his nature and manifests an entirely different set of attributes. That is the way man personified this play of Nature, through his
imperfect conception of the cause of this change. But to him it was,
and is, a truth, and man's effort to externalize these attributes in a
Divine personality was, and is, strictly from the plane of his mental
development and spiritual unfoldment.

The two pictures of this Astro-Theology, as set forth in the two
divisions of the Jewish Bible, will illustrate our meaning. The Sun
had entered the sign Aries some time prior to the exodus from Egypt.
Aries is the constellation of Mars, the fiery, destructive and warrior
element, or force, in Nature, and we find the Jewish conception of
God a perfect embodiment of these attributes: The Lord of Hosts,
a God mighty in battle, delighting in the shedding of blood and the
smell of burnt offerings, ever marshalling the people to battle and
destroying their foes and the works of his own hands; a God imbued
with jealousy, anger, and revenge. This was the type set up by the
Jewish savior and lawgiver, Moses.

After a period of 2,160 years, we find the Christian cosmology
ushered in. The Sun has entered the sign Pisces, which is ruled by
Jupiter, the beneficent father. The Christ, or mediator, of the Christian
Gospel was an embodiment of the joint qualities of the sign and ruling
planet. Gentle, loving and merciful, His words were messages of
love and peace; His work was with the poor, oppressed and fallen;
he eschewed sacrifices and burnt offerings; a contrite heart was the
best offering; He taught the people that God was their Father, loving
all, just, yet merciful. But a strong taint of the old conception has
remained with the human race, hiding, at times, the beauty of the
latter concept. These are, again, the refractions of eternal truths,
viewed by man from his material plane. The elements are here presented, the alphabet and its key clearly defined. Therefore, let each one
explore this tangled labyrinth of Astro-Theology for him or herself,
and work out the various correspondencies at leisure. It is enough
to indicate the starry originals of all this seemingly confused mass of
so-called Divine revelation in sacred books.

They, one and all, pertain to the same celestial phenomena, and
the various Bibles are the outcome of man's serious attempt to tabulate and externalize this heavenly order, to record his conceptions

of these starry aspects and movements with their corresponding effects upon the Earth.

Probably the purest system to us is that which may yet be derived from Chaldean sources. This sacerdotal caste were the most perfect in their astral conceptions and complete in their symbolic system of recording, and if the great work found in King Sargon's library in seventy tablets is ever translated, it will prove of priceless value to the student of these weird, but sublime, astrological mysteries.

In conclusion, as we reflect upon the fourfold aspect of the subject that we have presented in outline in these pages, the whole imagery passes in review before the mental vision. We see that the radiant constellations of the heavenly vault, with the beautiful reflection and counterpart, the shining Zodiac, are the two halves of the great *Cycle of Necessity*, the spiral of eternal, universal life, which binds the whole into unity, and unity into infinity. It is the grand scheme of creative life. The seven principles of Nature, or Divine Activities, are the forces producing the phenomena within seven angelic states, seven kingdoms, and, by seven planets, upon the external plane; the planets being the passive mediums of the positive spiritual forces. Upon this dual spiral, which reflects the seven rays of the solar spectrum is produced seven musical notes; one half of the spiral in sound and color being the complementary of the other half. Man, the Earth, and our solar system, are revolving, each orb in its own key, and its own peculiar ray, meeting and blending with other spirals, and the whole blending into one mighty spiral Cycle of Progressive Life, revolving around the Eternal, Infinite Ego—God, ever involving and evolving the attributes, powers and possibilities of the One great central source of Being.

It is a grand orchestra, pealing out in richest *melody* and sublime *harmony*, the grand Anthem of Creation: "We Praise Thee, O God."

CHAPTER V

The Astro-Mythological system of the ancients, though forming the last section, so to say, of the mysteries of the Divine Urania, is, perhaps, the most beautiful of its general features, and perfect in the complete fulfillment of the purpose for which it was intended, viz.:— to convey to the human mind a lesson, a moral, a truth in Nature; and last, but not the least, to serve as a basis upon which its inner aspirations and its more external faith might rest in security.

When we come to examine the deep, philosophical principles of such a wise system, we are almost astounded at the result of our researches and the wisdom of human nature displayed in formulating such perfect analogies of truth, semi-truth, and of falsehood, according to the plane occupied by the individual.

Let us take one instance, which will clearly explain all the rest, for they are built and formulated after the same model. Æneas, of Greek myths and fables, is reputed to be the son of Venus by a *mortal* father, upon the plane of reality. As that of actual *parent* and *child*, of course this is an utter falsehood. To the rural population of long, long ago, and their simple, rustic conceptions, *it was a truth*.

Why so? Because they believed it, and to them it taught the required lesson of obedience to the powers that be. But if in reality it was a falsehood, how can it become a truth by the simple addition of acceptance and belief? Because it possessed a metaphysical truth, though not a physical one, in the sense accepted.

Æneas, son of Venus, whose history is so beautifully preserved by the immortal Virgil, was (metaphysically speaking) son of the goddess, because he was, in his astral and magnetic nature, ruled and governed by Venus, born under one of her celestial signs and when she was rising upon the ascendant of the House of Life, even as Jesus Christos was born of a virgin, because Virgo was rising at His birth.

Thus Æneas was, in strict metaphysical reality, a son of Venus. Having satisfied the rural mind, which thus, unconsciously, accepts an absolute truth under a physical disguise, the metaphysical thinker, the philosopher, also accepts the same fable, knowing and realizing its more abstract truth.

But, again, we are met with the objection that such a truth is only apparently a truth; i.e., on the plane of embodied appearances, and naturally the question arises, where (if at all) is the real truth of the mythos? That truth which is beyond the mere metaphysical thinker and commonplace philosopher; the truth which the Initiates recognize—where is it? That truth lies far beyond the purview of Astro-Mythology. It is connected with the center of angelic life. Sufficient here to say that, as there are seven races of humanity, seven divisions to the human constitution, seven active principles in Nature, typified by the seven rays of the solar spectrum, so are there seven centers of angelic life, corresponding to the seven planetary forces formulated in "The Science of the Stars," and, as each one of us must of necessity belong to one of the particular angelic centers from which we originally emanated, the Initiate can see no reason why *Æneas may not in reality* belong to that celestial vortex represented by Venus upon the plane of material life. This being the case, we see how beautiful the ancients' system of temple worship must have been. The simple rustic, in reverence and awe, accepting the gross and physical meaning—the only one possible to his dark, sensuous mind. The scholar and philosopher bow their wiser heads with equal humility, accepting with equally sincere faith the more abstract form of the allegory; while on the other hand, the priest and the Initiate, lifting their loftier souls above the earth and its formulas of illusion and matter, accept that higher and more spiritual application, which renders them equally as sincere and devout as their less enlightened worshipers. It is thus we find these astro-myths true for all time, true in every age of the world, and *equally true of all nations.* And this is the real reason why we find every nation under the Sun possessing clear traditions relating to the same identical fables, under different names, which are simply questions of nationality. And when mythologists, archæologists, and philologists once recognize the one central, cardinal truth, they will cease to wonder why nations, so widely separated by time and space, possess the same basic mythology. They will then no longer attempt its explanation by impossible migrations of races, carrying the rudiments with them. They will find that this mythology was a complete science with the ancient sages, a *uni-*

versal mystery language, in which all could converse, and that it descended from the Golden Age, when there was but *one* nation on the face of the Earth, the descendants of which constituted the basic nucleus of every race which has since had an existence. In this light all is simple, clear, and easy to comprehend—all is natural.

The astronomer-priests of the hoary past, when language was figurative, and often pictorial, had recourse to a system of symbols to express abstract truths and ideas. In order to impress the minds of pupils with a true concept of the attributes of the celestial forces, we call planets, they personified their powers, qualities, and attributes. Just as the average mind of to-day cannot conceive of Deity apart from personality, so did primitive man clothe his ideas in actual forms, and in these impersonations, they combined the nature of the celestial orb with that of the zodiacal sign or signs, in which the planet exerted its chief and most potent activities. For instance, the planet Mars, whose chief constellation is Aries, was described as a great warrior, mighty in battle, fierce in anger, fearless, reckless, and destructive; while the mechanical and constructive qualities were personified as Vulcan, who forged the thunderbolts of Jove, built palaces for the gods, and made many useful and beautiful articles. Then, again, we find that Pallas Athene was the goddess of war and wisdom. She sprang from the head of Zeus. Aries rules the head, and represents intelligence. Athene overcame her brother Mars in war, which shows that intelligence is superior to brute force and reckless courage.

Here, we see three different personages employed to express the nature of the powers and phenomena produced. They were called gods and goddesses. This was quite natural, as the planets of our system are reflections of Divine principles. Esoterically, Mars symbolizes strength, victory—attributes of Deity.

Mars is said to have married Venus, teaching us that the union of skill and beauty are essential in all artistic work.

Mythology tells us that the god Mars was supposed to be the father of Romulus, the reputed founder of Rome. Romulus displayed many characteristics of the planet. The mythos is no doubt a parallel to that of Æneas. Rome was founded when the Sun in his orbit had entered the sign Aries, and Mars was the god most honored by the Romans. In time, with the degeneration of human races and their worship, to the rural mind, the subjects of the mythos became actual personalities, endowed with every human passion and godlike attribute, the former characterizing the discordant influence of the heavenly bodies upon man.

Gai, Rhea and Ceres, or Demeter (Greek), represent the triune attributes of Mother Earth. Gai signifies the Earth as a whole, Rhea the productive powers of the Earth, and Ceres utilizes and distributes the productive forces of Rhea.

In the charming story of Eros (Divine Love), son of Mars and Venus, he (Eros), we are told, brings harmony out of chaos. Here, we see the action of Aries and Taurus, ruled respectively by Mars and Venus.

The beautiful myth of Aphrodite, born of the sea foam, is Venus rising out of the waters of winter, to shine resplendent in the western skies at evening, and typifies the birth of forms, as all organic forms have their origin in water.

In all lands the Sun was known under various names, typical of solar energy, especially in reference to the equinoctial and solstitial colures.

Henry Melville, in his valuable work, "Veritas," says no reliance can be placed upon ancient dates, either of Europe, Asia, or anywhere else, and he conclusively shows that such dates are Astro-Masonic points on the celestial planisphere, the events recorded being, as it were, terrestrial reflections of the celestial symbols.

To attempt to wade through all the various systems of mythology, and explain each in its proper order, would be to write a large encyclopedia upon the subject. We have given a few examples as keys, and suggest works for study. We have here given the real key, and the student must fathom particulars for himself. The chief work, and most valuable in its line, is Ovid's "Metamorphoses." The next, also the most valuable in its line, is "The Mythological Astronomy of the Ancients," with notes (these latter are the gist and constitute the real value), by S. A. Mackey; and last, and, perhaps, in some sense, not the least, is the "Wisdom of the Ancients," by Lord Bacon. This is published in "Bacon's Essays."

A careful study of Ovid, with the key which this chapter supplies, will reveal *all* that pertains to ancient gods, demi-gods, and heroes, while a study of Mackey, and a careful comparison with "La Clef" and "La Clef Hermetique" will reveal all that pertains to cosmic cycles and astral chronology, which is the only chronology that is quite trustworthy, as far as ancient history is concerned.

While we are on this subject, we must point out some of the delusions, into which the subtle, magical teachings of the Orient would lead the student.

All the monster sphinx, half human, half animal, etc., which the ancients have preserved, are simply records of the past. They are chronological tables of cosmic time, and relate to eras of the past, of the Sun's motion, and not by any means to living creatures of ante-diluvian creations, as some wiseacres have imagined. Many of these ancient monuments, monstrous in form, are records of that awful period of floods and devastation known as the Iron Age, when there was a vertical Sun at the poles; or, in other words, when the pole of the Earth was ninety degrees removed from the pole of the ecliptic. To those who can read aright, every lineament tells as plainly as the written word the history of that awful past, marking the march of time, recording the revolutions of the Sun in his orbit of 25,920 years, and relating with wonderful accuracy the climatic changes, in their latitudes, which took place with each revolution of the Sun and corresponding motion of the Earth's pole of less than four degrees. All the greater myths of the dim past were formulated to express cosmic time, solar and polar motion, and the phenomena resulting therefrom. These monuments of antiquity prove that, the ancients knew a great deal more of the movements of heavenly bodies and of our planet than modern astronomers credit them with.

Madame Blavatsky, in her "Secret Doctrine," seriously states that all these monstrous forms are the types of actual, once living physical embodiments, and, with apparent sincerity, asserts that the Adepts teach such insane superstitions.

Such, however, is not the case, neither is there anything true, or even approaching the truth, in the cosmogony given in the work in question.

And, lastly, we have but one more aspect of the grand old Astro-Mythos to present to your notice. This aspect reveals the whole of the ancient classification of *work* and *labor*, and gives us a clear insight into the original designs, or pictorial representations, of the twelve signs and the twelve months of the year. It also clearly explains many things which are to-day attributed to superstitious paganism.

As each month possesses its own peculiar season, so are, or were, the various labors of the husbandman, and those of pastoral pursuits, altered and diverted. Each month, then, had a symbol which denoted the physical characteristics of climate and the temporal characteristics of work. As the Sun entered the sign, so the temple rites varied in honor of the labors performed, and the symbol thus became the object of outward veneration and worship. So we see that the twelve signs, and principally the four cardinal ones, became Deities, and the symbols sacred, but in reality, it was the same Sun to which homage was paid.

There is a large sphere of study in this direction, as, of course, each climate varied the symbol to suit its requirements. In Egypt there were three months when the land was overflowed with water; hence, they had only nine working months out of doors, and from this fact sprang the Nine Muses, while the Three Sirens represented the three months of inactivity in work, or three months of pleasure and festivity.

Mackey tells us that the great leviathan mentioned in the Book of Job was the river Nile.

In nearly all mythologies, we find that the gods assembled on some high mountain to take counsel. The Olympus of the Greeks and Mount Zion of the Hebrew Bible mean the same, the Pole-Star; and there, on the pictured planisphere, sits Cephus, the mighty Jove, with one foot on the Pole-Star and all the gods gathered below him. The Pole-Star is the symbol of the highest heaven.

With this we close, leaving the endless ramifications of this deeply interesting subject to the student's leisure and personal research, trusting the keys we have given in this chapter and their careful study may induce the reader and student of these pages to search out for himself the meaning concealed in all Astro-Mythologies.

CHAPTER VI

SYMBOLISM

At this point of our study it is necessary to make a halt; and, before proceeding further, to attempt to formulate and realize that, which, so far, we have been pursuing.

First, then, we have passed in review the Zodiac, and then the constellations. From this we mentally surveyed both Astro-Theology and Astro-Mythology; and now, it is our first duty to realize these in their real significance, and this consists in a clear comprehension of the Grand Law of Correspondences.

What is this law? It is the law of symbolism, and symbolism, rightly understood, is the one Divine language of Mother Nature, a language wherein all can read, a language that defies the united efforts of both time and space to obliterate it, for symbolism will be the language of Nature as long as spirit expresses itself to the Divine soul of man.

No matter where we turn nor where we look, there is spread out to our view a vast panorama of symbolic forms for us to read. In whatever form, angle, or color they present themselves, the true student of Nature can interpret and understand their symbolic language aright. It has been by the personification of Nature's symbols, that man has become ignorant of their language. There is no form, sound, nor color but what has its laws of expression; and only a perfect knowledge of symbolism will enable man to know the law, power, and meaning, lying behind such manifestations. The law of expression is exact, and as unalterable as Deity Himself. The physical senses cannot vibrate to these interior forces, and through them, comprehend their law. The physical senses vibrate to the spirit's expression, not to the powers, forces, and laws, which brought them into objective existence.

Countless numbers of mystics, if such they deserve to be called, among present-day students, speak and write very learnedly upon the "Law of Correspondence," and few, if any, of them really understand or know anything at all of that law. The intellect alone cannot solve the problems of this law. It cannot grasp the true, interior and spiritual meaning, except in just so far as intellect is capable of externalizing them. The inmost spiritual truths, that cannot be demonstrated to the outward senses, never have, nor never will, appeal to any one who has not the interior ability to comprehend them.

There was a time when men ruled by pure intellect, without its accompanying other half, intuition: they were looked upon as monstrosities. This state of purely intellectual development has been brought about by the positive, masculine principle, reason, absorbing its counterpart, the intuition, the feminine portion; and the result, by correspondence, *is* as fatal as upon the interior plane, where the positive, masculine soul denies the existence of his mate; thus setting upon his throne, only a portion of himself as his idol, and then, reasons himself into the belief that he is complete. Love has been cast out, ignored and forgotten until at last she departs, leaving a vacancy, that eternity cannot fill.

This is somewhat similar to their illusive Devachan, an ideal, a mere mystical sentiment to gush over, but a something they do not in reality comprehend. Therefore, we shall do our utmost to explain this universal law, and to point out wherein its first principles are manifest. Once these are mastered, the Golden Rule will explain all the rest: "As it is below, so it is above; as on the earth, so in the sky."

Here, then, is our first lesson on the subject of *reality,* which constitutes the Hermetic science of Correspondences.

First, realize that a line or an angle, for instance, is something more than its mere mathematical outline. It corresponds to some power, force, or principle within the great Anima-Mundi of the mysteries, that are trying to find expression, in their evolutionary journey, in forms. Let us illustrate our meaning. A point or dot is what? Well, externally it is the alpha of all mathematics. It is the first finite manifestation of the spiritual force. Within that dot lies concealed, in embryo, all the future possibilities of the manifesting principle.

This dot or point is a something to begin with, a form externalized. from which all future forms may spring forth, and they may be infinite. both in number and variety. First a primary, simple idea, from which all ideas and thoughts, intricate and complex, have their being.

A point extended is a straight line, scientifically expressed (whereas in real truth there is no such thing as a straight line); that is to say, it is a form increased or multiplied by itself, and therefore, is an extension in space that can be measured, and each extension means a new form, an additional symbol. It has taken on new aspects, new relations, hence contains the second principle of mathematics, so to say; but, besides being points, *they are symbols.* They are principles in Nature as clearly related to each other as the leaf and the stem of plant life.

Each monad, or point in the universe, is the beginning of something; equally so, it is also the termination of its own forces in that particular action, and will remain inert until it becomes acted upon by something else.

A point, then, is a primary, simple idea, a straight line. An angle is the same idea, rendered greater and more complex, and refers to the same forces upon a different plane, and the more we multiply the angles the more complex and far-reaching becomes the symbol and the more numerous and diverse become its planes of action. Here we will introduce an example. A trine represents three forces or angles, and, when united, form a trinity, hence harmony. Its apex (when above) is celestial, therefore represents the male forces of spirit.

A trine reversed also represents the same forces, with its apex in matter, hence it is negative. In these two complex ideas, clearly represented by these symbols, we have *all* matter and spirit; and yet they are but extensions of our point in space, rendered far-reaching and complex, by the position and the number of angles presented.

Let us turn the key once again, and we find that, both spirit and matter possess the same outline in their primal concept, except reversed (polarized).

Let us unite these two trines, and we have a still more potent form; a symbol almost infinitely complex. We have spirit and matter united, or, rather, three rays of force, positive, meeting three rays of force, negative, at a given point. Thus we have six points, also six sides, the ultimate of which is a cube. All are now equal. It is the first force of a crystallization (creation) of matter.

Once again let us turn the key, and we have our two conceptions in a metaphysical sense; the trine with its apex above is as the trine with its apex below, both the same in form, yet vibrating to very different planes, and a very different language is required to read and interpret their meaning aright. The spiritual, or the trine with its apex above, draws its influence from the celestial, and as it condenses and takes on form in the trine of matter, it transmits this same Divine force through its apex, which points below, to matter. The double trine is found upon every plane, obeying the Divine Law of Correspondences.

It is, in this sense, called "Solomon's Seal," because it is the grand hieroglyphic of the Hermetic law: "As it is above, so it is below; as on the Earth, so in the sky."

To continue this line of reasoning, or speculation, let us say, would lead us beyond the firm basis of human reason; it would escape the grasp of intellect, to which I am compelling this course of instruction to bend, but it would never take us beyond the real limits of the universe; yet, not to extend our investigations, we would ever remain in the lower trine, in the realms of effects, and lose sight entirely of the trine of spirit, from whence originated the force and potency in the form of matter.

Therefore it is, that the science of Symbolism has been evolved and formulated. The symbols, the manifestations, are ever present, and the study of effects will, to a developed soul, suggest the cause, the nature of the principle back of it, as well as the law which would produce such effects. Such is the science of symbolism; and it bounds and binds back into a religio-philosophical system, each class of symbols and each plane of manifestation; as securely as modern savants have defined the province of chemistry, magnetism, and mathematics; and, so far, these bounds are useful. But it is only a question of time and space, after all, because, when resolved back, or, let us say, evolved up into their abstract principles; chemistry, magnetism, and mathematics, are purely arbitrary terms to express special features of the same one eternal thing or science—which is *existence;* and it, in turn, is *consciousness;* not that external consciousness of existence, not that knowledge and love of living, but that interior, conscious knowledge, which tells us why and how we exist, by what force and power we are sustained and permitted to obey and carry out the law of mediumship, reception and transmission, attraction and repulsion, spiritual and material, that ultimately blend and become as one, the double trine, and, united with the Divine Ego of its being, becomes complete; seven, the perfected number of form.

The sum total, then, of all, and the value it may possess to the individual, is measured by his ability to perceive; for there is nothing external that is not in some sense mental, and there is nothing mental that is not in some sense spiritual. The sides of the triangle, physical, mental, and spiritual, and the apex where meet the mental and spiritual, forms the center of contact to higher trines in realms above.

Where mind is not, there are no symbols, no ideas, no manifestations. The spirit has not yet reached that point in its evolutionary journey where it can yet crystallize its projected force, power, or ideas, into forms; for everything that is, is the outcome of Divine thought, and expresses within itself the symbol of its being. This is the arcana of the Law of Correspondences.

Remember the above teaching, because upon its full comprehension rests the ability to read symbols aright. It will aid the soul to fully realize that, the vast universe is but the mental image of the Creator; that there is no such thing as manifested existence apart from mind; and consequently, the infinite worlds that float securely in space, blushing and scintillating with light of life and love of the Father, revealing to mortal minds some faint conception of the awful resources and recesses within Nature's star-making laboratory, are but the scintillating reflection of life, the reactions of mental phenomena. So, too, with the mental creative powers of the mind of man, for, not a vibration that proceeds from his every thought but what creates its correspondence in the creative realm of spirit. Hence, symbolism continues giving to the soul of man, throughout eternity, food for thought and contemplation.

All symbols, then, are objectified ideas, whether human or Divine; and as such possess a real meaning; and this meaning is altered, extended and rendered more complex with every additional thing or influence by which we find it surrounded, or with which, we find it correlated. For instance, $1.00 means one dollar; add six ciphers to the left 0000001., and it is still the same $1.00, and no more, because their position is previous, or before, the 1. But add the same number of ciphers to the right, $1,000000, and lo! we find a wondrous change of force, power, and consequence. We see all the mighty power of our million of money, and the possibilities and responsibilities with which, in these days, it becomes associated.

So it is with everything else in Nature. Man pays the penalty by increased responsibility, for every step in knowledge that he takes, as well as every dollar in gold he procures. Dollars, as well as talents, have to be accounted for, and their usefulness increased tenfold. The dollars must not be buried nor hoarded any more than our talents, but each, unfolded and doubled, so that we may be instrumental in helping our coworkers in their upward path, in the Cycle of Necessity. Knowledge is the basic foundation in reading Nature's language. Purity of thought, truth in motive, and unselfish benevolence, will lift the veil that now lies between the two trines, cause and effect, spirit and matter.

We have given the key and explained the alphabet of this wondrous law; therefore we close. Each must, by the same rules, work out the special links in the chain for him or herself. The angle from which each take their view determines the reading and interpretation of the symbols presented, whether that be from the apex, the sides or the base, for every symbol has its trinity in principles and form. Cause and effect are but the action and reaction; the result is the symbol which reveals the correspondence of both.

CHAPTER VII

ALCHEMY—PART I

What a weird yet strangely pleasing name the term Alchemy is. It is simple, yet so infilled and intermixed with the possible verities of exact science and the philosophical speculations on the infinite and the unknown, as to elude our mental grasp, as it were, by its own subtle essence, and defy the keenest analysis of our profoundest generalizers in science. And yet, in spite of this self-evident truth, how fascinating the sound of the word becomes to the mystic student's ear, and how pregnant with awful and mysterious possibilities it becomes, to the immortal powers embodied within the complex human organism termed man.

Words, if we but knew it, have the same innate, magnetic influence, and possess the same power of affinity and antipathy, that the human family possesses; as well as all organic and inorganic forms and substances; and how sad, to a developed soul, to witness the inharmony existing in our midst, caused by the misapplication of names.

Most human beings are very conscious of personal, or human magnetism, and its effects. But they stop right there, and do not dream of the subtle, silent influences emanating from a name, a word, and the power existing in words, when properly used. The human mind is so absorbed in Nature's manifestations, which are only the husks, that they fail to see the true, hidden meaning and realities, concealed beneath the material shell.

We will first notice the meaning of the words which constitute our subject, viz., Alchemy, then give a brief review of its physical correspondence, chemistry, and its true relation to its spiritual counterpart, Alchemy.

"Al" and "Chemy" are Arabic-Egyptian words which have much more in them than appears upon the surface, and possess a far different meaning from the one which the terms usually convey to the average mind. Terms, and the ideas we associate with them, vary according to the age in which we live. So with those, from which the word Alchemy is derived.

Let us penetrate beneath the mere verbal husk with which linguistic usage and convenience have clothed them, and which, in the course of ages, has become nothing but the dross of decomposed verbiage, and see if we can excavate the living germ, that has become buried within. If we can do so, we shall, at the commencement of our study, have attained unto a realization of the ancient meaning and real significance of the terms employed. And this will be no small gain, and will form no unimportant part of the equipment in our present research.

The Arabians, who derived the whole of their Occult arcana from the Egyptians, are the most likely to render us the most truthful and direct significance of the word, and so we find them. Thus, "Al," meaning "the," and Kimia," which means the hidden, or secret, *ergo* THE OCCULT, from which are derived our modern term Alchemy, more properly Al Kimia. This is very different from the popular conception to-day, which supposes that the word relates to the art of artificially making gold by some chemical process, and viewing it only as some sort of magical chemistry, forgetting that, the science of chemistry itself is also derived from the Kimia of Arabian mystics, and was considered as one and the same thing by every writer of the Middle Ages.

At this time, the physical man was not so dense and grasping for husks; hence the soul and spiritual part had greater control, and could impart the real, the alchemical side, of Nature to him; hence the Law of Correspondences was understood, and guided the educated in their considerations, researches, and conclusions.

Do you ask why, if they were so enlightened, they have veiled their knowledge from the world at large?

The power of mind over matter was as potent in those days as now, and the masses were as correspondingly corrupt as they are to-day. Therefore, to put this knowledge into the hands of the multitude would have been generally disastrous. So they wrote it in mystical language, knowing that all educated students in Nature's laws, at that time, would understand; yet they little dreamed how much their language would be misunderstood in the centuries to follow, by those who look to their ancient ancestry for aid on subjects that have become at the present day so lost in mystery.

Having ascertained, beyond question, that Alchemy was, and consequently is, the secret science of Occultism—not the philosophy, mind you, but the science; let us proceed, for, we shall find that these two aspects may often differ, or appear to differ, widely from each other, though they can never do so in reality, for the latter produces and establishes the facts, while the former occupies itself in their tabulation and deductions. The science constitutes the foundation, and the philosophy, the metaphysical speculations, which rest thereon. If these important distinctions are borne in mind, all the apparent confusion, contradiction, and other intellectual debris, will either disappear or resolve themselves into their own proper groups, so that we may easily classify them.

It is at this very point, that, so many students go astray amid the labyrinths of science and philosophy. They, unconsciously, so mix and intermingle the two terms, that nine-tenths of the students present only one side of the question—philosophy, which soon runs into theory, if not supported by the science, which they have lost in their volumes of philosophy.

You may say, one subject at a time. Yes, this may be true, if its twin brother is not absorbed and forgotten.

In this chapter, we shall deal especially with organic Alchemy.

Organic Alchemy deals exclusively with living, organic things, and in this connection differs from the Alchemy of inorganic matter. These two aspects may, in this one respect, be compared to organic and inorganic chemistry, to which originally they belonged; as astrology did to astronomy. Alchemy and astrology—twin sisters—were the parents of the modern offspring, known in chemistry and astronomy as exact science. These latter, however, deal with shadows and phenomenal illusions, while the former concern the living realities, which produce them. Therefore, there can be "no new thing under the sun." saith Solomon.

First, let us deal with the most lovely form of our art, that which pertains to the floral and vegetable kingdoms. Every flower or blade of grass, every tree of the forest and stagnant weed of the swamp, is the outcome of, and ever surrounded by, its corresponding degree of spiritual life. There is not a single atom but what is the external expression of some separate, living force, within the spaces of Æth, acting in unison with the dominant power corresponding with the type of life.

If science could only behold this wonderful laboratory within the vital storehouse of Nature, she would no longer vainly seek for *the origin of life*, nor wonder, what may have become of the missing link in scientific evolution, because, she would quickly realize that, biogenesis is the one grand truth of both animate and inanimate Nature, the central, living source of which is God. Science would also, further realize that, this biune life is ever in motion throughout the manifested universe; circulating around the focii of creative activities, which we term suns, stars, and planets, awaiting the conditions which are ever present for material incarnation; and under all possible combinations of circumstances and conditions, conceivable and inconceivable, adapting itself to continuous phenomenal expression. Links, so called, in this mighty chain of evolution, may appear to be missing here and there, and, for that matter, whole types may seem to be wanting, but, this is only because of our imperfect perception, and, in any case, can make no real difference with the facts, because, if such be a reality, if there be what *we* may term *missing links* in the scheme of evolution, it only shows that spirit, although associated with, is ever independent of matter.

But matter—what is to become of it? Is it independent of spirit? The kindness of the Divine spirit heeds not the unconscious mind of matter and its boasted independence, and works silently on, and at last, accomplishes its mission—the evolution of matter, the uplifting of the soul of man, as well as the universe. The blindness of man is dense, and the saddest part to admit is that, they will so stubbornly remain so.

If, for one instant, the penetrating eye of the soul could shine forth through the physical orbs of vision, and imprint the scenes, beheld behind the veil, upon the tablets of the brain of the physical organism, a fire would be kindled that, could never be quenched by the fascinating allurements of the material. perishable things, of matter.

That development of the real atom of biune life can, and does, go forward, irrespective of the gradation of physical types, needs no convincing proof, other than visible Nature.

Man is not the outcome of physical evolution, and produced by a series of blind laws, that lead him upward from protozoa to man, as a child climbs up stairs, advancing regularly, *one step as a time.* This latter conception, we know, is the theory of exact science, but not of Alchemy, not of the science of Occultism. Man, according to Wallace, Darwin, Huxley, and Tyndall, is what progressive stages of physical evolution have made him. But the very reverse is true. The fauna and flora of past geological periods are what the human soul has produced, by virtue of its gradual advancement to higher states and conditions of life, so that, so far from man being the outcome of the planet's development, such material progress is the outgrowth of man's advancement, proving again that, matter is not independent of spirit, neither can spirit be independent of matter for its expressions. They so interblend that, the dividing line cannot be detected by the untrained eye of the exact scientist. But, that time is not far distant, when the scientists will prepare and evolve their interior being to take up the spiritual thread, exactly where the visible thread ends, and carry forth the work, as far as the mortal mind of man can penetrate, while embodied in the physical form.

God hasten this day is my prayer, for then man will become more spiritual and aspiring for advancement and knowledge, thus, setting up vibrations that will create higher and loftier conditions for the physical man. Aye! then they will know that, even the birth of the world itself, owes its primal genesis to the desire of the human atom for earthly embodiment.

Here is where exact science, or the counterpart of Alchemy, becomes both profitable and helpful. Says Paracelsus: "The true use of chemistry is not to make gold, but to prepare medicines." He admits four elements—the *star*, the *root*, the *element* and the *sperm*. These elements were composed of the three principles, *sideric salt, sulphur,* and *mercury*. Mercury, or spirit, sulphur, or oil, and salt, and the passive principles, water and earth. Herein we see the harmony of the two words, Alchemy and Chemistry. One is but the continuation of the other, and they blend so into each other that, they are not complete, apart.

The chemist, in his analysis of the various component parts of any form of matter, knows also the proportional combinations; and thus, by the Law of Correspondence, could, by the same use of the spiritual laws of Alchemy, analyze and combine the same elements from the atmosphere, to produce the corresponding expression of crystallized form. By the same laws, are affinities and antipathies discovered and applied, in every department of Nature's wonderful laboratory.

Chemistry is the physical expression of Alchemy, and any true knowledge of chemistry is:—not the knowing of the names of the ex-

tracts and essences, and the plants themselves, and that certain combinations produce certain results, obtained from blind experiments,
yet, prompted by the Divine spirit within; but, knowledge born from
knowing the why and wherefore of such effects. What is called the oil
of olives is not a single, simple substance, but it is more or less combined with other essential elements, and will fuse and coalesce with
other oils and essences of similar nature. The true chemist will not
confine his researches for knowledge to the mere examination, analysis,
and experiments, in organic life; but will inform himself equally, in
physical astrology; and learn the nature, attributes, and manifested
influences of the planets, that constitute our universe; and, under
which, every form of organic matter is subject, and especially, controlled by. Then, by learning the influence of the planets upon the
human family; and that special planetary vibration that influences the
individual; he can intelligently and unerringly administer medicines
to remove disease in man.

A familiarity with the mere chemical relations of the planet to
man, makes still more apparent, the mutual affinity of both to the soil,
from which they appear to spring, and to which, they ultimately return; so much so that, we have become conscious, that, the food we
eat is valuable or otherwise as a life sustainer, in proportion to the
amount of life it contains. We are so complex in our organization
that, we require a great variety of the different elements to sustain all
the active functions and powers within us. Man, being a microcosm,
or a miniature universe, must sustain that universe, by taking into the
system the various elements, which combine to make up the Infinite
Universe of God. Animal flesh is necessary to certain organized forms,
both animal and man. When I say necessary, I do not mean an acquired taste and habit of consuming just so much flesh a day: but a
constitution, which would not be complete in its requirements, without animal flesh. I am thankful such do not constitute the masses.

Science would say, you only require certain combinations of
oxygen, hydrogen, nitrogen, and carbon, to sustain all the activities of
the physical body. Apparently, this is true. Upon the surface it is,
but in reality it is not; because if it were really true there could be
no famines. Science could make bread out of stones, as was sug-
gested at the temptation of Christ in the wilderness. And yet, no one
knows better than the academies of Science, themselves, that their

learned professors would quickly starve to death, if they were compelled to produce their food from the chemical properties of the rocks.
They can make a grain of wheat chemically perfect, but they cannot
make the invisible germ by which it will grow, become fruitful, and
reproduce itself. They can reproduce from the stones in the street the
same chemical equivalents that go to compose gluten, albumen, and
starch—the trinity which must always be present to sustain life; but
they cannot, by any known process, make such chemical equivalents
of these substances, do the same thing. Now, if not, why not? Science
cannot answer this. A very mysterious shake of the head and profound silence is the only answer. Ask Science *how the plant grows,*
what causes the atoms of matter to build up root, stem, leaf, bud and
flower, true to the parent species from which the germinal atom came.
What is there behind the plant that stamps it with such striking individuality? And why, from the same soil, the deadly aconite and
nutritious vegetable can grow, each producing qualities in harmony
with its own nature, so widely different in their effects upon the human
organism, *yet, so completely identical as regards the source from which
they appear to spring.* There must be a something to account for this,
and this something, ancient Alchemy alone can scientifically reveal and
expound; and, this knowledge lies just beyond that line which calls a
halt to material scientists, and says: "You can go no farther; this is
beyond your purview. The end of the material thread has been
reached, and unless you can connect it with the thread of the next
plane, your researches must stop."

Before entering upon and answering these vital questions, we
must digress a little, and make ourselves perfectly familiar with the
ideas and revelations of advanced physical science upon the subject, and for this purpose no more trustworthy guide can be consulted
than the new edition of "The Chemistry of Common Life," by the
late James F. W. Johnson, M. A., England, and revised by Arthur
Herbert Church, M. A. In chapter IV on page 56 of this work, upon
the anatomy of plant life, we read:

"How interesting it is to reflect on the minuteness of the organs
by which the largest plants are fed and sustained. Microscopic aper-
tures in the leaf suck in gaseous food from the air; the surfaces of
microscopic hairs suck a liquid food from the soil. We are accustomed
to admire, with natural and just astonishment, how huge, rocky reefs,

hundreds of miles in length, can be built up by the conjoined labors of myriads of minute zoophytes, laboring together on the surface of a coral rock; but it is not less wonderful that, by the ceaseless working of similar microscopic agencies in leaf and root, the substance of vast forests should be built up and made to grow before our eyes. It is more wonderful, in fact; for whereas, in the one case, the chief result is that, dead matter extracted from the sea is transformed into a dead rock; in the other, the lifeless matter of the earth and air are converted by these minute plant-builders into living forms, lifting their heads aloft to the sky, waving with every wind that blows, and beautifying whole continents with the varying verdure of their ever-changing leaves."

Further on in the same chapter, on pages 62-3, the same eloquent writer continues:

"But the special chemical changes that go on within the plant, could we follow them, would appear not less wonderful than the rapid production of entire microscopic vegetables from the raw food contained in the juice of the grape. It is as yet altogether incomprehensible, even to the most refined physiological chemistry, how, from the same food taken in from the air, and from generally similar food drawn up from the soil, different plants, and different parts of plants, should be able to extract or produce substances so very different from each other in composition and in all of their properties. From the seed-vessels of one (the poppy) we collect a juice which dries up into our commercial opium; from the bark of another (cinchona) we extract the quinine with which we assuage the raging fever; from the leaves of others, like those of hemlock and tobacco, we distil deadly poisons, often of rare value for their medicinal uses. The flowers and leaves of some yield volatile oils, which we delight in for their odors and their aromatic qualities; the seeds of others give fixed oils, which are prized for the table or use in the arts * * * These, and a thousand other similar facts, tell us how wonderfully varied are the changes which the same original forms of matter undergo in the interior of living plants. Indeed, whether we regard the vegetable as a whole, or examine its minutest part, we find equal evidence of the same diversity of changes and of the same production, in comparatively minute quantities, of very different, yet often characteristic forms of matter."

From the whole of the foregoing, we observe the exact position to be the one we have previously stated. If such wondrous things can be revealed to us through the physical science of chemistry, what think you must be hidden from our physical sight and knowledge by the veil which hangs between matter and spirit? Think you not, it is worth the effort to penetrate beyond that point where the atom disappears from the view of the scientist?

If plants produce such wonderful phenomena in their life and influence, what must the Divine organism of man have concealed within his microscopic universe, to study and comprehend? Plant life is merely the alphabet of the complex, intricate, and multitudinous processes, going on in the human body.

And, as the mechanical microscope of physical science cannot reveal the why and the wherefore, let us, for a brief moment, disclose some of the wonders that declare their existence, when subjected to the pentrating alchemical lens, of the inward spirit. The first thing that intrudes itself upon our notice, by virtue of its primary importance, is the grand fact of biogenesis—life emanating from life. We perceive every external form to be the physical symbol of a corresponding degree of spiritual life; that each complete plant represents a complete cycle, state, or degree of interior existence; that it is made up and consists of countless millions of separate atoms of life; that these atoms of spiritual activity are the real instigators of the life and motion of corresponding material atoms; that they ever obey the Divine impluse of co-operative unity, in their chemical, as well as their spiritual affinity. Consequently, everything in the form of material substance must be, and is, but the means for the phenomenal expression of incarnating spirit; the organism of man, a tree, a plant, or an animal, being no exception to this Divine, omnipresent law of creative life.

To the true Alchemist there can be no mystery surrounding the wonderful phenomena mentioned in the work we have quoted, in plants extracting from the same rocks, soil, and air, qualities so manifestly different—deadly poisons, healing balsams, and pleasant aromas, or the reverse, from the same identical plant foods. Nothing is more wonderful or mysterious, than, the same alchemical processes, which, are hourly being enacted within our own bodies. From the same breath of air and the same crust of bread do we concoct the blood, the bile, the gastric juice, and various other secretions; and distil the finer nervous fluids, that go to build up and sustain the whole of our mental and dynamic machinery. It is the same ancient story of the atoms; each part and each function endowing the same inorganic chemicals with their own spiritual, magnetic, and physical life-qualities, by what appears, to the uninitiated observer, a miraculous transmutation of matter, but which is, in reality, the evolution of organic form from inorganic materials, in obedience to the Divine law of spiritual progression. Who could stop with exact science? For, when we come to consider the apparent mysteries of life and growth by the aid of this alchemical light, the shadows flee, and all the illusions of Nature's phenomenal kaleidoscope vanish before the revelation of the underlying spiritual realities. We know that the plant, being the physical expression upon the material plane of a more interior life, endows its outward atoms with their peculiar qualities. *These qualities are not drawn directly from the soil;* the soil only becoming the medium for their complete or incomplete expression, as the case may be; i.e., supplying the necessary inorganic atoms. Hence, the deadly qualities of aconite, and the generous life-sustaining qualities of the nutritious vegetable, *being spiritual life endowments*, conveyed to the material substance, abstracted from the soil and withdrawn from the atmosphere, are no mystery; their effect upon the human organism being exactly that, which is produced by their spiritual affinity or antipathy, as the case may be. And this also shows and explains, why purely inorganic chemical atoms, though they be exactly the same as the organic substances, from a strictly scientific standpoint, *yet fail to support life*, because such chemical equivalents lack the organic spirituality of the interior life, which alone, gives them the power and function to support the same. They fail to fulfill the requirements of the alchemical law of life for the support of life—in other words, biogenesis.

And, too, this inorganic life may be parted from the plant or vegetable, if it be too long severed from the medium which transmits the spiritual life, from the inorganic world to that of organic matter. Vegetables, fresh from the ground, or parent stem, retain this life if at once prepared for food, if not overcooked, which is so often ignorantly done. This is the secret of sustenance from foods. Nature's perfected fruits and vegetables are overflowing with the life-giving essences, and, if eaten direct from the tree or parent stem, that life is not lost, but transmitted to our organisms, and replenishes the wasting system with a living life. Much less of such food is required to completely satisfy and nourish the body than if the life had partly departed or been destroyed.

Briefly stated, then, everything within organic Nature is the expressional symbolic manifestation of spirit; every form being a congregation of innumerable atoms of life, revealing their presence in material states; each organic form, or, rather, organism, evolving under the central control of some dominating Deific atom or soul, which, by virtue of past incarnations and labors in its cycle of evolution, from the mineral up to man, has achieved the royal prerogative to rule within its own state. Man being the highest representative form—the grand finale in the earthly drama—sums up and contains within himself everything below, and *the germs of everything beyond, this state.* He is truly a microcosm, and represents in miniature the grand Cosmic Man of the Heavens. Every living force beneath him corresponds to some state, part, or function, which he has graduated through and conquered, and which, in him, has now become embodied, as a part of his universal kingdom. Consequently, all things are directly related to him, in the grand universal unity of spiritual life.

This cannot be realized and comprehended by the physical man, nor conveyed to his outer senses by the physical sciences. He must bring into active use the inner man, the real being, which inhabits and controls the outer organism, and through its instrumentality, understand the interior source and workings behind the phenomena of manifested being. So we see that, exact science cannot take us far, yet, it is a mighty factor, in the evolution of the microcosm Man, and in consciously relating him to the Infinite Macrocosm—God, Spirit, All.

CHAPTER VIII

ALCHEMY—PART II

Paracelsus, the most celebrated of the alchemists of the Middle Ages, thus mystically speaks of his art:

"If I have manna in my constitution, I can attract manna from heaven. Melissa is not only in the garden, but also in the air and in heaven. Saturn is not only in the sky, but also deep in the ocean and Earth. What is Venus but the artemisia that grows in your garden, and what is iron but the planet Mars? That is to say, Venus and Artemisia are both products of the same essence, while Mars and iron are manifestations of the same cause. What is the human body but a constellation of the same powers that formed the stars in the sky? He who knows Mars knows the qualities of iron, and he who knows what iron is knows the attributes of Mars. What would become of your heart if there were no Sun in the Universe? What would be the use of your 'Vasa Spermatica'* if there were no Venus? To grasp the invisible elements, to attract them by their material correspondences, to control, purify, and transmute, them by the ever-moving powers of the living spirit—this is true Alchemy."

Thus, in a very few simple words, we find this master of the art revealing the whole arcana of that mysterious science, which has for its chief object and goal, the discovery of the "philosopher's stone," which confers upon its fortunate possessor the blessings of immortal youth. Therefore, we cannot possibly do better in the commencement of our present study than, to minutely examine each particular sentence and endeavor to discover his true meaning, which, like all mystical writing, is so apparent, yet cunningly concealed, as to excite the student's admiration.

"If I have manna in my constitution, I can attract manna from Heaven." The manna here spoken of does not specify any particular thing, but is of universal application, and is simply used as an unknown quantity, like x, y, z in mathematics. But, ever since the days of Paracelsus, half-initiated mystics and bookworm Occultists, have endeavored to discover what this manna really was. Some, the more

_____
*Astral germs of subjective life forms:—it is the latent, "to be".

spiritual, were of the opinion that, it was spiritual power, or purity of spirit; others imagined it to mean special magnetic qualifications, similar in nature to the so-called gifts of modern spiritualistic media. The concealment of the truth is unique, and consists in its very simplicity; and, when correctly expounded, should read: "I am the microcosm, and all the visible and invisible universe dwells within me, so that whatsoever power I have in my constitution, I can attract its correspondence from Heaven." Paracelsus must have smiled to himself when he wrote *"If I have manna,"* etc., because his whole writings strive to prove man the miniature of Deity. Further along, he explains himself by pointing out the real Law of Correspondence, thus: "Melissa is not only in the garden, but also in the air, and in Heaven. Saturn is not only in the sky, but also deep in the ocean, and Earth." The illustrations are beautiful. The life of the plant, the "anima floralis," pervades the atmosphere and the interior states of spiritual life, where it becomes in the highest degree beautiful, and beneficial to the soul. A reference upon this point to "The Light of Egypt" Vol., I, may not be considered out of place. Upon page 74 it is written: "The flower that blooms in beauty, breathing forth to the air its fragrance, which is at once grateful to the senses and stimulating to the nerves, is a perfect specimen of Nature's faultless mediumship. The flower is a medium for the transmission to the human body of those finer essences, and of *their spiritual portion to the soul;* for the aroma of the flower is spiritualized to such a degree as to act upon the life currents of the system, imparting to the spiritual body a nutriment of the finest quality."

Thus, here is where the knowledge of the alchemical attributes of plants, as applicable to man, can be most beneficially utilized. Plants and flowers, whose attributes and aromas harmonize with the complex organism of man, should be selected for the house and garden, for, they are mediums to transmit the finer essences and aromas to the spiritual constitution of man; the plant to the physical, and the aromas and essences of the flowers to the soul.

Antipathies in plants and flowers would bring a similar evil influence, as the discords of the antagonistic human magnetism. It would not be so apparent, but more subtle, yet nevertheless effective in result.

Our attention is next drawn to the planet Saturn, which, we are informed, is not only shining in his starry sphere of the heavens, but is also buried in the ocean depths and embodied in the stratas of the earth. It is almost needless to add that, our author refers to those substances naturally Saturnine in their quality of life and expression, such as lead, clay, and coal, among the minerals, and various deadly plants among the flora, the chief of which is the aconite or *monkshood*, so significant of Saturn and the isolated, monkish hermit. After some repetition, in order to impress the truth of correspondences, our author exclaims: "What is the human body but a constellation of the same powers that formed the stars in the sky?" Truly, what else? for, "he who knows Mars knows the qualities of iron, and he who knows what iron is knows the attributes of Mars." Could anything be plainer? We think not.

From the foregoing, which a long experience and much critical investigation and research have demonstrated as true, we cannot avoid the conclusion that Alchemy, equally as well as every other science, religion, or system of philosophy formulated by man, resolves itself, ultimately, in all its final conclusions, into the one universal parent of all wisdom.

ASTROLOGY, the Science of the Stars, in unison with the Science of the Soul, was, and still is, the one sublime center of real learning. It constituted the sacred fountain of living waters, from whose placid depths there rayed forth the Divine revelations of man, his whence, where, and whither; and under the careful conservation of a long line of gifted seers, it shone forth to the sons of men, as the sacred Hermetic light in the Astro-Masonic wisdom of Egypt's ancient priesthood.

It is not lost to us to-day. The same book lies open before us that faced our ancient forefathers. It is standing out clear and distinct, waiting to be read by the sons of men. We can learn its language, and from its pages, we ourselves can read our relation to God and our fellowman. Shall we not heed the whispering intuitions of the soul and place ourselves in conscious rapport with the whole?

This sublime Book of Wisdom was written by God Himself, to convey to His children the knowledge of His powers, attributes, and relation to all creative life. We cannot see that Divine Spirit which we call God. No; but as long as the finite form exists as such, we will have the spirit's manifestations to learn from. Never will the Book of God be closed to the searching eye of the soul. There will always be presented to his vision lessons to study, and practical experiments to perform, to lead the soul into deeper mysteries. Until man fathoms his own universe, he cannot understand God. "Know thyself" is as applicable to-day as when the famous, immortal and mystic utterance was inscribed on the porch of the temple at Delphi.

Before this wonderful, divinely elaborated, but complex system can be fully realized, it is necessary that the student should comprehend, very distinctly, the two states of existence, the internal and the external, and become familiar with the laws of correspondences. And it seems strange that of all Sciences, that of medicine should have so completely failed to grasp this living truth, since every atom of medicine administered, invariably acts upon this alchemical principle. When the human organism has become discordant in some of its parts, it is because the interstellar vibrations have aroused various states within the human kingdom into a condition of rebellion against the supreme will. Man's ignorance favors such seditious movements, and his general habits and code of morals stimulate them to undue activity. The final result is *disease*—disorganization of the parts and functions, and those medicines corresponding *to the same functional degree of life within the grand man,* cure the disorder, when administered properly and *in time,* whereas, if given to the perfectly healthy organism, *the atoms produce similar symptoms to the diseases they alleviate,* because it is their mission to either subdue or be subdued, and when disease prevails the medicinal atoms, acting in unison with the natural parts and functions they affect, conquer or subdue the inharmony, and vice versa, as before stated. In all cases of disease and medicine, it is a simple question of *a war between the atoms,* and, therefore, the most potential forces within Nature are always at the command of the true Alchemist, because he knows how and when to select his fighting forces, and when to set them in motion, for the best results.

Hahnemann, the founder of the Homeopathic system, has approached *the nearest* to this alchemical truth, and as a consequence, we find it is in actual practice, the most natural, scientific, and successful system of medicine, yet given to the world; based, as it is, upon the well-known law of affinites, "*Similia similibus curantur*," "like cures like," being a very ancient axiom in the astrological practice of physic.

Bulwer Lytton, who had become thoroughly convinced of the great value and importance of uniting ancient Alchemy with modern medicine, makes the hero of his immortal story declare: "All that we propose to do is this: To find out the secrets of the human frame, to know why the parts ossify and the blood stagnates, and to apply continual preventives to the effects of time. *This is not magic; it is the art of medicine, rightly understood.*"

It is a fact that, the molecules of the body are all changed within twelve months; that every cell in the human organism is born and grows to maturity within that space of time. Nature is absolutely impartial. She draws from the atmosphere that she may reproduce a fac-simile of everything she finds upon the surface of the body. So, if there be a sore, or festering ulcer, the atoms which are thrown off attract similar atoms, so as to reproduce the ulcer or sore, and thus prevent the disease from getting well of itself until it has worn itself out.

Further, every vein and canal throughout the entire body, from youth to maturity, is being coated with carbonate of lime, or lime in some form. The coating of the walls of the veins in such a manner, prevents the free circulation of the living matter; then, the real vitality of the food which we eat, is simply passed off through the pores, or through the bowels, or through the system, because it is unable to penetrate through the lime.

If that prevention which produces old age can be attained, then physical youth will continue.

The first step to take is to dissolve the lime in the body. Drink nothing but distilled water, in either tea, coffee, or any other form, and drink freely of the sweet juices of the grape and apple.

The food that we eat contains lime in a living form, and it is the living lime we need to build up the living bones, for the lime and the magnesia that we take in the water is crystallized dead mineral, possessing no responsibility of life, and the lime in our food is quite sufficient for all purposes. For everything we take in excess. Nature makes us pay the penalty.

The first principle of long living is to keep all channels of the body perfect and free from coatings of lime.

The second is that of youthful ideals of the mind. The soul never grows old.

The third principle is dynamic breathing, which is storing up the oxygen in sufficient quantities, to supply the tissues with sufficient fuel, for combustion.

These three principles, acting in unison, contain the true basis of physical life and a means of long living. Old age is simply the petrifaction of the body through lime, and the incorporating of erroneous thoughts into the organism.

It is the true Alchemy of human existence, and the preventives, in each and every case must contain the spiritual correspondence to the cause they seek to remedy; and, though the followers of Hahnemann base the whole of their procedure of treatment upon their master's fundamental law of "Similia similibus curantur," yet, there may be a few rare cases wherein, this undeviating method would not apply with the required effect. In such a case, the Alchemist would resort to the well-known law of opposites, and base his treatment upon the dogma of "Contraria contrariis curantur," so long the pet theory of the Allopathic school. They work upon the hypothesis that, like attracts like, and, if disease exist, those elements must be administered to set up the vibrations that will produce the polar opposite. If the body was racked with pain, those medicines would not be given that would create or increase similar conditions, but, their antipathy would be introduced into the system or applied locally to extinguish the foe.

So long as mankind remain within the semicrystallized state of soul development, so as to require the aid of external forces to support the human throne within its earthly temple, mercenary troops will exist to supply these supposed supports.

Unquestionably, the astrological law is the true system of medicine, which treats disease by sympathy or by antipathy, according to the nature of the case, and the efficacy of the remedies at hand. This method is the only natural one, and has been thoroughly demonstrated by the numerous "provings of drugs" under Hahnemann's law.

Happily, the time is not far distant when, the incarnated spirit will be able to use its own slumbering forces, and subdue all suffering and symptoms of disease in their very first inception, by virtue of its purer life and the dynamic potencies of its own interior, spiritual thought. Already, mental therapeutics is taking an advanced position among liberal, progressive minds, and nothing demonstrates so clearly and forcibly the grand, alchemical law of life-growth and decay, as the imponderable, invisible forces, which, constitute the materia medica, or remedial agents, of mental, magnetic, and spiritual healing.

Perhaps the most recondite subject connected with the healing art divine is, the modus operandi of medicinal action, upon the human body. A subject so simple and self-evident to the Alchemist, remains a profound mystery to the educated physician of the medical college; so much so that, we are tempted to ask of them: "Can you explain the modus operandi of drugs?" Dr. William Sharp, one of the most advanced physicians of the Homeopathic school, in one of his well-known "Essays on Medicine," says: "In respect to the manner of action of drugs we are in total darkness, and we are so blind that the darkness is not felt. *Knowledge of this kind cannot be attained;* it is labor lost and *time wasted* to go in search of it. True, hypotheses may be easily conceived; so may straws be gathered from the surface of the stream. But what are either of them worth? There is this difference between them—straws may amuse children, and hypotheses are sure to mislead physicians."

It is when the Occult Initiate observes to what helpless conditions the practice of medicine has fallen, that, he would, if he could with any possiblity of success, implore the angelic guardian of the human race to open the spiritual sight of men, that they might see, as he sees, the Divine relationship, and spiritual correspondence, of everything in the wide universe to man.

Nature's laws move slowly and imperceptibly, yet surely and exact, and the time will certainly come when man will be forced into consciousness of these laws, whether he will or no. Nature is no respecter of persons, and those who will not move and progress, in harmony with her laws of advancement, must, of necessity, pass out with the old.

Alchemy, as it relates to the healing art, is the most noble in its object and beneficial in its effects, of all the many subdivisions of the sciences, because, it alleviates the pains and morbid afflictions of suffering humanity. We have given quite sufficient of its astrological aspect in the second part of "The Light of Egypt," Vol. I, wherein the four ancient elements are translated into their chemical correspondences of oxygen, hydrogen, nitrogen and carbon, which still constitute the four primary elements of the most advanced chemistry to-day. They enter more or less into every organic form and substance, which is known, in various combinations and proportions. The human organism is principally composed of them; so, likewise, is the food that supports physical life, and the air we breathe is but modifications of the same atoms.

As man's constitution embraces a microscopic atom of all the essences and elements, corresponding to the whole; so does the air; and much, that we depend upon our food to supply, can be extracted from the atmosphere by breathing. Every breath we breathe is new life, or death.

Herein is the secret of success or failure, in certain localities, and under certain conditions. If we have iron within us, could we extract or attract iron from Saturn's district? Or, if the element within us could attract gold, could we obtain it from the coal fields?

Therefore, it is only natural that the medical remedies we employ to restore the organism, when afflicted with disease, should group themselves into similar correspondences, and so, in a general sense, we find them; for we note that the brain, the circulation, the lungs, and the stomach, are the four chief citadels of the body; the heart, of course, representing the center of circulation. And this also explains, further, if that were necessary, why the principal remedies of the homeopathic system are so speedy and direct in their action. The four principal drugs, which stand as representatives of their class, are aconite, belladonna, phosphorus, and pulsatilla. These represent the quadrant, for light is not more nicely adjusted to the eye, nor sound to the ear, than aconite to the circulation, belladonna to the brain, phosphorus to the lungs, and pulsatilla to the stomach; while ramifying in the seven directions indicated by the seven primary planets, we find stimulants, tonics, narcotics, nervines, alteratives, cathartics and diuretics, as the natural material correspondences thereof.

That we assign phosphorus to the lungs may appear startling to the orthodox student, especially when, he calls to mind the fact that phosphorus has long been recognized in medical science as a brain food and medicine. Anticipating such mental questions, we reply that in medicine, from the alchemical view, we are occupying a wholly different standpoint; i.e., the power of controlling the functional action of the body, in this view of the case, and the fact that, the lungs and the brain are in the most perfect affinity, there will remain no mystery upon the subject.

The Alchemy of stones and gems attracts our next attention. Affinites and antipathies to the human constitution, are to be found in these crystallized representatives of the subtle, invisible influences emanating from our planetary system. They are the mediums for the transmission of corresponding attributes and influences of existing powers and potencies, and if carried or worn upon the person, they will bring the person in direct rapport with the invisible forces within the universal system.

Here again Hahnemann's scientific philosophy would prove effectual, that "Similia similibus curantur." Would the fiery influence of a topaz attract much from the realms of a chrysolite? Or, the crystallized, airy forces of a sapphire be a suitable medium for the earthly forces of a jasper?

Gems and stones are dead or living realities. They live, slumber and die, and have their potent existence as do the organic forms of matter. They are, usually, imbued with the vivifying spark of Divinity, and shine forth and exert their influence through the magical powers attracted to them from the forces of Nature. A real, living entity abides within them that can be seen by the clairvoyant vision, and to the trained student in Occult lore, this entity can be made to become an obedient servant, giving warning of the approach of danger, impressions of men and things, and warding off discordant influences surrounding us; or that, which we may contact from the magnetic and personal environments in our relations in the social world; or that which may be projected to us from the invisible realms of life.

Think you the pryamids would be intact to-day, if the stones from which they were built had been promiscuously selected? They were chosen by Adepts in the knowledge of the Laws of Correspondence and antipathy and affinity. The sphinx also stand as monuments to the heights of wisdom that man can attain.

Metals also can be followed out on the same lines as the gems and stones.

Much as we would like to continue, we are compelled to bring this discourse to a close, even though in doing so we must of necessity omit much of vital interest to the student. We will, therefore, only add that the seven basic metals stand as the crystallized representatives of their respective groups: Gold for the Sun, Silver for the Moon, Tin for Jupiter, Copper for Venus, Quicksilver for Mercury and Lead for Saturn. Each finds it own sphere of action within the temporary abiding place of the human soul on earth—the physical body. So, likewise, the twelve constellations and their corresponding talismanic gems, representing in their glittering array the anatomical Zodiac of the human frame, and typifying the spiritual quality of the atoms, there congregated, in every degree of life. These, and a thousand other mysteries, had we the time, might be unfolded to the student's view with considerable advantage, but we are compelled to refrain. The philosopher's stone is near at hand. Seek it not in remote spheres or distant parts of the earth, for it is ever around you and within, and becomes the golden key of true wisdom, which prepares the soul for its higher life and brighter destiny. It is the still, small voice of the awakened soul, that purges the conscience from suffering, and the spiritual body from earthy dross. It is that, which treasures not the corrupting, delusive wealth of Earth, nor the transient powers of mammon, but garners the fruits which spring from the pure life, and treasures the jewels of heaven. Vainly will you seek for this stone of the wise philosopher amid the turmoils, sufferings, and selfishness of life, unless you accept your mission upon earth as a duty, delegated to the soul, from Heaven. Eschew the evil thereof, and hold fast that which is good. To do this, means to expand with the inward truth and become one of the "pure in heart," in which blessed state, the magical white stone, conveying *a new name*, reveals the living angel within, to the outward man. Then, and then alone, doth he know the Adonai.

Such are the Divine, spiritual principles upon which the higher Alchemy of life is based. They seek only to establish a Divine, conscious at-one-ment between the angel, the man, and the universe, and to this end, we conclude with the words of the immortal Paracelsus:

"To grasp these invisible elements, to attract them by their material correspondences, to control, purify, and transmute them by the ever-moving powers of the living spirit, *this is true Alchemy.*"

CHAPTER IX

TALISMANS

Words are the symbols of ideas, and bear the same correspondence to the physical brain as matter does to spirit, a medium of expression, and are subject to continual change in their application and meaning, in exact proportion to the changing mental and moral condition of the people. As the planet, as well as man, is continually progressing, so must there be a higher and nobler conception of ideas. Hence, words or expressions must change, to convey the progressive spirit, that is constantly taking place. Therefore, it is always interesting, as well as valuable, for the Occult student to go to the root of each word connected with his philosophy, in order to learn the real sense in which the word was used by the ancients, from whom his mystic lore has descended. The true meaning, as well as the words themselves, have become as mystical as the lore itself. Hence, each student must commence as a beginner in any foreign language, which he does not at present understand. In following this method of procedure he will, at least, escape the dense and interminable confusion of modern opinions upon subjects of which the writers thereof, are partially or wholly ignorant.

No better illustration of this can be afforded than by the word "Talisman," derived from the Greek verb "teleo," which means, primarily, to accomplish, or bring into effect. But, in its real, and therefore higher, sense, it means to dedicate, consecrate, and initiate into the arcana of the temple mysteries. But, in the present day it means a piece of imposture, connected with some magical hocus pocus of the ignorant and superstitious mind, a vulgar charm, that is supposed to bring the owner thereof some material benefit, irrespective of his mental, magnetic, and moral condition, "and," says the learned Webster, after describing his idea of such things, "they consist of three sorts, astronomical, magical and mixed." But in what sense the "astronomical" differed from the "magical" we are not informed, nor is any light thrown upon the peculiar nature of that class designated as "mixed." In fact, the lexicographer so mixes up his definitions that, we are unable to distinguish anything in particular, but his own individual ignorance.

So it has become, in every branch of learning. Words and their meanings have become so mixed in their use and application, that, the world is full of discords and misunderstandings, which lead into dissensions and contention, among all schools of thought, sects, and isms; and lastly, though not the least serious, it has reached into the close relations of the human family.

All writers and speakers, as well as the readers and listeners, should acquaint themselves with the derivation and meaning of words.

The fact stands very clearly defined that, Talismans are confused in the minds of the present generation with magical charms, which depend for their effects, upon the power of the idea or thought, which the formulating magician impresses upon the substance of which they are composed. If the magical artist be expert, and endowed with an exceedingly potent will, his charm may become very powerful, when worn by the person for whom it was prepared. But, if this one grand essential be lacking, no amount of cabalistical figures and sacred names will have any effect, because, there can be no potency in symbols apart from the ideas and mental force they are capable of arousing in the mind of the maker. Solomon's Seal is no more powerful, when drawn upon virgin parchment, with a weak will, or in a mechanical state of mind, than a child's innocent scribbling upon its slate. But, if the artist realizes the mysteries symbolized by the interlacing triangles, and can place his soul en rapport with the invisible elements they outwardly represent; then, powerful effects are often produced.

I am sorry to say that, the knowledge of charms is not confined to the creation of beneficial talismans. Its perversion has led to the diabolical practices of the Voodo and Black Magician, whose work is wholly, either for gain or revenge. Nothing, but the most extreme selfishness lies beneath such immoral practices, but, as there must be a light to reflect a shadow, so a charm must follow a talisman. Magical charms, then, are simply natural objects, possessing but little active virtue in themselves, but, owing to the mediumistic nature of their substances, are endowed with artificial powers, of temporary duration, by virtue of the idea and thought impressed upon them, through the mental magic of the maker; and in this sense, a charm must be clearly distinguished from "teleo," the Talisman. The very names suggest their difference, and, above all other men, students in Occultism should strive to become thoroughly educated in the true sense of the term, *men of letters,* by virtue of (as Ruskin calls it) "the kingship of words." "Charm" is derived from the Latin "carmen," a song that fascinates, and means to control by incantation, to subdue; while Teleo concerns the secret powers and wisdom of consecration and initiation. It is because of modern misuse of antique terms that, we have considered this somewhat lengthy explanation necessary, in order to clear away the accumulated debris of the ages, from the true foundation of our present study.

A Talisman is a natural object, containing the elemental forces of its own degree of life, in a state of intense activity, and capable of responding to the corresponding quality of life, *outside of itself,* that emanates from the same spiritual state, either by sympathetic vibration or antagonistic currents, the nature, power, quality, and degree of life, which the various natural objects represent, being a part of the temple curriculum of initiation. Hence, the name, by which the latent power of these natural objects became known, was in strict harmony with the facts involved.

In order to prevent any possible misconception upon the subject, let us briefly restate the definition in a different way: A Talisman is the exact antipodes of a charm. This latter is the artful and temporary result of man's mental power; the former, the natural production of universal Nature, and as permanent and enduring as the substance of which it is composed, *during the present cycle.* And yet in some sense, it may be quite correct to say that, a Talisman *acts like a charm,* and vice versa, that charms *act like a Talisman,* providing that, the real vital difference between them, is maintained in the statement.

Now that we have our subject clearly defined, let us carefully examine *how and in what sense* a given natural object becomes Talismanic, for it must appear self-evident to all that, one and the same substance cannot constitute a Talisman for everyone, and for everything. They must naturally differ, as widely in their nature and quality, as mankind differ in physical, mental, moral, ethical, and temperamental, development. And, yet, though, man may so differ from his fellow man; the ignorant Esquimau, killing seals in his kayak, may belong to the same spiritual quality of life as the Harvard professor, who obtains his subsistence by daily discourse upon the sublime harmony of the infinitely small with the infinitely great, throughout the manifested universe of matter, and wherever we find this *kinship* of the spirit, we shall find the same identical Talisman acting alike upon each, whenever they shall come en rapport with it. Mental, moral, and physical development, never alter the real nature of the internal man. Culture only brings to the surface, into active use, the latent possibilities lying concealed within the human soul. It only allows him to exercise his functions upon different planes, and with different effect.

Every natural department of Nature corresponds to some peculiar specific quality and degree of life. These have been divided, for the sake of convenience, into four primary groups; and each group again subdivided into three, corresponding to the four cardinal, four succedent, and four cadent houses, of the astrological chart; therefore, the twelve signs of the Zodiac; these constituting the Cycle of Necessity within physical conditions, wherein, the ever-measuring or decreeing tidal flow of life from solar radiation throughout the year, represents the twelve groups of humanity, of lower animated Nature, of vegetation, and crystallized gems. Every human being is ushered into the world under the direct influx of one or more of these celestial divisions, and by virtue of the sign occupying the horizon at the moment of birth, absorbs such influx, and becomes endowed with a specific polarity, by virtue of which, he ever afterward, during such expression within physical conditions, inspires with every breath, that specific life quality from the atmosphere, corresponding to the same degree of the universal spirit. Consequently, that gem, or those gems, representing and corresponding to *his House of Life*, become to him, a Talisman, because of their relationship—their spiritual affinity. These are all given in the second part of Vol. I. *The metals* never become Talismanic, because of their comparatively negative degree of life, and for this reason also, they make the most powerful charms. Certain combinations of metals, and in proper proportions, increase the potency and magnetic influence of a charm; and here, too, the laws of antipathy and affinity come into practical use.

A true expert will know his metals, or metal, and his client, before commencing his magical work.

Those persons who derive most virtue from a Talisman are those who belong to the most sensitive, or interior state, within such degree of life, and who are dominated by one sign only. Thus, if we find one sign occupying the whole of the House of Life, or practically so, as when the first face of a sign ascends, we may be sure, other things not interfering, that such a native will receive great benefit from wearing its Talismanic gem. If a person of good intellectual powers and sensitive spirituality, be born when the lord of the ascendant occupies the *rising sign,* as, for instance, Mars in Aries, or Sun in Leo, we may be sure that, the Talismanic gem, in their case, will be exceedingly powerful, because, all the Astro-physical conditions are then most favorable for the expression of natural forces, and, if worn upon, or near that part of the body which the sign rules, the power and influence is more powerful and beneficial.

In wearing them, take them to you as a part of yourself, a part of your higher self, a thing to be heeded, listened to and obeyed. They will usually make their presence most pronounced when something arises to disturb the harmonious vibrations that naturally and quietly go on between the person and the interstellar spaces above. They are like the sensor and motor nerves—they never make their presence known, except, when danger encroaches.

Having explained in what sense gems become talismanic, we have now to disclose the modus operandi—*the how.*

The gems contain the life quality of their own astral nature. Man, as a higher expression, only, of the same universal biune life, contains the same. Like two electric currents, *man, the positive pole* (comparatively), attracts unto himself *the mineral life of the gem,* which thus, becomes the negative pole. A complete circuit is formed and maintained, as long as they remain in contact. Gems belonging to a different quality of life, not being en rapport with his astral state, have no good effect, because, no current flows between them. Thus, the Talisman acts in unison with the psychic, or soul-principle, of man, aiding the organism to sustain health, stimulating the mental perceptions, and spiritual intuition, and affording in a remarkable manner. many premonitions of coming danger, when the individual is sufficiently sensitive to perceive them. And now, per contra, as there are gems that act in sympathy with man, there must be, and in fact are, gems that act upon contrary principles; i.e., antagonistic, and these belong to purely antagonistic elements, as Air to Earth and Fire to Water, unless the native be born under *both* forces, as Mars in Cancer (♋) rising, or the latter part of one sign and nearly the whole of another of an opposite nature, occupying the ascendant. Such natives are pure neutrals, and such might wear the gems that belong to the most powerful planet of the horoscope, or that triplicity holding the most planets; then, they are usually combined, the planet and the triplicity.

There are, of course, innumerable substances, more or less, capable of talismanic virtue to particular individuals. But those gems, and similar ones, that are given in "The Light of Egypt," Vol. I, are the most powerful. To these may be added the opal, under Scorpio (♏); the garnet, under Aries (♈); and the turquoise, under Cancer (♋), when Saturn is therein; and the aquamarine, under Pisces (♓); and among the temporary talismans of vegetation we may add that, the young shoots, bearing the flower and seed vessels, are the portions of chief virtue, and the young shoots of trees. These are often used in locating mines, wells, oils, etc., that lie hidden beneath the surface of the earth, and in the hands of a negative, sensitive person, seldom fail to reward the searcher with success. These should always be gathered when their ruling correspondences are rising, or, *better still, culminating upon the meridian.* These will be explained in the chapter on The Magic Wand.

We have now reached the limits of our present study, and have only to state that all gems, like the human organism, are in one of three conditions: alive and conscious, asleep and *unconscious,* or dead and powerless. These conditions can only be discovered, in stones, by the trained lucid or the instructed neophyte. Stones that are sleeping require to be awakened. This, also, can only be done by the trained student or Adept. Those that are dead, are *useless* as Talismans, no matter how beautiful they appear as ornaments.

Gems and stones are also sexed, and those who wear them would receive the best effect if they should wear those of opposite sex, although either is powerfully potent in their influence upon the individual. How very ignorant the children of men are, of the subtle, silent, yet obedient servants, that everywhere, surround them. Here, again, that Divine spark, which lies embedded within the crystallized forces of Nature, is exerting its subtle, spiritual influence, in making man's very selfishness, and love of ornament and show, a means, to bring forth these silent monitors, knowing ere long that, their true power and potency will be known, and consciously utilized by him, as potent factors in his soul's evolvement and physical development.

The twelve representative gems within the cold stratas of matter, stand as the material representatives of their stellar counterparts in the sky, and constitute the beautiful, glittering, but crystallized, Zodiac of man's physical anatomy.

CHAPTER X

CEREMONIAL MAGIC

The above title has been selected, chiefly, because, in most works treating upon magic we find it wrongly used, and therefore, take the opportunity of explaining the matter, for, there were no such terms in the vocabulary of the ancient Magi.

It is unfortunate, that, words of ancient origin are not more carefully used, and that, we should attach so many different meanings to the same word. The terms "ceremony" and "ceremonial" are nothing more nor less than, what that eminent critic, John Ruskin, would designate as "bastards of ignoble origin," which, somehow or another, have usurped the places of "rite" and "ritual." The word "rite" has descended to us from the Latin "ritus" of our Roman ancestors, and they received it from the more ancient "riti" of the Sanskrit, the Greek equivalent of which is "reo," and means the method or order of service to the gods, whereas, "ceremony" may mean anything and everything, from the terms of a brutal prize fight to the conduct of divine service within the church. But, no such chameleon-like definition or construction can properly be placed upon the word "rite," for it means distinctly, if it means anything at all, the serious usage and sacred method of conducting service in honor of the gods, or of superiors, and requires the attendance of the prophet or priest, or some one duly qualified to fulfill such sacred functions for the time being. The ritual of magic, then, is the correct title of this present study, and as such, we shall, henceforth, term it as we proceed with the course.

Man is especially, and above all creatures, an organizing force, and when to this fact, we add the most interior and powerful of his sentimental instincts—veneration for the powers that be, and for the higher, invisible forces of Nature, his "religiosity," as it has been aptly termed, we cannot wonder that, the earliest races of which we possess any record are chiefly distinguished for their imposing and elaborate religious rites. In fact, it is to the stupendous temples and a colossal sacerdotalism, that, we are indebted for nine-tenths of the relics and records which we possess of them. So true is this that, from what we have been able to discover, we are quite justified in asserting that the ancient races were, above all other things, a profoundly religious people. The temple was the center around which revolved all their genius and art, and the sacred edifice became their grandest achievement in architecture, and its high priest the most powerful individual in the state. In fact, it was in consequence of the real power invested in such sacred office that it was so intimately connected with the throne, and why royalty so frequently belonged to the priesthood or exercised priestly functions. And there can be no real doubt, but that, amongst the pastoral and more spiritual races of Earth's earliest inhabitants, the priest, by reason of his superior wisdom, was the first law-giver; and, by virtue of his sanctity of person and elevation of mind became their first, primitive king, a patriarchal monarch, whose scepter and symbol of power was the shepherd's peaceful crook; just as among the ruder nomads of the inhospitable North, we find the greatest hunters invested with the dignity of chief, whose significant symbol and scepter of royalty, upon their Nimrod thrones, was the trusty, successful spear. And the times in which we live have had their full effect upon these symbols, so significant of rule. The monarch has transformed the spear into the less harmful mace, while the Church has added an inch of iron to the crook. Therefore, the former has become less war-like, and the latter less peaceful, and, verily, in actual life we find them so.

The patriarchal sire, head of the tribal household, was the original priest; and the hearthstone the first altar around which the family rites were performed; and from this pure and primitive original have been evolved, through progressive ages, the stately temple and the sacred person of the despotic pontiff; from the sincere prayer the pure aspirations of the human heart and the joyous offerings of fruits and flowers to the invisible powers around them; and from the souls of their beloved ancestors has arisen the costly and complicated ritual of theology. And, if the theologians of to-day really knew the lost, secret meaning of their complicated rituals, and the unseen powers lying behind their external symbols, their anxieties for the continued life of their dying creeds would be turned to new hopes and faith, which could be demonstrated to their equally blind followers; that, that which they were teaching they knew, and could practically use the knowledge given forth in their sanctuaries; and, instead of offering up their supplications to an imaginary, personal Deity, their words, rites, and ceremonies, would take on the form and power that such should command, and they would become truly, what their title really means, a doctor of the soul. Then could they, intelligently, lead and direct the souls of their followers to the path of Christ (Truth), which leads up to salvation; not a vicarious atonement, but gaining the at-one-ment through the individual soul's development to a conscious relation, to that Divine spirit, we call God, where it can say "I know."

Out of those simple gifts, which were the spontaneous offerings of loving remembrance and unselfish charity, have grown the prayers, penances, sacrifices, and servile worship, of sacerdotalism. Out of the paternal consideration and love of the aged sire has evolved the haughty, chilling pride of the selfish, isolated priest, and which reflects its baneful influence upon the worshipers at their feet. They have also changed their once sacred, faithful, and reverent, obedience into suspicion and distrust, and with the educated to utter disgust. The light has been extinguished, and priest and people alike are groping about in darkness.

It is strange, yea, passing strange, the amount of human ignorance and folly that is revealed. When we look upon this picture and then upon that, verily we cannot help but ask the question, is mankind really progressing? We know that it is; we are keenly alive to the truth that the Anthem of Creation sounds out "Excelsior"—"move on," but how, and in what way (*spiritually*) we fail to comprehend. The cyclic development of the human soul is an inscrutable mystery.

All the considerations above presented must be thoroughly weighed and understood in order to arrive at the true value of "the dogma and ritual of high magic," as Eliphas Levi terms it; because, amid the vast array of tinselled drapery, the outcome of man's vain conceit and bombastic pride, we shall find very little that can be considered as vital and really essential to the rites of magic. The show, the drapery, the priestly ornaments and instruments, are to the really spiritual Occultist, but, as sounding brass and a tinkling cymbal. That they had, and still have, their legitimate uses, is true, but these uses do not concern magic, per se, nor its manifold powers. They awed the popular mind, and impressed upon the masses a due reverence for the powers that be. They were instrumental in holding the untrained passions of the common herd in check, by a wholesome fear of summary vengeance from the gods, so that this pageantry of magic, the outward priestly show, was more of a politic development than a spiritual necessity, an astute but, philosophical method of enabling the educated few to govern the uneducated many. And it was only when the educational and initiatory rites of the temple became corrupt, and the priest became the persecuting ally of the king—when, in real fact, the priest lost his spirituality in the desire for temporal power and place, that the people began to disbelieve his professions and rebel against his tyrannical control.

The powers that be, are now wielding their sword of justice, and unfurling the knowledge of freedom and truth to the aspiring mind of man. He has begun to feel his bondage and the yoke of oppression. The words of promise and love, instead of lifting him up to the God he has been taught to worship, bow him down in slavish obedience to his priest. Mankind cannot remain in this mental and spiritual darkness much longer. Already I see the break of day, the dawn of a new life, a new religion; or, rather, the re-establishing of the true, which is as old as Time itself. There is but One Law, One Principle, One Word, One Truth and One God.

The original requirements for the office of priest, and the rites of magic, were, as shown, a primitive, i.e., pure mind; one that had outgrown the lusts and passions of youth, a person of responsibility and experience; and even to this day the priest of the Roman Church is called by the familiar title of "father." And as Nature does not alter her laws and requirements in obedience to the moral development of the race, we may rest assured that the same requirements, of ten thousand years ago, still hold good to-day. You may enter your magic circle. drawn with prescribed rites, and you may intone your consecrations and chant your incantations; you may burn your incense in the brazen censer and pose in your flowing, priestly robes; you may bear the sacred pentacles of the spirit upon your breast and wave the magic sword to the four quarters of the heavens; yea, you may even do more—you may burn the secret sigil of the objurant spirit; and yell your conjurations and exorcisms till you are black in the face; but all in vain, my friend—all in vain. It will prove nothing but vanity and vexation of spirit unless the inward self, the soul, interblends with the outward Word, and contacting by its own dynamic intensity— the elemental vibrations of Nature—arouses these spiritual forces to the extent of responding to your call. When this can be done, but not until then, will your magical incantations have any effect upon the voiceless air. Not the priestly robes nor magic sword, not the incantations, *written word*, nor mystic circle, can produce Nature's response to Occult rite; but the fire of the inward spirit, the mental realization of each word and mystic sign, combined with the conscious knowledge of your own Deific powers—this, and this only, **creates** Nature's true magician.

Who and where can such be found? Are they so few that the echo answers back "Where and who?" Yet, there are many such upon the Earth at the present time, but the present mental conditions forbid them making their identity known. They would not be recognized and accepted as the *true* teachers, but reviled and persecuted and dubbed as insane. But silently, they are sowing the seed of truth that will spring up and bear fruit, where and when least expected.

Because evil is so active, truth is not lying dormant. The spirit of God, that Divine spark of Deity within every human soul, never sleeps, never rests. "On and upward" is its cry. "Omnia vincit veritas."

The grand sublimity of man's conception of at-one with the Infinite Father, at-one with the limitless universe of being, at-one with, and inheriting, all the sacred rights and inalienable prerogatives of the ineffable Adonai of the deathless soul, is the only test of man's qualification for the holy office; for, as Bulwer Lytton has truthfully said, "the loving throb of one great *human heart* will baffle more fiends than all the magicians' lore." So it is with the sacred ritual. One single aspirational thought, clearly defined, outweighs all the priestly trappings that the world has ever seen.

The success of all incarnations depends upon the complete unison of *voice* and *mind,* the interblend of which, produces the dynamic intonation, that chords with the inward rhythmic vibrations of the soul. Once this magical, dynamic, vibration is produced, there immediately springs into being the whole elemental world belonging thereto, by correspondence. Vocalists who hold their audiences spellbound do so by virtue of the magical vibrations they produce, and are in reality practical, even though unconscious, magicians. The same power, to a degree, lies in the voice when speaking, the graceful movement of the hand when obeying the will, and the eye rays forth the same dynamic power and becomes magical in its effects.

These powers are exercised more upon the physical plane, and no better illustration can be given, than, the power man is able to exert over the animal when gazing into its eyes.

Here, as well as in incantations and invocations, within the power of the will, lies the success or failure.

At this point it may be asked, what, then, is the use of magical rites, of symbols and priestly robes? We answer, in themselves alone, nothing, absolutely nothing, except the facility and convenience we derive from system, order and a code of procedure. To this may be added the mental force and enthusiasm of soul which such things inspire, just as men and women may feel more dignified, artistic, and refined, when dressed in accordance with their ideas. So may the average priest feel more priestly, holy; and consequently, more powerful mentally; when arrayed in the robes of his office and surrounded by the outward symbols of his power and functions. But, in themselves alone, there is not, nor can there be, any real virtue. The same may be said of the incantations. The words used in their composition are the hieroglyphics of mystical ideas. Therefore, the correct pronunciation of the words or the grammatical construction of a sentence is nothing, if the underlying idea is conceived in the mind and responded to by the soul. Will and motive form the basis of true magic.

One word more and we have completed our subject. Magic swords, rings, pentacles, and wands, may, and often are, powerful magical agents in the hands of the magician, by virtue of the power, or charm, that is invested within them when properly prepared; but apart from such preparation, by those *who know*, they are as powerless as unintelligible incantations.

All the foregoing are aids, but if physical manifestations of magical forces be required, there must always be present the necessary vital, magnetic pabulum, by means of which such phenomena are made to transpire; and in every case, to be successful, the assistance of a good natural magician, or seer, is necessary; for without this essential element the whole art, in its higher aspects, becomes abortive.

CHAPTER XI

THE MAGIC WAND

This is the last lesson of our present course that requires a clear definition of the terms employed in the title thereof, for the twelfth, and final study is, perhaps, fortunate in having for its title a word that has not, so far, been misused and distorted from its original sense.

The Magic Wand. The words savor of everything that the young tyro in Occult art can picture to his mind; of the midnight magician and his mysterious, if not diabolical, arts, muttering his incantations, working his gruesome spells, and raising the restless ghosts of the dead. Strange fancies, these, and yet, so corrupt and ignorant have become the conceptions of the popular mind regarding the once sacred Science of the Temple and the psychological powers of Nature, that we very much question, if the ideas above stated were not very similar to the originals of each modern student, before he had become acquainted with the deeper truths—the realities of Occult philosophy.

We will commence our study by a careful investigation of the original meaning of the words Magic Wand, since those who were the masters and originators thereof, are far more likely to know more about them than their degenerate offspring of a later age. Few, comparatively, would believe that the words *magic, mason,* and *imagination,* are the present unrelated descendants of the same original conception—*the root idea;* but such is the case. First, then, we will examine their modern meanings. Magic is the unholy art of working secret spells, of using invisible powers, and holding intercourse with the unseen world of ghosts and demons, by means of enchantments. It also means the expert deception of the senses by the tricks of a conjurer, *so-called* hocus-pocus and fraud, and a magician is either an evil-minded, superstitious mortal, fool enough to believe in charms, or an expert pretender and imposter of the first water, who cheats and deceives the people. A mason is the honorable designation of a builder, who works in stone; metaphysically, a member of a semi-secret society, whose sole advantage is social intercourse and standing; who proclaim fraternity and universal brotherhood theoretically and practice the reverse in reality; a man who apes the Egyptian Mason, knows nothing in reality of Hiram, his master; who knows nothing of the starry Solomon or his mystic temple in the heavens, which Hiram built; and who misconceives the import of the three villains, or assassins; and who, further, knows nothing of that wonderful sprig of myrtle:—in short, a Free Mason, speaking generally, is a man who delights in ideals, social equality, secret fraternity, and plays at mysticism; who parades on the Masonic stage and enacts a role he does not understand. The first meaning, that of a builder, is the most correct. Lastly, the imagination is the exercise of mental imagery—the picturings of silent thought.

And now we will proceed *backwards*. Imagination is from the word "image," a form, a picture, and has descended to us from the Latin "imago," which, in its turn, was derived from the old Semitic root, "mag." Mason comes to us from the Latin "mass," which means to mould and form, i.e., to build; and the word "mass," through various transformations, was also derived from the root-word "mag." Consequently, originally, there was but little difference in the ancient idea of building pictures in the mind and erecting the mental idea externally in stone. It is from this fact, that, we have to-day *Mental Masons,* a la the secret orders, and stone masons, who labor for wages. The Mental Masons have merely lost the knowledge of their art. They should, by rights, be as active and correspondingly useful to-day as their more physical brothers, the masons of stone.

This art would never have fallen into disgrace and disuse, if their daily bread, or material accumulations, had depended upon their efforts in building up the mental, moral, and spiritual attainments, of each other, and bringing their knowledge into more external use, by making the material edifice, the physical body, a purer and more fitting temple, for the Divine soul.

Magic comes from the Latin "magi" and the Greek word "magos," which means wise, learned in the mysteries, and was the synonym of wisdom. The initiated philosopher, the priest, and the wise men, are all of them included in the "magi." Again, tracing this word to its remote ancestor, we find it terminating in the same Semitic root, "mag," but of this strange root no one was able to say much, except that it seemed to belong to the Assyrian branch of the great Semitic race. But quite recently, thanks to our scientific explorers and archaeologists, versed in the mysterious meaning of cuniform inscription; Assyrian scholars now inform us that they have found the hoary, primitive original of it, of magic, magi and imago, etc. It is from an old Akkadian word, "imga," meaning wise, holy, and learned, and was used as the distinguishing title of their wisest sages, priests, and philosophers, who, as may be supposed, gradually formed a peculiar caste, which merged into the ruling priestly order. The Semites, who succeeded the old Akkadian race in the valley of the Euphrates, as a mere matter of verbal convenience, transformed many of the old Akkadian words to suit their own articulation, and "imga" became "mag," and thus "magi." *The blend* between the Semetic and the older Akkadian race, produced, by fusion of racial blood, the famed Chaldeans. So that we see how old are the words which many of us daily use, but with different meaning. Verily, it makes one feel, when he thinks of magic and its origin, as though he were quite nearly related to the people who honored King Sargon, the Wise, the earthly original of the mystic Solomon of Biblical tradition. The term Wand is an old Saxon word, which primarily signifies to set in motion, to move. From this we derive our word wander, i.e., to roam, and wandering, i.e., moving and continually restless.

We have now the original, therefore real, meaning of the words Magic Wand; thus an object that sets in motion the powers of the magician, and the magician, an Initiate of the sacred rites—*a master of wisdom*, possessing all the resources that enable him *to build*, mould, and form; to create in fact, by virtue of his knowledge of the secret powers of mental imagery and the potential use of his own imagination. He is both Mental Mason and learned philosopher.

The student may doubtless ask, why all this care and labor regarding mere definitions? We reply that, it is because, the real meaning of the words we have purposely selected for the title of our studies are, in themselves, a far better revelation than we could possibly have written. Originally, ideas and words were related as absolute expressions or correspondences, of each other. This is not so now. As the different races became interblended, the purity of both language and morals retrograded, and the people grew more to the external. The intuitions and spirit were compelled to retreat, giving place to only the intellectual and mental. The blending of the languages gave birth to many words wherein different meanings were transmitted; hence, the trouble arising to-day over the numerous interpretations of a single word.

Hybrid races have no such thing as a pure language. Their ideas and language, like their blood, is badly mixed up, confusing, and unsatisfactory, so far as the real meaning of the words are concerned. For this very reason we find so many different meanings for the same word; and also for this reason, we cannot formulate a legal enactment in the Anglo-Saxon tongue that, a learned lawyer, versed in this senseless jugglery of words, cannot demonstrate, to the satisfaction of the courts, means something the very opposite of the real intentions—the spirit—which the framers thereof, intended it to convey. Anciently, it required no artful cunning of the lawyer to interpret the laws. The words had only one simple and obvious meaning. If a language could be so constructed to-day, and the antiquated precedents of the courts annihilated; the legal profession would be exterminated inside of twelve months, and an affliction removed from the people.

The philosophy of the Magic Wand is this. It is a magnetic, electric conductor for the magician's will. It directs the flow of his thought and concentrates it upon a given point in space or an object. It is, magically, what the sights of a rifle are to a sportsman. It enables him to focus his powers with exact precision upon the mark against which, or upon which, his will is directed. Apart from this there is no power, per se, in the Wand itself, any more than there is in a lightning conductor without the electric storm. Ergo, the Wand is the conductor, in the magician's hand, for the lightnings of the soul; and just as the lightning rod is most useful and most powerful to protect, when the storm is the strongest; so is the Wand most powerful in the hands of the most potential magician. We can only transmit through this Wand the degree of force we may happen to possess in the soul.

In a properly prepared Wand lies the most powerful weapon, to protect or destroy, that can be placed within a magician's hands. With his own spiritual force and knowledge, combined with the magic power attached to the instrument, nothing can withstand its power, when directed with a determined and powerful will.

Many substances have been employed in the manufacture of these Magic Wands. Metals or stones will not serve this purpose, unless covered with some organic matter. In any case stones are worthless. The very finest Wands are made from the live ivory of a female elephant. A short Wand, twenty-one inches long, tipped with gold at the largest end and silver or copper at the other, is very powerful.

Next to these costly articles are Wands with a gold or copper core, a
wire, in fact, cased with ebony, boxwood, rosewood, cedar or sandal-
wood. English yew also serves the purpose; so does almond wood.
Simpler, less expensive, and almost as effective, are Wands made of
witch-hazel. In fact, apart from the Wands of live ivory, I consider
that witch-hazel is as powerful as the golden Wand. Next in force to
this witch-hazel are the shoots of the almond tree, and, lastly, the
peach and swamp willow.

The proper time to manufacture a Magic Wand is whenever you
can find the person who is able to do the work. But after it is constructed it must be thoroughly magnetized, with proper ceremony and
aspiration, the first or the second full Moon after the Sun enters Capricorn, at midnight, when the Moon will be culminating in her own
sign upon the mid-heaven.

The best time *to cut* a shoot of witch-hazel or other material for
a Wand is the first full Moon after the Sun's entry into Capricorn, at
midnight, and then magnetize it upon the next full Moon at the same
hour.

In conclusion, let us repeat that, the Magic Wand is but the highly
sensitive magical medium for transmitting and concentrating the force
of the learned magician; that it is equally powerful under great excitement of mind, *whether used consciously or not.* The stream of mental
fire will go in the direction the Wand happens to be pointed, and,
therefore, should never be in the hands of the wicked or foolish, any
more than firearms. It is potential or otherwise, in exact proportion to
the artist's wisdom and dynamic mentality, and is useless in the hands
of the idiotic or weak-minded. A Magic Wand requires brains and
vigorous mental force to make it effective, just as the steam engine
requires an apparatus for generating the steam, that moves it. With a
determined will, and a mental conception of one's inward power, any
man or woman can, by means of this sensitive Wand, defy all the
legionaries of Hell, and quickly disperse every form of spiritual iniquity.

The firearms which have become so intricate in their mechanism
and so destructive in their operations, are only a degeneration of the
Magic Wand. The first weapons of warfare and slaughter were very
crude and clumsy, then larger and more destructive, until at last they
have become as fine in texture and mechanical genius, compared with
their early brothers, as the Magic Wand is to-day, above and beyond,

the present weapons of warfare. At last, the original mode of defense will be rediscovered and become a utility in the hands of the majority of mankind. At the same time, the mental and moral nature will be evolving into better conditions, too, so that their use will not be given to the ignorant and evildoers, but placed in charge of the educated, those who are morally capable of leading and ruling.

Yes, we are now stepping upon the plane of reason and intuition, where right, not might, will prevail and rule the world. The present mode of government and rule will be changed, and one of humanitarian justice take its place.

God hasten the Millenium.

THE BOOK
WHICH IS CALLED
THE TABLETS OF ÆTH

THE SACRED SCROLL WHICH IS CALLED

THE TABLETS OF ÆTH

Now for the first time Transcribed from the
Astral records and done into a book,

By ZANONI, ⫫

To which is added a series of interpretative reflections

for the spiritual meditation of the faithful.

FOREWORD

Thy temple is the arch
Of yon unmeasured sky;
Thy Sabbath the stupendous march
Of grand eternity.

To my Brothers and Sisters of the Hermetic Brotherhood of Luxor:

GREETING—For some years it has been my desire to leave a spiritual legacy to the many devoted friends and followers who have braved so much amid present truth and error for my sake.

In choosing the present work for such a purpose, I have had in view the deeper spiritual needs of the soul—the prophetic element of the interior spirit, which can best exalt itself through the contemplation of Nature's arcane symbolism of the starry heavens—not the material expression of the glittering splendors of the midnight sky, but the spiritual soul-pictures of those blazing systems that reveal to the seeing eye the shining thrones of *the Rulers*—the Powers that Be.

Ever since the dawn of intellectual human life upon our Mother Earth, long before the days of the cave man, or even the first frost that heralded the coming of the Ice Age, souls have hoped and hungered and souls have quailed and fallen in their struggles with the mysteries of God. But ever and anon some bright flower of the race has gained the spiritual victory. A Messianic soul has responded to aspirations of a great-hearted, great-souled woman, pregnant with spiritual yearnings beyond her race, and she has unconsciously blessed her kind for the generations yet to come with that incarnated mystery—*the Son of God.* Blessed, O Woman, is thy patient mission on the earth, and transcendent are the holy mysteries of thy maternity. Every human birth is a Divine miracle in humanity, performed by the Motherhood of God.

Hence it is that, from the earliest ages of life, triumphant souls have stormed the gates of the sanctuary and penetrated Nature's most occult mysteries and there recorded their spiritual victories. Amid these sacred records lies one great scroll, that none but the brightest and bravest may read.

This sacred scroll, sealed with the seven mystic seals of the heavens, contains *The Tablets of Æth,* a record of the soul's experiences upon the planes of both conscious and sub-conscious life—spirit and matter, that are expressed in a series of universal symbols, which manifest to the seer the processes of creative life, of spiritual cause with material effect. And, finally, the mystery of the seven vials and the seven stars of Saint John are written therein; for the Tablets are the hieroglyphic keys which unlock the realities of truth involved within the unrealities of external life, and open up, to the aspiring soul, inconceivable vistas of knowledge yet possible of realization, within the Divine womb of the uncreated Æther.

Myriads of exalted spirits, who have toiled for the treasure which doth not corrupt, have added, and are adding, their portion of personal conception to this universal conception of life, so that the sacred symbols themselves, inscribed upon these imperishable Tablets, *are evolutionary*—are slowly unfolding through the eons of time, and revealing wider and yet deeper processes of the light, life, and love, of the Motherhood of God.

Therefore, all Divine revelation of infinite truth is limited and finite as to its conception, when revealed through a finite capacity. All Divine truths are universal; all personal conceptions of such truths are limited; hence springs the unquenchable fountain of the *one* eternal truth, enternally repeating itself, in cosmic as in human life, by the progressive unfoldment of Nature's unlimited potentialities.

> "The outward doth from the inward roll,
>   And the inward dwells in the inmost soul."

The true poet is always a seer, and he might have added that the *inmost soul* is the uncreate, and, the yet uncreated itself, lies buried in the ever eternal beyond; hence the immortality of the human spirit.

This sacred astral scroll, rightly and reverently studied by the disciple of the higher law, becomes a boundless source of knowledge and inspiriation. There is no mood of the mind or yearning of the soul that cannot be satisfied and refreshed from this inexhaustible fountain of spiritual truth, no passion of the human heart that cannot be eased of its burden and soothed of its pain. Its spiritual refreshment falls like the dew from heaven upon those who are weary and heavy laden with the trials and sufferings of external life.

Accept it, then, even as it is given unto you. My friends and brethren, accept it as Zanoni's last work on earth—his legacy to you, and may the spirit of the All-Father-Mother, the ineffable spirit of Life, Light, and Love,—the Unknowable, whom men call God, rest upon you and be with you now and forever.

Very Truly
T. H. Burgoyne.

INTRODUCTION

To the Book Which Is Called "The Tablets of Æth," Wherein Are Described The Formulas of Meditation.

THE FORMULAS OF MEDITATION,

TO THE DRAGON, FOUNTAIN OF YOUTH.

"When first, a musing boy, I stood beside
Thy starlit shimmer, and asked my restless heart
What secrets Nature to the herd denied,
But might to earnest hierophant impart;
When lo! beside me, around and o'er,
Thought whispered, 'Arise, O seeker, and explore.'"

The Tablets of Æth are the culminating expression of symbolical ideas, and the studious meditation thereof is to be approached and continued in this wise:

First, commit to memory, as near as may be, all the ideas involved in the astrological laws and principles laid down in "The Science of the Stars," formulated in the second part of "The Light of Egypt," Vol. I, especially as regards the symbolism there given and manifestation thereof on the intellectual plane. Mentally digest these aspects of truth most thoroughly.

Second, carry forward the same course of mental training with regard to the preceding chapters in this volume, from No. 1 to No. 12. There are thirteen chapters, but No. 13, the last one, being "The Penetralia," should not be included in this course, but, rightly used, should be reserved as the last and final revelation for spiritual contemplation.

The twelve chapters just mentioned continue the great astral laws given in "The Light of Egypt," Vol. I, from this plane to that of the soul life of the human monad (both prior to and after human incarnation). At this point we leave the finite and step into the realms of the infinite. From the sphere of limitations which surround the microcosm we enter the starlit path of the macrocosm, and here, with the illimitable ocean of eternal life sweeping onward before us, we hear the first strains of the Grand March of the Universe burst forth from the organs of God! The suns of creative life swell the infinite chorus of sound; archangels swing their fiery batons to the march of the heavenly host; and all earthly sound has ceased. We are absorbed in the music of the spheres.

We are now in the realm of universals, the domain of living realities. The Tarot of Mother Nature revolves before us, revealing her mystic meanings to the soul. All ideas are symbols, and symbols are reservoirs for the conservation of thought. And this is a very truth: Even so on earth as it is in heaven.

The Tablets of Æth, then, constitute a spiritual astrology, a spiritual science of the stars, void of mathematics, yet possessing all the exactitude of figures, constructed on the principles of astronomy, yet expressed by the methods of the Kabbalah.

The transmission of spiritual truth from inward to outward form, though differing according to the age in which it is expressed, is ever the same in principle. And in the same way that the sacred *clavicula* of Solomon became the Tarot of Bohemian gypsies, so did the Tablets of Æth manifest their mysteries in the starry science of Chaldean lore. But there is this sharp line of demarcation between them, namely, the Tablets of Æth deal with universal human life and nature, with infinite principles from which all finite laws radiate. The Tablets of Æth express and symbolize the cause. All other mundane systems of occult study, astronomical or metaphysical, are spirito-natural effects, the individual intellectual fruits, gathered from the one universal tree of knowledge. Uncreated, Unlimited Potentiality, is the one impersonal truth shining forever in the Great White Light of God. All the laws, powers, and principalities, manifested in the moving Universe, are but the colored rays, blazing with glorious life through the prisms of matter.

Having stated thus much, the neophyte will perceive in what meditative sphere of thought the Tablets may be used. The method of study is, as shown, a purely synthetic deduction of human ideas from spiritual symbols of universal principles. The Tablets themselves constitute a grand arcane Tarot of man, God and the universe, and of all the powers that dwell therein. They may be studied singly, as, for instance, meditating upon some one great universal idea or principle;

or they may be studied in trines, as they appear in each separate book, or chapter, or as squares, like two, five, eight, eleven, or as the seal of two trines, one, three, five, seven, nine, eleven, with No. twelve in the center, as the revealer of the mystery. And, finally, they may be contemplated as the Grand Oracle of Heaven, in the following manner:

Make a circle of the tablets, as you would with a pack of Tarot cards, beginning with No. 1, ♈, on the eastern horizon, and proceeding in the exact opposite order from a figure of the heavens—No. 2, ♉, being on the Twelfth House, No. 3, ♊, on the Eleventh, and ♋ on the M. C. of the figure, as in the Astro-Masonic chart, given in the second part of "The Light of Egypt," Vol. I, and so proceed with the rest of the twelve tablets of the stars. This figure will represent the potentialities of the macrocosm, the starry signs symbolizing the possibilities of things past or to be, and the rulers the active executors thereof. Study the figure in all its aspects as such, first singly, tablet by tablet, then as a whole—the cosmos. Next, place the ruler of any given tablet at the side of the Mansion, and try to penetrate its various meanings, powers and possibilities. Then proceed the same with a trine and a square, and, last, with all the rulers, in the order of their celestial lordship of the signs, each in his appointed place, as a whole Arcana.

In any grave crisis of mental or physical affairs, wherein nations, and not individuals, are concerned, the tablets may be used as a celestial scheme of the heavens, thus: Cast a figure of the heavens for the Sun's first entry into the sign Aries at the vernal equinox, calculated for the meridian of the capital city of the country under consideration. Degrees and minutes are not wanted. Then place the twelve tablets in place of signs, exactly as they would occur in an astrological figure. Then place the rulers of the Sun, Moon and planets therein (each having its own tablet), as they are found to be situated in an ephemeris for the time of the figure. This done, study the whole from a spiritual standpoint as the causes and ultimates of the crisis, according to astro laws.

The foregoing simple directions will, I think, be sufficiently plain for all purposes, never forgetting that this holy study is not a system of divination, as commonly understood, but of Divine revelation, in its highest and most holy religious sense. Long study and most reverent meditation will be required to master this mystery, and many errors of judgment will occur to the beginner.

The interpretative reflections are added for the purpose of guiding and guarding the spiritually untrained seer from possible error in fundamental conceptions only. They must not by any means be taken as a complete revelation of the tablets, but only as a series of skeleton keys by means of which all things may be revealed to the earnest seeker thereof. To have added more than is given would only be to defeat the object of this work. Each seeker for the truth must excavate the mines of knowledge, and dig further into this universal well of truth for himself.

Remember that all interpretation will be personal to each student. Of no one can it be affirmed, "thou hast said," and so endeth the matter. Not so. To each, according to his talent, shall the mysteries of the kingdom be revealed, to every one according to his humility, spiritual light, and merit. But from the arrogant, the selfish, and spiritually proud, shall all things be taken away, and truth shroud herself in the veil of delusion. In simplicity of mind, then, and purity of soul, approach the Holy of Holies. "Suffer little children to come unto Me," saith a messenger of the Most High, "for of such is the Kingdom of Heaven." Verily, therefore, I say unto you, that not until you can look upon all the works of Nature—beauty in her nakedness or vice and crime in their repulsiveness, with pure thought and holy feeling, can you inherit eternal life.

Here endeth the introduction to the book which is called "The Tablets of Æth."

PART I

OF THE TWELVE MANSIONS

Here beginneth Chapter I of the Book which is called "The Tablets of Æth," wherein is transcribed the First Quadrant of the Twelve Mansions.

"I sent my soul through the invisible,
  Some lesson of that after life to spell;
  And by and by my soul returned to me
  And answered, 'I, myself, am Heaven and Hell.' "

"The moving finger writes; and, having writ,
  Moves on; nor all your piety nor wit
  Shall lure it back to cancel half a line,
  Nor all your tears wash out a word of it."

TABLET THE FIRST

Aries

♈

SYMBOL

———

A deep blue Sky, a blaze,

as if something were

about to rise.

I

REFLECTION

TABLET THE FIRST

The blush of dawn of a new life, all nature quivering with the sense of coming, conscious life; Isis, vibrant with love of the coming child, her bosom flushed in expectation of the little son soon to breathe on her yearning breast.

In this we trace the great lesson of preparation, of sending the light before the form, of the prophecy before the fulfillment. Dawn must precede sunrise. What you expect will be your destiny.

It is the longing of centuries that incarnates a god, a real Sun-God, whose vibrant love-life can thrill other lives into prayer—aspiration, the struggle for eternal life. The dawn represents the expectant maternity of Nature—God.

O child of Adam! See that thou expecteth much, and that thy aspirations are reflected in thy outward life.

TABLET THE SECOND

Taurus

♉

SYMBOL

———

A red sun

on the horizon

of

an inky sea.

II

REFLECTION

TABLET THE SECOND

Nature has shown forth her glory, as brought forth by young Horus, but her creative force is still unreflected. The sea is black and inky. The Son of God is born, but the sea of human life still remains unconscious, in primeval darkness.

The angles of the Sun and the sea are not yet in right relation to each other. A few, standing on the watch-towers of life, seeing the red glow of the risen sun, call "Look!" But the unfortunate ones in the outer darkness cry, as they beat their breasts; "No! There is no light! You do but dream!" And yet the Sun of Life has risen—the Divine light glows.

O child of Adam! Remember that "In Him was life, and life was the light of man, and the light shineth in the darkness, and the darkness comprehended it not."

TABLET THE THIRD

Gemini

♊

SYMBOL

———

Two stars are rising at
angles to each other and
to the Polar star,
while eight stars shine
faintly in the black space
of background.   ★

★

★

III

REFLECTION

TABLET THE THIRD

The Divine symbol of soul-matehood is here signified in the two stars rising in the foreground; not only the soul-affinities of humanity, but the eternal father-mother forces manifested in the biune spirit of universal life and nature, the two great creative powers, Life and Light, whose harmony creates love, attraction and repulsion, and the straight lines of law and justice, which blend in the spiral of mercy.

The two stars are rising at an oblique angle to the pole-star, the center around which, material things revolve. So, too, life and love are balanced by the star of wisdom. Love in the spirit is adaption to the environment in matter and providence in universal life. The eight stars reveal the mystery of the tablet—universal death, present with life, the final end of all discord glimmers faintly afar off, and man questions the love of God, seeing that all things pass away, not realizing that death is the germinal promise of life, of transformation, of the realization of unrealized hopes, of the union of loving hearts in their starry pilgrimage back to the Father's home.

O child of Adam! Listen unto the words of the Teacher: "I and the Father are one." Suffer little children to come unto me, for of such is the Kingdom of Heaven."

PART I

———

Here beginneth Chapter 2 of the Book which is called "The Tablets
of Æth," wherein is transcribed the Second Quadrant of the
Twelve Mansions.

———

"How they struggle in the immense Universe!
How they whirl and seek!
Innumerable souls, that all spring forth
From the vast world-soul.
They drop from planet to planet,
And in the abyss they weep
For their forgotten land.
These are thy tears, O Dionysus,
O Spirit vast, Divine One, Liberator.
Draw back thy daughters to the breast of light."

———

"Ah, love! Could you and I with him conspire
To grasp this sorry scheme of things entire,
Would we not shatter it to bits? And then
Remould it nearer to the heart's desire."

TABLET THE FOURTH

Cancer

♋

SYMBOL

A woman's face

unconscious, in trance,

surrounded by

clouds.

IV

REFLECTION

TABLET THE FOURTH

The dreaming woman, whose brooding thoughts shape the coming man. The race is never any farther advanced than the average thought of the woman. She is yet sleeping, knowing not her powers. So, not until she awakes and recognizes herself as conceiving by the Holy Ghost and the mother of the incarnate God, will that God be brought forth unto universal knowledge.

In this is the great lesson to woman: Ever remember thy creative power as the mother of the humanity of the future. The sun in thy mansion exerts its highest power. Awake, therefore, O soul, and eclipse not its brightness with thy dreams of sublunary power.

O child of Adam! Ever honor the womb that gave thee birth, and know that all thy earthly greatness received its seed therefrom. A fountain cannot rise higher than its source.

TABLET THE FIFTH

Leo

♌

SYMBOL

———

A man's arm, bent,
exceedingly muscular,
a knife in the hand,
a streak of lightning
opposite the arm, which is
defying the lightning.

V

REFLECTION

TABLET THE FIFTH

Here we have the symbol of the incarnate fire of the spirit defying the mere natural fire of the heavens. The woman sleeps and broods and dreams, but the man she has brought forth is awake, and bids defiance to the fiery forces of Nature. He has armed himself with the keen knife of action, and with it has conquered the forces of matter. He has harnessed the lightning, and made the electric fluid his obedient slave. And thus has he mastered all forces inferior to spirit—that spirit of conscious life which is his birthright.

The lesson to be gleaned from this is that, the kingdom of Nature must be taken by·storm. Not for rest, but for work, has Mother Nature sent forth her man child; not for peace, but for battle; not for inertia, but for effort.

O child of Adam! Arm yourself with the sword—mayhap the sword of affliction —and, gallantly raising the strong right arm aloft, hurl defiance at the chaos of Nature, sure that the fire from the Sun of the spirit is burning in every vein of that arm.

TABLET THE SIXTH

Virgo

♍

SYMBOL

———

A Lotus, rising from the

water, coiled around

its stem a snake,

whose efforts fail to reach

the flower.

VI

REFLECTION

TABLET THE SIXTH

Here we have the sacred flower, symbol of the virgin soul, uncontaminated by the snake of passion, which can only enfold the body—the stem; the snake of matter—of lust—of evil. But the flower of the spirit—the soul—lifts its pure white petals upward as an incense cup to the Sun of the Spirit.

In this symbol read the great lesson of the experience of evil. If, the flower of the soul, blossoms; the mud of the soil and the snake of the passions are but the surroundings of its roots and stem. Both are necessary for the perfection of the flower. The roots sink deep into Mother Earth, and draw nourishment and life, lifting matter upward, while the snake of passion becomes, under another aspect, the serpent of wisdom. Coiled around the stem of this life, it gives to the incarnated soul that wisdom which later blossoms in the Seraph of the Sun spheres.

O child of Adam! Take suffering, if it forge the sword of the spirit. Take evil and passion, and turn them into deep lessons of life, blossoming the evil into good, changing passion into wisdom. Only "the pure in heart can see God."

PART I

———

Here beginneth Chapter 3 of the Book which is called "The Tablets of Æth," wherein is transcribed the Third Quadrant of the Twelve Mansions.

——————

"To know what really exists, one must cultivate silence with one's self, for it is in silence that the eternal and unexpected flowers open, which change their form and color according to the soul in which they grow. Souls are weighed in silence, as gold and silver are weighed in pure water."

——————

"The worldly hope men set their hearts upon turns to ashes; or it prospers, and anon, like snow upon the desert's dusty face, lighting a little hour or two, is gone."

TABLET THE SEVENTH

Libra

⌢

SYMBOL

———

A crowned king, with a
scythe raised in the
air, looks closely at two
boys wrestling
beneath him in a field of
grain, a red poppy
below them.

VII

REFLECTION

TABLET THE SEVENTH

The symbol of Nature's eternal war for the impossible equilibrium between spirit and matter; the symbol, also, of Time, which is but the illusion in which eternity clothes itself; forever putting on and forever putting off new garments of matter. The crowned king is the victorious soul, waiting, with the scythe of Time, to reap the harvest of the world; while incarnated man, as represented in the wrestling youths, is struggling for that which he did not produce. and which only death can reap. The poppy reveals the secret of the illusions of Nature's master-showman. All earthly things are unreal to the spirit, which is the only real thing. Man's effort to hoard and save the things of this world *is injustice to others.* The struggle is eternal, and no matter how careful or cunning man is to monopolize either power, truth or wealth, swift-footed time will readjust all things without error.

O child of Adam! "Lay not up for yourselves treasures upon earth, where moth and rust doth corrupt and where thieves break through and steal."

TABLET THE EIGHTH

Scorpio

♏

SYMBOL

———

A wide, arid plain, on it a

skeleton; a dull, grey sky,

in which an Eagle soars,

full-fed, it seems, from

the flesh of the skeleton.

VIII

REFLECTION

TABLET THE EIGHTH

A significant symbol to the seer, showing forth the two ultimates of life and death, of earthly things and sex. Scorpio is both the eagle of the spirit, soaring aloft, well fed with all that is worth carrying away from the earth; and also the scorpion, whose natural home is the desert.

In sex, either way, life is given. Shall it be to your spirit making fat and full your immortal self, or will the other interpretation be yours? And will you leave yourself dead and annihilated, a skeleton, to the Ego, the Divine spirit? For sex is indeed the foundation of all. Raised to the region of Libra, it is power and magnetism. To the bosom it is love; to the brain it is enthusiasm. It is the promethian fire of life, the creative force, giving vigor to whatever region to which it is raised; or, lowered, to be spent with no returns, it debases and renders life a desert of dry bones.

O child of Adam! Reflect on the fall of man from spirit to matter, and combine the wisdom of the serpent with the purity of the dove, and "lest ye partake of the tree of life ye shall surely die."

TABLET THE NINTH

Saggitarius

↗

SYMBOL

———

A child in a shell, holding

in its hand a feathered lance,

is drawn by five stars,

grouped in an under arc.

IX

REFLECTION

TABLET THE NINTH

The symbol of the conscious soul. The shell is the body, drawn by the five senses—stars—which form an under arc, to represent the world of material things and our relation thereto. The child, armed with the feathered lance, is the soul; riding thus, fully armed, in the shell of the body, it realizes the duality of truth; that all things are changeable; and that each thing is true upon the plane of its manifestation, while an illusion to that which is interior to its life, while the soul is in its dream state. Sagittarius represents conservatism and the permanence of crystallized institutions; but, when the spirit awakes and bursts the shell of matter, the senses, instead of being the guardians and jailors of its environment, become its servants, and the means by which, united as the one Ego, sense-perception, it races o'er the fields of Æth—a being of life and beauty, shining in the empyrean of God.

O child of Adam! Ever remember that temperament and environment constitute the north and south poles of human possibility, and that ability, combined with opportunity, is the measure of responsibility.

PART I

———

Here beginneth Chapter 4 of the Book which is called "The Tablets of Æth," wherein is transcribed the Fourth Quadrant of the Twelve Mansions.

———

"A hair, perhaps, divides the false and true.
Yes, and a single alif were the clue—
Could you but find it—to the treasure house,
And, peradventure, to *the Master*, too."

———

"Beware, O my son, of self-incense. It is the most dangerous on account of its agreeable intoxication. ❀ ❀ ❀ Learn, O my beloved, that the light of Allah's truth will often penetrate an empty head more easily than one too crammed with learning."

TABLET THE TENTH

Capricorn

♑

SYMBOL

———

A deep, black ground, o'er which shimmers a phosphorescent light; at each side an aurora borealis rises, mountain like; above all, a tiny star.

X

REFLECTION

TABLET THE TENTH

Here is revealed the symbol of the messenger of the Most High. The star hovers over the phosphorescent light cast on the darkness as the spirit hovers over the blackness of matter. The aurora borealis stands as the emblem for the magnetic attraction of Earth on spirit, the Christ soon to be born in the manger of the Goat; the descent of the Holy Ghost into material form, so that heavenly truth may illumine the drear speculum of earthly thought with the Divine iridescence of celestial light. It is the lowest arc of the cycle that reveals the new birth of death unto life—the divine egg of Brahma, containing the promise of the new law: "Peace on Earth, good will towards men."

O child of Adam! Be thou the star, and not a dweller of the outer darkness, and "Let your light so shine before men, that, they may see your good works."

TABLET THE ELEVENTH

Aquarius

≋

SYMBOL

———

A stormy sea is seen; above it the eight stars shine, brilliant and clear.

XI

REFLECTION

TABLET THE ELEVENTH

This tablet symbolizes the complete materialization of man—man, perfect on the earth and the lord thereof, in so far as material forces are concerned. The storm is the tempest of life, the whirl of the elements of matter in their battle with the spirit. The eight stars, brilliant now (for they are the same stars that were dimly seen in Gemini), show that the conquest of matter is complete, the great fall of spirit finished; the end of involution. And this would bring stagnation and death, if peace now ensued. The lesson taught is that, not in peace and rest can the soul grow; but amidst the earthquakes that shake thrones, the floods that overwhelm countries, the fires that reduce to ashes, has the strong man-soul grown to its present state and power. So fear not the storm, but the calm; not the unrest, but the quiet; fear not the battle, but the ignoble peace of the coward.

O child of Adam! The astral soul must learn to do and dare. Not over the brave man's grave shall it be written, "Rest in peace," but "I will arise, and go to my father."

TABLET THE TWELFTH

Pisces

♓

SYMBOL

———

A comet, beyond it infinite
things, only dreamed of
as yet, a world floating
in an ocean and in night,
beneath are two hands
clasped palm to palm.

XII

TABLET THE TWELFTH

A revelation of the to be. The comet is the twelfth Avatar, the herald, coming forth from the starry abyss of the infinite, staying with us a little while, and then flashing on his shining way to other worlds than ours, bearing *the Divine Word* from sun to planet, as the fiery messenger of God. And here the soul may well ask: "Who? Where? Whence and Whither?" For behold, he has come, and gone, and

> "Earth could not answer; nor the seas that mourn
> In flowing purple, of their Lord forlorn;
> Nor rolling Heaven, with all his signs revealed
> And hidden by the sleeve of night and morn."

The world floating in the sea of the infinite and resting in night shows the present state of humanity. But, "the blush of dawn" is ready to gladden the soul, and the expectant seer, from his lonely vigil on the hilltop, awaits the sunlight which will soon flood the world anew.

The two clasped hands point to many problems, chiefly soul-matehood, the message of the starry messenger, universal brotherhood, and the Father-Motherhood of God.

O child of Adam! Watch and pray, that a voice of the silence may speak unto you.

Here endeth the four Quadrants of the Tablets of the Twelve Mansions, wherein are revealed the signs and symbols thereof, as faithfully transcribed from the sacred roll in the astral records and called "The Tablets of Æth."

April, 1893.

PART II

of The Book which is called

THE TABLETS OF ÆTH

———————

OF THE TEN PLANETARY RULERS

PART II

———

Here beginneth Chapter I of the Second Part of the Book which is called "The Tablets of Æth," wherein is transcribed the First Trinity of the Planetary Rulers.

———

"The human heart is the true temple of God; enter ye into your temples and illumine them with good thoughts. The sacred vessels, they are your hands and your eyes. Do I say that which is agreeable to God—doing good to your neighbors? But, first embellish wherein dwells He, who gave you life."

———

"How small soever your lamp be, never give away the oil which feeds it, but only the light and flame, which crown it."

TABLET THE FIRST

The Sun

⊙

SYMBOL

———

A flaming splendor,

a center of

light, radiating in all

directions.

I

REFLECTION

TABLET THE FIRST

The symbol of all created life, spiritual and material; of all goodness, human or Divine; the center of all thought, from brutal instinct to Deific wisdom; of all creations, from starry systems to man, and from man back again to invisible gas; of all action, from the imperceptible vibrations of nerve energy to the awful destruction of worlds. All creative potency lies within a Sun sphere. Light is life. The planets are but the offspring of light and life. So in this symbol, we read the source of the human Ego, of our own life. We are, as it were, the planets of the spiritual Sun. Our souls are the attributes of the Sun, of the spiritual Ego. Only from the Ego can we receive life eternal and make immortality a fact. Obeying this spiritual life-force, the human monad is but an attribute, a reflection, of the Divine Ego, and if it fails to awake to a consciousness of this union, it withers and dies like a flower plucked from the parent tree of life.

O child of Adam, in reverence and awe do thou meditate upon this Tablet, for it is a thing of beauty, a being of light, life and love, manifesting its creative mission. It is the Vicegerent of God, flaming forth His splendors in the sky.

TABLET THE SECOND

Mercury

☿

SYMBOL

An elephant, kneeling between two square columns; on one an eagle, on the other a vulture.

At the side a boy, with bow and arrows, standing in doubt which to shoot.

Below these a human face, composed of various flowers, whose roots are snakes, a poppy, forming an eye, which winks.

II

REFLECTION

TABLET THE SECOND

A vision revealing the earthly drama of the microcosm. The elephant represents the highest expression of intelligence, minus the spirit; kneeling between the square columns of matter, i.e., guarded by them. The external mind is sleeping, or, at most, dreaming of the things of the spirit. Above sleeping mind sit the two birds, who represent spirit and matter, each waiting for the slowly preparing feast. The boy, the soul with its weapons, has a choice. Shall it be the sensuality of the flesh that he shall destroy, or the possibilities of the spiritual life on earth. The problem awaits solution. The eagle sits ready to bear aloft the spirit of the sleeper. The vulture hopes for sleep to end in death, that he may live upon the carrion thereof. The flowers of the external mind have for their roots the snakes; and, in a larger sense, the flowers of immortality have the serpent of wisdom for their roots. And the poppy winks. It knows its own power of illusion, and the double significance of the snake; the necessity of evil in the evolution of good. It is the Tablet of Wisdom.

O child of Adam! "Be ye therefore wise as serpents and harmless as doves."

TABLET THE THIRD

Venus

♀

SYMBOL

———

An altar; on it two cups, one full, the other spilled; near them two bleeding hearts. in one a snake, in the other a dagger.

Above––clouds, from which comes a woman's face, a wreath in the hand, coming out of the cloud; in the wreath an angel, going upwards, with wings out-spread.

III

REFLECTION

TABLET THE THIRD

There is but one altar, but one blood of the sacrament in two cups, but one flesh of the Christ—the Ego—in two hearts, two experiences in love, ecstacy, and pain; two results of experience, the serpent and the dagger, symbolizing wisdom and affliction. Above the altar the divine woman holds the wreath encircling the angel. The angel of immortal life rises from the altar of sacrifice. Some of the wine is spilled as offering. The cup that is filled is raised to "Ra." To serve at the altar of love is the soul-mission of all, even as Christ served his disciples. Each soul must find its own service, and then the pilgrims of the Sun return to the mansions of the blessed. The great mother-god, Venus, Urania, quivers and thrills as she holds forth her offspring—the angel, the young Eros of life eternal.

O child of Adam, this is the Tablet of Love. Meditate thereon, as the last of the triune God. In this Tablet lies the secret of suffering and pleasure. He who vibrates in pain will quiver in ecstacy. Only those who have agonized in Hell can thrill in Heaven.

PART II

———

Here beginneth Chapter 2 of the Second Part of the Book which is called "The Tablets of Æth," wherein is transcribed the Second Trinity of the Planetary Rulers.

————

"Thou art called forth to this fair sacrifice
For a draught of milk; with the Maruts
Come hither, O Agni!

They who know the great sky, the Visve
Devas without guile; with those Maruts
Come hither, O Agni!

They who are brilliant, of awful shape,
Powerful, and devourers of foes; with the
Maruts come hither, O Agni!

They who in heaven are enthroned as gods,
In the light of the firmament; with the Maruts
Come hither, O Agni!"

————

"Let us meditate on the adorable light of the Divine Rulers.
May it guide our intellects."

TABLET THE FOURTH

The Moon

꠱

SYMBOL

———

NIGHT

A wonderful spider's-web;

The web glitters in the faint moonlight against a dark background of blue; moon invisible; on the outside of web a star, in the center a spot of light, underneath a coffin filled with stones.

IV

REFLECTION

TABLET THE FOURTH

The web of life has caught the monad of the soul and thus incarnated the universe, for each soul incarnates its universe at birth, each one's world being different, and peculiar unto himself. At the first breath, the young child polarizes his relations to stars and earth, and it is the affinity and repulsion which make his life experience. And the stars weave the web in their lines of sextile, square and trine, of opposition and conjunction, thus enveloping the monad in the Circle of Necessity.

Outside the star of the spirit, the Ego, shines clear, free from the entanglements of the web and unaffected by the magnetic glamour of the Moon. And lo! the coffin is filled with stones, a symbol of death and the Moon, which is but a casket of stones. Therefore, little monad, caught in the tangle of the web of life and the glamour of earthly things, take heart, for, beyond all, is the star of your being. Call down the law of that star into yourself, and the web is broken and waves its tattered shreds in the breeze. The moonlight, the reflected light, pales as the Star-Sun of your being rises, and the moonlight of Earth gives place to the Sun-spheres of Ra.

O child of Adam! The beginning of sorrow is the dawn of spiritual life. The wise man rules the stars; the fools of Earth obey.

TABLET THE FIFTH

Mars

♂

SYMBOL

———

An immense helmet on

pedestal, across which a streak

of lightning flashes;

beside it a naked child painting

pictures on the helmet;

beneath, a broken sword.

V

REFLECTION

TABLET THE FIFTH

Can greater irony be shown than in this astral symbol. Mars is externally represented as a fierce warrior, awful to behold; the reality, a little child, painting toy pictures on the helmet, too big for his curly head. The lesson in this is indeed, that the pen is mightier than the sword; that the big and blustering helmet will become a plaything for the child. Soon, that the sword of bloodshed, rape, and ruin, will be broken and war relegated to the past, looked at, but, as pictures, painted with hideous reality by the childhood of the race.

The symbol also reveals the great executive forces of humanity, the child. The soul can paint, execute its ideas, its hopes and its fears in any color—the lurid red of blood, the black of ignorance and crime, or in the living light of beauty. All the same, it is the childhood of man painting its ideals in the material world.

O child of Adam, curb the anger of Mars, that thy painting may set the dove at liberty. Let the magic of thy soul transform the savage of the desert into the angel of mercy.

TABLET THE SIXTH

Jupiter

♃

SYMBOL

———

A cave in the mountain side; a face like the sphinx comes out of the cave; there is a blackness behind it; it looks with upturned head to a light that is way beyond; it is a face that means something awful. a godlike defiance to the things that are.

VI

REFLECTION

TABLET THE SIXTH

Again we are impressed with the contrast of internal and external things. Jupiter, the symbol of authority, conservatism, church, and state, and the stability of human institutions, and the things that are, as the things that are the best. But oh, how widely different the internal, the real Jupiter, that governing power of the spirit that hurls defiance at unjust authority, the cruelty and tyranny of the world. The soul sees the light beyond, and, emerging from the dark chasm of matter, knows the battle that must be fought against wrong. It is the awful—yea, terrible—symbol of defiance to gods and men who oppose its onward, upward march to the shining goal of light. Make way, then! Make way! For Earth has given birth to her giant son—the Spirit. For, listen closely, my friend, to the axiom of Immortality. What is soul? Not the spirit, mind you; not the deathless Ego, of which you at present, perchance, know absolutely nothing. Soul is mere memory; a scavenger in earthly states; and a gleaner, a hired help, in the fields of heaven; and to become immortal, there must be something more than soul as the result. It must take such a vital interest in its Lord's work that, finally it becomes too valuable to lose, and must be taken into partnership, so to say. The Ego—Lord—has found a valued servant, a trusted steward, after much seeking, and at once adopts it as its very own. And so the soul becomes heir to the heavenly estate and receives the immortal, vital principle of spiritual union, and awakes from the son of Earth a God-like being, free from the shackles of Time—a dweller in eternity. The soul must awake and realize the Deific atom around which it revolves before it is too late. Unless this is so, the seed of immortal life, sown in matter by the Ego, has not germinated, and it returns unfruitful and dies—it is an abortion. Many, many seeds never germinate. Many good orthodox, but animal-like lives, live, move, and die,—yes, die in very truth. Would to God I could make all mankind realize this awful, inconceivable privilege of life, that, Jupiter-like, they would turn and face the light.

O child of Adam! "It is easier for a camel to go through the eye of a needle than for a rich man to enter into the Kingdom of God."

PART II

Here beginneth Chapter 3 of the Second Part of the Book which is called "The Tablets of Æth," wherein the Third, and last, Trinity of the Planetary Rulers is faithfully transcribed.

"Thou hast entered the immeasurable regions. I am the Dweller of the Threshold. What wouldst thou with me? ° ° ° Dost thou fear me? Am I not thy beloved? Is it not for me that thou hast rendered up the delights of thy race? Wouldst thou be wise? Mine is the wisdom of the countless ages. Kiss me, my mortal lover."

"Thus man pursues his weary calling,
And wrings the hard life from the sky,
While happiness unseen is falling
Down from God's bosom silently."

TABLET THE SEVENTH

Saturn

♄

SYMBOL

———

A human figure with a

scepter of power,

a being of light crowned

with flames.

VII

REFLECTION

TABLET THE SEVENTH

In the external we remember Saturn as an old man, and as a skeleton with a scythe—as Time, in fact. But see, O immortal soul, the real Saturn, as the Angel of Life, having from time gathered the experiences which crown him with light, holding the rod of power; the Christ born in the manger of Capricorn, the Goat—life born of death; the conqueror of evil. He throws off the mask of age, and divine youth beams on us. He doffs the mantle of rags, and royal splendors clothe him. He lifts the hood, and behold the crown. He raises the crutch, and lo! the rod of power. He drops the scythe of death for the jewel of eternal life.

"Om Mani Padme Um."
(Oh the jewel in the lotus.)

O child of Adam! Meditate on the transmutations of life. Behold the earthly miracle of the caterpillar and the butterfly, of the toiling mortal and the transcendent God!

TABLET THE EIGHTH

Uranus

♅

SYMBOL

A human eye,

from which

darts lightning

upon

an ocean of matter.

VIII

REFLECTION

TABLET THE EIGHTH

The state of soul and spirit—penetration; the wonderful power of soul-perception, which sheds its light on all visible things, receiving their images and interpreting them into the spirit, the all-seer—what does it not convey? The perception that can see deep into your soul and see, as it were, the yet unborn thought; that can distinguish the motive of action; that judges the realities of your soul. Such is the Astral Uranian. For with us all, are three planes of mind: The drift plane, the intellectual, and the spiritual, or internal plane; and thought-reading can be on one or all of these different states. But only the Uranian seer can read the inmost mind, and so really know the possibilities of your spirit.

Imagine an image of soft wax, covered with a sensitive skin. All impressions on the skin shape the plastic wax, but go no deeper—do not reach the soul. You can separate these impressions from your real self, when calm and alone, and look upon emotion as a surface play. But the tragedies of life strike deep. They affect the soul, and go to the center of being. "*Verbum sap.*"

O child of Adam! Watch the tempest of life closely. The Ego may sit calm amidst the storm, but, if that be stirred—*beware!* The God acts: the soul alone watches.

TABLET THE NINTH

Neptune

ψ

SYMBOL

—

A

Winged

Globe.

IX

REFLECTION

TABLET THE NINTH

An unknown quantity, a hope of progression, ideal love, and all true mental and spiritual ideals; aspiration to become that which we feel to be noble and true; the symbol of the monad, the soul which, receiving its life from the Sun—the Ego—is constantly revealing new forces and potencies of that God-life. Each soul's Ego is its maker and God. The Ego is like the Deific potency of the universe, unlimited in potential power, but limited by its monad as to what will be evolved from its awful depth of being. Deity progresses through its expressions of the cosmos. The Ego, your God, finds progressive expression through you, through your soul. That soul is not immortal that becomes separated from its Ego—its God. So, soul, spread your spiritual wings and soar upward.

O child of Adam! Know these three things: Eternity is the creator of the universal life; universal life creates the world, and the world is the creator of time. And of these, the Universe is Life, and the World is Mind, and Time is the Soul. The sum total of all is Experience. And this is individual, conscious life—"*Jacta est alea*" (the die is cast)—the wings are spread.

TABLET THE TENTH

The Cypher — the unknown

O

SYMBOL

———

A Shining Nebulae;
within it a dot,
aimlessly wandering
around an unknown
center.

X

REFLECTION

TABLET THE TENTH

The unknown in very truth. It is everything—it is also nothing.
Inconceivable visions arise within the mental universe, but nothing
assumes definite form. It is all that is past. It is likewise everything
that the future has in store. Amen.

O child of Adam! "Canst thou bring forth Mazzaroth in his season? or loose
the bands of Orion?"

PART III

of The Book which is called

THE TABLETS OF ÆTH

————————

OF THE

TEN GREAT KABBALISTICAL POWERS

or

ANGELS OF THE UNIVERSE

PART III

VISION

Each angel standing in front of the symbol is dimly outlined and transparent. Through the angel's form is seen its symbol.

FIRST

A luminous something, which gives the impression of sleep.

SECOND

Something moving, like an ocean.

THIRD

A storm, and lightning.

FOURTH

A mist.

FIFTH

An animal moving, resembling a turtle.

SIXTH

A blue light; in the center a star with three points.

SEVENTH

An expanse of water, a blue sky, a shining disk rising on the horizon.

EIGHTH

A lurid sky, like a red dawn; in the water floats an egg.

NINTH

Five stars on a convex arc, like a rainbow; the shell of the egg is broken and forms continents.

TENTH

A man lying fast asleep under a magnificent palm tree, with his face turned toward the horizon of the sea.

EXPLANATION

Only the pure in heart can see God, and to those pure souls I commend the following brief explanation of the Vision of the Angels of Life, which I have here recorded for the benefit of all whom it may now and hereafter concern.

In the original Vision of the Tablets of Æth a great circle was seen, in the center a head, a faint shimmer above the head, as if the light were about to dawn; a dull, lurid glow beneath, as if of chaos or hell; the hair around the head like floating clouds, the beard like strange cloud-streaks. Each sign of the Zodiac surrounding the center head had within it a faintly seen face. Beginning with the first, it became more and more distinct and perfect with each sign until it evolved into godlike beauty in Pisces.

The symbolic planets were around the Zodiac, and beyond these, making a third grand circle, were the ten Evolutionary Angels. The vision is that of the evolution of all life, spiritual and material. We gaze at the cosmic sex mystery, and the discerning mind, the loving spirit, can read the correspondence of the great sacred conjugal act of both man and God; of its heights, of its depths, and of all that lies between.

To aid in meditation on the head at the center, herein is written a vision, an experience of the soul in the Sleep of Sialam.

The Hermetic brethren encircled my astral body, which was deeply entranced. *"From whence,"* the great question, quivered through my inmost being. To answer that awful problem of the soul the released spirit went on its fearsome journey, back through star systems; back, back beyond all stars, back to the blackness of nothing— that awful nothing, whose outside ring vibrated with fearful flames; the fiery cherubim, winged, taking all possible shapes, and unformed living shapes. A human flamed and changed and vanished. The tornado of whirling, flashing, chaotic life swirled and drove through the darkness of chaos of nothing from nothing—and that great, unknown abyss *is God!* But the life is *evolutionary.*

Deity is progressive, so never can man cease to be. Never can he return to that awful center of nothingness, or be absorbed within the bosom of the unmanifested being. On, and on, and on, with Deific power, God moves in ever-increasing whirls of evolution.

Thus came the answer of the ages: "From primeval force, from the mighty breath of unmanifested being, through every phase of action and reaction, from the energies of storm and lightning, from star-dust to sunlight, has come the spirit of man!"

And the Astral Brethren understood.

THE TWO SEALS OF THE EARTH

I

SYMBOL

———

A human being, with a
flaming, burning
heart.

II

SYMBOL

———

A round disk inside a light.
as from a sun, conceived,
but not seen.

So here endeth the Book which is called "The Tablets of Æth," transcribed
from the astral originals in the Year of Doom MDCCCXCIII.

"*Omnia Vincit Veritas.*"

"THY KINGDOM COME."

Very Truly
T. H. Burgoyne. H.

April, 1893

(*Zanoni*)

CHAPTER XIII

PENETRALIA

THE SECRET OF THE SOUL

We have now arrived at our final study, which we have approached step by step amid the labyrinth of the mysteries concealed beneath the Veil of Isis. We stand at last upon the very threshold of the sacred Adytum, the "Holy of Holies," from whence proceeds our final revelation of that inmost conception of Man's identity with his Creator—the Penetralia of his Being—the last secret of the incarnated soul.

The written word almost fails us—does fail in fact, when we come to the difficult task of externalizing ideas, the sublimity of which is so infinitely beyond the crystallized images of matter that, they can only be realized in their true glory, when the purified soul can view them from the ineffable heights of eternal spirit. We are lost, dazed, at the brilliancy of the spiritual imagery that opens out before us, in its fathomless stretch of the eternities that are past, of the ever-imperishable present, and the unborn eternities yet to be; all of them linked together in one grand chain of spiritual relationship and deathless identity; as Man, the Angel, God; and God, the Angel, Man; as the triune Cycle of Being, within the incomprehensible Cycle of Necessity; which constitutes Nature's cosmic university for the complete graduation, education, and purification, of that self-conscious, Deific atom of life, whose expression becomes the human soul. Ah! my brothers could you, but for one single instant, realize *who* you are, *where* you are journeying, and *what* your final destiny, every earthly moment at your disposal would be rightly used, and every hour considered too short for your efforts to aid your fellow-man. Selfishness, wealth, and power, would be so utterly contemptible in your sight that their possession would be considered a fearful affliction and a curse, the moment they exceeded the comfortable requirements of mundane existence.

Leave self and the world behind you for the present, and, for the moment, leave your life, with its manifold vanities, in the outer court, and together let us cross the threshold and enter the door of the Temple. There! At last we have entered the Sacred Sanctuary, my brother, and we stand face to face with the imperishable truth of our being—the truth which makes us free, the truth which must ultimately prevail, by virtue of its own inherent Divinity; and we realize Man as he really is, not as he outwardly seems to be. We view him as a molecule, composed of a congregation of separate atoms, all of them held in their places by the centripetal force of the central human atom of life. And yet, small as he is, small as his kingdom is, compared with the mighty creation of which he is a part, he possesses all the inherent qualities of the whole. This, then, is our first conception—Man, is a microcosmic molecule, an atom of divine life.

The scene changes within the chamber, and upon the shimmering, luminous veil, yet before us, we view the large and mighty planet called the Earth. Not as a revolving satellite of the Sun, but as she really is, a vital organ of the macrocosm, the stellar womb of the solar system, the matrix which produces the material organic form of humanity. When "the Earth was without form and void," as we are informed in the mystical language of Genesis, the human soul had not yet reached the state, or grade, in the celestial university that desired the Earth and its temporary illusions. Hence this state was void, an unborn idea, the To Be, and darkness, symbolical of complete lack of life and intelligence, "was upon the face of the deep," silent space.

Again the scene changes, and one by one the numberless planets, planetoids, moons, meteors, comets, and other attendant bodies, pass before the eye of the soul as we gaze upon the curtain of this Sacred Penetralia, each orb belonging to some portion of the Astral Man, each great planet constituting some vital function of the macrocosmic organism, and conferring those qualities upon each and every single atom pertaining to that degree of life, so that the solar system becomes individualized as a grand cosmic organism, its attendant satellites constituting its vital organs, and the shining Zodiac its outward form. So, also, each planet is a living, cosmic individual, intensely alive; living, moving, breathing, and bringing forth its offspring of like substance, matter, in obedience to the potential demand of incarnating spirit. The Sun is alive, glowing with life, and constitutes the heart and arterial center of all the circulating fluids of the stellar anatomy.

Scientists may continue to predict, as they have been predicting, the day when solar radiation will cease, but their predictions will prove as worthless as the sighing of the summer wind, so far as reality is concerned. "It is an incomprehensible mystery to science," says Sir Robert Ball, in his "Story of the Heavens," "how the Sun has been able to maintain its heat with such regularity in the past, for there has been no appreciable change in the Earth's temperature for thousands of years." What it is to-day it was ten thousand years ago—yea, Sir Robert Ball, and will be in ten thousand years to come. You may wonder, and the Royal College may wonder, but in the meantime the mighty, pulsating Sun continues beating out its rhythmic vibrations of spiritual and dynamic life—continues, and will continue, to send the exhilarating current throughout every atom, to the remotest part of his solar dominions, and the same current *returns to him again, undiminished*, for the purification which his glowing, transmuting photosphere alone, can give, to be sent forward again. upon its mission of light, life, and love, around the vital, organic worlds of the astral organism. There is nothing lost, no radiation of energy dispersed upon the unformed, lifeless ether. From the radiating solar focus of Divinity it comes, and to him, undiminished it returns, and so on forever and ever; until the last Deific atom has won its laggard way back to the shining throne of God.

The Sun breathes. The pulsating process of dynamic respiration, eternally repeated during the grand period of a solar lifetime, renews its vital energies, and supplies itself, with the full abundance of the ever-living spirit, transmitted from the shoreless ether in which it lives. It needs no other food, except the magnetic nutriment it receives from each vital organ, or planet, in return for the electrical life current it transmits to them. Just as the human lungs inflate themselves with the vital atmosphere, (which is only the ether, dynamically diluted by the Earth to harmonize with our conditions), to oxygenate the blood and add fresh fuel to the physical furnace, or supply finer essences to the nervous centers. Just as the human heart, with its continual, rhythmic pulsations, propels forth the circulating fluid to every part of the human frame; so does the central heart and lungs of the Grander Man of the Skies, (the Sun) send forth its vitalizing energy to every part of the universe.

Such are the crowding thoughts, born of interior knowledge, that flood the mind as we view these sacred revelations within the sacred chamber of the soul. As yet, we are gazing upon the undulating flow of the astral light. We yearn within our utmost being to become the center of the Penetralia and gaze upon the glorious radiance of the Adonai, from whose ineffable presence we are only screened by the last shining veil of semi-transparent matter, that waves and trembles with every spiritual aspiration. The soul sends forth its pleading cry for light: "Who and what is God?" Faintly, as the distant vesper sounds upon the cooling eve, comes the answer: "Who and what art thou? What canst thou see? What delectable blessing does Nature vouchsafe to the pure in heart?" We tremble with the awful, yet thrilling, revelation. We know dimly, yet fail to realize in our outward consciousness the full import thereof. We realize wherein the mistaken selfhood hath become the only begotten of the Father, but the revelation is too much, and too little. We know that, faint as the voice seemed to the yet unprepared soul, an echo only, *it was the voice of the Adonai behind the veil.* And now we crave the knowledge of the Where and Whither.

Again, we see the Earth as the vital function of the interplanetary being. It is composed of substance termed matter, which substance is the aggregation of countless atoms, which science has not, and never can, resolve into their individual selves. These atoms are rings of the atomless ether, which, thus differentiated from the formless ether, become centers of force, the center of such force being a vacuum within the atomic ring—a center so small that a microscope with lens one thousand times as powerful as the most perfect modern instrument would fail to reveal it. These atoms form systems, under the control of another apparent vacuum; or, rather, this vacuum seems to be the focus, or center, about which they revolve. *This system constitutes a scientific molecule of matter,* and, in response to the innumerable vibrations, they assume different forms or dimensions, and become, indifferently, molecules of oxygen, hydrogen, nitrogen, or carbon, as the case may be, all of which are but different modes of motion of the same primitive atoms, there being in Nature but three things—Ether, Intelligence, and Motion. What Ether is, no one knows. We call it the formless spirit, the unmanifest, etc. But, there can be no doubt but, that Motion is the product of Intelligence, since we never see Motion but as the manifestation of evolution, and this is the expression of Mind. Therefore, we have a duality—Ether and Intelligence; one the living spirit, the other the eternal substance for its manifestation.

Every molecule of matter is the outward form, the center of which, is the incarnating spirit, in some degree of progress. Man's physical organism is a system of life and development for countless billions of them. So the Earth, in its functional expression as the womb of Nature for the outward expression of Man, is only so in a material sense. *He is prior to the planet.* He (Man) is only the off-spring of the planet by virtue of his material body being a part of the substance of the Earth. This life is a stage, only, of his material journey; and, just as Man's body is continually throwing off useless dead matter and replacing the same with new life, so, too, the count-less organic forms of Earth are hourly returning to the ground from which they sprang, and new forms, rising from the same dust, are taking their places.

Here, then, is the sum total: First is revealed to us the grand Astral Man, the Zodiac being the outward idea or form, the Sun and his system the vital functions thereof. The Earth, apart from its functional expression or place, is also an individual. Man, apart from forming a molecule of the planetary womb, by comparison, is also an individual. And, lastly, every molecule of Man's organism is also, in reality, an individual, and small only by comparison with the human frame. And as there are the high Solar Archangels of the Sun, and a chief amongst these seated upon his throne of fire, so there is an Archangelic Chief of the Earth, surrounded by descending degrees of wisdom and power to Man, who also, in his turn, stands as the Deific center and chief of his being, his soul being the sphere of conscious-ness, which, when united to the feminine soul, constitutes the Angel of Life, Eternal. Down still we go, and find that this Divine scale of life and being is, from the lowly molecule, system upon system climb-ing, sphere upon sphere, upward and onward, forever, evermore, and all eternity cannot bring nearer the end of Man's glorious immortality.

In the full revelation of this divine scheme of creation, so full of light, life, love, joy and harmony, a scheme void of death and annihila-tion, the mind once more reflects upon the physical illusions of slowly advancing scientific thought. Camille Flammarion, the great psycho-materialist of France, has painted, in his various novels, a lurid, almost horrible, picture of what the mighty universe must become from the

logical deductions of his own school of thought; a school which would
be best named as transcendental materialism. According to this conception, "thousands, aye, millions of worlds are rushing through space,
inert, frozen, and dead. Suns have cooled down and ceased to give
forth the life-sustaining element of light, but have still retained their
mighty attraction upon their attendant planets, according to the laws
of gravity, by virtue of their material mass, and thus hold their planetary offspring in the eternal, cold, icy grasp of death. Our Sun,
too, is cooling fast; the Earth has already lost a great portion of her
own internal heat. She has passed her prime of life, and death—cold,
icy death—has already begun to encroach upon her extremities. The
South pole (the feet) is now practically lifeless in one perpetual
covering of ice. So, too, her head; her locks are the white of perpetual
snow. No longer has she the blush and beauty of youth, no longer
adorned with the healthy covering of verdue which youthfulness gives,
and as our geologists prove was once the case. So that, although the
time may still be long, according to our reckoning of years, it is only
a brief moment in eternity when this fair Earth, and also the beauteous
splendor of the silent stars, will be locked forever in darkness, and
the final sleep of doom." If this be so, we ask of the inmost soul, if
life be but the fitful awakenings of the indestructible spirit, ebbing
and flowing in response to the rise and fall of Nature's cosmic ba-
rometer and the transmutations of matter; if life is, in reality, but a
brief and passing moment, eternally repeated, from the flush of youth,
"the gilded salon to the bier and the shroud, then why, O why should
the spirit of mortal be proud?" Why aspire to penetrate the inward
realities of life and enter the Holy of Holies—to seek and find out
God? As the rushing torrent of this thought swept o'er the mental
chambers of the soul and saturated the spirit with its icy sting, as it
lay still chained within the prison house of matter, the higher self rose,
sublime in its grandeur, and consciousness of divine relationship, and,
in the last earthly appeal for light, for divine truth, as to Man and
his immortality, it turned in reverence and awe before the still, shimmering veil of the sacred Penetralia. The trial had come, the crucial
test, whether of life or death, the final revelation to Man. In purity of
heart and humility of soul we await in agonizing suspense. There is a
thrilling sensation, as though of ten thousand electric currents consuming the frame, and a swaying to and fro, as if drifting upon an

ocean of fire; then a dead silence, so profound that whole eternities seem to pass, without either beginning or end. And the sight of the inward spirit is opened slowly. Who? Where? What? For the shadows have fled, the luminous curtain fades, is gone, and flashing before the inward sight stands the ineffable Adonai. It is I—you! There is no God but this, and in one moment the interior consciousness becomes at-one-with-self, God, and from that inconceivable height of profound vision we again look upon Nature. Behold Sun, Moon and planets in all the original magnificence of their nebulous luminosity; from nebulous rings we proceed, stage after stage, each producing its own degrees of life. On, on we pass the ages, the geological cycles of inconceivable duration in time, but only a mere instant in eternity; and on and on, as the changes roll, until we see Earth as she is now; still on, at the ever-urging desire of the triumphant Soul, and a remarkable change is apparent. From forces, at present latent, there comes a change; and, instead of so-called physical; electrical races have superceded the present humanity. Crystallization has ceased; and all things become lighter in density and more ethereal in nature; *and the orbit of the Earth grows less.* Nearer and nearer shines the mighty Sun; first Vulcan, then the swift messenger of the gods are indrawn within the solar vortex, each absorption producing a cataclysmic change upon our Earth. Then comes the turn of Venus, while slowly and surely the orbit of the Earth contracts, and nearer shines the Sun. And, finally, the beautiful Earth, her mission over, the last atom of life beyond her rule, inward she sweeps, and is lost in the mighty ocean of fire as a stone is lost in the lake. Verily is the word of prophecy a literal truth: "The Earth shall be destroyed with fire." And so on with the rest, each planet in its proper turn fulfilling the functions at present performed by the Earth, each becoming the grand theater of material and ethereal life, and the cometary bodies, to-day chasing unknown orbits in the realms of ether, gradually fall into line when their erratic cycle is ended, taking the places of the present outermost planets.

No such thing as death, no such thing as the dark silence of eternal night, for any organic creation of the Most High. From the Sun they come, and unto the Sun each must ultimately return, even as the body of Man, coming from the dust of Earth, must also return thereto, to be taken up in new forms and furnish substance for other degrees of life. And thus will it be, until the Sun, in its mighty solar heavens of purified spiritual life, will form the last, the final battle ground of matter, receiving *its new life from a greater center than itself*. A glorious solar world, well typified in the last Battle of the Gods, and the new Earth—a World whereon the Angels tread in superlatively beautiful forms, clothed with the ideals and emanations of their own divine purity—Souls clothed in Air, treading the ethereal Realms of Light, as the children of God, and the inheritors of the Kingdom of Heaven.

Must the searching eye of the Soul seek further? Must the insatiable thirst of the Spirit launch out upon the trackless infinities of the yet To Be? Must it still penetrate further in the profound beyond, where time ceases to be, where the past, present, and the future, are forever unknown, but exist only as the Deific consciousness of the eternal Now? No. The Soul at last rests satisfied. The final revelation is over.

My brother, we have done; and, in closing, have only to add that, not until the speculating philosophy of earthly schools blends with the Science of the Spheres in the full and perfect fruition of the wisdom of the ages, will Man *know* and *reverence* his Creator, and, in the silent Penetralia of his inmost being, respond, in unison with that Angelic Anthem of Life: "We Praise Thee, O God!"

FINIS

CPSIA information can be obtained at www.ICGtesting.com
Printed in the USA
LVOW051833171012

303263LV00002B/272/P